SCOTTISH COMMUNITIES ABROAD
IN THE EARLY MODERN PERIOD

STUDIES IN MEDIEVAL AND REFORMATION TRADITIONS

History, Culture, Religion, Ideas

VOLUME CVII

ALEXIA GROSJEAN AND STEVE MURDOCH

SCOTTISH COMMUNITIES ABROAD
IN THE EARLY MODERN PERIOD

SCOTTISH COMMUNITIES ABROAD IN THE EARLY MODERN PERIOD

EDITED BY

ALEXIA GROSJEAN AND STEVE MURDOCH

BRILL
LEIDEN · BOSTON
2005

Brill Academic Publishers has done its best to establish rights for the use of the illustration printed on this volume. Should any other party feel that its rights have been infringed, we would be glad to hear from them.

This book is printed on acid-free paper.

Library of Congress Cataloging-in-Publication Data

A C.I.P. record for this book is available from the Library of Congress.

ISSN 1573-4188
ISBN 90 04 14306 8

PRINTED IN THE NETHERLANDS

For Gemma and Scott Murdoch
(Currently members of the Scottish Community in Asia)

CONTENTS

SECTION III: COMMUNITIES OF MIND
AND INTEREST

FOREWORD

From at least as early as the Hundred Years War, when the Scots in their thousands fought for pay, land and honour in French service, to the interwar years of the twentieth century, when they flooded out to Canada and other trans-oceanic destinations, the Scots were a people quick to seek their fortunes abroad by temporary or permanent migration. It was a national propensity only checked after 1945 by the collapse of the British Empire, which ended several centuries of movement by officials, soldiers and fortune hunters to Africa, Asia and the West Indies, and by the new restrictions on immigration to the United States and the white dominions, as the wide open spaces filled up and the better jobs in their economies were reserved to the native-born.

The scale of the population movement relative to the size of Scotland was extraordinary, and it resulted in a diaspora of many millions of Scottish descent scattered across the earth, some with a warm sentimental regard for their roots, others with barely any consciousness of them. The great exodus from Scotland has received varying degrees of attention from historians.[1] Broadly speaking, the Atlantic and Antipodean migrations of settlement have been the focus of much attention from scholars in several countries, with analyses of varying depth and sophistication. There has likewise been distinguished work, some published and some in progress, on the Scottish contribution to the British Empire.[2] But these events took place

---

[1] Among the best are B. Bailyn, *Voyagers to the West: Emigration from Britain to America on the Eve of the Revolution* (London: 1986); N. C. Landsman, *Scotland and its First American Colony, 1683–1765* (Princeton: 1985); A. W. Parker, *Scottish Highlanders in Colonial Georgia, 1735–1748* (Athens, Georgia: 1997); D. Meyer, *The Highland Scots of North Carolina, 1737–1776* (Chapel Hill: 1957); M. Harper, *Emigration from North-East Scotland*, 2 vols. (Aberdeen: 1988); M. Harper, *Emigration from Scotland Between the Wars: Opportunity or Exile* (Manchester: 1998); D. S. Macmillan, *Scotland and Australia, 1788–1860* (Oxford: 1967); M. Roe, *Australia, Britain and Migration 1915–1940: A Study of Desperate Hopes* (Cambridge: 1995).

[2] T. M. Devine, *Scotland's Empire, 1600–1815* (London: 2003). A further volume is forthcoming. M. Fry, *The Scottish Empire* (Edinburgh: 2001). Much of the wider writing on empire is full of references to the Scots: see, for example, J. M. Mackenzie, *The Empire of Nature* (Manchester: 1988).

mainly after 1700. The biggest relative gap in modern scholarly effort
has lain earlier, especially in the seventeenth century, when the direction of Scottish movement was primarily to Ireland and to Europe.
This is curious, since the scale of this earlier movement was very
large, involving perhaps one young man in five of the Scottish population. This outmigration was paralleled in contemporary Europe
probably only by Switzerland, and in proportion to the total population it was not seen again in Scotland, except, briefly, in the high
Victorian period.

Of course, this academic neglect has not been absolute, and a
complete bibliography of the study of seventeenth-century Scottish
migration published in the course of the twentieth century would be
quite lengthy. Its first highlights, in the years 1902–7, are the three
remarkable volumes by the German scholar, Thomas Fischer, on the
Scots in Sweden, Germany and in East and West Prussia. These
were described by his editor James Kirkpatrick, professor of history
at Edinburgh, as "primarily a contribution to Scottish genealogy",
but in reality they are much more, an early eye-opener as to the
extent and depth of the Scottish movement abroad.[3] Two important
but unhappily unpublished theses were undertaken on the Scottish
mercenaries, merchants and pedlars in Sweden, and Thomas Riis
completed a two-volume study of Scots in Denmark.[4] The Scottish
History Society presented source books on Scots in Poland, and on
Scots fighting in Dutch service, while the commercial side of contact with the Netherlands was served by early studies of the staple
at Veere.[5] The Scottish adventurers in Russia were expertly pursued

[3] T. A. Fischer, *The Scots in Germany* (Edinburgh: 1902); *idem*, *The Scots in Eastern
and Western Prussia* (Edinburgh: 1903); *idem*, *The Scots in Sweden* (Edinburgh: 1907).

[4] James Dow tragically died before his thesis on Scots in Sweden could be presented: his focus was mainly on the sixteenth century, but see his two articles on
'Scottish Trade with Sweden, 1512–1622', in *Scottish Historical Review*, vol. 48, 1969,
64–79, 124–50; J. A. Fallon, 'Scottish Mercenaries in the Service of Denmark and
Sweden, 1626–1632', unpublished University of Glasgow Ph.D. thesis, 1972, was
equally pioneering. T. Riis, *Should Auld Acquaintance Be Forgot: Scottish-Danish Relations,
c.1450–1707* (2 vols., Odense: 1988).

[5] A. F. Steuart, ed., *Papers Relating to the Scots in Poland, 1576–1793* (Scottish History
Society, Edinburgh: 1915); J. Ferguson, ed., *Papers Illustrating the History of the Scots
Brigade in the Service of the United Netherlands* (Scottish History Society, Edinburgh), vol.
1, *1592–1697* (1898), vol. 2, *1698–1782* (1899); J. Davidson and A. Gray, *The Scottish
Staple at Veere: A Study in the Economic History of Scotland* (London: 1909); M. P. Rooseboom, *The Scottish Staple in the Netherlands* (The Hague: 1910). An engaging picture
of the Scots kirk in Rotterdam emerges in J. Morrison, *Scots on the Dijk* (Kirkpatrick,

by Paul Dukes,[6] and three edited volumes of collected essays in the 1980s and 1990s brought together scholars (some of them from overseas) to examine the inter-relationships of Scotland with Scandinavia, the wider Baltic and the Netherlands.[7] The movement to Ulster was the subject of two good but not exhaustive monographs.[8] On the other hand, France, despite its importance, was largely neglected apart from a study of the Scots College in Paris,[9] and virtually nothing was written about the Scots in Spain or the Habsburg Empire, although David Worthington's monograph has recently addressed this gap.[10]

It may seem a not unimpressive list, yet what twentieth-century historians partly failed to grasp themselves, and failed totally to convey to the outside world, was the scale and significance of the early Scottish movement abroad. Most of the work, however good, was very particular and closely focused. The modern Troubles in Ireland forced on public consciousness their origins in the seventeenth-century Ulster plantations, though they inspired no-one in a Scottish university to undertake any significant work on seventeenth-century movements between the three kingdoms. There was certainly little awareness that this movement was far eclipsed in scale by the simultaneous one to Poland, "Scotland's America" as a contemporary described it, or even of the scale and political significance of the

---

Durham: 1981). An important recent study is D. Catterall, *Community without Borders: Scots Migrants and the Changing Face of Power in the Dutch Republic, c.1600–1700* (Leiden: 2002).

[6] J. W. Barnhill and P. Dukes, 'North-East Scots in Muscovy in the Seventeenth Century', *Northern Scotland*, vol. 1 (1972), 49–62; P. Dukes, 'Scottish Soldiers in Muscovy', in P. Dukes *et al.*, *The Caledonian Phalanx: Scots in Russia* (Edinburgh: 1987), 9–23; P. Dukes, 'Problems Concerning the Departure of Scottish Soldiers from Seventeenth-Century Muscovy', in T. C. Smout, ed., *Scotland and Europe, 1200–1850* (Edinburgh: 1986), 143–56. For an important earlier study, see A. F. Steuart, *Scottish Influences in Russian History from the End of the Sixteenth Century to the Beginnings of the Nineteenth Century* (Edinburgh: 1913). I. G. Anderson, *Scotsmen in the Service of the Czars* (Edinburgh: 1990) is rather slight.

[7] T. C. Smout, ed., *Scotland and Europe, 1200–1850* (Edinburgh: 1986); G. G. Simpson, ed., *Scotland and Scandinavia, 800–1800* (Edinburgh: 1990); G. G. Simpson, ed., *Scotland and the Low Countries, 1124–1994* (Edinburgh: 1996); see also G. G. Simpson, ed., *The Scottish Soldier Abroad, 1247–1967* (Edinburgh: 1991).

[8] M. Perceval-Maxwell, *The Scottish Migration to Ulster in the Reign of James I* (London: 1973); R. Gillespie, *Colonial Ulster: The Settlement of East Ulster, 1600–1641* (Cork: 1985).

[9] B. M. Halloran, *The Scots College in Paris, 1603–1792* (Edinburgh: 1997).

[10] D. Worthington, *Scots in Habsburg Service, 1618–1648* (Leiden: 2003).

Scottish hosts fighting on behalf of the Scandinavian kings in the
Thirty Years War. And we had no inkling of the significance of
what were to become the Baltic states in the overall story of the
Scottish diaspora.

The present volume is a breakthrough, surely the biggest single
advance in the field for a hundred years, since the days of Thomas
Fischer. The editors' own research on Scots in the service of the
Scandinavian kings provided a starting point for a new understanding of their political significance to Scotland, and more important
still in this context, created a starting point for a collaboration between
scholars from all over Europe, of which this collection forms the first
fruits.[11] The time was ripe. First, the collapse of Soviet power in the
1990s made it possible for scholars in Scotland to make readier contact with those in countries like Poland and Lithuania who had been
working, sometimes over a considerable period and unknown to the
West, on the ethnic composition of immigrants into their own communities. Second, the establishment in the University of Aberdeen
of a Research Institute of Irish and Scottish Studies created an inspir-
ing environment for outward-looking and comparative research, which
broadened over the years from its initially narrowly focused interest
on the Scottish-Irish axis to examine a much wider range of Scottish
external contacts with other countries in the seventeenth century.
Large databases were built up, and the possibility of linking these
to databases constructed in other countries suggests future prospects
for network analysis of an entirely new kind which the editors intend
to continue from their new base at the University of St Andrews.

This, however, is to run beyond what this volume offers, into possible future agendas. This collection of essays is both a taster of the
archival riches for Scottish history that lie abroad, and a substantial
meal of different approaches from different places, applied to the
common purpose of examining the Scot outwith Scotland. It is not
the business of a foreword to usurp the editor's own introduction.
But this book will take its readers to nine or ten countries ranging
from America to the Baltic, give new insights on relatively familiar
Scottish communities in the Netherlands and Scandinavia, and intro-

---

[11] S. Murdoch, *Britain, Denmark-Norway and the House of Stuart, 1603–1660: A
Diplomatic and Military Analysis* (East Linton: 2003); A. Grosjean, *An Unofficial Alliance:
Scotland and Sweden 1569–1654* (Leiden: 2003).

duce them to totally unfamiliar ones in Lithuania and Poland. It will uncover Scots identifying themselves abroad as Scots still, or as that new-fangled seventeenth-century thing, a Briton, or as loyal denizens of their adopted countries—sometimes the same individual being all three, depending on context. It will show Scots as merchants, soldiers, students, farmers, pedlars, artisans, sailors, preachers, and political refugees, all pursuing their careers in other people's territories, integrating, standing apart, marrying, staying and coming home. We are starting now really to understand the culture of migration, that distinctive, non-parochial side of Scottish history, and it is very exciting.

T. C. Smout
Historiographer Royal in Scotland

ACKNOWLEDGEMENTS

The editors of this collection would like to express their thanks to the numerous people and institutions that have helped make this collection possible. The collection itself was first conceived of during a conversation between the editors in 1999 in Jakarta when, while staying with close family there, they found themselves surrounded by a group of Scots who had formed something of an identifiable Scottish community abroad, albeit immersed in plural identities with their Welsh, English and Australian companions in Indonesia. From there the idea matured and a workshop was organised in Aberdeen in May 2002 under the auspices of the AHRB Centre for Irish and Scottish Studies at which several of the authors in the collection delivered papers. After a process of selection it was decided that we had the core of a collection and approaches were made to scholars known to have an interest in the field and the present collection is the result. We thank all the authors for their contributions and willingness to discuss ideas with each other, particularly those who have never met yet felt happy to give and receive advice in a positive spirit throughout. Further to the obvious thanks owed to the contributors, special thanks must be accorded to Professors T. C. Smout, Lex Heerma van Voss, Sølvi Sogner and Dr Thomas O'Connor who, in addition to their own contributions, read the complete manuscript and provided both the editors and the contributors with much valuable advice during the editing process. Other academic colleagues who gave valuable counsel and insights on the subject matter of this collection also include Professor Allan Macinnes and Dr Marjory Harper, both of the University of Aberdeen.

Alison Duncan deserves massive thanks for her copy editing and indexing of the collection as well as the generous help she gave to many of the non-native English speakers in ensuring that their essays were presented with appropriate eloquence. Irene van Rossum and Tanja Cowall at Brill have also been very helpful in the production stages of the book as has our good friend Marcella Mulder, particularly during the early stages of the project. Finally, we would like to thank the director of the AHRB Centre for Irish and Scottish

Studies at the University of Aberdeen, Professor Tom Devine, for supporting the 'Communities Workshop' in 2002 and for that Centre's financial contribution to the production of this collection. The School of History, University of St Andrews, also aided with aspects of the production of the book and in encouraging the editors to complete the project throughout the winter of 2004–2005. To all involved with the project, our most heartfelt thanks.

LIST OF CONTRIBUTORS

DR DOUGLAS CATTERALL is Assistant Professor of History at Cameron University of Oklahoma and is interested in the cultural impact of migration, social memory, and community/state relations. His publications include the monograph *Community without Borders: Scots Migrants and the Changing Face of Power in the Dutch Republic, c.1600–1700* (2002). He is currently at work on two projects, one concerning eighteenth-century European and trans-Atlantic Scots migration, the other addressing women's position in the informal public sphere in northern Europe during the seventeenth century.

DAVID DOBSON was educated at the universities of Abertay Dundee, St Andrews, and Aberdeen. He is the author of numerous books concerned with emigration from Scotland to North America and the West Indies. These include *Scottish Emigration to Colonial America, 1607–1785* (1994); *The Original Scots Colonists of Early America, 1612–1783* (1989), and *Ships from Scotland to America, 1628–1828* (2 vols., 1998–2002). He is at present an Honorary Research Fellow and doctoral candidate of the Research Institute of Irish and Scottish Studies, University of Aberdeen.

DR PATRICK FITZGERALD is Lecturer & Development Officer at the Centre for Migration Studies at the Ulster-American Folk Park, Omagh, Northern Ireland. He teaches a Queen's University Belfast Masters course in Irish Migration Studies and has published widely on aspects of Irish migration history, including, as editor, *Atlantic Crossroads: Historical Connections Between Scotland, Ulster and North America* (2001).

DR GINNY GARDNER is a history graduate of the Universities of Glasgow and Oxford. Her D.Phil. research was published by Tuckwell Press as *The Scottish Exile Community in the Netherlands, 1660–1690* (2004). She has also contributed to the *New Dictionary of National Biography* (2004) and is currently a civil servant with the Scottish Executive.

Dr Alexia Grosjean is Research Fellow in the University of St Andrews Scottish Parliament Project. Her main publications include: *An Unofficial Alliance: Scotland and Sweden 1569–1654* (2003) and a co-authored volume with Steve Murdoch, *Belhelvie: A Millennium of History* (2001). She has also published numerous articles on aspects of Scottish and Swedish history and twenty two entries for the *New DNB*.

Waldemar Kowalski is professor of history at the Department of Humanities, Holy Cross Academy, Kielce, Poland. His main interests are: culture, ethnicities and religious denominations in central Europe in the late middle ages and in the early modern epoch. His recent main publications include: "New interpretation of medieval and Renaissance sources in Poland," *Intellectual News. Review of the International Society for Intellectual History* 6–7 (2000): 20–27; "From the 'Land of Diverse Sects' to National Religion: Converts to Catholicism and Reformed Franciscans in Early Modern Poland," *Church History* 70.3 (2001): 482–526; "The Jewish population and family in the Polish-Lithuanian Commonwealth in the second half of the 18th century," *The History of the Family*, 8.4 (2003): 517–530 (with Zenon Guldon); "To One's Resurrection, following Christ, the Steadfast Master." *The Medieval and Early Modern Inscriptions of North-western Little Poland* (Kielce, 2004).

Andrew Ross Little is a doctoral student at the University of Exeter, focusing on British personnel in the Dutch navy, c.1650–1720. He has contributed chapters on these themes to A. J. Brand & D. E. H. de Boer, eds., *Trade, diplomacy and cultural exchange in the North Sea and Baltic region (ca. 1350–1750)* (2004); and Paul Rees, ed., *New Researchers in Maritime History, 2004* (2004), along with a co-authored article, 'Scots Privateering, Swedish Neutrality and Prize Law in the Third Anglo-Dutch War, 1672–1674' in *Forum Navale* (2003).

Dr Esther Mijers graduated in 2002 from the University of St Andrews and is currently employed as a Research Fellow at the A.H.R.B. Centre for Irish and Scottish Studies at the University of Aberdeen. She is interested in the political, intellectual and educational history of seventeenth- and early eighteenth-century Scotland and the Netherlands. She is the author of several articles on Scottish-Dutch relations.

DR STEVE MURDOCH lectures in Scottish history at the University of St Andrews. He has published widely on aspects of British and Scandinavian history, including *Britain, Denmark-Norway and the House of Stuart 1603–1660: A Diplomatic and Military Analysis* (2003), and, as editor, *Scotland and the Thirty Years' War, 1618–1648* (2001). With Andrew Mackillop he co-edited, *Fighting for Identity: Scottish Military Experiences, 1550–1900* (2002), and *Military Governors and Imperial Frontiers c.1600–1800* (2003).

DR THOMAS O'CONNOR teaches history in the National University of Ireland, Maynooth. He has published extensively on Irish migrants to Europe in the early modern period, notably, *An Irish Theologian in Enlightenment Europe: Luke Joseph Hooke 1714–96* (1995). As an editor he has published, *The Irish in Europe 1580–1815* (2001), and as co-editor with Marian Lyons, *Irish migrants in Europe after Kinsale, 1602–1820* (2003). Since 1997 he has directed the 'Irish in Europe' research project in N. U. I. Maynooth. He edits *Archivium Hibernicum*, the Irish history sources journal.

NINA ØSTBY PEDERSEN, Cand. Philol., is a Senior Executive Officer with the Norwegian Directorate of Immigration. Her Masters dissertation focused on Scottish migration into Norway in the early modern period with an emphasis on Bergen. This is her first publication and builds on her previous research work.

PROFESSOR T. C. SMOUT (Thomas Christopher Smout) is Emeritus Professor of Scottish History at St Andrews University and Historiographer Royal in Scotland. In addition to his contribution to domestic Scottish history, his main publications in relation to this volume include *Scottish Trade on the Eve of Union* (1964), and, as editor, *Scotland and Europe* (1986), and *Scotland and the Sea* (1992).

PROFESSOR SØLVI SOGNER is Emeritus Professor of Early Modern History at the University of Oslo. Her main fields of interest are historical demography, women's history, and historical criminology. She has published, *i.a.*, *Folkevekst og flytting* (1979); *Fra stua full til tobarns kull* (1984); *Far sjøl i stua og familien hans* (1990); *Ung i Europa* (1994); *Krig og fred* (1996), and co-authored *Norsk innvandringshistorie* vol. 1 (2003).

PROFESSOR LEX HEERMA VAN VOSS is Senior Research Fellow at the International Institute of Social History in Amsterdam and Professor of the History of Labour and Labour Relations at the University of Utrecht. He co-edited *Dock Workers. International Explorations in Comparative Labour History, 1790–1970* (2000), and *The North Sea and culture in early modern history (1550–1800)* (1996).

KATHRIN ZICKERMANN studied history at the University of Kiel, Germany, where she completed her Masters degree researching the British community in Hamburg. Her interest in Scottish history developed during an undergraduate exchange year at the University of Aberdeen in 1999. She has previously co-authored an article with Hartmut Ruffer entitled 'German reactions to the Scots in the Holy Roman Empire during the Thirty Years' War' in S. Murdoch, ed., *Scotland and the Thirty Years' War, 1618–1648* (2001).

RIMANTAS ŽIRGULIS is Director of Kėdainiai Regional Museum. His Masters thesis, undertaken at Vilnius University in 1993, concerned 'The Monastery of Kėdainiai Carmelites in the 18th and the 19th centuries'. He has subsequently published numerous articles in Lithuanian and, in English, has co-authored with A. Juknevicius and A. Stanaitis, *Kėdainiai and Environs* (1998). He also published 'Kėdainiai Jewish Community in the 16th–19thC' in the Vilnius University collection *The Gaon of Vilnius and the Annals of Jewish Culture* (1998), and 'Three Hundred Years of Multiculturalism in Kėdainiai' in G. Potasenko, ed., *The Peoples of the Grand Duchy of Lithuania* (2002).

ABBREVIATIONS

AOSB	Axel Oxenstiernas Skrifter och Brefvexling (unpublished)
APC	English Privy Council, *Acts of the Privy Council of England* (25 vols., London: 1890–1964)
ARA	Algemeen Rijksarchief (Dutch National Archives), The Hague
BL	British Library, London
CSPD	*Calendars of State Papers, Domestic Series,* First Series, 1547–1625 (13 vols., London: 1856–1992) Second Series, 1625–1649 (23 vols., London: 1858–1897) Third Series, 1649–1660 (13 vols., London: 1875–1886)
CSPV	*Calendars of State Papers and Manuscripts relating to English affairs, existing in the archives and collections of Venice and in other libraries of Northern Italy* (38 vols., London: 1864–1947)
DNB	*Dictionary of National Biography*
DRA	Danish Rigsarkiv (Danish National Archives), Copenhagen
EUL	Edinburgh University Library
HMC	*Historical Manuscripts Commission*
HP	Hartlib Papers
KRA	Krigsarkiv, Stockholm
NAS	National Archives of Scotland, Edinburgh
NLS	National Library of Scotland, Edinburgh
NRA	Norwegian Rigsarkiv (Norwegian National Archives), Oslo
PRO	Public Records Office, London
RAOSB	*Rikskansleren Axel Oxenstiernas Skrifter och Brefvexling* (22 vols., Stockholm: 1890–1977)
RGSS	Register of the Great Seal of Scotland (11 vols., Edinburgh: 1984
RPCS	Scotland, Privy Council, *Registers of the Privy Council of Scotland,* First Series, 1545–1625 (14 vols., Edinburgh: 1877–1898) Second Series, 1625–1660 (8 vols., Edinburgh: 1899–1908)
SAÄ	G. Elgenstierna, *Den Introducerade Svenska Adelns Ättartavlor, med tillägg och rättelser* (9 vols., Stockholm: 1925–36)
SP	State Papers
SRA	Swedish Riksarkiv (Swedish National Archives), Stockholm
SRP	N.A. Kullberg, et. al., eds., *Svenska Riksrådets Protokoll, 1621–1658* (18 vols., Stockholm: 1878–1959)
UU	*University of Utrecht*

INTRODUCTION

Migrations are a feature of the human experience.[1] Since prehistoric times groups of humans have left their homes for a variety of reasons which largely boil down to two motivations: flight from the old, or curiosity for the new. They are either fleeing something or seeking something. They might leave their homes and move no farther than the neighbouring village. Alternatively they might find themselves settled at the other side of the world, according to their ease of mobility at any given time. For some the migratory process reflected a temporary shift from their 'home', as sojourners. For others it meant a permanent resettlement in a new location, whether intended or otherwise.[2] Many found that the process was ceaseless. In whichever capacity the movement took place, the numbers involved could amount to tens, hundreds or thousands and, ultimately, all sought to find security within whichever society they found themselves. The main way people did that historically—and still do today—was through their participation in communities. These are what sociologists variously describe as specific forms of human association, be they of ties of blood, ethnic origin, territory, or simply lifestyle and common interest.[3]

As in the innumerable experiences of other peoples throughout time, Scots engaged in a spectrum of migrations. Examples abound, and these vary from the experience of other British migrants just as

---

[1] For two impressive surveys of comparative global migrations see T. Sowell, *Migrations and Cultures: A World View* (New York: 1996); D. Hoerder, *Cultures in Contact: World Migrations in the Second Millennium* (Durham and London: 2002).

[2] Sowell, *Migrations and Cultures*, 4.

[3] R. König, *The Community* (London: 1968), intro. 1–6 and 22–30; J. R. Gusfield, *Community: A Critical Response* (Oxford: 1975), xiv, 1–15, 21, 83; A. Macfarlane, *Reconstructing Historical Communities* (Cambridge: 1977), 1; G. Delanty, *Community* (London and New York: 2003), intro. 2–4, and 186–195; K. A. Lynch, *Individuals, families, and Communities in Europe, 1200–1800: The Urban Foundations of Western Society* (Cambridge: 2003), 15–18. These works describe in detail the numerous definitions of 'community' as debated by sociologists and social-anthropologists while Macfarlane, for one, observes that a lack of definition dominates the sociologist's debate on the subject.

much as the histories of the nations of the British Isles vary.[4] Some
migrants were accepted in their chosen destination without contest.
Others either failed to be accepted, or themselves rejected the new
location and so moved on. Many fell victim en route as a result of
catastrophies like shipwreck, death in battle, or disease. Not all the
migrations resulted in the establishment of anything we could mean-
ingfully call a 'Scottish' community. Some ventures were so short-
lived that community formation was impossible. In other cases, the
arrivals were scattered or integrated into much larger societies where
their presence as individual Scots was hardly noticeable, or largely
irrelevant. Indeed, for a variety of reasons many individuals sought
to opt out of any kind of ethnically orientated community.[5] Obviously
such men and women developed their own networks to fulfil their
social needs and thus they fall outside the scope of this survey.
Instead, this collection discusses those groups of migrants who moved
to new locations from their native country and constructed 'communities' which would facilitate the fulfilment of their personal
aspirations.

Community can be a problematic word for historians and it is
unlikely that any one definition will meet with the approval of all
scholars in the field. Joseph Gusfield suggested that "rather than con-
ceiving of 'community' and 'society' as groups and/or entities to
which persons 'belong', it would seem more useful to conceptualise
these terms as points of reference brought into play in particular sit-

---

[4] Sowell, *Migrations and Cultures*, 3–4.
[5] The devout Calvinist merchant Patrick Thomson, a resident in Norrköping for
fifteen years, sought self-imposed exile from his countrymen in Stockholm as he felt
that "All the Scots here are Lutherans or Atheists, the English are worse if worse
can be [. . .] so I come heir alone." Lord George Murray, the spectacularly successful Jacobite general, imposed a harsher exile on himself than he needed to in
1746, explaining that he went to Germany rather than France as "I thought it
much more eligible to live in a country where I had no acquaintances, the language of which I know not a syllab" than in France, which he believed had betrayed
his forces during the 1745 uprising. For others, the new life completely replaced
the old one and no value was seen in clinging to what had been given up. One
Englishman wrote to a Swedish friend in London "Let me assure you that since
my coming abroad, I never seriously thought of England till the friendly expres-
sions in your letter caused me to reflect." See variously NAS, Russell Papers,
RH15/106/608. Patrick Thomson to Andrew Russell, Stockholm, 22 April 1686;
S. Murdoch, 'Soldier, Sailor Jacobite Spy', in *Slavonica*, vol. 22 (1996), 27; SRA,
Anglica 190, Brev från utlänningar till Christoffer Leijoncrona, 1689–1709. Volume
C; Robert Child to Leijoncrona, Rome, 14 July 1708.

uations and arenas".[6] They might include such examples of self-identification as local (Aberdonian), national (Scottish), political (British), confessional (Presbyterian) or geographical (European). Indeed, pluralistic arenas in which individuals could express themselves on a variety of levels were the norm for both the indigenous and the migrant Scottish communities.[7] Lyndon Fraser has observed that the migrant could pursue any of these identities, dependent on the situation he found himself in. The resulting "ethnic mutualism was a powerful resource enabling immigrants to infuse unfamiliar surroundings with some degree of collective meaning and coherence".[8] This collection scrutinizes a variety of Scottish communities established in numerous 'unfamiliar surroundings' in the sixteenth and seventeenth centuries. The volume does not attempt to study every overseas Scottish community in the early modern period, particularly if, like Greifswald and Elsinore, they have already received serious scholarly attention.[9] Instead, the collection is broken down into three distinct sections, each revealing different aspects of the Scottish historical community abroad that may be applicable to communities elsewhere.

Section I: Migrant Destinations, Colonies and Plantations

In this section, the authors offer general survey essays that contextualise Scottish migratory patterns in three geographic locations: Ireland, Poland-Lithuania and the Americas. These represent several general types of population movement. The first is to the

---

[6] Gusfield, *Community*, 41; Macfarlane, *Reconstructing Historical Communities*, 2–3. For an excellent description of Irish Catholic migrant community development in New Zealand see L. Fraser, *To Tara via Holyhead* (Auckland: 1997), 51, 79–80 and *passim*. I thank Dr Fraser for providing me with a copy of his very informative book.

[7] S. Murdoch and A. Mackillop, eds., *Fighting for Identity: Scottish Military Experiences c.1550–1900* (Leiden: 2002), intro, xxiii–xxix.

[8] Fraser, *To Tara via Holyhead*, 79.

[9] Examples of studies of early modern Scottish communities (or at least clusters of Scots) are numerous. A few worthy of note include: J. Dow, '*Skotter* in Sixteenth-Century Scania' in *Scottish Historical Review*, 44 (1965), 34–51; Von Ilse von Wechmar and R. Biederstedt, 'Die schottische Einwanderung in Vorpommern im 16. und frühen 17. Jahrhundert' in *Greifswald-Stralsunder Jahrbuch*, Band 5 (1965), 7–28; T. L. Christensen, 'Scots in Denmark in the sixteenth century' in *Scottish Historical Review*, 49:2 (1970), 125–145. The citations in the chapters that follow are replete with many more equally interesting examples.

'near-abroad', the second to the 'middle-abroad' and the third to the
'far-abroad'.[10] These are, of course, flexible definitions but nonetheless
they offer a broad concept of how and why communities might establish themselves in particular ways in given places. There is no doubt
that migrants living not far from their place of origin can perceive
differences with their close neighbours that are indiscernible to those
from farther afield. The further the move from home, and the more
alien the new surroundings become, the easier it is to forget local
rivalries and concentrate on the similarities. Thus Scots who moved
into nearby countries were able, for the most part, to leave behind
their regional differences due to the need to bind more closely together
in an alien (and often hostile) environment. Whether a couple of
days' or a couple of weeks' travel away, Scots in the 'near-abroad'
were also close enough to home to return without many problems
should the need arise. Ulster was a day from Glasgow, Bergen only
a few days from the eastern Scottish ports and Rotterdam the same.
Even Norrköping on the east coast of Sweden could be reached in
nine days from Scotland.[11] These communities were therefore frequently reinforced by a regular stream of fresh immigrants, short-
term visitors and those simply passing through on their way to other
destinations.[12] These often came directly from Scotland and might

---

[10] The concepts of the 'near', 'middle' and 'far' abroad are not new. In 1994,
Andrew McKay published an article entitled 'Russians in the Near Abroad', in
Spectrum: The Current Affairs Magazine of Aberdeen University, No. 3 (1994). A paper of
the same title and similar content was presented at a conference on nationalism
previously that year in Swansea by Dr Sasha Ostipenko, Moscow University, and
usage can undoubtedly be traced back much farther. More recently it has been
used to describe 'migrants from the near Continent'. See E. Edwards, 'Interpretations
of the influence of the Immigrant Population in Kent in the Sixteenth and Seventeenth
Centuries' in *Archæologia Cantiana*, Vol. CXXII (2002), 275. Due to the mapping of
the world by Western imperial powers and the importance of the Greenwich Meridian
to global navigation, the concept exists in such geographic descriptions as the Middle
East and Far East.

[11] This was a good time, achieved by the Bo'ness skipper John Gibb. See NAS,
Russell Papers, RH15/106/607. James Thomson to Andrew Russell, Norrköping,
30 September 1686. It is often contested that the geographical position of cities
denoted where migrants would go, *i.e.* that Glaswegians would go to Ulster and
east coast Scots to Europe. See T. M. Devine, *Scotland's Empire, 1600–1815* (London:
2003), 9. That is perhaps an over-simplification. Most 'undertakers' in the western
plantation of Lewis came from Fife, as did many in Ulster. Also, Glasgow had a
thriving trade with Scandinavia at the end of the seventeenth century, while many
of the East New Jersey settlers in colonial America came from Aberdeen.

[12] This was certainly the case in Ireland. See N. Canny, 'The Origins of Empire;
An Introduction' in N. Canny, ed., *The Origins of Empire* (Oxford: 1998), 13.

even be visiting simply for social purposes. William Thomson, writing from Newcastle in 1680, told his friend Andrew Russell that "My wife has a mynd to spend some tyme this summer at Rotterdam".[13] This was to be a social visit during which he hoped she would not place any burden on his friends there. Scots could also reinforce each other from Scottish communities outside Britain. James Thomson's Scottish wife arrived in Norrköping to be with him, not from Scotland but from Rotterdam, where she had lived for many years.[14] It is abundantly clear from this collection that family members in Scotland, England, the Dutch Republic and Scandinavia frequently sent relatives to spend time with friends elsewhere, reinforcing their wider community through continual and reciprocal personal and written contact.

Immigrant community development was, of course, dependent on the nature of the society the migrant moved into, and theoretical models seldom reflect historical reality. In some cases there was a smooth resettlement while in others communities formed in the face of hostility. These movements have a difficult historiography due to the subtleties of the words used to describe them, particularly with regard to 'colony' and 'plantation'. Both words can have imperial connotations, though both were also used historically to describe non-imperial dynamics in addition to those concerned with empire building. Apart from its obvious colonial meaning, 'colony' can simply mean 'community'. Similarly 'plantation' was also used historically to describe anything from a particular agricultural system to a utopian community ideal.[15] While plantation schemes in the Americas undoubtedly formed part of the mechanism of European control of

---

[13] NAS, Russell Papers, RH15/106/387/29. William Thomson to Andrew Russell, Newcastle, 4 March 1680.

[14] NAS, Russell Papers, RH15/106/574. James Thomson to Andrew Russell, Norrköping, 9 October 1685.

[15] For more on 'communitarian utopias', see Gusfield, *Community*, 97–99; Canny, 'The Origins of Empire', 9. Canny also noted the utopian idea and expressed his belief that the use of the word 'plantation' was a deliberate attempt to soften the term 'colony' with a horticultural term. Nonetheless, just as we plant in different ways, so too does the word plantation have different meanings. But there is a prevalent view that plantation *must* be colonial in nature and usually involve an agricultural system which is used to extract 'native wealth' through the exploitation of slaves, creoles and the poor white group. Such views run through V. Rubin, *et al.*, eds., *Plantation Systems of the New World* (Washington: 1959). See particularly the following: Rubin, 'intro', 1; J. H. Steward, 'Perspectives on Plantation', 6–8; E. Padilla,

indigenous and slave populations, there was more to the concept than that. In the context of the British Isles, 'plantation' was used as a mechanism to ensure stability both by the English in their 'private plantations' in Ireland in the 1580s, and by pro-Government Scots through the attempted 'plantation of Lewis' in the 1590s and early seventeenth century. The end goal for the various governments was the civilisation of 'savages', the planting of 'true religion' and an economic return for the 'undertakers' involved.[16] After the Union of Crowns of 1603, James VI of Scotland, now also James I of England and Ireland, felt it appropriate to continue the 'plantation policy' by moving still more Scots and English into the 'Ulster Plantations' as equal partners in what Nicholas Canny describes as "a British experiment".[17] From the king's viewpoint, these moves were hardly colonisation in the imperial sense as he could send his subjects anywhere in his dominions he saw fit, so long as they strengthened the society the king hoped to rule over.[18] The society James's

---

'Colonization and the Development of Plantations', 54. Padilla in particular believes that the plantation system was "born in the Caribbean" as a mechanism for European control, without consideration of the internal European plantation schemes discussed below.

[16] An excellent account of the 'Lewis Plantation' by a Lowland Scottish minister who participated in it can be found in NLS, Wodrow Manuscripts, Wod. Qu. Vol. XX, ff. 352–357. It encapsulates the above sentiment by showing that James VI wished to "Reduce that countrie into civilitie And to plant religion unto it, Whereby it might be maid profitable to the whole kingdome in regaird of the com[m]odities that it wes abill to afford being anes maid peaceable & civill." I thank Aonghas MacCoinnich, a doctoral student at the University of Aberdeen, for this source. See also J. Spottiswoode, *The History of the Church of Scotland* (London: 1655, 1972 Scholar Press reprint), 466–467; J. Ohlmeyer, 'Civilizinge of those Rude Partes: Colonization within Britain and Ireland' in Canny, *Origins of Empire*, 124–147; Devine, *Scotland's Empire*, 21; A. I. Macinnes, *The British Revolution, 1629–1660* (Palgrave: 2004), 62–70.

[17] Canny, 'The Origins of Empire', 12.

[18] With Lewis already part of his dominions in the 1590s, the fact that he encouraged his subjects to move from one part of his kingdom to another reflected James's pragmatic politics. That this upset the indigenous population of the islands was probably, in his opinion, hardly worthy of consideration. When the culturally alien Lowland Scots could not suppress the Macleods, the Mackenzies were called in to finish the job. See NLS, Wodrow Manuscripts, Wod. Qu. Vol. XX, ff. 354–357. That the Mackenzies were also Gaels mattered little so long as they remained loyal to the king. Similarly, James encouraged the plantation of Ulster as an expedient with little regard to what the indigenous Irish population felt about it. After all, in law any Scots, English or Irishmen born after 1603 were considered *post-nati* subjects of the same monarch, albeit this was not settled until the Colville/Calvin case was upheld by English common law in 1608. See J. R. Tanner, ed., *Constitutional*

subjects were to build in Ireland was supposed to reflect a utopian model and to encourage entrepreneurs who were willing to develop the economic opportunities afforded by participation. Given James's world-view, the simultaneous development of these types of British plantations in the Americas is unsurprising.[19] Neither was the establishment of plantations and communities by foreigners in Britain rejected, so long as they could contribute to these goals. Thus we find small Dutch communities in locations as diverse as Maidstone in England in the 1580s (115 Dutch adults) and Stornoway in the Western Isles of Scotland in the 1630s (12 Dutch adults), while numerous other foreigners established communities across Britain, even developing 'stranger churches' to accommodate their own confessions of faith.[20]

Plantation as a concept need not have been as controversial as is often portrayed. Indeed evidence exists to show that there was more

---

Documents of the reign of James I (Cambridge: 1930), 24; S. Murdoch, *Britain, Denmark-Norway and the House of Stuart, 1603–1660* (East Linton: 2003), 17–18. I thank Prof Allan Macinnes for discussing the Colville case with me, considered at greater length in his book, *The British Revolution*.

[19] The description of Virginia as a British rather than an English experiment is noted in I. N. Hume, 'First look at a lost Virginia settlement' in *National Geographic*, vol. 155, no. 6, (June 1977), 735 and *passim*. Hume believes the design of the planned settlement of 'Martin's Hundred', built c.1619 and destroyed 1622, was "tantalizingly close" to the settlements established by English colonists in Ireland. Some fifty-eight settlers were killed in Martin's Hundred, along with about 300 others in the surrounding area, in one morning in March 1622 in raids orchestrated by Native Americans. For discussion of the Britishness of the American colonies see Canny, 'The Origins of Empire', 8–12.

[20] While the Dutch community in Kent evolved over time, the Dutch on Lewis were designated 'undertakers' in the same way as other planters in Lewis and Ireland. Aonghas MacCoinnich is working on contextualising the Dutch settlers in Lewis for an article which will be published in due course. I thank him for passing this information to me. Dutchmen are also mentioned participating in the Fens drainage scheme in A. Calder, *Revolutionary Empire: The Rise of the English Speaking Empires from the Fifteenth century to the 1780s* (New York: 1981), 123. 'Stranger churches' were common in most large trading ports. In Britain, Calvinist churches were founded soon after the Reformation in England (in Canterbury and London in the 1550s), although Scandinavian Lutherans had to wait until the second half of the seventeenth century to found their own church in London. For a thorough treatment of the stranger churches in London see A. Pettegree, *Foreign Protestant Communities in Sixteenth-Century London* (Oxford: 1986). See also Edwards, 'Interpretations of the influence of the immigrant population in Kent', 279, while the rest of her article is replete with information on foreign communities in England. For the Lutherans and the thanks they owed to Karl XI of Sweden for the establishment of their church in London see SRA, Anglica 190, Brev från utlänningar till Christoffer Leijoncrona, 1689–1709. Volume E–F. J. Edward to Leijoncrona, London, 16 April 1697.

to these schemes than a desire to inflict imperial tyranny over the Gaelic, slave or Native American populations. Alexander Forbes, Master of Forbes (whose own family was involved in the Ulster Plantation), hoped to be allowed to establish a plantation in the heart of the growing Swedish Empire in the mid-1630s.[21] This example is interesting as it presents a clear demarcation between the establishment of strong Scottish communities in Sweden (such as that in Gothenburg) and a proposed Scottish plantation in Swedish dominions (Ingermanland), following a quest for a 'communitarian utopia' and with the same desire for religious uniformity discussed by David Dobson in several examples in the American colonies. It is not that the Swedes rejected the idea of such a scheme; they simply would not agree to Forbes' request to allow the Scots freedom of religion, for "he having demannded liberty of religion for a plantacon as the first condicon, it was refused".[22] Had the Scots simply eliminated this obstacle the plan would have gone ahead. Nevertheless, the scheme did not end there; it found an influential sponsor in the person of John Durie, who felt it was worth another try. He offered to sponsor any English 'Transplanters' who would go to Germany or Sweden to join the Scots as "it is most seasonable for them to worke joyntly with others of the same mind to strengthen one anothers suit".[23] In effect, he was arguing for the proposed Scottish plantation to be turned into a British one—just like those that existed in Ulster—with a broader theological remit than desired by Forbes. The important point about this plantation scheme is that it could not have been 'colonial' in nature. Durie and Forbes were too politically astute and *au fait* with Swedish and German politics for that. Rather it was an attempt to establish a community within an existing and largely sympathetic society, in which the planters could build a life for themselves *without* any imperial ambition.[24]

---

[21] G. Westin, ed., *John Durie in Sweden, 1636–1638: Documents and Letters* (Uppsala: 1936), 5. John Durie to Samuel Hartlib, 18/28 May 1636. Forbes's scheme to populate Ingermanland with Scots (and other similar schemes) were discussed both directly and indirectly in the Swedish Riksråd. See *Svenska Riksrådets Protokoll*, vol. 6, 16 December 1636, 771–772.

[22] Westin, *John Durie in Sweden, 1636–1638*, 5. John Durie to Samuel Hartlib, 18/28 May 1636.

[23] Westin, *John Durie in Sweden, 1636–1638*, 5. John Durie to Samuel Hartlib, 18/28 May 1636.

[24] For the sympathetic attitude of the Swedes to the Scots in this period and

Patrick Fitzgerald's essay examines the issue of migration to the Ulster Plantation more through the vehicle of Scottish community formation in an English colonial environment rather than as an attempt at Scottish imperialism. In Ulster, the transplantation of Scots represented a formally authorised movement *within* the fledgling British state, with the Scots as theoretical if not actual partners in the venture.[25] However, Fitzgerald demonstrates that the Scots chose not to limit themselves to the official settlements the monarch set aside for them in Ireland. Indeed, these settlements were effectively treated as points of entry, undermining their very existence as Scottish enclaves. After only a few years the settlers often spread out to the more lucrative centres in Ireland, in particular Dublin and Cork.[26] Many others scattered into the wider diaspora beyond the Stuart kingdoms. A large Scottish community (or cluster of communities) did survive in Ulster, though neither in the form nor with the results envisaged either by the king or presumably by the original planters themselves.

When the Scots and English were thrust together outside Britain they found they actually had a lot in common. Most spoke languages on the same linguistic continuum, and the majority shared a belief in a reformed confession of faith, despite the differences in interpretation.[27] The move to the 'middle-abroad' often compounded the self-evaluation expressed by many migrants regarding who they were

---

why they may have contemplated such a scheme, see A. Grosjean, *An Unofficial Alliance: Scotland and Sweden 1569–1654* (Leiden: 2003), particularly chps V and VI. Calvinism was illegal in Sweden, though many Scottish Calvinists settled there with no problem due to their excellent military service. The idea of an entirely Calvinist enclave was something the Lutheran bishops could not allow.

[25] Canny, 'The Origins of Empire', 12.

[26] Even as late as 1797 it was observed by one French traveller to Cork that "The principle merchants are nearly all foreigners, Scotch for the most part, and in the short period of ten years are able sometimes to make large fortunes." See Jacques Louis de Bougrenet (Le Chevalier de La Tocnaye), *A Frenchman's walk through Ireland 1796–1797: Translated from the French of De La Tocnaye by John Stevenson 1917* (Belfast: 1984 edition), 73. Stephen Dornan, a doctoral student at the University of Aberdeen, kindly provided this reference.

[27] The languages meant here are Scots and English. Scots is a Germanic language and not to be confused with Scottish Gaelic which is on the same linguistic continuum as Irish Gaelic. For more on the Scots language see C. Jones, ed., *The Edinburgh History of the Scots Language* (Edinburgh: 1997). The importance of the Scots language in overseas Scottish communities is admirably dealt with in D. Horsburgh, 'The political identity of the Scots-speaking community in Scotland and Ulster, 1545–1760' in W. Kelly and J. R. Young, eds., *Ulster and Scotland 1600–2000: History, Language and Identity* (Dublin: 2004), 142–160.

and where they came from. When surrounded by populations largely
of the Roman Catholic faith, speaking starkly distinct languages,
many of those from Britain had even more reason to work together
and build integrated 'British' communities, albeit these often arose
out of expediency.[28] Thus even before 1603 a mixed Scottish-English
community had formed in Elbing, with a Scottish Presbyterian
preacher in their 'stranger church' by the 1620s.[29] In Middelburg,
a Scottish Calvinist preacher, Reverend William Spang, ministered
to the 'English' congregation throughout the middle seventeenth century. Although it was observed by some transient English travellers
in 1663 that he used some peculiarly Scottish forms during his service, neither they nor the congregation he ministered to appear to
have minded.[30]

In Poland-Lithuania a different set of problems arises when trying to ascertain the strength of the Scottish community. This is the
great 'Polish question' posed by William Lithgow and his claim that
30,000 Scottish families were settled in Poland by 1620.[31] Waldemar
Kowalski tackles the issue of Scottish communities in this 'middle-
abroad' head on. Given that the largest communities settle in urban
centres, Kowalski looks at the Scottish settlement in a number of
Polish centres and questions the nature of the institutions they built
up to support themselves. While discussing several locations in a general way, he establishes a clear framework for understanding the
move to the European East and evaluates this aspect of Scottish
diaspora studies in a most illuminating way. The distance from home
meant that there were certain realities the migrants had to deal with.
From central Poland, they were no longer days or weeks from home
but most probably months. Indeed, when the young Patrick Gordon
found himself hoping to return to Scotland from Danzig in 1653, a

---

[28] Canny, 'The Origins of Empire', 3.
[29] T. Fischer, *The Scots in Germany* (Edinburgh: 1902), 175; *DNB*, VI, 261.
[30] Philip Skippon, 'An Account of a Journey made thro' part of the Low-Countries, Germany, Italy and France, 1663' published in *A COLLECTION of Voyages and Travels, some now first printed from original manuscripts, others now first published in English. In SIX VOLUMES* (London: 1746), VI, 398. Spang had earlier been minister to the Scots congregation in Campveere in the 1630s–40s. See D. Laing, ed., *The Letters and Journals of Robert Baillie, Principle of the University of Glasgow, 1637–1662* (3 vols., Edinburgh: 1841), I and II, *passim.*
[31] William Lithgow, *The Totall Discourse of the Rare Adventures and Painefull Peregrinations of long Nineteene Years Travayles from Scotland to the most famous Kingdomes in Europe, Asia and Affrica* (Glasgow: 1906 edition), 368.

group of Scottish merchants told him "it would be nyne or ten mon-
eths ere I should fynd an occasion by sea to Scotland; to travell by
land would be very expensive, and to stay there no lesse".[32] Journey
times were dependent on the season, as well as on the political situation at given times. There were fewer 'social visitors' and the environment was more alien. It was small wonder that local rivalries
appeared trivial to the Scottish settler in this world. Scots found
themselves seeking out fellow Scots, but also Englishmen and
Dutchmen. Even when they could not speak each other's language
they were thankful for the security the company of a fellow 'western' European could bring. Patrick Gordon seems to have sought
out such company on several occasions, even when he suspected one
individual of plotting some serious crime against him.[33]

As the Scots spread even further across the globe, they entered
the 'far-abroad'. It took five to six months to reach the East Indies,
with the round trip usually taking up to eighteenth months.[34] Few
would want to simply get off the boat only to turn straight back
again, and indeed round trip journeys of several years were quite
common.[35] Many found themselves in lands where the populations

---

[32] Spalding Club, *Passages from the Diary of General Patrick Gordon of Auchleuchries*
(Aberdeen: 1859), 12.

[33] While most of the men Gordon found himself travelling with appeared friendly
in 1653, he did keep company with one he thought might be plotting to murder
him. Although warned that this man was a rogue by a fellow Scot, Gordon obviously decided he was still better than no company at all and continued with him
for several more days. See *Diary of General Patrick Gordon*, 8–11.

[34] NLS, Adv. MS 33.3.14. 'The Woyage of Cap: Jhone Andersone. Pilat Maior
of a Fleit of Hollanders which went out from Halmorsluiss in South Holland in
AD 1640 and Returned from Thence to ye Flee in ye monnth of Julay 1643',
ff. 2, 17. Anderson left the Dutch Republic on 29 December 1640 and arrived at
his destination in Batavia on 10 May 1641. Drummer Major James Spens left
Swedish service to join the Dutch East India Company (VOC) in 1631. He wrote
to his parents from Africa en route to Java, assuring them that he would see them
again. He had signed up to the VOC for five years which, he explained, meant a
seven-year journey once the year-long travel there and back was added to his time.
He wrote: "for it is plisit god yt I was borne to travill always I prais god for I
have greit contentment be it [. . .] I must be fyve zeire in ye Land and a zeir cum-
ing and ane zeir going and pliss god to spair me so lang days yt qn my fyve zeirs
is out I sall cum hame and see yow". See NAS RH9/2/242. James Spens to his
parents from the Guinea Coast, 23 February 1632.

[35] NLS, Adv. MS 33.3.14. 'The Woyage of Cap: Jhone Andersone', ff. 79–80.
Nonetheless, some casual 'visitors' do seem to have made the trip. See the case of
Elizabeth Couper who apparently 'visited' her brother in Batavia in the 1670s. S.
Murdoch, 'The Good, the Bad and the Anonymous: A Preliminary Survey of the
Scots in the Dutch East Indies 1612–1707' in *Northern Scotland*, vol. 22, (2002), 67.

practised cultural traditions and religions most Europeans found
abhorrent. In addition, the striking physical attributes of the indigenous populations often meant that European travel-journals dwelt
heavily upon them.[36] In Africa, South America and Asia, the locals
looked different to Europeans just as Europeans looked alien to them,
so much so that one skipper observed that in Africa "the blacks,
who in odium of the colour, say, the devil is white, and so paint
him".[37] In such circumstances, Scottish Protestants could mingle with
Portuguese Catholics or any number of other Europeans in a way
they were less likely to at home. Thus we find that in the 'far-
abroad', the likelihood of finding any mono-ethnic European community is extremely remote.[38] Whether Scottish, English, Dutch,
Portuguese, French or Swedish, in the 'far-abroad' the communities
that established themselves were almost universally multi-ethnic from
the outset, although the degeneration of ethnic and commercial rivalries into hostilities was not uncommon.[39] In attempts to found either

---

[36] For an endless assortment of such references see *A COLLECTION of Voyages
and Travels, some Now first Printed from Original Manuscripts, others Now first Published in
English. In SIX VOLUMES* (London: 1746). This collection of travelogues is replete
with descriptions of indigenous populations throughout the globe. Scots also engaged
in the discussion of indigenous people and distant places; see NLS, Adv. MS 33.3.14.
'The Woyage of Cap: Jhone Andersone', ff. 17–18, 27–28, 31–47, 49, 53, 64–69.

[37] Thomas Phillips, 'A Journal of a Voyage Made in the HANNIBAL of London,
Ann. 1693, 1694 From England, to Cape MONSERADOE, in AFRICA; And
thence along the Coast of Guiney to Whidaw, the Island of St. Thomas, And so
forward to BARBADOES. WITH A Cursory ACCOUNT of the COUNTRY, the
PEOPLE, Their MANNERS, FORTS, TRADE. &c.', published in *A COLLEC-
TION of Voyages and Travels*, VI, 235. Phillips was a remarkable slave captain with
strong views on Christianity and paganism. He also wrote in his journal: "excepting their want of Christianity and true religion, (their misfortune more than fault)
[Africans] are as much the works of God's hands, and no doubt as dear to him
as ourselves; nor can I imagine why they should be despised for their colour, being
what they cannot help, and the effect of the climate it has pleased God to appoint
them. I can't think there is any intrinsick value in one colour more than another,
nor that white is better than black, only we think it so because we are so, and are
prone to judge favourably in our own case."

[38] N. E. S. Griffiths and J. G. Reid, 'New Evidence on New Scotland, 1629', in
The William and Mary Quarterly, vol. 49, no. 3 (July 1992), 499. This article contains
a very illuminating transcription of an eye-witness account of the Scots in Nova
Scotia in 1629 by one Richard Guthry.

[39] Victor Enthoven makes the point that it is impossible to distinguish between
English, Irish and Dutch settlers from Flushing who settled on the 'Wild Coast' in
the Amazon Delta. This was due to the fact that the English community in Flushing
employed Zeeland ships, while Zeeland settlements included English speakers in
their populations. V. Enthoven, 'Early Dutch Expansion in the Atlantic Region,

a colony or a plantation at a great distance, those who were to go had to be the hardiest, the most willing, the most adaptable or, preferably, the most capable. There was no room to exclude any willing contributor; hence (as David Dobson argues) the desire of the Virginia colony to recruit even Scottish criminals, who would surely be more acceptable or at least useful to them than the pagan indigenous population, particularly in terms of their renowned martial abilities. The English in both Ireland and the Americas perceived the Scots in terms of a defensive barrier between them and the 'savages'.[40]

Dobson traces the numerous endeavours and routes taken by Scots in their move to the 'far-west'. He demonstrates that from the earliest attempts to establish communities in Nova Scotia in the 1620s, there was never *intended* to be a mono-ethnic Scottish community in the Americas, although particularly Scottish institutions like the Scots' Charitable Society of Boston, Massachusetts, were established to support them.[41] Dobson confirms previous studies which have highlighted that the English were an integral part of the Nova Scotia scheme from the outset, and were also initially intended to be involved in any plantation scheme to be undertaken by the Company of Scotland in the 1690s.[42] Similarly, most English schemes involved numerous Scots and Irish, while members of these nations also found their way into other European colonies. Underpinning the Scottish-English interaction were several interpretations of pan-British identity which varied in the rigour of their implementation throughout the century. There was of course an exception. Although the Company of Scotland initially had support from English investors, the Darien scheme it engaged in resulted in physical disaster for 3000 Scottish settlers and a financial catastrophe for hundreds of investors. The Honourable

---

1585–1621' in J. Postma and V. Enthoven, eds., *Riches from Atlantic Commerce: Dutch Transatlantic Trade and Shipping, 1585–1817* (Leiden: 2003), 34.

[40] Griffiths and Reid, 'New Evidence on New Scotland', 492; Canny, 'The Origins of Empire', 13.

[41] W. Budde, 'The Scots' Charitable Society of Boston Massachusetts', Appendix 5 in J. Taylor, *A Cup of Kindness: The History of the Royal Scottish Corporation, A London Charity, 1603–2003* (East Linton: 2003), 255–257. Founded in 1657 by twenty-eight Scots to support indentured servants, the society gained thirty-four new members over the next eight years. After a moribund period, it then took on 154 new members between 1684–1692.

[42] Previous works have suggested that the Scots were even in the minority among the settlers. See Griffiths and Reid, 'New Evidence on New Scotland', 497.

East India Company and other London-based institutions like the
Muscovy Company had a history of protecting their monopolies
against other Englishmen (particularly those from Hull) as well as
Scots, if they threatened their monopoly.[43] It has been a feature of
Scottish historiography to turn both the king and the English into
scapegoats for the failure of the venture. Yet, as Dobson argues, had
the Scots established a plantation 'lawfully' as directed by the king
in one of his colonies, it would probably have been far better supported, hardly have aroused the concern of the East India Company,
and developed eventually into another integrated British colony.[44]
Instead those Scots who bought into the company defied their monarch

---

[43] *APC*, IV, 70–72 and 77. 15 and 18 March 1618. Revocation of Patent, and
Order of Reimbursement for Sir James Cunningham; *CSP Colonial*, II, 1617–1621,
113–114, 137, 162, 218. Various East India Company minutes against James
Cunningham, March–December 1618; Calder, *Revolutionary Empire*, 162; Murdoch,
'The Good, the Bad and the Anonymous', 65–66. See also G. P. Herd, 'General
Patrick Gordon of Auchleuchries – A Scot in Seventeenth Century Russian Service',
unpublished Ph.D. thesis, Aberdeen (1994), 20. Herd notes that the Muscovy
Company sought to prevent "interlopers in the shape of Scottish and Dutch merchants, as well as those from Hull and York, attempt to break their self-awarded
monopoly." Hull merchants had been trading with Russia since at least 1580. See
also G. Jackson, *Hull in the Eighteenth Century: A Study in Economic and Social History*
(Oxford: 1972), 5. Another famous episode of a company community protecting
itself from interlopers occurred in the East Indies at Ambon in 1618. The memory of the Ambon massacre is often repeated as an act of Dutch barbarity against
the English nation. Too often scholars forget that there were Britons *with* the Dutch
in Ambon and that the victims of the massacre included Japanese and Portuguese
equal in number to the unfortunate English who died, *plus* an equal number of
Englishmen were set free to those killed. The point is that a VOC community eliminated their perceived competition. What they did not do was execute them simply because the one side were 'Dutch' while the others were 'English'. The VOC
officers attacked a rival mercantile community threatening their own, albeit the
English were still publishing propaganda pamphlets to the contrary in 1688. See
*The Prince of Orange. His Declaration: Shewing the Reasons Why he Invades England. With
a Short Preface, and some modest remarks on it. Printed by Randal Taylor* (London: 1688).
The author stated "We love our country, and we love Honour, and before England
shall become the prey of Holland, we will take order they shall find nothing in it,
but Grass and Trees, no Men for them to use as they did at Amboina". I thank
Emma Bergin, a doctoral student at the University of Hull, for passing on this
reference.
[44] William of Orange ordered the Marquis of Tweedale to instruct the Scottish
parliament "to pass an Act for the encouragement of such as shall acquire and
establish a plantation in Africa or America, or in any other part of the world where
plantations may be lawfully acquired, in which Act you are to declare that we will
grant to our subjects of that kingdom [Scotland], such rights and privileges as we
grant in the like cases to the subjects of our other dominions, the one not inter-
fering with the other". *CSPD*, 1694–1695, 428. 17 April 1695.

to establish a colony that was illegal; the king (or his navy) could not have supported them without risking war with Spain. At the same time, however, other Scottish planters headed to legal settlements in the Americas with the aid of English shipping. Indeed, in 1696 *The Lily* of London left Montrose with 112 passengers bound for Pennsylvania, with little fuss made by anyone about it.[45]

Section II: 'Located' Communities

Over the course of the early modern period numerous Scottish communities evolved, several of which have received much scrutiny by historians, while others remain largely unknown. It is an accepted fact that migrant destinations are seldom random and were often bound by a tie between a point of origin and a point of destination, based on highly localised information sent to one place from the other. As Thomas Sowell observed, "behind such migration patterns often lay particular beginnings of a new community in a new land where one pioneering individual, family or group of families decided to try their luck overseas".[46] This process leads to 'chain migration', a recurring theme in the following chapters which highlight several communities located in particular urban centres.

Remembering that the Swedes rejected the attempted plantation by Scots in the 1630s, it is interesting to note that a similar scheme appears to have been implemented in the private city of Kėdainiai in Lithuania within three years of the rejection of the Forbes proposal. Kėdainiai undoubtedly reflects both a small 'plantation' followed by chain migration. Rimantas Žirgulis notes that those who settled there possessed qualities admired and shared by the town's owner, Duke Radziwill. In this case, the majority of those who migrated from Scotland were Calvinists. Such 'Reformation from above' was not uncommon and happened elsewhere in communities like Colmar (Alsace) in 1575.[47] However, in Colmar's case the civic authorities decreed that the population *could* practise Protestantism

---

[45] NAS, RH15/14/58.
[46] Sowell, *Migrations and Cultures*, 5–6.
[47] P. G. Wallace, *Communities and Conflict in Early Modern Colmar, 1575–1730* (New Jersey: 1995), 2, 16.

and 'overnight' it became a 'bi-confessional' town. In Kėdainiai's case a whole new set of citizens were brought in with the explicit design of inclining the community towards Calvinism. The parachuting in of a community of Scots to this city occurred relatively quickly and their domination of the city infrastructure took a little over twenty years. That this community successfully survived for over a century challenges the prevalent notion that Ulster drained Scotland of the resources required for the Scots to form plantations elsewhere.[48] Žirgulis' findings are striking. To some degree they are the result of the breaking down of linguistic barriers and the historical amnesia towards Lithuanian history that dogged the study of the country until the 1990s. However, Kėdainiai was only one 'private' town of the Radziwill dukes. Among the others were towns of equal importance in areas of Lithuania now in the modern countries of Ukraine and Belarus. There were also Scottish communities in these towns, and even a Scottish governor, William Paterson in Slutsak/Sluck.[49] These communities await the kind of detailed examination undertaken by Žirgulis and may be of equal significance to Scottish history. Until such work is done, we may never actually know the full extent and numbers involved in the Scottish communities established in the east of Europe.

While the Lithuanian situation highlights an example of an effective 'eastern plantation', Nina Østby Pedersen discusses the somewhat different case of Bergen. Sustained contact and existing mercantile exchanges in that city over several hundred years resulted in episodic influxes of Scots. Their presence was encouraged by the Danish-Norwegian monarchy, and the resulting numbers in the new burgess structure were designed to challenge the power of the Hanseatic League in the city. They effectively hobbled the Hansa merchants through sheer presence of numbers, and operated an integrationalist strategy (by accident or design) that allowed both fellow Scots

---

[48] For example as argued in Canny, 'The Origins of Empire', 15–16. Other, largely forgotten, Scottish communities developed elsewhere in Europe throughout the century. Some twenty Scottish families moved into Finnmark in Norway to take advantage of the patronage of the Scottish governor, John Cunningham. See R. Hagen, 'At the Edge of Civilisation: John Cunningham, Lensmann of Finnmark, 1619–1651' in A. Mackillop and S. Murdoch, eds., *Military Governors and Imperial Frontiers, c.1600–1800: A Study of Scotland and Empires* (Leiden: 2003), 35–37.

[49] This information was kindly provided by Andrej Kotljarchuk, Baltic and East European Graduate School, Södertorn Högskolan, Sweden.

and the Copenhagen-based government to benefit from their presence. As in Norway, there was a long-standing presence of Scottish enclaves in the Dutch Republic. Douglas Catterall's research on Rotterdam provides a case study that shows the 'informal' community actually grew stronger than the 'official' one. The city of Veere was designated as the Scottish staple port in the Dutch Republic.[50] A Scottish Conservator remained in residence there and all Scottish trade in staple goods was theoretically targeted to that city and that city alone. A small but vibrant Scottish community remained in the town throughout the seventeenth century, with their own social and religious institutions, while the last Conservator did not leave office until 1799.[51] As Catterall makes clear, however, while Veere represented the official centre for the Scottish merchant community in the Dutch Republic, Rotterdam proved to be far more influential as the hub of Caledonian enterprise. Indeed, the establishment of the Scots Kirk in the city in 1642 stands as testament to the strength of community there.[52] Yet such cultural acceptance of the Scottish community was far from universal. Despite the strength of their presence and the immense impact they had on the culture within Kėdainiai or Bergen, it was never made explicit in these cities that the Scots were present because they were Scots. Because the Reformed community in Kėdainiai was multi-cultural from the outset, there were no specific civic, regal or cultural institutions set down to formalise the 'Scottishness' of the community within the wider society of the city. The same was true in Bergen. Therefore the recorded contact with Scotland and apparent Scottish community structures that existed were often of an informal nature, built upon a variety of social and commercial networks and private initiatives such as the provision of poor relief for Scots in foreign communities.[53] Informality was not

---

[50] M. P. Roosenboom, *The Scottish Staple in the Netherlands* (The Hague: 1910); V. Enthoven, 'The last straw: Trade contacts along the North Sea Coast: the Scottish staple at Veere' in Juliette Roding and Lex Heerma van Voss, eds., *The North Sea and Culture, 1550–1800* (Verloren: 1996), 209–221.

[51] Enthoven, 'The last straw', 209, 219.

[52] The Scots Kirk in Rotterdam has been written about on numerous occasions, most recently by D. Catterall, *Community Without Borders: Scots Migrants and the Changing Face of Power in the Dutch Republic, c. 1600–1700* (Leiden: 2002), 245–253.

[53] Douglas Catterall goes into detail about the provision of poor relief in Rotterdam. In London too, Scots established a 'poor box' which eventually led to the formation of the Royal Scottish Corporation of London. See Taylor, *A Cup of Kindness*, 25–27. The success of less structured Scottish settlements reflected the internal

the case in the newly established city of Gothenburg in 1621. Just as in Bergen, the Scots were favoured because of existing contact with the region, through the older towns of Älvsborg and Lödöse. But Gothenburg was a fresh start, where the royal patent enshrined a Scottish presence as a formal part of the city council from its inception by allocating two seats on the council to members of the Scottish nation. No wonder then that those Scots already resident nearby ensured that the best was made of this privilege, and a strong and vibrant community flourished. This was despite the fact that there could be no sanctioned Calvinist community as there was in the less 'formalised' community of Rotterdam, resulting in an anomalous situation for many Scottish communicants of the Kirk living in Sweden.

While the urban centres just mentioned all hosted distinguishable Scottish communities, albeit at various degrees of integration with the host community, Hamburg was different. As Kathrin Zickermann makes clear, to talk of a settled Scottish community in Hamburg is problematic. The city was an English staple port, and the presence of the 'English Court' has drawn the historiography of the city in a direction that simply cannot conceive of any meaningful Scottish presence. Nonetheless, over the course of the 1600s there were several hundred Scots living in the city, many of them settled for significant periods of time and forming a web of networks. Where this community became demonstrably different was in the application of 'British' concepts within the English community in a way traditionally associated only with Ulster. Scots and Englishmen lived and functioned together in a British community that neither nation could contest was fully theirs. Zickermann's evidence suggests that, although there was no British 'plantation' in Hamburg, the building of a British community during the same period that the plantations in the Americas and Ulster were still evolving had some startlingly successful effects.

Though Zickermann's is probably the most overtly pluralistic chapter of this section, it must not be forgotten that there could be more than one form of pluralism. As evidenced throughout this collection,

---

situation in Scotland, where Lowland Scots did better at informally transplanting communities to Orkney and Shetland than in the formal plantation of Lewis. See Ohlmeyer, 'Civilizinge of those Rude Partes', 135.

groups of Scots demonstrably described themselves as Scottish *and* British, but also as Scottish *and* Swedish, Scottish *and* Dutch and a variety of other combinations, which gives the lie to the belief that if Scots once described themselves as anything other than Scots their Scottish identity became redundant. They qualified who and what they represented as a given occasion demanded, and undoubtedly varied their definitions at different stages of their lives. Importantly their pluralism suggests a far more complex process of cultural assimilation and distinctiveness to that offered for 'the Scots' by Thomas Sowell.[54] While arguing that linguistic factors encouraged quick assimilation of Scots into the American colonies, his theory was never tested against areas like Scandinavia, Poland-Lithuania and the Dutch Republic, where it is obvious that the Scots could, and usually did, integrate linguistically into the host society rather quickly. That they did not feel the need to overtly demonstrate their ethnicity suggests a more nuanced process at work, in which integration took place while ethnically based community structures and ties operated on a more covert, less intrusive level. Therein undoubtedly lay their success: their ability to exploit all the avenues presented to them by their native and host societies alike.

Section III: Communities of Mind and Interest

As discussed above, the question 'What makes a community?' is something of a subject in itself. In the previous sections, both general trends facilitating the establishment of communities, and some examples of communities in specific locations are discussed—what sociologists describe as 'bounded' communities. Yet there is a different form of community that can be described—the 'unbounded' communities of mind and interest.[55] The three essays in this section discuss several varieties of such communities "orientated towards the

---

[54] Sowell, *Migrations and Cultures*, 47. Sowell suggests that the process of assimilation may have linguistic constraints, hence the tenacious nature of German-speaking populations in the Americas as opposed to the Scots who were 'readily absorbed'.
[55] Macfarlane, *Reconstructing Historical Communities*, 1, 8–9; Delanty, *Community*, 112. Delanty describes these as essentially communicative in their organisation and composition and not located in either the classic rural or urban models usually discussed.

ways in which group members co-operate and conflict—to the existence or absence of bonds of similarity and sympathy".[56] Sowell made
the case well that migrant populations are frequently "atypical of the
population in the country from which they came".[57] Gerard Delanty
describes "the radical dimension of community as expressed in protest,
in the quest for an alternative society or the construction of collective identity in social movements".[58] In the Scottish case they were
often refugees with a political consciousness, the expelled or self-
imposed religious exiles of the sort described throughout this volume. Ginny Gardner discusses one such group of people who fled
from Scotland and established a community in exile, albeit not settled in a single 'bounded' location. They were spread by ill-fortune
at home and necessity abroad. The Dutch Republic simply could
not absorb them into any one existing Dutch community. Thus soldiers, sailors, scholars, lawyers, clergymen and their families lived in
exile but formed something of a 'correspondence community' within
the Dutch provinces and frequently beyond. This united them, kept
them in touch with their Protestant *raison d'etre* and ultimately saw
them return to the greater Scottish community after various periods
of exile. Both the home and foreign-based Calvinist communities
reinforced each other's adherence to a contested confession of faith
in their homeland through constant reaffirmation of the importance
of the one community to the other. This could take place through
direct contact from the Scottish Kirk or as evidenced by some of
the still-extant personal testimonies that circulated between the various Scottish communities.[59] This community did not integrate like

---

[56] Gusfield, *Community*, xv–xvi.

[57] Sowell, *Migrations and Cultures*, 4.

[58] Delanty, *Community*, 4 and 112. Delanty believes this form of community-building to be representative of the modern period, though the examples discussed by
the authors in this section fit his description rather well. See also Lynch, *Individuals,
families, and Communities*, 16.

[59] See for example *An Exhortation of the Generall Assembly of the Kirk of Scotland unto
the Scots Merchants and others our Country-people Scattered in Poleland, Swedeland, Denmark,
and Hungary* (Edinburgh: 1647). For examples of the overseas Scottish Calvinist communities lending each other support, see for example NAS Russell Papers,
RH15/106/532/16–17. Alexander Davidson to Andrew Russell, Riga, 20 October
1684; NAS Russell Papers, RH15/106/576/17 James Adie to Andrew Russell,
Danzig, 6 July 1685, on Rev James Brown's request for information from Scotland;
Laing, *The Letters and Journals of Robert Baillie*, numerous examples of Baillie's letters
to foreign-based Scottish Calvinist ministers, vols. I–III, *passim*, particularly William
Spang.

the others discussed, as both exiled and home-based Scots hoped for the former's return to Scotland to strike off the bonds of tyranny, as they saw them. The exiles were galvanised by assurances of a positive reception on their return and, as Gardner highlights, with some success.[60] Indeed, according to David Ogg this refugee community grew so strong that there was a kind of reverse cultural assimilation, as they had migrated to the Dutch Republic "in such numbers that, before his accession, William had probably more experience of the Scottish than of the English language".[61]

The exile community were not the only Scots to live in the Dutch Republic, as evidenced by Catterall's contribution. There was of course the Scots-Dutch Brigade, but also the hugely significant student community. Like the exiles, this was something of a community of the mind. There was no total separation between the exile, military and academic Scottish populations in the Republic, nor indeed from the communities at Veere, Rotterdam or elsewhere. Though Esther Mijers talks in terms of thousands of individuals, they never inhabited the same space at the same time. They were spread over a number of years across the various Dutch universities and academies. Nonetheless, on one level they formed a continuous community, with many being brought or sent to their seat of learning by previous members of the academic community, in another facet of chain migration. On another level, Mijers identifies the fact that within the wider student community there were others who had specific attachments to particular universities for reasons of religion, politics or patronage. The impact these individuals had on wider Scottish society was immense, particularly with regard to the expertise re-imported by returning academics in spheres as diverse as law, metaphysics and theology.

Another community of interest with a strong presence outwith Scotland was the Scottish maritime population. In a most interesting comparative assessment of Scots in the 'English' and Dutch naval

---

[60] See also, among others, NAS Russell Papers, RH15/106/710/17. Rev James Brown to Andrew Russell, Königsberg, 28 April 1690.

[61] D. Ogg, *England in the Reigns of James II and William III* (Oxford: 1955), 264. For more on the use of the Scots language in European politics and diplomacy, including its use by other European potentates, see D. Horsbroch, '*Nostra Vulgari Lingua*: Scots as a European Language 1500–1700' in *Scottish Language*, no. 18 (1999), 1–16.

services, Andrew Little contrasts Scots in the Royal Navy with contemporaries in the Dutch marine (and other foreign navies), once
more raising the spectre of community pluralism. Cautiously examining the difficult issue of whether the Royal Navy was an 'English'
or a 'British' institution, Little targets groups of sailors drawn from
specific towns and questions their motive for enlistment in the service they chose at given times. In contrast to the supposition that
such individuals were simply part of the general seventeenth-century
maritime labour market, Little not only postulates but demonstrates
their desire and repeated insistence to remain together with fellow
Scots. Thus ships in the navies of the two maritime super-powers
could be entirely populated by Scots who had refused to be dispersed. In foreign service they may have been, yet the *desire* to form
a Scottish community remained overwhelming and clearly stated, if
not always permitted by their superiors.

The Historical Significance of the Scottish Community Abroad

Arguments against 'community studies' abound, and one of the most
virulent is "that 'communities' tend to lie in the eye and the method-
ology of the beholder".[62] There are certainly historical difficulties for
the historian in trying to locate historical communities, though the
rigorous use of available data has certainly yielded positive results
for the contributors to this volume.[63] Indeed, the historical importance that the presence of a strong Scottish community outside the
country could embody cannot be overstated. On several occasions
throughout the seventeenth century the overseas communities demonstrably impacted militarily, economically and/or politically in Scotland
and throughout the rest of Great Britain and Ireland. Had there not
been such a strong Scottish community in Sweden, among other
places, it is doubtful that the Covenanting Revolution would have
had the success it did, with all that implied for the 'British' civil
wars.[64] As Gardner demonstrates, Scottish refugees also had a pro-

---

[62] Macfarlane, *Reconstructing Historical Communities*, 14–15.
[63] Macfarlane, *Reconstructing Historical Communities*, 8–10.
[64] Murdoch and Mackillop, *Fighting for Identity*, intro, xxx–xxxii; Grosjean, *An
Unofficial Alliance*, particularly chps V and VI.

found influence on the outcome of the Williamite succession in the British Isles. Economically, too, Scottish communities abroad were vitally important. James Foulis in London observed that "if our gentry had not beine numerous heir at present" then the Scottish rate of exchange in England would have declined quite seriously in April 1678, well ahead of the usual annual fluctuation.[65] Yet quite what Foulis meant by his 'numerous' community is uncertain in the light of comments by other contemporary London Scots. Writing only a few months after Foulis, John Robertson described his situation in London as being in "unknowne company", suggesting a dearth of fellow countrymen.[66] Similarly, two years later, William Jamieson observed that there were enough of "our folk" in the city to support him, but not enough to find him employment.[67] What these letters *do* reveal is the importance of the connection between the two émigré Scottish communities in London and Rotterdam. The exact strength of Scottish communities in England is yet to be established, though with a population of around 575,000 at the end of the seventeenth century it is probable that London supported numerous Scottish communities, at a variety of social levels, that were not necessarily connected at all.[68] However, the establishment of the Royal Scottish Corporation provided an important focal point, particularly after it became formalised by Royal Charter in 1665, in what Allan Macinnes has described as "the premier ethnic anchor for Scots in the city".[69]

---

[65] This annual fluctuation was despite the fact that the exchange rate was officially set at a rate of 12:1 after the accession of James VI to the English throne in 1603. See NAS, Russell Papers, RH15/106/305/12. James Foulis to Andrew Russell, London, 23 April 1678. Foulis served as Treasurer of the Royal Scottish Corporation in London in 1674 and Master of the Corporation in 1679. See Taylor, *A Cup of Kindness*, 45.

[66] He wrote to Andrew Russell that he intended to leave the city for want of company, although his comrade William Lamb would still be around with him for a further two weeks. See NAS, Russell Papers, RH15/106/305/24. John Robertson to Andrew Russell, 6 August 1678.

[67] NAS, Russell Papers, RH15/106/387/11 and 12. William Jamiesson to Andrew Russell, 23 March and 9 April 1680.

[68] For instance in 1650, at a time when Scotland and England were in a state of conflict, one English observer noted the presence of a community of Scottish women in London who retained the "Art of brewing". See Hartlib Papers, EPHEMERIDES, 1650 PART 4, HP 22/1/79B. It is unlikely that they were connected to numerous higher status Scots resident in London who sympathised with the Cromwellian regime or continued trading from London in spite of it.

[69] Quoted from the preface by A. I. Macinnes to Taylor, *A Cup of Kindness*, xi.

This volume does not claim that the Scottish experience of migration or community establishment is in anyway unique, or that those communities were in any way self-sufficient or isolated from the wider societies that hosted them. As Fraser pointed out, a community was not continually cohesive, but could combine and divide as circumstances dictated.[70] Rather, these essays confirm the dependency of the communities on other institutions in order that they could flourish. What the contributors have shown is that the studies, as well as being meaningful in their own right, illuminate valuable lessons in a world in which the migratory process has arguably reached an apex when cheap global transport facilitates the evolution of new communities across continents. These studies have been placed in an international perspective by three respected experts in the field of migration and social integration, and their chapter is of no less relevance than any editorial comment.

Steve Murdoch and Alexia Grosjean
University of St Andrews

Taylor's book is a welcome and important contribution to the study of the Scottish community in London. A systematic survey of that community and other Scottish communities elsewhere in England in the early modern period is currently underway in the School of History, University of St Andrews.
[70] Fraser, *To Tara via Holyhead*, 80.

SECTION I

MIGRANT DESTINATIONS, COLONIES
AND PLANTATIONS

SCOTTISH MIGRATION TO IRELAND IN THE SEVENTEENTH CENTURY

Patrick Fitzgerald

Writing in 2000 on the subject of Irish emigration in the nineteenth century, Donald McRaild suggested that "Migration history is a particular beneficiary of comparative methodologies. Because it links countries and continents migration studies in a sense really has to be comparative".[1] This broad point retains its validity when we move backwards from the nineteenth to the seventeenth century and shift our focus from Ireland to Scotland. The wealth of fresh research being undertaken into Scottish migration in the seventeenth century, much of which is presented in this volume, reminds us of the impressive scope and scale exhibited by the emerging early modern Scottish diaspora. In considering Scottish migration to Ireland over the course of these hundred years, an awareness of the wider context of migration from contemporary Scotland can only enhance our understanding. Historians studying migration from Britain to Ireland in the seventeenth century have not always fully developed the domestic context from which migrants departed or considered departure for Ireland as one of several potential migrant strategies open to individuals.[2]

The aim of this paper is to review current knowledge and thinking about Scottish migration to and settlement in seventeenth-century Ireland. Given the context in which Scottish migration occurred, it is also necessary to refer where appropriate to British or English migration and settlement. In order to provide a platform for some initial outline comments I would like to reflect upon what I would

---

[1] D. M. MacRaild, 'Crossing Migrant Frontiers: Comparative Reflections on Migrants in Britain and the United States during the Nineteenth Century' in D. M. MacRaild, ed., *The Great Famine and Beyond: Irish Migrants in Britain in the Nineteenth and Twentieth Centuries* (Dublin: 2000), 42.

[2] A notable exception in relation to framing Ireland as one destination amongst a range of others is N. Canny, 'English Migration into and across the Atlantic during the Seventeenth and Eighteenth Centuries' in N. Canny, ed., *Europeans on the Move: Studies on European Migration 1500–1800* (Oxford: 1994), 39–75.

identify as four main impressions about this movement which retain influence in the domain of what could be called 'popular history'.

Revising Popular Misconceptions

The first of these popular impressions relates to the chronology and relative volume of migration. That James VI and I instituted a comprehensive plan for the plantation of the six escheated Ulster counties of Armagh, Cavan, Donegal, Fermanagh, Londonderry and Tyrone in January 1609 is well known. This was to be part of what Nicholas Canny has described as a 'British' rather than an 'English' colonisation of the island, albeit somewhat forced.[3] A second 'landmark' date in the popular narrative of Irish history is 23 October 1641, when natives erupted in rebellion against planters in Ireland. I would suggest there is a widely-held perception that it was these three decades which were critical in establishing a planted British community in Ireland and in establishing a predominant Scottish influence in Ulster.[4]

Whilst these trends were clearly developing by 1640, the estimates offered for British migration to Ireland during the course of the seventeenth century serve to confirm that the volume of migration was significantly greater during the second half of the century.[5] Looking specifically at migration from Scotland, it has been suggested that 14,000 Scots came to Ireland between the beginning of the century and 1625.[6] Nicholas Canny has suggested that Scottish migration in the four decades prior to 1641 was unlikely to have exceeded 30,000.[7] It was the 1650s which witnessed a significant further wave of Scottish movement, with an estimated 24,000 crossing the North Channel during that decade.[8] Migration continued spasmodically during the

---

[3] N. Canny, 'The Origins of Empire' in N. Canny, ed., *The Oxford History of the British Empire: The Origins of Empire to 1689* (Oxford: 1998), 12–13.

[4] This perception is based to some extent upon fairly regular interaction with individuals from Britain, Ireland and North America who are primarily interested in pursuing their family history.

[5] Canny, 'English Migration into and across the Atlantic', 62–63.

[6] M. W. Flinn, ed., *Scottish population history from the 17th century to the 1930s* (Cambridge: 1977), 8.

[7] Canny, 'English Migration into and across the Atlantic', 62.

[8] R. A. Houston, *The Population History of Britain and Ireland 1500–1750* (Basingstoke: 1992), 62.

following three decades but it was the 1690s which witnessed a reju-
venation of large-scale migration. The combination of a powerful
pull factor (favourable conditions for the acquisition of land in the
wake of the Williamite War of 1689–91) and a powerful push factor (devastating famine in Scotland during the four years after 1695)
produced a migration flow which may have seen as many as 50,000
Scots entering Ulster during the course of one decade.[9] Thus, it must
be stressed that the migration from Scotland to Ireland in one
decade—the 1690s—was at least three times as voluminous as that
which occurred during the British reign of James VI and I (1603–28).
This *fin de siècle* migration was arguably less a final 'topping up' to
Scots settlement in Ulster than the critical dynamic in shaping a predominant Ulster-Scots and Presbyterian influence in the northern
province. There can be little doubt that had the 1690s migration
not occurred the subsequent Scottish presence and influence in Ulster,
particularly in the western and interior region, would have been
significantly weakened. Although in part pushed outwards by famine
conditions, it cannot be assumed that the migrants of the 1690s were
uniformly poor subsistence migrants. Men of means migrated in agricultural crises as well as the impoverished and marginal. At least
some of those Scots, attracted by the lure of the Williamite army in
Ireland, did well provisioning it and remained in Ulster.

A second popular impression concerning Scottish migration to
Ireland in the seventeenth century is that those engaged in the movement were drawn exclusively from the Scottish Lowlands and were
exclusively Protestant in religion. Whilst there is little doubt that
Lowland Scots Protestants were a strong group within this migration, we need to be aware of migrants who did not fit this desig-
nation. During the Jacobean plantation of the six escheated Ulster
counties, some of the 'undertakers' who took advantage of the opportunity to acquire areas of land from the Crown were drawn from
what might be described as Gaelic Scotland, and remained Roman
Catholic in religion.[10] Some of them have been characterised as being

---

[9] P. Fitzgerald, 'Black '97?: Scottish Migration to Ulster in the 1690s' in W. Kelly
& J. R. Young (eds.), *Ulster & Scotland: history, language and identity* (Dublin: 2004).

[10] Sir Randall MacDonell's lands in the two eastern counties of Ulster are said
to have been better planted with both English and Scots than the six escheated
counties. See A. Calder, *Revolutionary Empire: The Rise of the English Speaking Empires
from the Fifteenth Century to the 1780s* (London: 1981), 129.

among the more successful 'undertakers' in establishing the economic viability of their estates.[11] Given the very strong links which existed between Gaelic Ulster and the west of Scotland before 1600, this pattern should not surprise us. We should also be wary of laying too much emphasis upon the religious zeal of the under-tenants who crossed to Ulster in the decades after 1600. Presbyterianism was well established before the first presbytery was formed in 1642, and Ulster had already demonstrated its appeal to the more radical and fervent Scottish Calvinists. Nonetheless the religious preferences of the person from whom a tenant ultimately rented their holding could count for a good deal in deciding their public denominational allegiance.[12]

Thirdly, we might observe that both continuity and isolation are characteristics which arguably distort the popular conception of this migration. As indicated above, the pattern of Scottish migration to Ireland tends to be characterised by distinct peaks and troughs: the decades of the 1610s, 1650s and 1690s define periods when the migration flow was heaviest. During the later 1630s and particularly the early 1640s and again in the later 1680s migration not only slowed, it shifted into significant reverse. Re-migration was most pronounced when planter society was under direct political and military threat, as it was in 1641–2 and 1688–9.[13] The economic cycle was also significant and failed or poor harvests in Ireland could influence settlers to retreat across the Irish Sea.[14] However we should not lose sight of the fact that these migrants were all individuals who were exposed to a myriad array of personal factors which could influence their choices. The geographical proximity of Ulster to Scotland facilitated constant movement, a case of coming and going rather than always leaving or staying for good. It is important to bear this pattern of cyclical migration in mind and to remember

---

[11] J. Michael Hill, 'The Origins of the Scottish Plantations in Ulster to 1625: A Reinterpretation' in *Journal of British Studies*, 32, (1993), 24–43.

[12] M. Perceval-Maxwell, *The Scottish Migration to Ulster in the Reign of James I* (Belfast: 1973), 273.

[13] K. J. Lindley, 'The impact of the 1641 rebellion upon England and Wales 1641–5' in *Irish Historical Studies*, vol. 18, no. 70, (Sept. 1972), 143–76; J. R. Young, 'Scotland and Ulster in the seventeenth century: the movement of peoples over the North Channel' in W. Kelly & J. R. Young (eds.), *Ulster & Scotland: history, language and identity* (Dublin: 2004).

[14] R. Gillespie, 'Harvest Crises in Early Seventeenth Century Ireland' in *Irish Economic and Social History*, vol. XI, (1984), 13.

that some Scots settlers 'failed' in Ireland and returned to Scotland, whilst others frequently retained business or landed interests and family connections in Scotland. When Ulster Scots Presbyterians made the decision to leave Ulster for colonial America in the late 1710s and 1720s, it is almost certainly the case that only a minority were the descendants of settlers in the Jacobean plantation of Ulster.

There is also a strong sense in which the Scots in seventeenth-century Ulster have been popularly viewed as a people apart. The evolution of this view, of course, has a long and complex history and could well threaten to draw us away from our central purpose here. The main point is that whilst there was a material and non-material cultural legacy of Scots migration to Ulster by 1700, there was by no means an absence of cultural interplay between migrants from Scotland, England and Wales and the native Irish.[15] A second sense in which these migrants are viewed in isolation relates to the point developed above concerning the tendency not to consider migration to Ulster as part of a wider Scottish diaspora. It would be fair to claim that it is not widely appreciated in contemporary Ireland that many more Scots, in the opening decades of the seventeenth century, were headed east to Scandinavia and the Baltic states than were moving the short distance west to Ulster.[16] Nor was it the case that these migration streams remained unconnected from each other. One prominent example of this was Gustavus Hamilton, who lived at Monea castle in County Fermanagh and was elected Governor of Enniskillen in 1688. Gustavus was the son of Lewis (also Ludovick) Hamilton, a Scot who had distinguished himself in Swedish military service, became Baron of Deserf in Sweden and married a Swede, Anna Catherina.[17] More widely, as Steve Murdoch and Alexia Grosjean have demonstrated, some Scots who had settled in Ireland were

---

[15] Useful starting points for those interested in this subject are R. A. Gailey, 'The Scots element in north Irish popular culture: some problems in the interpretation of historical acculturation' in *Ethnologia Europea*, vol. VIII, (1985), 2–21 and L. Lunney, 'Ulster Attitudes to Scottishness: the Eighteenth Century and After' in I. S. Wood, ed., *Scotland and Ulster* (Edinburgh: 1994), 56–70. Canny, 'The Origins of Empire', 13.

[16] T. C. Smout, N. C. Landsman and T. M. Devine, 'Scottish Emigration in the Seventeenth and Eighteenth Centuries' in N. Canny, ed., *Europeans on the Move: Studies on European Migration 1500–1800* (Oxford: 1994), 85.

[17] P. Livingstone, *The Fermanagh Story* (Enniskillen: 1969). I am grateful to Steve Murdoch for drawing my attention to this connection.

engaged throughout the Thirty Years' War in both the Danish-
Norwegian and the Swedish armies. They also brought native Irishmen
into those armies with them.[18] One result of this large-scale martial
migration of Scots was increased trade with Ireland, as family groups
like the Hamiltons maintained trading links with each other in both
destinations. Given this information it would be fair to speculate that
Matthew Scott, trading sugar from Belfast to Danzig, or Thomas
Stand trading herring to the same city in the 1680s, did so using
existing trading networks established by their Scottish neighbours.[19]

    The fourth and final popular misconception, admittedly in steady
retreat, is that Scottish settlement in seventeenth-century Ireland was
confined to the six escheated counties which made up the official
plantation. That settlement in the two eastern and nearest Ulster
counties, Antrim and Down, was successfully established before 1609
and proceeded apace thereafter is of course difficult to neglect. A
wider appreciation of its significance has followed on from the works
of Michael Perceval-Maxwell and Raymond Gillespie.[20] Less well
appreciated, however, is the fact that internal migration by the Scots,
or 'colonial spread' as it has been described by one historian, was
no respecter of county or provincial boundaries.[21] Thus, where land
or other economic opportunities beckoned, Scotsmen moved to take
advantage. Already by 1641 the Leinster county of Longford had
experienced significant overspill of Scots from Ulster, and one area
in the north of the county was being referred to as "the Scots

---

[18] S. Murdoch, *Britain, Denmark-Norway and the House of Stuart, 1603–1660* (East
Linton: 2003), 205, 223–5; A. Grosjean, *An Unofficial Alliance: Scotland and Sweden
1569–1654* (Leiden: 2003), 29–31, 57, 66, 89, 106, 255–256.

[19] Danish Rigsarkiv, Da. Kanc. 1681–83, Skab 15 N.252, c.63c, 'Den af Isak
Holmes fulmægtig, Seneca Torsen holdte journal fra alle engelske og skotske skip-
pere saavel fra vestersoen som fra Østersoen som har passeret Øresund'. Record
216 re. Matthew Scott of Belfast passing the Sound for Danzig with 4,800 pounds
of sugar and a quantity of white leather, 15 June 1682 (returned through the Sound
on 19 July with hemp and flax). Record 321 re: Thomas Stand of Londonderry
on *St Jacob* with 46 lasts of herring plus two more for the master and crew passing the Sound for Danzig, 2 October 1682. I would like to thank Steve Murdoch
for passing on this information.

[20] M. Perceval-Maxwell, *The Scottish Migration to Ulster in the Reign of James I* (Belfast:
1973); R. Gillespie, *Colonial Ulster: The Settlement of East Ulster 1600–1641* (Cork:
1985).

[21] P. Robinson, *The Plantation of Ulster: British Settlement in an Irish Landscape* (Belfast:
1984), 117.

quarter".[22] We should also take note of the detectable expansion (from an admittedly low base) of Presbyterianism in Dublin during the last decade of the seventeenth century. The majority of Presbyterians in the capital at this time appear to have originated from England rather than Scotland but it is clear that Scots and Ulster-Scots merchants were trading out of the second largest city in the British Isles in the 1690s.[23]

Mapping and Conceptualising Settlement Patterns

The partition of Ireland in the 1920s may seem a curious point from which to embark on a discussion of the representation of British settlement in seventeenth-century Ireland. Nevertheless partition left a distinct imprint in terms of the way both Northerners and Southerners subsequently conceived the historical geography of the island. That sense of Ulster's apartness and uniqueness, which became increasingly apparent in the writings of many northern unionists after partition, also took root at a more popular level. The establishment of the Northern Ireland State following the Government of Ireland Act in 1920 cemented the association of Unionism, Britishness and Protestantism with the 'North'. The 'North' was different because plantation in the seventeenth century, particularly by loyal and 'doughty' Scots, had been successful in a way it had not been in the other three provinces. So ran the popular version.

The traditional view of the plantation enterprise at work in early seventeenth-century Ulster tended to stress the impact and controlling hand of the Crown and of government in shaping the population process. Whilst the plantation scheme was clearly government-sponsored, the actual movement of individual migrants from Britain was much less obviously conditioned by centralised regulation. The paucity of primary source material detailing the migration experience

---

[22] R. Gillespie, 'A Question of Survival: the O'Farrells and Longford in the Seventeenth Century' in R. Gillespie & G. Moran, eds., *Longford: Essays in County History* (Dublin: 1991), 19.

[23] R. Gillespie, 'Religion and Urban Society: The Case of Early Modern Dublin' in P. Clark & R. Gillespie, eds., *Two Capitals: London and Dublin 1500–1800* (Oxford: 2001), 224; J. Agnew, *Belfast Merchant Families in the Seventeenth Century* (Dublin: 1996), 184–5.

and motivation of individuals crossing the Irish Sea at this time makes it difficult to write with assurance about the character of the movement. However, the very propensity for Scottish and English under-tenants to migrate within the six escheated counties and beyond, within Ireland, reminds us of the 'natural' dynamic at work. We are much more aware today of the extent to which migration and set-tlement patterns in seventeenth-century Ireland reflected the indi-vidual agency of migrants as well as the state formation policies of government. Plantation had, of course, been an instrument in gov-ernment policy in Ireland well before 1609. The plantation of King's and Queen's (later Leix and Offaly) counties in the Irish midlands had been initiated under Mary Tudor (1553–58) and large tracts of former Desmond lands in Munster were planted from 1584 on. Furthermore, we are reminded by Jane Ohlmeyer of James VI and I's campaign to "civilize those rude parts" of his own Scottish king-dom through plantation. It is instructive to note that royal efforts to sponsor official plantations on the forfeited island of Lewis and Harris between 1595 and 1609 met with less success than the informal col-onization of Orkney and Shetland.[24]

The Earl of Essex and Sir Thomas Smith, both enterprising courtiers, had pursued plantation in east Ulster during the early 1570s. In pondering on how this phenomenon of plantation was pre-sented to a wider public through the maps which were produced and reproduced in the historical literature, it is interesting to note recent innovations, reflecting changes in the way historians interpret and represent the process. Map 1 (above), depicting Tudor planta-tions, was first published in volume III of the Oxford New History of Ireland in 1976. The map describes a pattern of English settle-ment which was clearly segmented and specific to designated areas. The actual pattern of settlement by migrants from England in the period between the 1530s and 1603 was actually much more dis-persed and untidy than the map suggests. The historical geographer William J. Smyth, drawing on the earlier work of Rolf Loeber, pub-lished Map 2 in 2000 in an article on colonial settlement patterns. Here we find the expansion of English settlement in the six decades after 1550 represented as a frontier moving gradually outward from

---

[24] J. H. Ohlmeyer, 'Civilizinge of those Rude Partes': Colonization within Britain and Ireland, 1580s–1640s' in Canny, *The Origins of Empire*, 124–47.

the Pale, the early Tudor core of English governance on the island which was centred on Dublin. In a way we are reminded here of the notion of an expanding frontier in terms of settlement in contemporary colonial America. Map 1, focused more on the theory rather than the practice of settlement, nonetheless shaped and confirmed the general conception of actual patterns of settlement, whilst Map 2 (below) inevitably sharpened the boundary between settled and unsettled land. Even by 1641 no Irish county was untouched by British settlement and the evolving urban network across the island acted as the crucial framework for the expansion of settler society.[25] The most comprehensive recent work on British settlement in Ireland in this period (by Nicholas Canny) reinforces the message that settlers were not neatly constrained by political or administrative boundaries. Dublin, for example, so often neglected in the classic plantation story, was an increasingly important location for migrants from Britain and a political, economic, religious and legal hub for settler society.[26] In the context of Scottish migration to and settlement in the north of Ireland, the concept of 'an expanding frontier' may be helpful in terms of representing the generally observable southward and westward expansion of Scottish landholding and wider cultural influence. Thinking in terms of 'a closing frontier' may help us to understand the forces which propelled Presbyterians of largely Scottish stock to leave Ulster in the early eighteenth century for that wider and still very much open frontier across the Atlantic Ocean.

Scottish Settlement: Three micro-studies

In order to better appreciate the diversity of the migration and settlement experience undertaken by the Scots in seventeenth-century Ireland let us review the phenomenon in three different local contexts. In looking at Scottish settlement in the Ards district of north Down, the barony of Strabane in north-west Tyrone and in County Sligo, I will draw upon the work of those who have studied these

---

[25] L. Proudfoot, 'Markets, Fairs and Towns in Ireland, c. 1600–1853' in P. Borsay & L. Proudfoot, eds., *Provincial Towns in Early Modern England and Ireland: Change, Convergance and Divergence* (Oxford: 2002), 69–97.

[26] N. Canny, *Making Ireland British 1580–1650* (Oxford: 2001), 362–74.

areas in depth for the seventeenth century and try to establish some
meaningful comparisons between them.

The Ards

The context within which settlement by Scottish migrants occurred
in the Ards during the seventeenth century came to be largely defined
by its position within one of the two eastern counties of Ulster which
remained outside the territory set aside by the Crown for the official
plantation scheme of 1609. British settlers in counties Down or Antrim
were therefore not subject, in the opening decades of the century,
to the levels of regulation and inspection by government that prevailed in the six escheated counties to their west. In examining the
context within which significant numbers of Scottish settlers arrived
into the Ards after 1600, it is perhaps sensible to reflect initially
upon the geographical location of the region. As Map 3 (below)
demonstrates, the Ards lies upon the north-eastern seaboard of County
Down, facilitating easy and relatively rapid access to Scotland. Already
by the opening decade of the seventeenth century it was reported
that Scots pedlars would cross from Stranraer or Portpatrick to
Donaghadee on the Down coast, hire horses there and ride on to
Newtownards to sell their wares before returning across the North
Channel that same evening.[27] The central fact of geographical proximity would consistently bear heavily upon the establishment and
sustenance of a Scottish presence here.

     Two aspects of settlement in this area prior to 1600 should also
be taken into account by way of context. John de Courcy had exposed
this area of County Down to Anglo-Norman influence following his
incursion into Ulster in the 1170s. Subsequent to the establishment
of the Earldom of Ulster in 1205 under Hugh de Lacy, the town
of Newtown was formed close to the site of the Movilla monastery.
Despite Gaelic revival in the period after 1400 we should bear in
mind the extent to which settlers from Britain during the later
Elizabethan and Jacobean period were grafting onto an existing
Anglo-Norman infrastructure, particularly in terms of the built environment.[28] The second element relating to pre-existing settlement

---

[27] J. Stevenson, *Two Centuries of Life in Down* (Belfast: 1920), 48–9.
[28] T. E. McNeill, 'County Down in the Later Middle Ages' in L. Proudfoot, ed.,

legacies for the post-1600 Scots was the fact that this area had been subject to English plantation under the direction of the Elizabethan courtier Sir Thomas Smith. Smith's highly theoretical plans met with very little success on the ground as he encountered substantial native opposition during the early 1570s. Whilst the dominant native sept, the Clandeboye O'Neills, effectively fought off Smith's initiative, some vestiges of this enterprise remained in place and mapping and geographical knowledge of the region had been comparatively advanced.[29] Smith's family continued to lay claim to the lands he had been granted by Elizabeth and unsuccessfully challenged the grants made to Scottish landholders in the opening decade of the seventeenth century.[30] It is interesting to speculate how successful Scottish settlement in this area might have been had the Elizabethan 'private enterprise' plantations of Smith and the Earl of Essex established a more sizeable and enduring English presence in the Ards.

In 1605 Sir Hugh Montgomery of Braidstone in Ayrshire and James Hamilton, a personal favourite of the king, each took possession of a third share of what had been the estates of Conn O'Neill. From 1605 on these two grantees enjoyed significant success in attracting large numbers of Scottish settlers into north Down. As a major landowner in Scotland, Montgomery was well placed to draw upon his lands there in order to encourage the peopling of the estate he had acquired in the Ards. Many quite substantial tenants were encouraged to cross to Ireland and settle under what might be described as Montgomery's more paternalistic regime. Hamilton, although keen to attract those from Scotland with the necessary means to establish settlement, was nonetheless conscious of the risks in encouraging those who might become too powerful and troublesome. Montgomery in particular sought to recreate the landed hierarchy with which he was familiar in Scotland and can be seen to have attracted significant numbers of Scots from lower down the social scale. This class of sub-tenant included those who sought to escape the forces of law in Scotland and others who were either landless or under pressure from

Down: History & Society (Dublin: 1997), 103–22; T. McCavery, _Newtown: A History of Newtownards_ (Belfast: 1994), 32–41.

  [29] H. Morgan, 'The colonial venture of Sir Thomas Smith in Ulster, 1571–1575' in _Historical Journal_, 28, (1985), 261–78.

  [30] R. Gillespie, _Colonial Ulster: The Settlement of East Ulster 1600–1641_ (Cork: 1985), 17.

the increasingly constrained tenurial regime evolving in south-western Scotland during the opening decades of the seventeenth century.[31] In this migration flow were to be found families from Ayrshire in particular, but also from Lanarkshire, Renfrewshire, Stirlingshire, Argyllshire, Bute, Arran, the Borders, Kirkcudbrightshire and Dumfries.[32]

As Philip Robinson has demonstrated in relation to British settlement within the six counties of the official plantation, one of the surest indicators for predicting intensive settlement by newcomers in the seventeenth century was the existence of better quality land. On the basis of the valuation of land in Ulster in 1860 we can determine that land within the Ards was almost all of category A or B (*i.e.* the two highest valuation bands of six).[33] Well-drained and more fertile land suitable for arable cultivation, lightly peopled and thus at reasonable rental was one obvious and very attractive pull factor exercising influence upon migrants from Scotland. The fact that settlers experienced few harvest failures and several abundant harvests in the early years of settlement was also important in establishing momentum in the movement. For example, had the subsistence crisis of the late 1620s come two decades earlier it might have significantly retarded Scottish population expansion in the critical initial phase of settlement. An urban settlement providing a market was another important factor in determining the success of plantation settlement. Clearly in the Ards the old Anglo-Norman centre of Newtown provided an important base for new urban growth and this appears to have been swift after 1605. As early as 1611 it was reported to the government that "Sir Hugh Montgomery, Knight, hath repaired part of the abbey of Newtowne for his own dwelling and made a good town of a hundred houses or thereabouts, all peopled with Scots".[34]

Montgomery's efforts at establishing an urban core in the early decades of the seventeenth century clearly helped to provide a firm base for continuing Scottish immigration during the remainder of the century. Whilst Newtown's growth was not spectacular it did reflect the predominance of settlers over native Irish and of Scots over English planters. The census of 1659, though registering only

---

[31] Gillespie, *Colonial Ulster*, 28–63; Perceval-Maxwell, *The Scottish Migration*, 49–60.
[32] T. McCavery, *Newtown: A History of Newtownards* (Belfast: 1994), 53.
[33] Robinson, *Plantation of Ulster*, 10–17.
[34] Quoted in McCavery, *Newtown*, 56.

those liable for taxation, listed 332 adults in the town of whom 207 were identified as Scots and 125 as Irish. It may be observed from a survey of the town compiled by John Sloaner in 1720 that there had been significant development since the mid-seventeenth century. It is likely that the significant Scottish immigration of the 1690s provided something of a demographic fillip to the Scots and Presbyterian community in the town. By 1723 theological disputes had split the town's Presbyterians into a conservative, Old Light congregation and a liberal, New Light congregation. Nonetheless the meeting houses in which they met were both larger structures than the neat but small church in which the Anglican congregation gathered.[35]

Today's visitor to Newtownards is reminded of this strong Scottish influence in the town's evolution. In terms of architecture, layout and the prospect which it presents, Newtownards bears a strong resemblance to many towns in the south-west of Scotland. Recognising the strong if not complete correlation between affiliation to Presbyterianism and Scottish roots, it may be pertinent to conclude by pointing out that the 2001 census recorded 38% of the population within the Ards local government district as being Presbyterian, as compared to 16.5% Anglican (Church of Ireland) and 10.5% Roman Catholic.[36]

Strabane

The barony of Strabane, which covers an area of some 400 square miles in the north-west quarter of County Tyrone, came into being when the latter territory was shired on the English pattern in 1585. The most obvious and critical difference between Strabane and the Ards in relation to British settlement in the seventeenth century was that Strabane as part of the escheated county of Tyrone fell within the territory set aside for the official plantation scheme of 1609. In establishing a context in which to analyse that process, it again makes sense to observe briefly the geographical features of the area and to reflect upon its preceding historical experience. As a plantation environment Strabane could be contrasted with the Ards on the basis of the much greater extent of upland, most of which would have

[35] McCavery, *Newtown*, 62–82.
[36] Consulted on the Internet at www.nisra.gov.uk/census.

remained as afforested or barren moorland c. 1600. The more fertile lowland tended to be concentrated along the river valleys that drained into the Foyle basin. In general terms land quality here was inferior to that in the Ards but productive farming, settlement patterns and transport routes in the area before the seventeenth century correlated closely with these river valleys. The existence in the early part of the century of significant woodland in these same river valleys only added to their attraction for commercially-aware settlers.[37] North-west Tyrone remained well beyond the boundaries of the Earldom of Ulster. Prior to 1607 and the departure of Hugh O'Neill, Earl of Tyrone, the O'Neills were the leading Gaelic family in the region. Although at the heart of Gaelic Ulster in the sixteenth century, the O'Neills retained links with Gaelic Scotland and it should be noted that these links led to the presence of Scots from the western Highlands in the Strabane area in the later sixteenth century. Turlough Luineach O'Neill's accession in 1567 to the premier position of 'The O'Neill' augmented the power of an individual whose power base lay in the area around Strabane. However this overlordship remained contested by Hugh O'Neill, whose power base lay in east Tyrone. In 1569 Turlough married Lady Agnes McDonnell, daughter of the Earl of Argyll. As a part of the marriage settlement Turlough acquired the services of 1,000 Scottish mercenaries, of whom a proportion settled more permanently in and around Strabane. Turlough O'Neill remained embroiled in warfare with Hugh O'Donnell, the Gaelic chieftain whose overlordship bordered O'Neill to the west. In 1583 the settlement known as Strath Bán (Strabane) was burned by O'Donnell. New development on this site seems to have been slow and a second fire in 1608 no doubt retarded the town's recovery still further. Thus a developed urban infrastructure for the early seventeenth-century planters to graft onto seems to have remained fairly limited.[38]

As part of the allocation of lands in accordance with the plans laid down after 1609, grants of land in the barony of Strabane were reserved for Scottish 'undertakers'. The largest allocation of planta-

---

[37] *The Strabane Barony During The Ulster Plantation 1607–1641* (Londonderry: 1974), 3–5. This booklet was produced by historians and extra-mural students at Magee College in Derry in the early 1970s.

[38] J. Dooher & M. Kennedy, eds., *The Fair River Valley: Strabane Through the Ages* (Belfast: 2000), 23–29.

tion acreage went to one of the leading Scottish families, the Hamiltons of Paisley. Three of the most significant grantees were James Hamilton, created first Earl of Abercorn in 1603, and his brothers Sir Claud Hamilton and Sir George Hamilton. Whilst James was a Protestant, his two younger brothers were both practising Catholics and following the death of Claud in 1614 and then James in 1618 their two eldest sons, William and James respectively, were brought up as Catholics in accordance with the preference of their Scottish guardian, Sir George Hamilton of the Largie and Dirrywoon estates.[39] This fundamentally contravened one of the central requirements of the plantation scheme, namely that all 'undertakers' who took up lands in Ulster should be Protestant. As might be anticipated in the context of the early seventeenth century, the confessional preferences of the landed elite had an impact more broadly within settler society. Whilst the members of the Hamilton family varied their pattern of residence and their allocation of time between estates in Scotland and north-west Tyrone, they appear to have enjoyed reasonable success in attracting tenants to Strabane from Scotland, certainly by comparison with English 'undertakers' elsewhere in Tyrone. Nonetheless there is a good deal of evidence that Scottish Catholics were a part of the incoming tenant population. Both the Archbishop of Glasgow and the nearby Bishop of Derry decried the number of Scottish Catholics who settled in the vicinity of Strabane during the 1620s. The muster roll of 1630 for the town of Strabane identified both Protestants and Scottish Catholics amongst the 208 citizens who were male settlers.[40]

In the barony of Strabane, as throughout much of plantation Ulster, there remained a strong economic incentive for British landholders to retain native Irish tenants on their estates. While only a small minority of estates saw a total removal of Irish tenantry, it would appear that where there was a sufficient supply of British labour in Tyrone a pattern of significant spatial segregation between British and Irish emerged at a local townland level. Attention can also be drawn to the continuing extent to which English and Scottish settlement remained quite segregated. While there would appear to have been a relatively high level of internal migration and movement

[39] Dooher & Kennedy, *Fair River Valley*, 60–61.
[40] Dooher & Kennedy, *Fair River Valley*, 65–66.

towards the plantation settlements which were founded on the best
land and seen to be most secure, this area remained predominantly
Scots.[41] Despite the limited base from which to develop the town of
Strabane, it seems that Abercorn's personal energy contributed a
dynamic stimulus to urban growth. It is significant to note, however,
that the emerging settlement was able to exploit its riverside location for the purposes of trade with Scotland. We know from the few
surviving port records from the second decade of the century that
a Strabane ship, the *Gift of God*, plied regularly back and forth from
Londonderry to Renfrew, close to Abercorn's Scottish estate and that
the Scots captured most of the Londonderry trade and came to out-
number the English inhabitants there.[42] This mercantile connection
helped to sustain links with Scotland during this early phase of settlement, and further British migration into the barony of Strabane
later in the century was also predominantly Scottish.[43] Indeed, the
significance of the major Scottish immigration of the 1690s was
even more pronounced in western counties such as Tyrone than it
had been in settlement core areas like north Down.[44] By the close
of the seventeenth century the town's evolving merchant community
reflected the enduring Scottish influence in the peopling of the district and in its economic exploitation.

  In considering the longer-term fortunes of the descendants of these
seventeenth-century Scottish settlers we should bear in mind the fairly
heavy and consistent emigration which characterised the Presbyterian
community in this area in the century after 1715. Scottish Catholics
who had settled in the early seventeenth century and earlier would
appear to have integrated into the local Catholic community, but
evidence relating to inter-marriage and this process in general is limited. Despite the disproportionate draw of New World emigration
upon Presbyterians from Strabane in the eighteenth century, one historian profiling the church's history in the area identified the nine-

---

[41] P. Robinson, 'The Ulster Plantation and its Impact on the Settlement Pattern
of Co. Tyrone' in C. Dillon & H. A. Jefferies, eds., *Tyrone: History & Society* (Dublin:
2000), 261–63; W. Roulston, 'The Ulster Plantation in the Manor of Dunnalong,
1610–70' in Dillon & Jefferies, *Tyrone*, 286–7.

[42] Calder, *Revolutionary Empire*, 129.

[43] Dooher & Kennedy, *Fair River Valley*, 63, 78.

[44] W. Macafee & V. Morgan, 'Population in Ulster, 1660–1760' in P. Roebuck,
ed., *Plantation to Partition: Essays in Ulster History* (Belfast: 1981), 58–59.

teenth century as "an era of expansion".[45] The 2001 census figures for the Strabane local government district indicate that today Roman Catholics make up 63% of the area's population whilst the remaining segment of the population is fairly evenly divided between Presbyterians (17%) and Anglicans (11%).[46]

Sligo

Sligo, as a county in the province of Connacht, obviously lay outside the boundary of the official Ulster plantation scheme of 1609. On the Atlantic coast, some seventy miles south-west of Strabane and over 100 miles west of Newtownards, it was also more geographically distant from Scotland. The town of Sligo itself had an interesting pre-seventeenth century history as an Anglo-Norman foundation in the thirteenth century which continued to expand and prosper during the medieval period under Gaelic rather than Anglo-Norman rule. In the fifteenth century, for example, the port town of Sligo had a number of Gaelic Irish merchants who were trading within the British Isles and beyond. Thus from an early juncture Sligo could be said to have looked outwards, through its seagoing trade, to a wider commercial world. The town's position on the coastal strip linking the provinces of Connacht and Ulster also served to mark it out as occupying an important strategic location and it suffered attack and changed hands regularly during the wars of the sixteenth century.[47]

As has already been pointed out, British settlement in Ireland during the early seventeenth century did not remain restricted within the bounds of counties set aside for plantation. Settlers from Ulster spilled over into north Leinster and it is equally clear that similar expansion from Ulster occurred south and west into the counties of north Connacht, particularly Leitrim (itself subject to a separate plantation scheme), Sligo and Mayo. While settlers with roots in England and Wales were present within the British settler community in these three counties before 1641 it is clear that the significant majority of

---

[45] Dooher & Kennedy, *Fair River Valley*, 313.
[46] Consulted on the Internet at www.nisra.gov.uk/census.
[47] M. O'Dowd, *Power, Politics & Land: Early Modern Sligo 1568–1688* (Belfast: 1991); M. O'Dowd, 'Sligo' in A. Simms & J. H. Angrews, eds., *Irish Country Towns* (Dublin: 1994), 142–53.

newcomers in north Connacht hailed from Scotland.[48] In order to help explain the influx of Scots entering western counties such as Sligo it may be worthwhile to focus on settlement in those areas which were closest to Connacht within the six escheated counties designated for plantation by Scottish 'undertakers'.

One such area was the barony of Boylagh, effectively the south-western quarter of County Donegal. Boylagh was in many ways the most remote and inhospitable environment on offer to those who took up land in the Ulster plantation and it is not entirely surprising to find that all eight Scottish 'undertakers' who took up estates within the barony disengaged within a relatively short period. British settlement was most successful in the coastal corridor between Donegal town and the small fishing settlement of Killybegs but both these urban settlements disappointed government officials. Robert Hunter, surveying British settlement in the county during the early seventeenth century, concludes that "both in terms of plantation and of social regulation, society in west Donegal remained transitional up to 1641".[49] Equally, the evidence relating to settlement in the largely upland barony of Magheraboy in western Fermanagh, which had likewise been set aside for Scottish 'undertakers', suggests genuine difficulties in establishing and sustaining plantation settlement.[50] Although direct evidence relating to the background and migration paths of Scots coming into Sligo after 1610 is very limited, Mary O'Dowd, who has studied early modern Sligo society in most detail, offers a convincing reconstruction of the settlers' response to initial settlement. O'Dowd writes of "Scottish families arriving in remote parts of Donegal or Fermanagh and looking around them with despair and fear at the isolation and barrenness of their new homes. Some may have decided to look elsewhere, moving southwards or westwards towards the sea. Sligo, as an existing port, may have offered better prospects than the hills or lakes of Donegal or Fermanagh".[51] As in Strabane, the relative abundance of mature woodland in Sligo did not go unnoticed by settlers further north who were keenly aware

---

[48] O'Dowd, *Power, Politics & Land*, 103.

[49] R. J. Hunter, 'Plantation in Donegal' in W. Nolan, L. Ronayne & M. Dunlevy, eds., *Donegal: History & Society* (Dublin: 1995), 293–95.

[50] P. Livingstone, *The Fermanagh Story* (Enniskillen: 1969), 72–3.

[51] O'Dowd, 'Sligo', 147. It should be noted that O'Dowd fully acknowledges the influence of Robinson on this point.

of the ready and rapid profits to be derived through the felling and sale of timber.

A sense of security contrasted with awareness of the exposure in an isolated holding in the uplands of west Donegal or Fermanagh may have been one factor spurring this internal migration towards Sligo. It is interesting to note that by the 1630s the Ballymote estate, some twenty miles south of Sligo town, had attracted a cluster of merchants and craftsmen with distinctively Scottish surnames. Then in the hands of Viscount Taffe, Ballymote had formerly been in the possession of George Bingham, sheriff of the county from 1588–95, who had lived in a well-fortified and well-repaired castle. The sites of other garrisons also attracted Scots settlers.[52] However it was not only English or Scottish landholders who sought to attract British settlers into Connacht. There is clear evidence that native landholders in the province were keen to augment their rent rolls by offering holdings to English and Scottish tenants.[53] Nonetheless, the heaviest concentration of Scottish settlers was to be found within the town of Sligo. On the basis of the depositions offered by those settlers who had suffered losses in the rising of 1641, just under half of the 140 British families resident in Sligo county were dwelling in the county town.[54] Sligo town during the opening decades of the seventeenth century developed significantly in stature and scale. This port town was a more dynamic model of urban growth than most of the incorporated boroughs within the six counties of the official plantation. The town at this stage also demonstrated a mixture of Old English Catholic, New English and Scottish Protestant inhabitants. In 1622, following incorporation in 1612, Sligo was created a statute staple town and the surviving list of those who became members of the staple indicates that there were English, Irish and Scottish merchants residing in and trading out of Sligo.[55] It is known that there was trade through the port with Scotland and it would appear that individual merchants were also masters of trading vessels. Exports strongly reflected Sligo's close ties with its rural hinterland and the strong dependence upon agricultural produce. The most significant

---

[52] O'Dowd, *Power, Politics & Land*, 35, 96.
[53] Canny, *Making Ireland British*, 387.
[54] O'Dowd, *Power, Politics & Land*, 103.
[55] O'Dowd, *Power, Politics & Land*, 151–54.

portion of Sligo's trade continued to be directed to continental European ports, particularly in France and Spain.[56] Despite the hiatus caused by warfare in the 1640s and the massacre of British settlers in Sligo which occurred in 1641, Scottish settlement in the town recovered rapidly and strongly in the 1650s and 1660s. Many of these new Scottish settlers were soldiers or former soldiers who chose to settle permanently in Sligo, but it is also possible to detect the presence of a new body of Scottish merchants, many of whom were men of some substance.[57] By the 1680s members of the Delap and Johnston families (who came to dominate the Dublin wine trade by the beginning of the eighteenth century) were present in Sligo.[58] The town's importance within Ireland as a market for agricultural produce was growing during these years and by the last quarter of the century barrelled beef was being exported across the Atlantic to the American colonies and the West Indies. We also know that at least one Sligo merchant, William Davis, was engaged in trade with Greenock on the Clyde and it is not inconceivable that vessels such as these provided the transport for the Scots pedlars noted by Charles O'Hara as trading in the county during the Restoration period.[59] In the 1620s and 1630s we know that Scottish ministers, men like Archibald Hamilton and Archibald Adair, were attracted to the united see of Killala and Achonry, of which Sligo was a part. These ministers (and presumably those who followed them into Connacht) became a part of the established Church of Ireland.[60] It would appear that the first Presbyterian minister recorded in the town was the Rev Samuel Henry who came from Convoy in County Donegal in 1695.[61] During the early eighteenth century, as Sligo was increasingly drawn into the orbit of the developing linen industry in Ulster, a meeting house was erected with the assistance of local landowners keen

---

[56] O'Dowd, *Power, Politics & Land*, 154–56.

[57] O'Dowd, *Power, Politics & Land*, 119–20, 158–9, 162–3.

[58] O'Dowd, *Power, Politics & Land*, 163. Further information on the Delap and Johnston families and their commercial interests can be found in L. M. Cullen, 'The Dublin merchant community in the eighteenth century' in P. Butel & L. M. Cullen, eds., *Cities and merchants: French and Irish perspectives on urban development, 1500–1900* (Dublin: 1986).

[59] O'Dowd, *Power, Politics & Land*, 160–62.

[60] O'Dowd, *Power, Politics & Land*, 108.

[61] *A History of Congregations in the Presbyterian Church in Ireland 1610–1982* (Belfast: 1982), 753.

to promote the settlement of what were seen to be industrious Protestant tenants.[62]

In terms of trying to measure the impact in Sligo town of the significant immigration of the 1690s, we are hampered by the limited sources relating to urban demography. However, on the basis of what is available, O'Dowd suggests that by 1680 roughly two-thirds of the town's population of 1,500–2,000 was of British origin and that by 1749 when the total population was closer to 3,000, the proportion of Protestants was about half that total.[63] Whilst proportionately this represents something of a decline in the Protestant population, it indicates stability if not slight expansion in gross terms. Given the relatively limited extent of fresh immigration from Britain after 1700, the figures for 1749 would suggest that the Protestant population of the town was augmented by British settlers (predominantly Scottish) in the 1690s and that this inward flow of migrants may have been sustained to some extent by Ulster Presbyterians drawn south and west thereafter. Given that the Scottish immigration of the 1690s had a proportionately greater impact in expanding Scottish settlement in west Ulster and in stimulating migrants of Scottish stock in east Ulster to spread west, it would seem likely that the Scottish and Protestant component of Sligo's population was at least strongly consolidated in the 1690s.[64] A similar pattern, for example, has been identified in relation to the north Leinster county of Longford.[65]

Those of Scottish ancestry settled in Sligo remained particularly drawn by the prospects of emigration across the Atlantic during the following century and a half. As early as 1718 it was being reported to Dublin Castle that thousands of Presbyterians had sailed for America from the north of Ireland and Sligo was one of the ports specifically mentioned as being involved in this emigrant traffic.[66]

---

[62] T. C. Barnard, 'The Government and Irish Dissent, 1704–1780' in K. Herlihy, ed., *The Politics of Irish Dissent 1650–1800* (Dublin: 1997), 14.

[63] O'Dowd, *Power, Politics & Land*, 159; O'Dowd, 'Sligo', 150.

[64] McAfee & Morgan, 'Population in Ulster', 58–9.

[65] L. Kennedy, K. Miller with M. Graham, 'The Long Retreat: Protestants, Economy and Society, 1660–1926' in R. Gillespie & G. Moran, eds., *Longford: Essays in County History* (Dublin: 1991), 35.

[66] This source has been consulted on the Irish Emigration Database at the Centre for Migration Studies, Ulster-American Folk Park, Omagh, hereafter cited as IED and followed in brackets by the original source; IED 9907362 (PRONI; T. 1809).

Emigration to British North America in the 1820s and 1830s further depleted Presbyterian and Anglican ranks in the area and it was reported by the *Sligo Guardian* in 1849, at the tail end of the Great Famine, that more than one half of those on board a vessel recently departed for Quebec were 'respectable Protestants'.[67] According to the census of 1891 there were 691 Presbyterians living in the county of Sligo. A century later this figure had fallen to a mere 121. Thus in 1991 only 0.2% of the population of Sligo county was Presbyterian in denomination as compared to 0.37% of the population of the Republic of Ireland as a whole. The demographic vestiges of seventeenth-century Scottish settlement in Sligo were in steady decline by the closing stages of the twentieth century.[68]

Conclusion

Whilst the government throughout the early 'British' Stuart period was keen to see the development of new towns and new buildings on an English model, particularly in the six escheated counties, evidence on the ground often reveals a desire to graft onto existing settlements and structures. Pragmatic instincts and economic realities tended to influence settlers towards development from an existing nucleus rather than 'green field' construction. Montgomery was clearly building on earlier Anglo-Norman foundations in the development of Newtownards, which in turn reflected continuity from the monastic settlement of Movilla. Although Strabane suffered degradation in the generation before the official plantation, it was nonetheless a recognisable nucleus, again stemming from an earlier monastic foundation. Over the course of the seventeenth century the town developed significantly, reflecting the sponsorship of the Earls of Abercorn and the importance of mercantile trading links with the port of Londonderry and the world beyond. The inclination of Scottish settlers to gravitate towards the established urban and commercial network, even where this lay beyond the bounds of government plans,

---

[67] C. J. Houston & W. J. Smyth, Irish Emigration and Canadian Settlement: Patterns, Links & Letters (Toronto: 1990), 36–7; IED 9803688 (*Sligo Guardian*: 7 May 1849).

[68] I am grateful to Michelle Guiney of the Irish Central Statistics Office for supplying me with the relevant census data.

is evident in the case of Sligo town's role as an active port during the sixteenth century. The internal migration towards Sligo by Scots settlers from within the official Ulster plantation was no doubt a commentary on the very real problems associated with meeting the stringent requirements of government in terms of building in the most hostile and remote environments.

Acquisition and exploitation of land was of course the fundamental dynamic propelling migrants from Scotland to Ireland throughout the seventeenth century. In the opening decades of the century, in particular, it was the primary natural resource of Irish timber which helped to shape settlement patterns. However, Scottish settlers seeking opportunities to till the soil and plant crops, or more likely graze livestock, consistently sought out or gravitated towards the best quality land. No other factor correlates as strongly as land quality with patterns of British settlement in the seventeenth century. The relationship between fertile soils, lush grasslands and Protestant habitation was a remarkably enduring feature of rural life in the north of Ireland. Their impact was large enough for Nicholas Pynnar to observe that had it not been for the efforts of these Scots, many parts of Ulster would have starved.[69]

Although the fundamental importance of agricultural ambitions should not be underestimated in seeking to penetrate the 'settlement psychology' of Scottish migrants to Ireland, it is worthwhile pondering one of the most distinguishing features of seventeenth-century Scottish society: high levels of outward migration. It has been estimated that during the first half of the seventeenth century approximately one in every five young men left the country.[70] The majority of these migrants were destined for continental Europe. Warfare and military recruitment absorbed the greatest proportion, but from an early point commercial trading networks were an important dimension of this outflow. Placing Scots migrants to seventeenth-century Ireland into the wider context of the evolving Scottish diaspora may serve to adjust the picture slightly, sensitising us to the potential connections and links which not only bound the migrant to the Scottish homeland but also to the Scottish diaspora. Access to the sea and

---

[69] Calder, *Revolutionary Empire*, 128.
[70] I. D. Whyte, *Migration and Society in Britain in Britain 1550–1830* (Basingstoke: 2000), 114.

the potential to sustain relatively easy contact and trade with Scotland
and the wider world favoured all three of the areas studied here.
From the 1680s, but most voluminously after 1715, Scottish settlers
and their descendants in the north of Ireland migrated further west
to a wider frontier in North America. By the outbreak of the American
War of Independence in 1775 somewhere in the region of 50,000
Presbyterian 'Ulster-Scots' had crossed the Atlantic, where they joined
an estimated 35,000 migrant Scots, often replicating the 'Scottish
enclaves' of Ulster.[71] An intriguing question which remains to be sat-
isfactorily answered is the extent to which these migrant streams
interrelated in America and expressed a sense of shared diasporic
cultural identity.

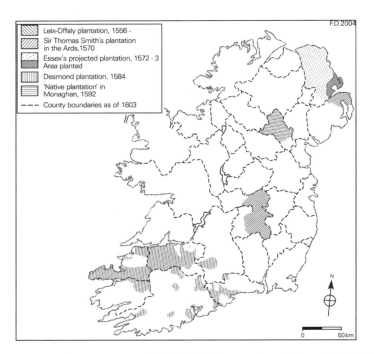

Map 1. Tudor Plantations by K. W. Nicholls reproduced from T. W. Moody,
F. X. Martin & F. J. Byrne, eds., *A New History of Ireland, Vol. III Early
Modern Ireland 1534–1691* (Oxford: 1976), 77

---

[71] Canny, 'The Origins of Empire', 12; P. J. Marshall, *The Oxford History of the
British Empire: The Eighteenth Century* (Oxford: 1998), 9; Whyte, *Migration and Society*,
125.

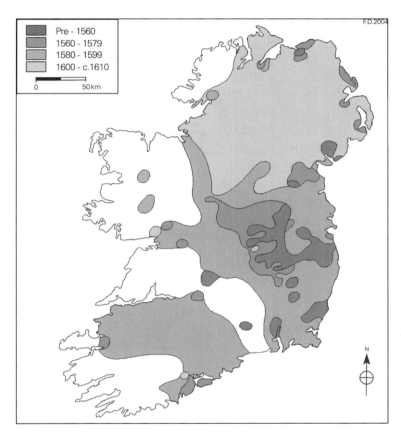

Map 2. The expansion of English military and settlement frontier, 1534–1609 by W.J. Smyth reproduced from T. Barry, ed., *A History of Settlement in Ireland* (London: 2000), 160

Map 3. Location of the three study areas

THE PLACEMENT OF URBANISED SCOTS IN THE POLISH CROWN DURING THE SIXTEENTH AND SEVENTEENTH CENTURIES*

Waldemar Kowalski

The issue of urbanised Scots in the Polish Commonwealth has not been entirely neglected, but literature on Scottish immigrants in Old Poland and bordering territories published up to the 1970s reveals that the authors had little or no appreciation of the wider socio-economic background.[1] This social context cannot be ignored if we wish to understand fully why Poland was attractive to immigrants from Scotland and how the multi-national and multi-denominational environment influenced their lives. Considerable progress has been made during the last thirty years in diaspora research, and studies on the Scottish settlements in Little Poland are worth noticing here. However, there is still a need for a thorough presentation of the socio-economic aspect of migration from Scotland. Extensive post-war studies into Polish economic history and more recent research on ethnic groups—especially on Polish Jewry—have facilitated a general overview of the Scottish presence in the urban society of early modern Poland. In this essay, the stage we have reached to date will be shown and routes to follow in the future will be suggested. It has not been possible to refer to all the local studies dealing with particular urban communities, nor to their archives. However, we owe much of this

* A paper based on this article was presented at the Research Institute of Irish and Scottish Studies, University of Aberdeen, on 7 November, 2001. I am grateful to Dr Steve Murdoch for his kind assistance with some of the recent literature. The article has been supplemented with research findings in Aberdeen City Archives (hereafter ACAs) and Aberdeen University collections. This research was possible thanks to a grant the author received from the Caledonian Research Foundation and the Royal Society of Edinburgh in 2003.

[1] A general overview of the problem and the basic literature has been provided by A. Biegańska in 'A Note on the Scots in Poland, 1550–1800,' in *Scotland and Europe, 1200–1850*, ed. T. C. Smout (Edinburgh: 1986), 157–165, and 'The Learned Scots in Poland (From the Mid-Sixteenth to the Close of the Eighteenth Century),' *Canadian Slavonic Papers* 43.1 (2001): 1.

increase in knowledge *exempli gratia* to Zenon Guldon's valuable studies on the diaspora in the Sandomierz Palatinate.[2]

Around 1500 the population of Poland was about 4,000,000 in a
territory of 265,000 square kilometres. At the end of the fifteenth
century it was made up of three ethnic regions. One consisted of
Mazovia, Cuiavia, Great Poland and most of Lesser (Little) Poland,
excluding its southern borders. Polish ethnicity was dominant in this
region, particularly in the rural areas. Royal Prussia, parts of the
northern Carpathians and a few enclaves of some towns and cities,
for instance Olkusz and Poznań (Posen), were areas populated to a
high degree by German migrants. Other ethnic groups were the
Kashubes in the north and the Wallachians and the Slovaks in the
south. The south-eastern areas of the Polish Kingdom (the Crown)—
Red Ruthenia (Red Rus'), western Podolia and the Land of Bełz—
formed a region dominated by Ruthenians with Polish, German and
Wallachian minorities scattered among them.[3]

These ethnic divisions, which were relatively clear in the country,
were far more complicated in the towns. Poles were the dominant
urban population in the first region, as were Germans in the second; the Ruthenian towns, colonized or founded during the fourteenth and fifteenth centuries, were multi-ethnic. The Germans, Poles,
Ruthenians, Wallachians, Jews and Armenians who lived in them
were the most numerous but not the only urban nationalities in the
region. However it is worth remembering that this multi-ethnic social
structure was a common feature of numerous towns and all the cities
of the kingdom in late medieval times. Poles, Germans and Jews
had the highest population figures, but in large urban areas like
Cracow, there were also Bohemians, Hungarians, Wallachians and
a few English. This multicultural diversity was the norm in the early
modern period, even in provincial settlements.

It is estimated that by 1500, Poles accounted for 70% of the state
population. The remaining 30% consisted of Ruthenians (5%), Germans

---

[2] See his 'Szkoci w miastach województwa sandomierskiego w XVI–XVII wieku,'
in his *Żydzi i Szkoci w Polsce w XVI–XVIII wieku. Studia i materiały* (Kielce: 1990),
7–47.

[3] H. Samsonowicz, 'Grupy etniczne w Polsce XV wieku,' in *Ojczyzna bliższa i
dalsza. Studia historyczne ofiarowane Feliksowi Kirykowi w sześćdziesiątą rocznicę urodzin*, eds.
J. Chrobaczyński, A. Jureczko, M. Śliwa (Kraków: 1993), 461–464.

(more than 10%) and the Jews, who were the most noticeable minority (15%).[4]

As a result of the 1569 Lublin Union between the Kingdom of Poland (the Crown) and the Grand Duchy of Lithuania, a new state was created which was the largest in Europe, excluding the Grand Principality of Muscovy. As of 1582, the Polish-Lithuanian Commonwealth covered 815,000 square kilometres, which was enlarged in 1634 to 990,000 square kilometres. This vast land was inhabited by over 8,000,000 people in the 1580s, and the estimate for the first half of the seventeenth century is 11,000,000. Compared with the fifteenth century, the percentage of Polish nationals dropped to around 50% after the 1569 union. Lithuanians and Ruthenians constituted 40% of the entire population, and the remaining 10% was comprised of mainly Germans, Armenians and Wallachians, with less significant minorities in relatively unchanged proportions.[5]

Scottish settlement and population

The Scots began to settle in Polish territories as early as the fourteenth century. The first area they reached was Gdańsk (Danzig), where the settlement was fostered by the close commercial links which the German Order had maintained with Scotland from the turn of the fifteenth century.[6] Scottish goods constituted about 10%

---

[4] Samsonowicz, 'Grupy etniczne,' *passim*. The ethnic situation in Cracow has been analysed recently by K. Friedrich, 'Nationale Identität und Pluralität in Krakau und Prag im 16. Jahrhunderts,' in *Geisteswissenschaftliches Zentrum Geschichte und Kultur Ostmitteleuropas e.V. Berichte, Beiträge*, 2 (1999): 60–79 and L. Belzyt, *Kraków i Praga około 1600 roku. Porównanie topograficznych i demograficznych aspektów struktury społecznej i etnicznej dwóch metropolii Europy Środkowo—Wschodniej* (Toruń: 1999).

[5] J. Topolski, *Polska w czasach nowożytnych. Od środkowoeuropejskiej potęgi do utraty niepodległości (1501–1795)* (Poznań: 1999), 12, 124–127; S. Litak, *Od Reformacji do Oświecenia. Kościół katolicki w Polsce nowożytnej* (Lublin: 1994), 29; Z. Guldon, 'Ludność i gospodarka Rosji i Polski w XVI–XVIII wieku. Wybrane problemy badawcze,' in *Z dziejów Europy wczesnonowożytnej*, ed. J. Wijaczka (Kielce: 1997), 127–128, 133–134.

[6] Th. A. Fischer, *The Scots in Eastern and Western Prussia* (Edinburgh: 1903), 7–13; his *The Scots in Germany* (Edinburgh: 1902), *passim*; M. Biskup, 'Rozwój gospodarki czynszowej i utrwalenie ustroju stanowego na Pomorzu Wschodnim pod rządami krzyżackimi (1310–1466),' in *Historia Pomorza*, ed. G. Labuda, vol. 1 (Poznań: 1972), 663; Samsonowicz, 'Grupy etniczne,' 467; his 'Dynamiczny ośrodek handlowy,' in *Historia Gdańska*, ed. E. Cieślak, vol. 2: 1454–1655 (Gdańsk: 1982), 150. A little-known early episode of contacts with England has been presented by P. T. Dobrowolski,

of the total imports to Gdańsk in the sixteenth century, and in the first half of the seventeenth century ships with Scottish and English captains constituted around 12% of all ships plying the harbour. Between the years 1588–1649 Gdańsk citizenship was granted to 101 Scots. However this is not an exact figure for Scottish immigrants to the city, because the majority were either not interested or unable to get burgess rights. The total number of Scots in the early modern city has been estimated at around 500.[7]

The Scots in Gdańsk were mostly Presbyterians, and probably as early as the 1570s they gathered for services in the churches of Saints Peter and Paul and St Elisabeth. In addition, a so-called 'English' (although it included Scots) Calvinist congregation existed in the city from at least the mid-seventeenth century.[8]

The immigration process must have been far advanced in Royal Prussia by 1537, as in that year the first edict was issued against wandering pedlars. It was presumably ineffective, as it was followed by others in the years 1551, 1556 and 1580,[9] indicating that administrative attempts by the state authorities to discourage immigrants were insufficient. In the sixteenth and seventeenth centuries, Scots were living not just in the Gdańsk urban area but also in almost every Prussian town. The Scottish communities were usually small, rarely comprising more than a few families.[10] Nevertheless, large and

---

'Food Purchases of a Travelling Nobleman: The Accounts of the Earl of Derby, 1390–1393,' *Food and Foodways* 2 (1988): 289–308; Z. Guldon, L. Stępkowski, 'Ludność szkocka i angielska w Polsce w połowie XVII w.,' *Kwartalnik Historii Kultury Materialnej* 30.2 (1982): 203.

[7] M. Bogucka, 'Scots in Gdańsk (Danzig) in the Seventeenth Century,' in *Ships, Guns and Bibles in the North Sea and Baltic States, c.1350–c.1700*, eds. A. I. Macinnes, T. Riis & F. Pedersen (East Lothian: 2000), 39–40; her 'Obcy kupcy osiedli w Gdańsku w pierwszej połowie XVII w.,' *Zapiski Historyczne* 37.2 (1972): 68, 79; her 'Przemiany społeczne i walki społeczno-polityczne w XV i XVI w.' in *Historia Gdańska*, vol. 2, 213; J. Stankiewicz, 'Urbanistyczny i przestrzenny rozwój miasta,' in *Historia Gdańska*, vol. 2, 438.

[8] Bogucka, 'Scots in Gdańsk,' 40–41; J. Baszanowski, *Przemiany demograficzne w Gdańsku w latach 1601–1846* (Gdańsk: 1995), 75–79. Cf. Biegańska, 'In Search of Tolerance. Scottish Catholics and Presbyterians in Poland,' *Scottish Slavonic Review* (hereafter *SSR*) 17 (1991): 42, who writes that the Gdańsk Scots and English had not been allowed to open a place of worship by 1711.

[9] A. F. Steuart ed., *Papers Relating to the Scots in Poland 1576–1793* (Edinburgh: 1915), [hereafter *Papers Relating to the Scots in Poland*] 92–100; Guldon, Stępkowski, 'Ludność szkocka i angielska,' 203 and by the same authors, 'Szkoci i Anglicy w Koronie w połowie XVII wieku,' *Kieleckie Studia Historyczne* 2 (1977): 32; Fischer, *The Scots in Eastern and Western Prussia*, 157.

[10] S. Gierszewski, 'Szkoci w mniejszych miastach Pomorza Gdańskiego (XVI–XVIII

wealthy minorities lived in Chełmno (Culm) and Elbląg (Elbing).[11]
In 1614 the latter became the home town of the Ramsay family,
who held important municipal offices through the generations until
the mid-nineteenth century.[12] Although neither Scots nor Jews were
entitled to settle in Toruń (Thorn), in the Land of Chełm, some
lived temporarily in the suburbs.[13] The local *Wettgericht* articles from
1634 explicitly declared a ban on Scottish and Jewish peddling.[14] In
1651, immigrants from the British Isles were noted in thirty six towns
in Royal Prussia, or 97% of the towns in the region.[15]

However it must be remembered that town records identify first
of all those immigrants who gained citizenship. Those who were
refused or could not afford to obtain citizenship are extremely difficult
to trace. Pedlars probably made up the majority of newcomers, and
the restrictive royal ordinances issued during the sixteenth century
relate to this class. Wandering paupers were persecuted in the same
way, regardless of their nationality.[16]

This explains why in the second half of the sixteenth century Scots
were noted in only three towns in Great Poland.[17] One of them was
Poznań (Posen), where sixty two Scots were registered in the *Album
Civium*.[18] Ten Scottish merchants were admitted to the official community of the city between 1575–1600.[19] However it is impossible

---

w.),' *Zeszyty Naukowe Wyższej Szkoły Pedagogicznej im. Powstańców Śląskich w Opolu. Historia*
26 (1988): 49–58.

[11] See M. G. Zieliński, 'Catholic Scottish Burghers in Chełmno in the 17th–18th
Centuries,' a paper presented at the conference *Polish-Scottish Relations in the 15th–18th
Centuries*, Warsaw, September 20–23, 2000; Gierszewski, *Elbląg. Przeszłość i teraźniejszość*
(Gdańsk: 1970), 68–69, 71–72.

[12] Biegańska, 'The Learned Scots,' 16–17.

[13] S. Cackowski, 'W czasach Rzeczypospolitej szlacheckiej,' *Toruń dawny i dzisiejszy*,
ed. M. Biskup, (Warszawa: 1983), 161.

[14] Guldon, 'Artykuły wetowe miasta Torunia z 1634 roku,' *Zapiski Historyczne* 38.3
(1973): 95–96. James Fraser, who travelled in Poland in 1656 as an ensign in
Swedish service, was an exception. Once the Swedes made peace with Poland, he
settled in the city and became a merchant; for more on him see S. Murdoch, A.
Grosjean, *Scotland, Scandinavia & Northern Europe, 1580–1707*, database.

[15] Guldon and Stępkowski, 'Szkoci i Anglicy,' 35.

[16] This social stratum in early modern Poland has been studied by B. Baranowski,
Ludzie gościńca w XVII–XVIII w. (Łódź: 1986).

[17] Guldon, Stępkowski, 'Szkoci i Anglicy,' 33: Poznań, Kalisz, Pyzdry.

[18] Biegańska, 'In Search of Tolerance,' 40; *Papers Relating to the Scots in Poland*,
passim.

[19] Gierszewski, *Obywatele miast Polski przedrozbiorowej. Studium źródłoznawcze* (Warszawa:
1973), 73.

to obtain an exact figure for the Scots in Poznań. In 1576, King Stephen Batory's decree obliged city authorities to remove those Scots who had not purchased property.[20] Only five Scottish families are listed in a 1590 register, and twenty one Scots were included in a 1601 register. Thus not all the Poznań Scots could have been dwelling within the city walls. Nevertheless they continued to live in Poznań in the following decades, at least until the turn of the eighteenth century.[21]

In 1568, hucksters were forbidden to settle in Bydgoszcz (Bromberg),[22] although a relatively affluent Scottish community existed there at that time. They were engaged in trade and floating timber, and often held high town offices. The number of constant Scottish town dwellers does not seem to have exceeded twenty adults.[23] Scottish settlement is known to have occurred in other towns in Great Poland, but there is little we can say about its range and social impact.[24] As elsewhere, the poor must have constituted the majority of newcomers, as a royal mandate against "Jews, Scots and other vagabonds" was also issued for this province in 1594.[25] One recent find is an almost unknown Scottish community living in a peripheral town in Koniecpol at least until the beginning of the eighteenth century. It reveals the vast scholarly potential available in the huge number of parochial and town records which to date have not been exploited.[26]

---

[20] S. Abt, 'Ludność Poznania w XVI i pierwszej połowie XVII w.,' in *Dzieje Poznania do roku 1793*, ed. J. Topolski (Warszawa – Poznań: 1988), Vol. 1, Pt. 1, 449; Fischer, *The Scots in Eastern and Western Prussia*, 209; Guldon and Stępkowski, 'Szkoci i Anglicy,' 47; A. B. Pernal, R. P. Gasse, eds., 'The 1651 Polish Subsidy to the Exiled Charles II,' *Slavonic Papers*, 32 (1999): 21–22. I am grateful to Professor Pernal who kindly mailed me an offprint of his work.

[21] *Papers Relating to the Scots in Poland*, xxix–xxx.

[22] *Ibidem*, xiv, xxix.

[23] Z. Guldon, R. Kabaciński, *Szkice z dziejów dawnej Bydgoszczy XVI–XVIII wieku* (Bydgoszcz: 1975) 96–97.

[24] Kabaciński, 'W czasach staropolskich (do roku 1772),' in *Dzieje Pakości*, ed. W. Jastrzębski (Warszawa: 1978) 77–78; *Koronowo. Zarys dziejów miasta*, ed. M. Biskup (Bydgoszcz: 1968) 34. Pakość and Koronowo were small towns in Cuiavia, which was part of Great Poland.

[25] Fischer, *The Scots in Eastern and Western Prussia*, 33.

[26] In the years 1609–1626(†) Alexander Gierner 'civis et famatus' lived and died there. Martin Gierner, a tailor, noted in 1678 and 1679, was one of his numerous children. Martin's relatives must have been Marianna and Regina Gierner [or as in the source: 'Giernerowicowe'], who married in 1707 and 1709 respectively. Peter Scotus was noted in the local parochial records in 1609 or 1624. In 1631 Simon Russel was mentioned, and in 1651 a John 'Szotek' died. In the same year the

In 1651, the English and Scots were listed in 48% of settlements in this region,[27] which is only 18% of the total number of towns. In the first decades of the seventeenth century, at least three Scots were citizens of Sieradz.[28]

Little is known about the Scots immigrants in Mazovia. They were present in Warsaw from the sixteenth to the eighteenth centuries, and the first migrants received citizenship in 1571.[29] In 1651 they lived in at least seventeen towns, 16% of the total number of towns in the province.[30] We know, too, that Scots were still living in several of these towns in the following decades. In 1674, the poll tax list for Zakroczym opened with the name of Wojciech (Albert) Kalwak 'Scotus', who was followed by his wife and a servant, Willim, of the same nation.[31]

In Little Poland, considerable Scottish communities existed in the main cities of Cracow, Lublin and Lvov. Permanent Scottish residents were noted in Cracow for the first time in 1509, although students from Scotland enrolled in the Jagiellonian University there as early as the first half of the fifteenth century.[32] Up to 1611, citizenship was granted to forty five Scots, around 0.7% of the entire

demise of an Alexander was commemorated. In the 1680s a burgess named Alexander Blair was noted. Laurentius Szotowicz was a curate to the local church in the same period; Archiwum Państwowe w Kielcach, Księgi metrykalne parafii Koniecpol, MS 1: 69, 90, 104, 177, 123, 153, 154, 166, 169, 172, 199, 224, 235, 298, 327; MS 2: 38, 54, 74; MS 3: 17, 27, 166, 185, 237, 238; MS 4: 83–84, 96, 100, 105–106, 198, 203.

[27] Guldon, Stępkowski, 'Ludność szkocka i angielska,' 206, Table 1; Pernal, Gasse, 'The 1651 Polish Subsidy,' passim.

[28] Papers Relating to the Scots in Poland, 59–61.

[29] Fischer, The Scots in Germany, 257–258; Biegańska, 'Scottish Merchants and Traders in Seventeenth and Eighteenth Century Warsaw,' SSR 5 (1985): 18–34; Bogucka, 'Podstawy gospodarczego rozwoju Warszawy,' in her et al., Warszawa w latach 1526–1795 (Warszawa: 1984), 45–46, 57–60; W. Kowalski, 'The Scotsmen in the Cracow Market in the mid-17th Century,' a paper delivered at the conference Polish-Scottish Relations, 15th–18th Centuries, Warsaw, September 20–23, 2000 [to be published], Table 2.

[30] Guldon, Stępkowski, 'Ludność szkocka i angielska,' 206, Table 1; Pernal, Gasse, 'The 1651 Polish Subsidy,' 31–35.

[31] Archiwum Główne Akt Dawnych w Warszawie, Archiwum Skarbu Koronnego, Dział I, MS 66, f. 265v. No-one of this name exists among the twelve local Scots who paid the tithe for Charles II; Pernal, Gasse, 'The 1651 Polish Subsidy,' 32–33. As early as the 1640s the Scottish presence in Zakroczym was testified to by Alexander Tudy [Tweedy]; Biegańska, 'Scottish Merchants,' 21.

[32] Papers Relating to the Scots in Poland, 347–351; Fischer, The Scots in Germany, 256–257; Biegańska, 'The Learned Scots,' 3.

immigrant population registered in local burgh admittance records.[33] Of a group of thirty Scots who arrived in Cracow, twenty one were listed by city scribes as coming from Aberdeen, and one of them, the Cracow merchant Andrew Hunter, served his home town's city council as a factor in 1619.[34]

In the years 1601–07 only eleven Scots were listed. Like their compatriots who settled in Cracow before them, they were mostly merchants and stall-traders.[35] During the seventeenth century, Cracow citizenship was granted to around thirty merchants from Scotland. There is source evidence that the trading community who lived temporarily in the urban area without consent must have been much larger, but unfortunately we have no grounds for any estimate.[36] In 1632, about forty Scots lived in the Cracow satellite town of Kazimierz.[37] By that time Scots had also settled in Kleparz, another municipality of the Cracow area. Several of the merchants in this township must have been quite rich, for instance John Roth (1572), James Dromont "ex familia magnificis baronis de Borlandt oriundus," or Kilian Buchan, a Scottish elder in 1603. Some of these well-to-do members of the Kleparz community aspired to Cracow citizenship; in this way they could improve their social status as well as business opportunities.[38]

Between 1583 and 1660, no less than forty Scottish merchants became citizens of Lublin, but there were at least twice as many living temporarily or permanently without citizenship.[39]

---

[33] T. C. Smout, N. C. Landsman, T. M. Devine, 'Scottish Emigration in the Seventeenth and Eighteenth Centuries,' in *Europeans on the Move. Studies on European Migration, 1500–1800*, ed. N. Canny (Oxford: 1994), 77, 80; Belzyt, 'Grupy etniczne w Krakowie około roku 1600. Próba opisu topograficznego,' *Studia Historyczne* 40.4 (1997): 469–470.

[34] *Aberdeen Council Letters* [hereafter *ACL*], ed. Louise B. Taylor, vol. 1 (1552–1633) (London: 1942), no. 167, 168.

[35] Belzyt, 'Kraków i Praga,' 279–281.

[36] Kowalski, 'The Scotsmen in the Cracow Market,' *passim*. According to S. Kutrzeba and J. Ptaśnik, 'Dzieje handlu i kupiectwa krakowskiego,' *Rocznik Krakowski* 14 (1910): 113. From the mid-sixteenth century to the end of the seventeenth, seventy five Scots were granted Cracow citizenship. See also *Papers Relating to the Scots in Poland*, 39–58.

[37] Belzyt, 'Kraków i Praga,' 228–229.

[38] *Papers Relating to the Scots in Poland*, 40, 45, 55; J. Bieniarzówna, J. M. Małecki, *Dzieje Krakowa. Kraków w wiekach XVI–XVIII* (Kraków: 1984), 226–227.

[39] R. Szewczyk, *Ludność Lublina w latach 1583–1650* (Lublin: 1947), 85–96. Twenty six Scots were listed in the city in 1635; J. Sadownik, *Szkoci w Lublinie XVII wieku* (Leszno: 1937), 1–5.

There is little we can say about the Lvov community. In the second half of the seventeenth century, the Forbes family had their base in Lvov, and ran a commercial enterprise throughout Ruthenia, with branches in many regional towns.[40] Those of Charles II's subjects who ran into tax collectors in Lvov in 1651 declared themselves to be sojourners from other places.[41] This may have been the case, as the Lvov fairs attracted merchants from the commonwealth and abroad.[42] The city records for the first half of the seventeenth century list Scottish merchants from the following places: Brody – 64; Jarosław – 2; Krasnystaw – 1; Krosno – 1; Lesko – 1; Lvov – 13; Łomża – 2; Ostróg – 3; Pińczów – 14; Przeworsk – 4; Sambor – 1; Tarnów – 22, and Zamość – 35. Moreover, two other Lvov Scots were noted in the sixteenth century: William Alland (1567–1576) and Albert Alland (1573).[43]

In the mid-seventeenth century, more than twenty Scottish merchants lived in Zamość, in the Land of Chełm, and some Scots arrived in the area even earlier.[44] From the 1630s–50s, sixty Scots were citizens of the town of Brody, in the Ruthenian Palatinate.[45] At the beginning of the seventeenth century several traders settled in Krosno, in the same palatinate, and a Scottish presence was documented up to 1651.[46]

---

[40] See R. V. Shiyan, 'Diyalnist shotlandskih kuptsiv na miskih rinkah ruskogo voevodstva v drugiy polovini XVII st.,' in *Z istorii starodavnosti i serednovitchtchya, Vysnik Lvivskogo Universitetu, Istoria* (Lviv: 1984), 19–23. The Central Historical State Archive of the Ukraine in Lvov [hereafter CHAL], Correspondence, fond 52, 132: information on Lvov Scots kindly imparted by Professor Zenon Guldon.

[41] Guldon, Stępkowski, 'Szkoci i Anglicy,' 60–61; Pernal, Gasse, 'The 1651 Polish Subsidy,' 28–29.

[42] Guldon, 'Szkoci w miastach,' *passim.*

[43] R. V. Shiyan, *Rol gorodov russkovo y bel'zskovo voevodstv v torgovih svyazyah vostochnoy Evropi s tsentral'noy y zapadnoy Evropoy v 16-pervoy polovinye 17vv.*, Lvov 1987, unpublished thesis in the Lvov University library, Appendix 1. Seven of the fourteen Pińczów Scots are not mentioned in the quoted thesis and were additionally found in CHAL fond 52, d. 402, *passim.*

[44] R. Szczygieł, 'Zamość w czasach staropolskich,' in *Czterysta lat Zamościa*, ed. J. Kowalczyk (Wrocław: 1983), 108; Biegańska, 'Andrew Davidson (1591–1660) and His Descendants in Poland,' *SSR* 10 (1988): 7–18; Guldon, Stępkowski, 'Szkoci i Anglicy,' 59; Pernal, Gasse, 'The 1651 Polish Subsidy,' 28; and further in this article.

[45] Guldon, 'Ludność szkocka w Brodach w pierwszej połowie XVII wieku,' in his *Żydzi i Szkoci w Polsce*, 65–85.

[46] F. Leśniak, *Krosno w czasach Odrodzenia. Studia nad społeczeństwem miasta* (Kraków: 1992), 123–124; his *Rzemieślnicy i kupcy w Krośnie (XVI—pierwsza połowa XVII wieku)* (Kraków: 1999), *passim.*

The register of 1651 lists Scots in only eighteen Little Polish towns, equal to 8% of the towns in the province. The unwillingness of individuals to pay the 1651 subsidy (well-known among scholars dealing with the Scottish diaspora in Poland-Lithuania) limits the usefulness of the register for research into Scottish settlement.[47] According to this source, there were Scots in eight towns of the Sandomierz Palatinate, which was part of Little Poland. However Appendix 1 of this essay shows that from about the turn of the seventeenth century through to the 1660s they were living in twenty two towns, both large (Sandomierz, Radom, Chęciny, Pińczów, Tarnów) and small. The Scottish presence in this area will be examined in greater detail elsewhere in this study.

Scottish settlement as shown in Appendix 1 is the result of research into source collections of different provenances which have been only partially preserved, and not to the same extent for every locality. Due to this uneven preservation of town records, relatively large numbers of Scottish burgesses have been found where sources have fortunately survived, which is the case for Tarnów (sixty eight Scottish traders) or Szydłowiec (thirty one). Although to date most of the sources for the Sandomierz Palatinate have been used, it seems likely that more data could be collected from town records[48] or parochial registers.[49] The authors of town monographs referred to in Appendix 1 give short shrift to Scottish immigrants, generally just listing them in a sequence of ethnicities once active in local society. These records should be examined again to shed more light on Scottish immigrants and their relations with local towns.

The research results I refer to have shown that city records of the main trade centres such as Cracow, Lvov and Lublin (including their toll registers) are promising sources. These records have been used far too little in the areas under consideration, and this is also true

---

[47] Guldon and Stępkowski in their articles mentioned above, and recently Steve Murdoch, 'The Scottish Community in Kėdainiai in its Scandinavian and Baltic Context,' a paper given at the *Colloqium Balticum* in Kėdainiai, June 2001. I am most indebted to the author who kindly sent me the article in its pre-print version. Also Anna Biegańska ('A Note,' 159) knows of 141 Scots mentioned in sources other than the 1651 census.

[48] Which mainly deal with Sandomierz.

[49] Of which Radom and Iłża are good examples. Only the 1590–1607 and 1621–1636 Radom registers have been employed in the search for Scottish immigrants; see Appendix 1.

of the state coffers documentation, including registers of the sixteenth-
and seventeenth-century property collections and poll taxes in the
1660s and 1670s. An unknown number of Scottish immigrants and
their descendants with Polonised and Germanised names cannot be
identified unless their Scottish roots have been documented. Thus
Appendix 1 is merely an illustration of the widespread presence of
Scots in early modern Poland. The list allows us to show that Scots
reached even remote peripheral towns in central and southern Poland.

A dearth of emigration statistics from before 1774,[50] as well as a
lack of immigrant registration, makes it difficult to pinpoint any pre-
cise population figure. All that we can do is generalize for a possible influx range. The population of Scotland in the 1650s has been
estimated at 1–1.2 million, with 862,000 being the highest estimate
for 1691.[51] The estimates for immigrants who reached Poland up to
1650 have shifted from roughly 30,000 to as many as 50,000.[52] The
latter suggests that the Scottish minority could be as high as 0.4%
of the population of the Polish-Lithuanian Commonwealth in the
first half of the seventeenth century. According to Jerzy Topolski,
however, "around the turn of the 16th–17th centuries, there were
no more than a few thousand Scots, but they were recorded all over
the country because of their agility in trade".[53] Antoni Mączak also
maintains that "there are no grounds for the 30,000 estimate".[54]
Neither scholar offers reasons for these assertions.

William Lithgow, author of one of the very few first-hand accounts
of Scottish settlement in Poland, mentions "the youth and younglings
of Scotland, who are yearly sent hither in great numbers . . . besides
thirty thousand Scots families." This number seems to be simply
an exaggeration typical of the epoch, as commented on by Neil

[50] See M. Flinn *et al.*, *Scottish Population History from the 17th Century to the 1930s*
(Cambridge: 1977), 91–92.
[51] Smout, 'Scottish Emigration,' 85; Flinn *et al.*, *Scottish Population*, 187–200; A. I.
Macinnes, 'Regal Union for Britain, 1603–38,' in *The New British History. Founding
a Modern State, 1603–1715*, ed. G. Burgess (London-New York: 1999), 47.
[52] Smout, 'Scottish Emigration,' 85; Biegańska, 'Żołnierze szkoccy w dawnej
Rzeczypospolitej,' *Studia i Materiały do Historii Wojskowości* [hereafter *SMHW*] 27
(1984): 86; R. I. Frost, 'Scottish Soldiers, Poland-Lithuania and the Thirty Years'
War', in *Scotland and the Thirty Years' War, 1618–1648*, ed. S. Murdoch (Leiden:
2001), 192; Murdoch, 'The Scottish Community in Kėdainiai'.
[53] Topolski, *Polska w czasach nowożytnych*, 131.
[54] A. Mączak, 'Od połowy XV wieku do rozbiorów,' in *Społeczeństwo polskie od X
do XX wieku* (Warszawa: 1988), 330.

Ascherson.[55] It is possible, however, that the supposition of there being 30,000 Scottish families in Poland was shared by contemporaries in Britain.[56]

As a comparative, the Jewish population, whose considerable influx to Poland is documented for the late Middle Ages, continues to provide many more fruitful avenues for research.[57] The number of Jews in the 1560s and 1570s can be estimated from 30,000 to no more than 100,000.[58] A figure of 300,000 was once suggested, but this seems highly improbable if we consider, *exempli gratia*, toll registers for 1662 and the 1670s, even taking into account a heavy demographic loss resulting from war and natural calamities between the years 1648–1665.[59] From 1662–76, poll tax was paid by no more than 20,000 Jews, which is of course the minimum for the diaspora's real figure.[60]

Any further attempts to estimate Scottish immigration to Poland should be preceded by complex studies of the demographic situation, based on parochial lists of Easter Communion recipients as well as 1662 poll tax evidence. For the time being, there are no grounds to refute the estimate of 30,000 or maybe even 50,000 Scots in seventeenth-century Poland-Lithuania.

Mass emigration from Scotland has been explained in Polish historiography as primarily a result of the political and social conflicts

---

[55] W. Lithgow, *The Total Discourse of Rare Adventures and Painfull Peregrinations* (rpt., Glasgow: 1906), 362; N. Ascherson, *Stone Voices. The Search for Scotland* (London: 2003), 244–245.

[56] The number was mentioned in 1621; M. A. Everett, ed., *Calendar of State Papers, Domestic Series, of the Reign of James I. 1619–1623* (London: 1858), 237.

[57] A useful introduction to the multifarious aspects of Jewish life in the commonwealth has been provided by Gershon David Hundert, 'Poland: Paradisus Iudæorum,' *Journal of Jewish Studies* 48.2 (1997): 335–348.

[58] See Z. Guldon and Kowalski, 'Between Tolerance and Abomination: Jews in Sixteenth-Century Poland,' in *The Expulsion of the Jews. 1492 and After*, ed. R. B. Waddington and A. H. Williamson (New York-London: 1994), 162–164.

[59] Guldon, 'Straty ludności żydowskiej w Koronie w latach Potopu,' in *Rzeczpospolita w latach Potopu*, ed. J. Muszyńska and J. Wijaczka (Kielce: 1996), 289–303; J. Raba, *Between Remembrance and Denial. The Fate of the Jews in the Wars of the Polish Commonwealth during the Mid-Seventeenth Century as Shown in Contemporary Writings and Historical Research* (New York: 1995); A. Karpiński, *W walce z niewidzialnym wrogiem. Epidemie chorób zakaźnych w Rzeczypospolitej w XVI–XVIII wieku i ich następstwa demograficzne, społeczno-ekonomiczne i polityczne* (Warszawa: 2000), 362–363.

[60] Z. Guldon and Kowalski, 'The Jewish Population of Polish Towns in the Second Half of the 17th Century,' in *Studies in the History of the Jews in Old Poland in honor of Jacob Goldberg*, ed. A. Teller, *Scripta Hierosolymitana. Publications of the Hebrew University of Jerusalem*, Vol. 38 (Jerusalem: 1998), 67–81.

which originated with the outbreak of the Reformation and continued during the sixteenth and seventeenth centuries.[61] The conditions
which made adequate food production difficult were also discussed,
but these points were not high on the authors' agenda.[62] The emphasis on the Reformation as an incentive for people to immigrate to
Poland has resulted from the dominance of political history in nine-
teenth-century traditional Positivistic historiography. According to this
view, the religious Reformation was primarily a sequence of political events. This perspective, coupled with a common ignorance of
economic history, resulted in the popularising of this hypothetical
motivation for immigration.

In 1598 Fynes Moryson noted that the Scots "flocke in great numbers into Poland, abounding in all things for foode, and yielding
many commodities. And in these kingdoms they lived at this time
in great multitudes, rather for the poverty of their owne kingdome,
then for any great trafficke they exercised there, dealing rather small
fardels, then for great quantities of rich wares".[63] This is not the
only contemporary opinion pointing to economic reasons for migration from Scotland. As early as 1648 Łukasz Opaliński, a well-known
Polish political commentator, wrote in his polemical treatise 'Polonia
defensa contra Ioannem Barclaium' that: "This nation [Scots], having come to loathe their poor and infertile fatherland flees overseas
because of poverty, looking for livelihood with us".[64] These judg-
ments agree with the view of contemporary British historiography,
which emphasizes recurrent famines combined with other natural
calamities as a 'push' factor from Scotland.[65] Last but not least, it

---

[61] The religious reasons have been widely commented on by S. Tomkowicz,
'Przyczynek do historyi Szkotów w Krakowie i w Polsce,' *Rocznik Krakowski*, ed.
S. Krzyżanowski, 2 (1899): 157, 158–160. Cf. W. Borowy, 'Prześladowani katolicy
angielscy i szkoccy w Polsce XVI wieku,' *Przegląd Powszechny*, 219 (1947): 111–124.
Also according to Gierszewski ('Szkoci w mniejszych miastach,' 49) the migration
was caused by 'mainly religious conflicts'. In his valuable book *Protestantyzm w Lublinie
i w Lubelskiem w XVI–XVII w.* (Lublin: 1933), 17–18, Aleksander Kossowski writes
that "in Lublin, the Scottish colony was particularly numerous as they were persecuted for their faith in their fatherland and looked for shelter in Poland in the second half of the 17th century."

[62] Borowy, *Scots in Old Poland, Scottish-Polish Society Publications*, No. 2 (Edinburgh-
London: 1941), 7; Sadownik, *Szkoci w Lublinie*, 1; Biegańska, 'Żołnierze szkoccy,'
85–86; Guldon and Stępkowski, 'Ludność szkocka i angielska,' 202.

[63] *Papers Relating to the Scots in Poland*, xiii.

[64] Cited after Guldon and Stępkowski, 'Ludność szkocka i angielska,' 202.

[65] Flinn *et al.*, *Scottish Population History*, 116–186; Smout, 'Scottish Emigration,'

was war which drew Scots to the Polish-Lithuanian Commonwealth.[66]

There is no doubt that Scots were present throughout Poland as early as the 1570s, and their numbers are said to have increased since that date. Widely-known evidence, such as Sir John Skene's comment,[67] can be supplemented by advice given by the most famous Polish Renaissance poet, Jan Kochanowski.[68] More recent research on the directions and range of seventeenth-century Scottish emigration noted that "movement to two traditional areas, Scandinavia and Poland, had by then [c.1650] dropped to an insubstantial trickle, and never subsequently revived".[69] Nevertheless, Antoni Mączak's categorical statement that "in the second half of the 17th century the ethnic group disappeared due to assimilation and 'the Scottish problem' was no longer raised"[70] has been revised. Scots certainly lived in numerous towns in both the Crown lands and Lithuania, for example in Chełmno, Cracow and Lublin and in some burghs of the Sandomierz Palatinate (see Appendix 1). As a rule, the sources tell us about townspeople who lived permanently in a place. Generally we cannot be sure whether those bearing Scottish names were the first generation or their descendants. In the case where a name was followed by nationality (such as the above-mentioned 1670s Zakroczym burgess), this suggests assimilation was under way. New immigrants arrived in Kėdainiai after 1660,[71] but an initial search into the mid-seventeenth-century Cracow toll records suggests that the period during which Scots were found in most Little Polish provincial towns must have come to an end by 1649.[72] It seems possible that in the

---

81. Steve Murdoch is undoubtedly right when he points to the confusion of Scottish and English history, which results in an English perspective on the migration from Scotland ('The Scottish Community', fn 35).

[66] See Frost, 'Scottish Soldiers,' 191–213; Biegańska, 'Żołnierze szkoccy,' 81–111, and also Murdoch, 'The House of Stuart and the Scottish Professional Soldier 1618–1640: A conflict of Nationality and Identities,' in *War. Identities in Conflict 1300–2000*, ed.: B. Taithe & T. Thornton (Stroud: 1998), 43; M. Nagielski, 'Gwardia przyboczna Władysława IV (1632–1648),' *SMHW* 27 (1984): 116.

[67] Borowy, *Scots*, 6; Smout, 'Scottish Emigration,' 80; Biegańska, 'A Note,' 158.

[68] Pieśń [Song] xix: 'Bodaj się przepadło/ To twoje zwierciadło/ [- -] Popatrz między Szoty/ Prawdziwszej roboty [- -]' ['I wish that looking-glass of yours got lost [- -]/ You better look around with the Scots for a better handiwork']; J. Kochanowski, *Dzieła polskie*, ed. J. Krzyżanowski (Warszawa: 1972), 264.

[69] Smout, 'Scottish Emigration,' 87.

[70] Mączak, 'Od połowy XV,' 331.

[71] Murdoch, 'The Scottish Community.'

[72] Kowalski, 'The Scotsmen in the Cracow Market'.

aftermath of the wars of 1648–60, trade by Scottish pedlars was significantly limited, but a number of relatively affluent merchants continued to do business in Poland. This matter needs further scholarly attention.

The Scots who entered Poland in the sixteenth and seventeenth centuries to trade can generally be divided into two categories. The comparatively rich, who applied for and often received city rights, visited fairs all over central Europe. The poor who traded as pedlars carried cheap haberdashery on their backs or with the help of a horse. Even hypothetical demographical figures suggest that the latter category was predominant. Craftsmen were another but minor group of Polish urbanised Scots. One of these was John Guntar, a goldsmith in Warsaw, who in 1643 applied for a birth-brieve from Aberdeen City Council.[73] A common feature of the migration was young people who left Scotland in search of a better life.[74]

Polish historiography maintains that the poor were able to make money quickly in the commonwealth, and they eagerly availed themselves of their opportunities. This judgment is based on numerous opinions expressed by contemporary observers such as Fynes Moryson (1598), William Lithgow (1632), Adam Grodziecki (1639) and Łukasz Opaliński (1648). All of them, particularly Grodziecki, stress that when the newcomers who "once wandered from village to village on foot" became richer, they bought property in the towns and even began to "trade oxen and furs".[75] Władysław Stanisław Jeżowski, a minor Baroque poet and pamphleteer, referred before 1638 to the class structure of Polish society, which was sanctioned by law and tradition and included trading merchants and the gentry who profited from farming. After a sentimental introduction, in which he said that "once husbandry was the best trade for the gentry", the poet added that "Our forefathers held husbandry dear. They never heard of faked contracts, plenty of which you can see in Poland nowadays as there is no way to buy a village competing against Scots and Jews".[76]

---

[73] ACAs, Propinquity book, f. 24v. See also Bieganska, 'Scottish merchants,' *passim.*

[74] J. Stuart, ed., *Miscellany of the Spalding Club*, vol. 5 (Aberdeen: 1852), 323–368; see also Fischer, *The Scots in Germany*, 33–34.

[75] W. Guldon, Z. Guldon, 'Saga szkockiego rodu Russellów w Szydłowcu w pierwszej połowie XVII wieku,' in *Szydłowiec. Z dziejów miasta*, ed. J. Wijaczka (Szydłowiec: 1999), 35–37; Guldon and Stępkowski, 'Ludność,' 202.

[76] W. S. Jeżowski, 'Ekonomia abo Porządek zabaw ziemiańskich,' in *Staropolska*

Information about purchasing villages from the gentry by substitutes who acted on behalf of those who were banned from such possessions seems true, although there is no way to estimate the range of such fraud.

Scots in the multi-denominational society, and their economic role

As a rule, Polish urbanised Scots lived in an international environment of Armenian, Italian, German and Hungarian traders and artisans, to note the most common nationalities living in the Republic of Nobles in the sixteenth and seventeenth centuries. The multi-ethnic economic environment of early modern Poland was noticed by the famous polemicist Szymon Starowolski, who wrote in his 'Polonia sive status Regni Poloniæ descriptio' (published in 1632): "There are very popular fairs in Lublin itself thrice a year, which attract Englishmen, Scotsmen, Italians, Germans, Muscovites, Persians, Armenians . . .".[77]

Until the mid-seventeenth century, the Jewish stake in Polish trade was rather small, assuming that the results of comparatively poorly advanced research are representative.[78] An analysis of the role of Jews and Scots from the Sandomierz Palatinate in the turnover at the Cracow market allows us to note that between 1600 and 1604 Jews appeared more often. Merchants of both nations were engaged in similar trade, in which tawdry woollen cloth and so-called 'Nuremberg goods' prevailed. The 'Nuremberg goods' or general stall merchandise was imported from abroad and distributed in small towns and villages all over the country. A further fragmentary observation of the same toll records, this time for the year 1649, leads to the conclusion that the Sandomierz Palatinate Jews prevailed significantly over the Scots.[79] In the sixteenth century, Jews were pre-

---

poezja ziemiańska, ed. J. S. Gruchała and S. Grzeszczuk (Warszawa: 1988), 247. See also M. Nadav, 'Jewish Ownership of Land and Agricultural Activity in 16th Century Lithuania,' in Studies in the History of the Jews in Old Poland, 161–165.

[77] S. Starowolski, Polska albo opisanie Królestwa Polskiego, ed. A. Piskadło (Kraków: 1976), 84.

[78] Guldon and Karol Krzystanek, Ludność żydowska w miastach lewobrzeżnej części województwa sandomierskiego w XVI–XVIII wieku (Kielce: 1990), 98–100.

[79] Guldon, Krzystanek, Ludność żydowska w miastach, 99–100; Guldon, 'Żydzi i Szkoci,' 8, Table 1; Kowalski, 'The Scotsmen in the Cracow Market,'; J. M. Małecki

sent in thirty six towns, and in 1662–76 in fifty six towns in the area, respectively 32% and 49% of the towns in the palatinate.[80] Other sources confirm that in the seventeenth century, Scots lived in at least 19% of the Sandomierz Palatinate municipalities, which has been shown in Appendix 1.

The mid-seventeenth-century trade regression, which was preceded by the credit crisis of the 1620s and 1630s, made Christian towns-people shift to farming, and husbandry became a much more common means of support than before. This stimulated agrarian influence on the towns, and this increased in the aftermath of the war and epidemics which raged at the beginning of the eighteenth century. The Jews gave up trade for craft and inn-keeping and moved out to the country.[81] These changes were seen to a greater extent in Lesser Poland than in Great Poland.[82] Despite all this, Jewish participation in the Cracow market trade was still significant. The Jewish share became even more conspicuous as a result of the rapid and permanent drop in turnover after the Swedish occupation of the city.[83]

The overwhelming economic depression which followed the mid-seventeenth-century wars and natural calamities led citizens to open

---

in cooperation with E. Szlufik, *Jewish Trade in Cracow at the End of the XVI Century and in the XVII Century. Selected Records from Cracow Customs Registers, 1593–1683* (Kraków: 1995); his 'Handel żydowski u schyłku XVI i w 1 połowie XVII w. w świetle krakowskich rejestrów celnych,' in *Żydzi w dawnej Rzeczypospolitej*, ed. A. Link-Lenczowski, T. Polański (Wrocław: 1991), 220. See also J. Bieniarzówna, 'The Role of Jews in the Polish Foreign Trade, 1648–1764,' in *The Jews in Poland*, vol. 1, ed. A. K. Paluch (Cracow: 1993), 101–109.

[80] Guldon and Kowalski, 'The Jewish Population,' 71, 77; J. Muszyńska, 'The Urbanised Jewry of the Sandomierz and Lublin Provinces in the 18th Century,' *Studia Judaica* 2.4 (1999): 223–239; Guldon, 'Skupiska żydowskie w miastach polskich w XV–XVI wieku,' in *Żydzi i judaizm we współczesnych badaniach polskich*, ed. K. Pilarczyk & S. Gąsiorowski, (Kraków: 2000), vol. 2, 17.

[81] Guldon and Krzystanek, 'Ludność żydowska,' 98; Guldon, 'Ludność żydowska w miastach małopolskich i czerwonoruskich w drugiej połowie XVII wieku,' in his *Żydzi i Szkoci w Polsce*, 102; Kowalski, 'Ludność żydowska a duchowieństwo archidiakonatu sandomierskiego w XVII–XVIII w.,' *Studia Judaica* 1.2 (1998): 178–186.

[82] The dualism has been explained by Topolski, 'On the Role of the Jews in the Urbanization of Poland in the Early Modern Period,' in *The Jews in Poland*, Vol. 1, 45. See also his *The Manorial Economy in Early-Modern East-Central Europe: Origins, Development and Consequences* (Aldershot, Hampshire-Brookfield, Vt.: 1994) and Muszyńska, 'The Urbanised Jewry,' 232–234. A general view of the state's economic decline has been sketched recently by J. A. Gierowski, *The Polish-Lithuanian Commonwealth in the XVIIIth Century: From Anarchy to Well-organised State* (Kraków: 1996), 105–113.

[83] Małecki, *Jewish Trade in Cracow*, 40. Swedish troops occupied the city from October 1655 through to August 1657.

their gates to all newcomers rich enough to invest in property and a stall. In this way, Jews were able to settle in many more royal and private towns than before, although on rare occasions religiously-motivated refusals occurred.[84] Despite such cases banning settlement, Jewish traders entered even ecclesiastical property on fair days, although as a rule their permanent residence was strictly forbidden.[85] Jews were, however, allowed to live on the estates of religious orders, and even episcopal complaints to the Roman Curia were ineffective.[86] Of course a policy of attracting settlers to join the local urban economy regardless of creed or nationality was in place before the 1660s, and it was not only the Jews who benefited.[87]

Private owners and royal demesne administrators created favourable conditions including granting city rights to migrants willing to increase their capital in a town. Zamość and its founder, Chancellor Jan Zamoyski, are good examples of such an attitude. According to the first charter of 1580, only Catholics were entitled to settle in the newly established town. As this policy of creating a mono-religious society failed, Zamoyski renewed the foundation charter in 1588, and this time the invitation was extended to all. Within three years, there was a total of one Scottish and two Jewish householders, along side the established Polish population.[88]

---

[84] Muszyńska, 'The Urbanised Jewry,' 236; Topolski, 'On the Role of the Jews,' 45–50; Guldon and Krzystanek, *Ludność żydowska w miastach*, 67–68; A. Kaźmier-czyk, *Żydzi w dobrach prywatnych w świetle sądowniczej i administracyjnej praktyki dóbr magnac-kich w wiekach XVI–XVIII* (Kraków: 2002).

[85] There is a wide range of literature on this point. J. I. Israel, *European Jewry in the Age of Mercantilism, 1550–1750* (London-Portland Or.: 1998) must be still appre-ciated for its broad range, although the author undoubtedly overestimates the role of the 'De non tolerandis Judæis' privilege. See also G. Dahan, *The Christian Polemic against the Jews in the Middle Ages* (Notre Dame: 1998).

[86] W. Müller, 'Żydzi w relacjach ad limina biskupów polskich z XVII i XVIII wieku," in *Religie, edukacja, kultura. Księga pamiątkowa dedykowana Profesorowi Stanisławowi Litakowi*, ed. M. Surdacki (Lublin: 2002), 82–85. In the sixteenth century Jewish colonies existed even in two bishops' towns; see H. Węgrzynek, 'Kościół katolicki a Żydzi w Małopolsce w XVI wieku,' in *Kościół katolicki w Małopolsce w średniowieczu i we wczesnym okresie nowożytnym*, ed. Kowalski, Muszyńska (Kielce: 2001): 226–227, 233–234.

[87] A. Cowan, *Urban Europe 1500–1700* (London-New York: 1998), 115–120. On various aspects of the Jewish presence in the town see H. Zaremska, 'Jewish Street (Platea Judeorum) in Cracow: The 14th—the First Half of the 15th C,' *Acta Poloniae Historica* 83 (2001): 27–56 and E. Fram, *Ideals Face Reality. Jewish Law and Life in Poland, 1550–1655* (Cincinnati: 1997), 19–25 and *passim*.

[88] Guldon and Kowalski, 'Between Tolerance and Abomination,' 162; Szczygieł, 'Zamość,' 105–108; J. Morgensztern, 'Żydzi w Zamościu na przełomie XVI i XVII w.,' *Biuletyn Żydowskiego Instytutu Historycznego w Polsce*, 43–44 (1962): 3, 16; Biegańska,

Numerous international communities were created as a result of citizens' desires to set up firm sources of steady income. A settlement action leading to a well-developed town might take only a few years; Pińczów is a good example of this at the end of the sixteenth century. In 1592 a new municipality named Mirów was located on the eastern suburbs of Pińczów. Once a village, it had been granted urban rights in 1428. The two separate towns formed an agglomeration in the Sandomierz Palatinate which was soon populated by a multi-ethnic society of merchants and craftsmen from several west European countries, with Jews and Scots predominating.[89] The town's owners, the Margraves Myszkowski, offered protection to their subjects. Two of these, James Johnson, a Scot, and David Bocheński, a Jew, appeared before the magistrates of neighbouring Raków in 1633. They presented a letter from the margrave in support of their demands as creditors of a Scottish merchant in Raków, Jacob Łaszan (Lawson). Thanks to the letter, judgement was in their favour, but Łaszan's property had already been seized by a local townsman.[90]

At this time Tarnów was another multi-denominational town, where a large group of Scots settled and created a separate Reformed Evangelical community. Some of the local Scots appear to have had close relations with the town owners; one example was Peter Bernath, who was named as a servitor of Prince Ostrogski.[91] In 1617, Prince Janusz Ostrogski asked King James VI and I of Great Britain and Ireland for protection for another Tarnów burgess, David Gurleius, who was travelling to Scotland.[92]

In the light of these urban policies, it seems likely that a considerable number of Scottish immigrants entering Poland-Lithuania were

'Andrew Davidson (1591–1660) and His Descendants in Poland,' *SSR* 10 (1988): 7–18; her 'In Search of Tolerance,' 39; *Papers Relating to the Scots in Poland*, 40, 74, 290–291.

[89] Małecki, 'Zarys dziejów Pińczowa do końca XVIII w.,' *Zeszyty Naukowe Uniwersytetu Jagiellońskiego. Prace Historyczne* 62 (1979): 20–28; Kowalski, 'Benedykt Briott,' *Studia Kieleckie* 3/43 (1984): 141–149.

[90] Biblioteka Jagiellońska [hereafter BJ], Protocolum advocatiale Racoviæ a[nno-rum] 1633–1659, MS 145, ff. 5ᵛ, 9ᵛ, 10ᵛ.

[91] F. Kiryk, 'Miasta regionu tarnowskiego: Tarnów, Tuchów, Ciężkowice do końca XVI w.,' in *Tarnów. Dzieje miasta i regionu*, ed. F. Kiryk and Z. Ruta (Tarnów-Rzeszów: 1981), 267.

[92] *Res Polonicae Iacobo I Angliae Regnante Conscriptae Ex Archivis Publicis Londoniarum*, ed. Carolus H. Talbot, *Elementa Ad Fontium Editiones* [hereafter *EFE*], VI (Roma: 1962), no. 138.

affluent people hoping to increase their wealth. A letter by William Bruce, sent from Gdańsk to Robert Cecil in 1606, emphasizes this probability. Bruce wrote "I haiwe wryttine to the Earle of Dumbaire thresorer of Scotland of Greatte sowmmes of our kinges Majestie coigne transported in this country be our Scottis merchantis against our Kinges ordinance . . .".[93] In the following decades, emigration was a way to avoid being deprived of personal property.[94]

City and town councils had different opinions on Scottish immigration. Attitudes towards the admittance of strangers into the community were influenced by several factors, including conflicting interests between local social classes, and the degree of freedom granted to the council by the town's owner. As a rule, royal town authorities were less constricted in implementing civic developments. Decisions were made according to current circumstances; Poznań, where a ban on granting citizenship to Scots had not been introduced by 1652, is a good example of this.[95] In 1667, the council of Bydgoszcz accused Andrew and Gasper Wolson, who did not have civic rights and were 'alienæ religionis' (Evangelical) of trading various merchandise, including goods such as salt and corn which they were not entitled to sell. They even began floating timber, which was in contradiction of the trade freedoms which the local Scots had been granted. According to that privilege, Scots could trade only a number of articles, including English cloth. The council ordered the confiscation of the timber, and threatened other retributions to deter Scots from acting against the town regulations in future.[96] Foreign merchants living permanently in Gdańsk were in competition for custom from the middle strata of the local townspeople. They were not powerful enough, however, to make the city council remove those traders who were not entirely legal, but also wealthy and influential.[97] This may explain why an attempt to gain citizenship might follow a ten-year

---

[93] *Ibidem*, no. 16.

[94] *ACL*, vol. 3 (1645–1660), no. 52, p. 44 (1646). Effectively these men were refugees from the Covenanting government.

[95] *Papers Relating to the Scots in Poland*, xxx; Gierszewski, *Obywatele miast*, 73. The ban was ineffective; see Fischer, *The Scots in Eastern and Western Prussia*, 212–214.

[96] Guldon and Kabaciński, *Szkice z dziejów*, 99.

[97] They arrived mostly from Amsterdam and German cities, but there were representatives of other nationalities including Scots; See Bogucka, 'Obcy kupcy,' 59–81; her 'Scots,' 40–41.

residence, as in the case of Alexander Kemp, an Aberdonian who applied for a birth-brieve in 1658.[98]

In 1633, in Chęciny, a royal town in the Sandomierz Palatinate, those Scots who had been granted citizenship were obliged by the local council to pay an extra tax for the urban community.[99] Migrants who arrived in Radom, in the same palatinate, around the turn of the seventeenth century, stayed either in the town or in the surrounding villages.[100] We know little about their material status, but the Scots who lived on the outskirts must have been relatively poor. All the examples given suggest that generally it was material status which influenced a council's attitude for or against a newcomer.

A Scottish merchant's material wealth is not usually easy to estimate. This obscurity is mainly due to the dearth of scholarly attention; city records, including those of Gdańsk,[101] often suggest that Scots were successful businessmen. So far, only the merchandise relating to the Forbes' enterprise has been investigated. The far-flung commercial activity of Samuel Edwards (Edward, Edwedt, †1654) has been studied thoroughly, but his Scottish roots are only hypothetical.[102] Thus a list of wealthy Scots in the Polish Crown which we could refer to today would not be long. It would include, however, the Davidsons in Zamość,[103] Robert Gilbert Porteus [Porteous] de Lanxeth in Krosno,[104] as well as John Pontius [Pont]. The latter was a citizen of Lvov, Zamość and Elbląg. He was also an agent for the London merchant Richard Stapper.[105]

The fiscal duties imposed on the Cracow merchants in 1643 and 1651 suggest that this must have been a small but affluent group. James Karmichel [Carmichael] and Albert Blackal [Blackhall], who

---

[98] ACAs, Propinquity book, f. 56v.

[99] Guldon, 'Szkoci w miastach,' 9.

[100] Archiwum kościoła parafialnego p.w. Św. Jana Chrzciciela w Radomiu, Księgi metrykalne parafii Nowego Miasta, Liber baptisatorum 1590–1649, MS 1, p. 33, 34, 59, 62.

[101] Bogucka, 'Scots,' 41 and passim.

[102] Guldon and Wijaczka, 'Kupiec zamojski i toruński Samuel Edwerdt,' Almanach Historyczny 3 (2001): 93–108.

[103] Biegańska, 'Andrew Davidson,' 7–18.

[104] Papers Relating to the Scots in Poland, xxxix; Leśniak, Rzemieślnicy i kupcy, passim.

[105] CHAL, fond 52, op. 2: d. 248, p. 367; d. 269, p. 492; d. 386, p. 488; W. Łoziński, 'Kupiectwo lwowskie w XVI wieku,' Biblioteka Warszawska 51.3 (1891): 436; H. Zins, Anglia a Bałtyk w drugiej połowie XVI wieku (Wrocław: 1967), 105, 109–110. The sources present Latinised versions of the surnames; cf. G. F. Black, The Surnames of Scotland (Edinburgh: 1999), 668, 669.

were at the top of the financial hierarchy, possessed capital of about 20,000 *florens*; other merchants evaluated their assets at some thousand *fls* or less. The fact that only six Scots out of the Crown residents who paid the Stuart tithe were charged from 1,000 to 5,000 *fls* led Andrew B. Pernel and Rosanne P. Gasse to the conclusion that "the Scots in the Kingdom of Poland did not constitute a wealthy minority".[106] However, it should be remembered that not all Scots in Poland were automatically pro-Stuart; certainly many may simply not have wished to support a monarch whom they felt had been duplicitous in his actions toward Scotland.[107] Pernel and Gasse's statement also needs the clarification that there was no ethnic group in Poland at that time which could be called "a wealthy [national or ethnic] minority". All the ethnic groups differed significantly as regards their material conditions. The Lvov judicial records studied by Zenon Guldon leave no doubt that Scottish merchants commonly ran into debt (often to their compatriots) to sums of several thousand *fls*. There is evidence that one merchant's assets were evaluated, perhaps excessively, at 30,000 *fls*.[108] The practice of running a commercial enterprise on credit was widespread. It often led to a loss, and the likelihood of this increased in times of war and economic decline. The particularly acute monetary crisis in the years 1620–23 is a good example of this.[109] Many experienced the fickleness of fortune by gaining and then losing wealth. In 1651, Alexander Russell, a Szydłowiec burgess, estimated his possessions at 1,152 *fls*, but it was noted that "the debts he has made with numerous creditors *valorem substantiæ ipsius superantur*". Nevertheless, he also owned some property in Scotland. Thus it may be safe to say that a measure of personal wealth could be based on the social status achieved within the local community. Russell, as well as his compatriots living in Szydłowiec, belonged to the local upper class.[110]

---

[106] *Papers Relating to the Scots in Poland*, 80–86; Pernal, Gasse, 'The 1651 Polish Subsidy,' 16. See also Bieniarzówna, Małecki, *Dzieje Krakowa*, 204.

[107] For a wider contextualisation see Murdoch, *Britain, Denmark-Norway and the House of Stuart 1603–1660. A Diplomatic and Military Analysis* (East Linton: 2003), 157–158 and *passim*.

[108] Guldon, 'Szkoci w miastach,' *passim*.

[109] Fram, *Ideals Face Reality*, 26, 67–163; J. Rutkowski, *Historia gospodarcza Polski do 1864 r.* (Warszawa: 1953), 156. That is why Andro Thoree, a Danzig merchant who asked for a birth-brieve in 1645, was named as 'ane hazardelis in merchandise;' ACAs, Propinquity book, ff. 29–29v.

[110] Guldon and Guldon, 'Saga,' 45–46.

Belonging to a Christian denomination other than the privileged one was not usually an insurmountable obstacle to citizenship. It was even easier for all those content only with the status of legal resident. However this assumption has been based on a relatively small number of cases of Evangelical merchants admitted to Catholic urban corporations. The Lublin city council and artisan guilds were satisfied with declarations of readiness to convert in the future. Such declarations were often lip service, to which city authorities turned a blind eye. There were also instances of people simply buying a forged document confirming conversion to Catholicism.[111] The case of a Dutch merchant, Michael Heydeman, once again proves that a high social position eliminated bureaucratic barriers in everyday city life. Being a Protestant, he acted as a so-called 'papal syndic' and transacted business for the local Reformist-Franciscan cloister for over twenty years. He decided to convert to Catholicism only in his article of death in 1710, probably tempted by the possibility of burial in the friars' church.[112] The Lublin authorities' attitude toward non-Catholics could not have been substantially different from the policy in other royal towns. Despite this, in 1635 the king's intervention was needed to make the Cracow council change its negative stance on granting citizenship to a group of Protestants, including Scots—but this was the exception rather than the rule.[113]

Both in Cracow and Lublin, Scottish merchants strongly supported the local multi-national Evangelical-Reformed congregations.[114] The Lublin congregation voted for alms distributions to the Scottish paupers in this district.[115] Denominational bonds were tightened in response to the permanent oppression of the Catholic environment. Self-sufficiency was undoubtedly a powerful tool. Relations with

---

[111] Sadownik, *Przyjęcia do prawa miejskiego w Lublinie w XVII w.* (Lublin: 1938), 35–41. See also Biegańska, 'In Search of Tolerance,' 39–42.

[112] See Kowalski, 'From the 'Land of Diverse Sects' to National Religion: Converts to Catholicism and Reformed Franciscans in Early Modern Poland,' *Church History* 70.3 (2001): 510–511.

[113] Bieniarzówna, Małecki, *Dzieje Krakowa*, 226–227; Biegańska, 'In Search of Tolerance,' 39–41.

[114] Biegańska, 'In Search of Tolerance,' 42–43; Kowalski, 'The Scotsmen in the Cracow Market,'; M Sipayłło ed., *Akta synodów różnowierczych w Polsce*, Vol. 3: *Małopolska (1571–1632)* (Warszawa: 1983), 249–250, 265, 288–289, 509. *Ibidem*, 379 on their integration into the Lublin evangelical community; also Sadownik, *Szkoci w Lublinie*, 4.

[115] Kossowski, *Protestantyzm*, 166.

co-religionists may well have played a more important role on an everyday basis than national self-consciousness. Ethnic and religious differences traditionally fostered ties within an urban national and denominational society.[116] There is no doubt that in seventeenth-century Cracow and Lublin the citizens saw this minority as a distinct group of Evangelicals and Scots. Most of these were probably not interested in assimilation, although there were individuals who saw themselves as part of the city community. Such integration was testified to by Alexander Dixon in Cracow in the mid-seventeenth century.[117]

Calvinists found unlimited confessional freedom in private towns owned by the nobility. Tarnów is an example of this, as is peripheral Jedlińsk, a small town in the vicinity of Radom in the Sandomierz Palatinate. In this private town, Scots were protected by the Evangelical owners from at least 1619. That year, the local Scots had a bell founded with the following inscription: 'Comonitas[!] gentis Scoticæ ecclesiæ evangelicæ dicat'.[118] No sources have survived to estimate how numerous the congregation was. It came to an end in 1629, when Jedlińsk was inherited by new Catholic owners. Most of the local Protestants, including the Scots, must have left the town at this time or in the following year. Nevertheless, a small Scottish community continued to exist in Jedlińsk. Kilian Wilim, a Scot, remained Evangelical together with his wife until 1650, as the only 'heretic' and also the only merchant in the township.[119]

An analysis of the data collected in Appendix 1 leaves no doubt that it was a town's economic status which was a deciding factor in settlement, and religious aspects must have been of secondary importance. Although the Scottish settlement in the Sandomierz Palatinate (25,790 sq. kms) has been reconstructed from badly-preserved sources, it seems reasonable to conclude that the chosen towns must have been commercially advantageous.

---

[116] *Cf.* J. Rossiaud, 'The City-Dweller and Life in Cities and Towns,' in *Medieval Callings*, ed. J. Le Goff (Chicago: 1996), 154–161; Zaremska, 'Jewish Street,' 27–29; Cowan, *Urban Europe*, 75–79, 107–120 and *passim*.

[117] Kowalski, 'The Scotsmen in the Cracow Market'. *Cf.* Friedrich, 'Nationale Identität,' *passim*.

[118] *Corpus Inscriptionum Poloniæ* [hereafter *CIP*], vol. VII: *Palatinatus Radomiensis*, fasciculus I: *Radom et Iłża regioque*, recensuit et annotavit Valdemarus Kowalski, qui edendo præfuit Zeno Guldon (Varsoviæ: 1992), no. 34.

[119] Kowalski, "Comonitas gentis Scoticæ' w Jedlińsku w pierwszej połowie XVII stulecia,' *Kieleckie Studia Historyczne* 9 (1991), 23–32.

In the second half of the sixteenth century, roughly thirty of 114 towns in the region had a population of at least 1000.[120] Table 1 shows possible population numbers in those towns inhabited by Scots. Jewish presence has been indicated if relevant. The numbers are estimates based on property taxes of the 1560s to 1580s and on poll taxes raised in the years 1662–74.

Table 1[121]

Possible population of the Sandomierz Palatinate towns containing Scottish settlers in the second half of the sixteenth century and the second half of the seventeenth century.

| Town | Ownership | 1560s–1580s | | 1662–1674 | |
		Total population	Jewish settlement	Total population	Jewish settlement
Bodzentyn	ecclesiastical	1,500	–	1,400	–
Busko	ecclesiastical	1,200	–	750	–
Chmielnik	private	250	–	1,400	+
Chęciny	royal	2,000	+	1,200	+
Iłża	ecclesiastical	1,500	–	1,000	–
Jedlińsk	private	100	–	400	+
Kielce	ecclesiastical	700	–	500	–
Koprzywnica	ecclesiastical	1,200	–	1,000	–
Kunów	ecclesiastical	1,000	–	900	–
N. M. Korczyn	royal	1,000	+	1,200	+
Opatów	private	2,700	+	1,700	+
Opoczno	royal	2,000	+	800	+
Pacanów	private	1,000	+	1,200	+
Pińczów-Mirów	private	1,000	+	3,700	+
Połaniec	royal	2,000	+	1,100	+
Radom	royal	2,000	+	900	–
Raków	private	500	+	1,600	+
Sandomierz	royal	4,500	+	3,000	+
Secemin	private	1,000	–	1,400	+
Skrzynno	ecclesiastical	1,200	–	700	–
Szydłowiec	private	2,000	+	1,000	+
Tarnów	private	2,000	+	1,200	+
Total	22	32,350	12	28,050	14

---

[120] Anna Dunin-Wąsowiczowa, 'Charakter i wielkość osiedli,' in *Atlas historyczny Polski, Województwo sandomierskie w drugiej połowie XVI wieku*, ed. W. Pałucki, pt. 2: *Komentarz, indeksy* (Warszawa: Wydawnictwo Naukowe PWN: 1993), 81–82.

[121] Sources: Archiwum Główne Akt Dawnych w Warszawie, Archiwum Skarbu Koronnego, Dział I, MS 67; Biblioteka Czartoryskich w Krakowie, MS 1099; Guldon,

Table 1 shows that Scottish presence has been confirmed for around 70% of the largest towns in the palatinate, although only for 20% of the entire number of towns in the region.[122] Almost all the municipalities in the table lay on routes which were sections of international highways, except for Bodzentyn, Kielce and Chmielnik. Bodzentyn and Kielce were, however, hubs for the Cracow bishops' landed property as well as centres of ecclesiastical administration. Chmielnik, a private town erected in 1551, soon became an important Protestant centre in Little Poland. From the early 1560s through to the 1590s, Anti-Trinitarians were predominant; subsequently, until 1692, their Calvinist opponents predominated, with Catholic and Jewish minorities. With crafts and trades developed enough to satisfy the needs of the local market, the town may have been more attractive for newcomers through its school and famous anti-Arian polemicists, Evangelical theologians and ministers to the local congregation.[123]

The Chmielnik Evangelical college competed successfully with a neighbouring Anti-Trinitarian centre in Raków. This peripheral township was founded a short time before 1567. In 1569 its owner, Jan Sienieński, urged radical opponents of the Calvinist persuasion to overlook unfavourable economic conditions. The town's status improved from 1602 onwards, with a well-known school, 'the Polish Brethren's Academy' and a printing house being set up in 1604. The Anti-Trinitarian 'Catechism' printed by the local press in Latin after 1605 was dedicated to King James VI and I, who unfortunately took umbrage and ordered the work to be burnt. Despite the dominance

---

Krzystanek, 'Ludność żydowska,' *passim*; Kiryk, *Urbanizacja Małopolski. Województwo sandomierskie XIII–XVI wiek* (Kielce: 1994), *passim*; Małecki, 'Zarys dziejów,' 22, 36; Muszyńska, *Żydzi w miastach województwa sandomierskiego i lubelskiego w XVIII wieku* (Kielce: 1998), 21–34; L. Stępkowski, 'Bodzentyn nowożytny. Z dziejów miasta biskupiego w XVI–XVIII wieku,' in *Bodzentyn. Z dziejów miasta w XII–XX wieku*, ed. Krzysztof Bracha (Kielce: 1998), 86–90; his 'Ludność Iłży w XVII i XVIII wieku,' *Studia Kieleckie* 1.5 (1975), 52–65.

[122] The sixteenth- to seventeenth-century municipal and parochial records of Sandomierz Palatinate have been preserved for only about 15% of the 114 burghs. To date no Scots have been found in two of the extant source collections of peripheral Ożarów (BJ, MS 4) and Skrzynno (Biblioteka Wyższego Seminarium Duchownego w Sandomierzu [hereafter BSDS], MS 1430).

[123] Kowalski, 'Zarys dziejów Chmielnika w czasach przedrozbiorowych,' *Almanach Historyczny* 1 (1999): 64–71. In 1674 a merchant named Allan founded a scholarship for students willing to enter the university in Frankfort.

of Anti-Trinitarianism, all Protestant religions and Judaism could be practised freely, and only Catholics were refused a place of worship. The 'Sarmatian Athens,' as this intellectual centre was called, attracted Evangelical youths and their noble parents regardless of stern admonitions from the Reformed Church elders.[124]

Neither freedom to express religious beliefs nor the reasonably good economic standing of the town in the seventeenth century attracted significant numbers of Scottish migrants to settle in the 'Arian Rome.' Undoubtedly, Scots did live in the town. On 26 July 1642 an adult, Anna Gutry [Guthrie], was baptised at the Jedlińsk parochial church. She was a daughter of Arian (Anti-Trinitarian) parents, Dorothy and Peter, who had come there from Raków. According to a local Jedlińsk tradition, some of the teachers at the Evangelical school came from Raków.[125] At least one Scot stayed there at the time of re-Catholicization, which began in 1638.[126] But the three renowned cultural and religious centres do not appear to have had large Scottish settlements, and these towns' appeal to Scottish merchants lay only in relation to the economic opportunities they offered. This suggests that the situation already noted in Kėdainiai did not take precedence in Little Poland.[127]

It appears that small numbers of Scottish Protestants who lived in peripheral towns with the Catholic majority tended to convert. Conversion, as well as marriage to a local inhabitant, could be an important step on the way to assimilation. This process was noted all over the kingdom.[128] There were also exceptional cases of non-

---

[124] Stępkowski, 'Religia i gospodarka. Z dziejów gospodarczych Rakowa w drugiej połowie XVI i w XVII wieku,' in *Ojczyzna bliższa i dalsza*, 215–226; W. Urban, 'Polish Brethren,' in *The Oxford Encyclopedia of the Reformation*, ed. Hans J. Hillerbrand, vol. 3 (New York-Oxford: 1996), 289–290; A. Séguenny, 'Raków,' *Oxford Encyclopedia of the Reformation*, vol. 3, 385–386. See also J. Friedman, 'Unitarians and New Christians in Sixteenth-Century Europe,' *Archiv für Reformationsgeschichte* 81 (1990): 216–238.

[125] Kowalski, '"Comonitas gentis Scoticæ" 25; Urban, *Chłopi wobec Reformacji w Małtopolsce w drugiej połowie XVI w.* (Kraków, 1959), 197.

[126] This was John Russ, who sued a Polish merchant in 1655; BSDS, Księga radziecka miasta Rakowa.

[127] L. Eriksonas, 'The Lost Colony of Scots: Unravelling Overseas Connections in a Lithuanian Town,' in Macinnes, et al., *Ships, Guns and Bibles*, 173–187.

[128] For example the Russells and the Sanxters in Szydłowiec as well as the Petersons in Łowicz; *CIP*, vol. V: *Palatinatus Squiernieviciensis*, cui edendo praefuit R. Rosin, fasciculus II: *Civitatis Loviciensis*, recensuit et annotavit I. Szymczak (Warszawa-Łódz: 1987), no. 123, p. 216.

Catholics being encouraged to settle on the Church's landed property, or being granted freedom of religion by Catholic bishops.[129]

There were undoubtedly many more Scottish pedlars than rich merchants, and the poor often acted as representatives for the rich.[130] However, because of the overt conflict of interests between the two trading groups, the role of the so-called Scottish brotherhoods could not have been significant. The brotherhoods were organised during the sixteenth century, and there were twelve of them in 1603. Their elders collected taxes for the maintenance of Evangelical congregations, and the organisations also acted as judicial courts. The elders judged according to written laws, and appeals could be lodged with the 'Main Diet', which met at Epiphany—in Toruń around the year 1603 and before 1639 in Elbląg (Elbing).[131]

The ruling group's desire to subordinate the paupers, including newcomers, was one reason for the setting up of brotherhoods. The wealthy increased their incomes, among other ways, by usury benefiting from court fines. Such attempts at imposing formal control on the diaspora failed or had limited success. Numerous examples of Scots suing each other in Polish courts suggest that the influence of the brotherhoods' judicial system must have been extremely weak, at least in the seventeenth century.[132] On the other hand, the power the *kahal* had over the official Jewish community, the *kehilla*, was impressive, but not without exceptions, which became common at the turn of the eighteenth century. Traditional law said that Jews who intended to litigate against one another must take the case to the rabbinic court or the lay court of community elders. The practice of going to gentile courts began around the seventeenth century, in contradiction to this tradition which had been generally cultivated from the Middle Ages. Such disregard for traditional law resulted from the progressive disintegration of self-government, and

---

[129] Chełmno (Gierszewski, *Obywatele miast*, 71) and Stare Szoty at Gdańsk, for which see E. Kizik, *Mennonici w Gdańsku, Elblągu i na Żuławach wiślanych w drugiej połowie XVII i w XVIII wieku* (Gdańsk: 1994), 25–28; *Res Polonicae Elisabetha I Angliae Regnante Conscriptae Ex Archivis Publicis Londoniarum*, ed. C. H. Talbot, *EFE*, IV (Romae: 1961), no. 68, p. 117; cf. Biegańska, 'In Search of Tolerance,' 47.

[130] Guldon, 'Szkoci w miastach,' *passim*; Sadownik, *Szkoci w Lublinie, passim*.

[131] *Ibidem*, 2–3; Tomkowicz, 'Przyczynek do historyi Szkotów,' 163; Guldon and Guldon, 'Saga,' 36; *Papers Relating to the Scots in Poland*, xiv–xv.

[132] Mączak, 'Od połowy XV,' 331; Tomkowicz, 'Przyczynek do historyi Szkotów,' 163; Guldon, 'Szkoci w miastach,' *passim*.

was a response to internal conflicts within Polish Jewry.[133] These social changes are instructive for a better understanding of almost unknown similar processes of disintegration that seem to have occurred even earlier in the Scottish communities.

The Scottish brotherhoods' history suffers from a lack of serious attention from contemporary scholars, and almost all our knowledge of them comes from the records of the Lublin organisation. This source should be published again, not only because of the errors included in the Lublin protocols in the 1915 edition.[134] This unique extended self-commemoration by part of the Polish diaspora does not meet the standards of modern critical editions.

An initiative to regulate the Scottish judiciary by submitting it to self-government, set up for the Scots in Poland in 1603 by King Sigismund, was a fiasco.[135] The Armenians and Jews, who also had the privilege of self-government, were also in charge of collecting state taxes from local diaspora communities. The fiscal aspect was an integral part of the initiative, but it was extremely difficult to put into effect. After Ian Authenlect [Auchinleck], a high-ranking royal official, fulfilling the 1658 Diet's law, stood security with his own 5,000 *fls* for the dues of the whole diaspora in Poland-Lithuania, the king turned to all state and urban offices in order to make local Scots repay the debt. They had refused to pay both tax and reimbursement. This reveals the lack of effectiveness of the Scots' self-government and the dearth of national solidarity, although the latter seems understandable.[136] It was different, however, with the Jews.

Numerous royal edicts and Diet acts published in the sixteenth and seventeenth centuries, particularly those of 1562–63, instructed urban authorities to remove poor foreign hucksters with no citizenship and no fiscal obligations.[137] Since paupers could not afford the burden of city rights, and probably saw neither the possibility nor the need for compliance, parliament decided to impose taxes upon

---

[133] Fram, *Ideals Face Reality*, 38–47 and *passim*; Kaźmierczyk, *Żydzi w dobrach*, 135–156 and *passim*; also M. J. Rosman, *The Lord's Jews* (Cambridge: 1990).

[134] Some of the errors have been noted by F. Bujak in his review of *Papers relating to the Scots in Poland, 1576–1793* in *Kwartalnik Historyczny* 45 (1931): 88–89.

[135] Tomkowicz, 'Przyczynek do historyi Szkotów,' 162–167.

[136] *Materiały do historii miasta Lublina*, 1317–1792, ed. J. Riabinin (Lublin: 1938), no. 356, 358.

[137] Guldon, Stępkowski, 'Ludność szkocka,' 203; Gierszewski, *Obywatele miast*, 69.

traders regardless of their legal status. In 1639 King Władysław IV
called on all foreigners who were wine merchants in Lublin, including Scots, to pay excise to the city coffers. The tax was imposed
upon both tenants and those who owned property in the city.[138]

Scots were obliged to pay the 'collection', a tax common in the
sixteenth and seventeenth centuries, and the 'merchant donative',
introduced in 1629. The edicts directed against hucksters found favour
with the majority of citizens, many of whom earned a living by stall-
trading. All over the kingdom, from Cracow to Gdańsk, stall-traders
and artisans who belonged to the urban community appealed to
their authorities to drive away illegal pedlars, and townspeople began
to use violent means against competitors with more initiative.[139]
Scottish traders wandering from village to village and offering cheap
everyday articles to the peasants led to the latter staying away from
local markets, causing financial loss to the monarchy and gentry.[140]
This was explicitly referred to by an English resident in Elbląg in
1584.[141] There is no doubt that pedlars served as an important connection between the town and the peasantry. Their personal access
to the urban markets had been cut off or seriously restricted by the
gentry, who pressured them to purchase goods from country markets controlled by the landowners.[142] Thus it was not always the case

---

[138] *Materiały do historii miasta Lublina*, no. 320.

[139] *Papers Relating to the Scots in Poland*, xxxix; Samsonowicz, 'Dynamiczny ośrodek,'
151; Bogucka, 'Podstawy gospodarczego rozwoju,' 58–60; Karpiński, *Pauperes. O
mieszkańcach Warszawy XVI i XVII wieku* (Warszawa: 1983), 71–76; Kowalski, 'The
Scotsmen in the Cracow Market,'.

[140] According to the then legal code, landowners benefited from markets in their
demesne.

[141] 'Upon his retourne he declared afore us in the Senat, the king by his man-
dat, not to have meant, thereby to inhibit any marchants that traded in Townes
and Cityes, Where fre markets were appointed, not any that traded by sea to any
port of haven, but onely to forbid common pedlars, and namely certen Scottes who
disorderly, to the preiudice of his nobility, and of his chiefs Townes, wandered from
village to village, and mayd privat sale, to the derogacion of his and of his Nobilityes
Tolles levied in the ordinary markets.'; *EFE*, IV, no. 30.

[142] See especially: M. Małowist, 'Über die Frage der Handelspolitik des Adels in
den Ostseeländern im 15. und 16. Jahrhundert,' *Hansische Geschichtsblätter* 75 (1957):
29–47; his 'The Problem of the Inequality of Economic Development in Europe
in the Later Middle Ages,' *The Economic History Review*, S II, 19.1 (1966): 15–28;
Mączak, *Money, Prices and Power in Poland, 16–17th Centuries: a Comparative Approach*
(Aldershot, Hampshire-Brookfield, Vt.: 1995); Topolski, *The Manorial Economy in Early-
Modern East-Central Europe: Origins, Development and Consequences* (Aldershot, Hampshire-
Brookfield, Vt.: 1994); M. North, 'Die Entstehung der Gutswirtschaft im südlichen
Ostseeraum,' *Zeitschrift für Historische Forschung* 26.1 (1999): 43–59.

that "Scottish peddling [was] accepted by the gentry as a factor restraining the peasants' contacts with the market".[143]

It seems, however, that the palatinate gentry imposed taxes on the 'trading nations' for many reasons and not only as a means of reprisal. For example, they believed that Scots, Jews, Armenians and Wallachians did not participate enough in the Crown army's maintenance.[144] Moreover, the 'collections' and poll taxes imposed both by the Diet and 'dietines' on all vagrants were intended to make this group settle.[145] Another purpose was to discourage Scots from inviting new immigrants.[146] The Scottish hucksters must have been particularly clever at avoiding taxation, because the 1654 Diet's law imposing a donative mentions "the Crown traders *cuiuscunque nationis*, including the Scots".[147]

The prejudice against the Scots in Polish society was not unique, for preconceptions about the Jewish presence,[148] although not always the same, were even more deep-seated. The Jews, however, were far more engaged in economic activities connected to the gentry and the Church.

Pedlars had to be vigilant to avoid royal tax collectors. Drunken peasants were another potential threat; when loitering along public roads, especially on Saturdays, they often behaved aggressively to travellers.[149] Country peddling ran a serious risk to life.[150] It was not

---

[143] A. Manikowski, 'Szkoci,' in *Encyklopedia historii gospodarczej Polski do 1945 roku*, ed. Antoni Mączak (Warszawa: 1981), Vol. 2, 359.

[144] Kaźmierczyk, *Sejmy i sejmiki szlacheckie wobec Żydów w drugiej połowie XVII wieku* (Warszawa: 1994), 38, 45, 55.

[145] *Papers Relating to the Scots in Poland*, 86–87; See R. Rybarski, *Skarb i pieniądz za Jana Kazimierza, Michała Korybuta i Jana III* (Warszawa: 1939), 173–174.

[146] In January 1612, Andrew Aidy wrote to Robert Cecil from Gdańsk about the capitation imposed during the war against Muscovy: '[The King of Poland] has laid gryt imposits upon all marchants and strangers and hes maid Inglish and Scotis a lyk with Jewis and Armenians and will have 7 sh. 6. d. stirling from every on man wyf and child every yeir, a havie burden to poor ons travelling heir.'; *EFE*, VI, no. 94; *cf. Papers Relating to the Scots in Poland*, xvi–xvii.

[147] J. Ohryzko, ed., *Volumina legum*, Vol. 4 (Petersburg: 1859), 210.

[148] See J. Tazbir, 'Images of the Jews in the Polish Commonwealth,' in *From Shtetl to Socialism*, ed. A. Polonsky (London-Washington: 1993), 26–38.

[149] Tazbir, 'Stosunek do obcych w dobie baroku,' in his *Szlaki kultury polskiej* (Warszawa: 1986), 199.

[150] 'Rozbije gdzie na lesie potkawszy kto Szota' [One will rob a Scot having met him in a forest]; Wacław Potocki, *Dzieła*, ed. L. Kukulski, Vol. 3: *Moralia i inne utwory z lat 1688–1696* (Warszawa: 1987) [hereafter Potocki, vol. 3], 103.

an easy job, even compared to military service; in fact the latter was considered more profitable—at least according to Wacław Potocki, an intent observer of his world and an eminent poet of the Baroque period (†1696).[151] This may explain why many former hucksters or even merchants were drafted (or enlisted on a voluntary basis) and when the war was over, shifted to trade again.[152]

Explaining the continued deterioration in the political state, Potocki pointed to the growing number of those entering the gentry.[153] During the reign of both the Vasa dynasty and the following so-called 'King-Compatriots', the number of knighted Poles and of foreign nobles admitted to the ruling class increased significantly. In the period under discussion, the number of knighted men was 902, but by that time only 471 had been bestowed the honours. Although burgesses were the majority of the knighted, immigrants from the British Isles comprised only a small number of the 'new gentry',[154] as has been shown in Appendix 2. Potocki's opinion that "Grocery doesn't make a Scot a nobleman"[155] seems to refer to the merchants who managed to enter the gentry class as a whole.

In the huge poetical output Potocki has left us, there is much nostalgia for 'the good old times', when the nobility were closely connected to their homes and splendid family traditions, and both valour and religiousness legitimised noble status. Potocki pointed to increasing neglect of these values, which were replaced by an admiration for wealth. The Scots and Jews personified these evils, and the two nationalities were often combined, as for example in a poem addressed 'To the new not-yet-lords', in which the author says "They do have money, the Jews and the Scots in Cracow".[156] However he saw these nationalities (sometimes including the Armenians) as integral to Polish

---

[151] *Ibidem*, 89.

[152] Guldon, 'Szkoci w miastach,' *passim*. 'Nie trzeba by nam Niemców zaciągać i Anglów/Chłopów od cepów ani Szotów od ich handlów' [We wouldn't have to draft Germans and Englishmen/Pull peasants from flails nor Scots from their merchandise]; Potocki, *Dzieła*, Vol. 2: *Ogród nie plewiony i inne utwory z lat 1677–1695* [hereafter Potocki, vol. 2], 622.

[153] Potocki, vol. 2, 351; vol. 3, 251, 336–337.

[154] See B. Trelińska, ed., *Album armorum nobilium Regni Poloniae XV–XVIII saec.*, (Lublin: 2001), 15.

[155] Potocki, vol. 3, 336.

[156] 'Do nowotnych niedopanków' ('Mają pieniądze Żydzi i Szoci w Krakowie'); Potocki, vol. 2, 539.

society, and this view was shared by many contemporary authors.[157] Whenever he intended to expose foreigners' styles of dress and cuisine, he usually called on the Italians, French or Spaniards, and less frequently on the Scandinavians or the English. Only once, describing the parental indecision of a nobleman who hesitated where to send his son abroad for schooling, and finally sent him to Gdańsk "to learn German", Potocki says that the son "returned a Scot in three years".[158]

Conclusions

Scottish mass immigration into the Polish Crown seems to have come to an end by the 1660s, but there is no doubt that new immigrants continued to arrive, although not necessarily directly from Scotland. During the whole early modern period, it appears that the majority of immigrants were poor, but a relatively significant number of newcomers may have had considerable assets to multiply. Although there were no consistent policies towards Scottish immigrants throughout the country, fiscal restrictions were imposed upon pedlars. They were made to leave the towns where they had managed to settle, although they returned, as a rule, to be removed again after some time. On the other hand, it was relatively easy to obtain citizenship, or at least the right to stay permanently in a town, if one was rich enough to enter the local upper class. With this status, a religion different from that which was locally dominant was no impediment, and conversion was not always required. Anna Biegańska is correct when she says that when city councils pointed to lack of religious compliance, it was usually in cases which were economically motivated.[159]

Future exploration of the Scottish diaspora in the Polish-Lithuanian Commonwealth should concentrate upon the relations which immigrants developed within their new environments. Studies should make use of city authorities' records, especially toll documentation, as well as parochial registers. It is also important to add that more attention

---

[157] See Tazbir, 'Stosunek do obcych,' 187.
[158] Potocki, vol. 2, 277.
[159] Biegańska, 'In Search of Tolerance.' 40–41. This was also the case with other

must be given to the contacts which settlers maintained with their homeland,[160] and to the above-mentioned brotherhoods. The fruits of existing scholarly work have provided a good basis for further serious, long-term research.

---

minorities, including the Jews; Kowalski, 'Ludność żydowska a duchowieństwo,' 198.

[160] They are documented, among other sources, with certificates of ancestry, which were required by town authorities from those applying for citizenship; see M. Górny, ed., 'List pochodzenia Dawida Urquharda z 1663 roku. Źródło do dziejów osadnictwa szkockiego w Polsce,' *Genealogia* 1 (1991): 81–84. Other birth-brieves, apart from those employed in this work, are known; see *Papers Relating to the Scots in Poland*, *passim*.

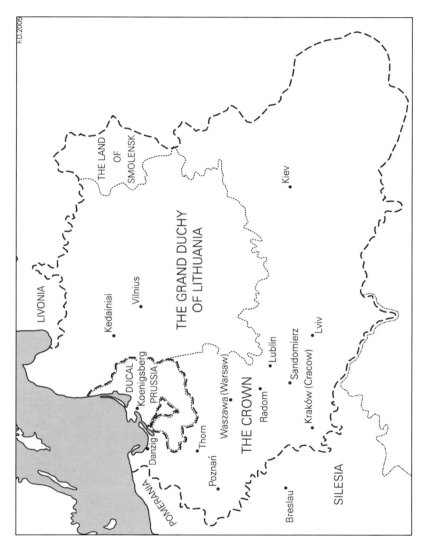

Poland (The Crown)—Lithuania 1569–1648

APPENDIX ONE

THE SCOTTISH SETTLEMENTS IN THE SANDOMIERZ PALATINATE (*WOJEWÓDZTWO SANDOMIERSKIE*) IN THE SIXTEENTH–SEVENTEENTH CENTURIES

List of abbreviations used in more than one entry

ADK, A par K—Archiwum Diecezjalne w Kielcach, Akta parafii Kielce
ADK, A par P—Archiwum Diecezjalne w Kielcach, Akta parafii Pińczów
AKKK I—Archiwum Kapituły Katedralnej w Krakowie, Inwentarz biskupstwa
  krakowskiego z lat 1644–1645, MS I–119
AKKK II—Archiwum Kapituły Katedralnej w Krakowie, Inwentarz
  biskupstwa krakowskiego z 1668 roku, MS I–120
BSDS—Biblioteka Wyższego Seminarium Duchownego w Sandomierzu
CIP VII/I—*Corpus Inscriptionum Poloniæ*, volumen VII: *Palatinatus Radomiensis*,
  fasciculus I: *Radom et Iłża regioque*, recensuit et annotavit Valdemarus
  Kowalski, qui edendo præfuit Zeno Guldon (Varsoviæ: Societas Scientiarum
  Radomiensis—PAE, 1992).
G I—Zenon Guldon, 'Szkoci w miastach województwa sandomierskiego w
  XVI–XVII wieku,' in his *Żydzi i Szkoci w Polsce w XVI–XVIII wieku. Studia
  i materiały* (Kielce: Wyższa Szkoła Pedagogiczna, 1990), 7–47
G II—Zenon Guldon, 'Żydzi i Szkoci w miastach województwa san-
  domierskiego w XVI–XVII wieku,' in *Ludność Żydowska w regionie święto-
  krzyskim* ed. Z. Guldon (Kielce: Wyższa Szkoła Pedagogiczna, 1989), 9–37
K I—Waldemar Kowalski, 'The Scotsmen in the Cracow Market in the
  mid-17th Century,' paper delivered at the conference 'Polish– Scottish
  Relations, 15th–18th Centuries', Warsaw, September 20–23, 2000 (to be
  published)
K II—Waldemar Kowalski, "Comonitas gentis Scoticæ' w Jedlińsku w pier-
  wszej połowie XVII stulecia,' *Kieleckie Studia Historyczne* 9 (1991): 23–32
KMKR 2—*Księgi metrykalne kościołów radomskich z lat 1591–1795*, Series A:
  Metryki chrztów, vol. 2: Kościół Św. Jana Chrzciciela 1621–1636, ed.
  Jan Orzechowski, Andrzej Szymanek (Radom: Radomskie Towarzystwo
  Naukowe, 2001)
PS—'The 1651 Polish Subsidy to the Exiled Charles II,' ed. Andrew B.
  Pernal, Rosanne P. Gasse, *Slavonic Papers*, 32 (1999): 1–50
Wijaczka—Jacek Wijaczka, 'Zarys dziejów Szydłowca w okresie prze-
  drozbiorowym,' in *Z dziejów Szydłowca*, ed. idem (Szydłowiec: Burmistrz
  & Muzeum Ludowych Instrumentów Muzycznych, 1993), 3–16
Note: when a first name only is given, it is followed in the source by a
  reference to the nationality ('Scotus', 'Schot', 'Szot' or 'Sot').

Bodzentyn, *an ecclesiastical town*

Kielianek, a locksmith, noted in 1668; AKKK II, f. 351.
Mandis, Thomas, a house owner, noted in 1668; AKKK II, f. 351.

Busko, *an ecclesiastical town*

A Scottish house owner in the first decades of the 17th C; G I, 24.

Chęciny, *a royal town*

Achterlon, Casper, present in Chęciny in 1638, renounced citizenship in
    1640; G I, 9.
Anchenchriff, Ian (John), present in Chęciny in 1638, renounced citizen-
    ship in 1639 and left for Kleparz at Cracow; G I, 9.
Baran, Kilian, trader, brought cloth and stall merchandise from Cracow in
    1600; G I, 7–8.
Berne, Jacob, merchant, in 1631 gifted a silver seal made in Wrocław
    (Breslau) to the local council, present in Chęciny in 1638, renounced cit-
    izenship in 1640; G I, 7–9.
Dinoff, Samuel, merchant, in 1631 received citizenship, which was con-
    firmed in 1633, present in Chęciny in 1638; G I, 7–8.
Gordon, William, merchant, received citizenship in 1631, present in Chęciny
    in 1638; G I, 7.
Ian (John), in 1600 brought cloth and stall merchandise from Cracow;
    G I, 7–8.
Jacob (James), in 1601 brought cloth and stall merchandise from Cracow;
    G I, 7–8.
Jonston, Ian see Pińczów.
Jonston, Jacob, noted as a burgher in 1636; G I, 9.
Lessels, Petrik (Patrick), present in Chęciny in 1637–1638, renounced citi-
    zenship in 1644 but in 1647 received it again; G I, 9.
Wood, Albert, merchant, received citizenship in 1633, in the Cracow mar-
    ket in 1635, present in Chęciny in 1638, renounced citizenship in 1639;
    G I, 7, 9.

Chmielnik, *a private town*

Fremtz, Samuel, noted in 1651; PS 23.
Hiton, Albert, noted in 1651; PS 23.
Moray, Ian, noted in 1651; PS 23.
Ross, John, noted in 1651; PS 23.

Iłża, *an ecclesiastical town*

Bik, Thomas, a building lot owner in 1668; AKKK II, f. 409.

Burnosz, a house owner in 1668; AKKK II, f. 408.

Burnosz, [Paul], a house owner in 1668; AKKK II, f. 409.

Czamer, a building lot owner in 1668; AKKK II, f. 408.

Fideth, Czycon[?], a house owner in 1668; AKKK II, f. 409.

Gordon, owned two houses and two building lots in 1668; AKKK II, f. 408, 408 v, 409v, 410.

Gordon, Patrick, buried his four-year-old son Robert in 1663; CIP, VII/I, no. 12.

Kiliankowski, a building lot owner in 1668; AKKK II, f. 409.

Kloch, Kempay, owned two building lots in 1668; AKKK II, f. 410.

Maxenti, Lawrence, a merchant, noted in Cracow in 1618–1619; Zenon Guldon, Lech Stępkowski, 'Iłżeckie wyroby garncarskie na rynku krakowskim w XVII wieku,' *Rocznik Świętokrzyski* 8 (1980): 18.

Oranski, a house owner in 1668; AKKK II, f. 407v.

Samson, David, noted in 1639; G I, 46.

Samson, possessed two houses and a building lot in 1668; AKKK II, f. 408, 409.

Scringier, John, a poor man, noted in 1651; PS, 23.

Simon, carried pottery to Cracow in 1600, G I, 23.

Stewards, possessed a house in the Main Square in 1668; AKKK II, f. 407v.

Jedlińsk, *a private town*

Dolary, John, a son of Eva and Martin, born in 1645; K II, 27.

Dolary, Lawrence, noted in 1640; K II, 27.

Dolary, Martin, married to Eva; John born in 1645; K II, 27.

Guthrie (Gutry), Anna, a Socinian baptized on 26 July 1642; K II, 25.

Inglin, Adam, married to Magdalene; Hedvigis baptized in 1643; K II, 27.

Inglin, Albert, married to Anna; Agnes baptized in 1644; K II, 27.

Inglin, Casper, married to Anna; Marina baptized in 1645; K II, 27.

Inglin, Hedvigis, a daughter of Magdalene and Adam, baptized in 1643; K II, 27.

Inglin, Hedvigis, a godmother in 1645; K II, 27.

Inglin, Marina, a daughter of Anna and Casper, baptized in 1645; K II, 27.

Inglnz, Dorothy, a godmother in 1641; K II, 27.

Inglnz, Dorothy, a daughter of Anna and John; baptized in 1641; K II, 27.

Inglnz, John, married to Anna; Dorothy baptized in 1641; K II, 27.

Kilian, Agnes, noted in 1657; K II, 27.

Kilian, Alexander, Willim's son, baptized in 1645; K II, 32.

Kilian, Hedvigis, noted in 1645; K II, 27.

Kilian, Jacob, Willim's son, baptized in 1647; K II, 32.

Kilian, Sophia, noted from 1645–1652; K II, 27.

Kilian, Willim, a merchant, married to Sophia, with Alexander and Jacob, noted in 1645–1652; K II, 27, 32.

Kielce, *an ecclesiastical town*

Alexander, a son of Catherine and Thomas, baptized on 6 October 1608; ADK, A par K, MS 2, 127.

Catherine, a daughter of Catherine and Thomas, baptized on 27 June 1606; ADK, A par K, MS 2, 75.

Catherine, Marina and Daniel's daughter, christened 16 November 1615; ADK, A par K, MS 2, 321.

Clemens, a son of John and Anna, baptized on 5 November 1611; ADK, A par K, MS 2, 216.

Daniel, married to Marina; Catherine baptized on 16 November 1615; ADK, A par K, MS 2, 321.

Daniel, married to Regina; Jacob christened on 4 August 1614; ADK, A par K, MS 2, 288.

Dyn, Thomas, noted from 1606 through to 1611; G I, 24; Archiwum Kurii Metropolitalnej w Krakowie, Acta episcopalia, MS 38, f. 385v.–386v.

Gier, Catherine, Jacob's wife, noted in 1617; ADK, A par K, MS 1, 16.

Gier, Jacob, married to Catharine, noted in 1617; ADK, A par K, MS 1, 16.

Gier, Stanislaus, a son born to Jacob and Catharine on September 30, 1617; ADK, A par K, Metrica baptizatorum, MS 1, 16.

Jacob, Regina and Daniel's son, christened on 4 August 1614; ADK, A par K, MS 2, 288.

John, noted from 1606 through to 1611; G I, 24.

John, married to Anna; Margaret baptized on 11 July 1606 and Clemens baptized on 5 November 1611; ADK, A par K, MS 2, 75, 216.

John, Catherine and Thomas's son, baptized on 1 October 1611; ADK, A par K, MS 2, 211.

Lang, Daniel, noted from 1614 through to 1633; G I, 24.

Lang, Saviel, 'incola protunc Kielcensis'; his wife Eva Raban was noted on 12 March 1633; ADK, A par K, MS 4, 27.

Lextan, a house owner, noted in 1645; AKKK I, [f. 209] 309.

Margaret, a daughter of Anna and John, baptized on 11 July 1606; ADK A par K, MS 2, 75.

Thomas, married to Catherine; Catherine baptized on 27 June 1606, Alexander baptized on 6 October 1608 and John baptized on 1 October 1611; ADK, A par K, MS 2, 75, 127, 211.

Waldun, a house owner's wife, noted in 1645; AKKK I, [f. 210] 311.

Koprzywnica, *an ecclesiastical town*

Hey, John, carried cloth and stall merchandise from Cracow in 1601; G I, 8, 22–23.

Hui, Peter, carried stall merchandise from Cracow in 1601; G I, 8, 22–23.

Kilian, carried stall merchandise from Cracow in 1602; G I, 8, 23.

Kin, Thomas, a trader, bought stall merchandise in Cracow in 1600; G I, 8, 22.

Lasle, Alexander, stayed in Lvov in 1603; G I, 23.

Milczan, Joseph, carried cloth from Cracow in 1605; G I, 8, 23.

Kunów, *an ecclesiastical town*

Dzafra, Alexander, noted in 1651; PS 23.

Rabans, had a building lot in 1668; AKKK II, f. 351.

Samson, Richard, David Walwod's servant, noted in 1651; PS 23.

Walwod, David, noted in 1651; PS 23.

Walwod, George, noted in 1651; PS 23.

William, noted there initially in 1592, opened a mason's workshop at the end of the 16th century; G I, 23.

Nowe Miasto Korczyn, *a royal town*

Andrys, carried swords and stall merchandise from Cracow in 1600; G I, 8, 23.

Opatów, *a private town*

Ines, John, sued by a Lvov merchant, John Watson, in 1671; G I, 24.

Murray, Richard, a trader noted at the Rzeszów fair in 1650. Maybe the same mentioned in 1687; G I, 24.

Ross, Alexander, a trader noted at the Rzeszów fair in 1650; G I, 24.

Thompson, Andrew, a merchant noted in 1715; Adam Kaźmierczyk, *Żydzi w dobrach prywatnych w świetle sądowniczej i administracyjnej praktyki dóbr magnackich w wiekach XVI–XVIII* (Kraków: Uniwersytet Jagielloński, 2002), 161.

Walwod, Thomas, a burgher noted in 1659; G I, 24.

Opoczno, *a royal town*

Kilian, carried stall merchandise from Cracow in 1603; G I, 8, 23.

Russell, Jacob (†1647 a.q.), a son of Alexander and Margaret Sanxter, Szydłowiec burghers, a merchant and sub-bailiff at Opoczno, married to Maryna Wygnańska. On 23 August 1631 he was noted in Radom; *KMKR* 2, no. 566; Guldon, 'Saga,' 38–39; G I, 23.

Stanisław, carried wine from Cracow in 1603; G I, 8, 23.

Pacanów, *a private town*

First, Jacob, carried stall merchandise from Cracow in 1603; G I, 8, 23.

Pińczów & Mirów, *private towns*

Alexander, carried stall merchandise from Cracow 'on his back' in 1600; G I, 9.

Bartrum, Thomas, a Pińczów merchant trading in Lvov in 1628; G I, 10.

Chory, Richard, merchant, noted in Lvov in 1631; R. V. Shiyan, *Rol gorodov russkovo y bel'zskovo voevodstv v torgovih svyazyah vostochnoy Evropi s tsentral'noy y zapadnoy Evropoy v 16-pervoy polovinye 17vv.*, Lvov 1987, (unpublished thesis in the Lvov University library), Appendix 1.

Derumpel, Mathew, a Pińczów merchant trading in Lvov in 1628; G I, 10.

Dombar, Albert, a Pińczów burgher[?] in 1630; G I, 13.

Dombar, Peter, Albert Dombar's representative in Lvov in 1630; G I, 13.

Gier, Jacob, carried stall merchandise from Cracow in 1616; G I, 10.

Giery, William, noted in Lvov in 1650, 1651; G I, 10.

Gordon, Peter, traded in the Ruthenia (Red Rus') in 1630; G I, 10.

Gultrie (Gultne), Lorens, in 1650 in Lvov, exempted from the Stuart tithe in 1651; G I 13; PS 23.

Hinnigus, Albert, noted as a godfather on 4 April 1638; ADK, A par P, MS 635, f. 99 [46].

Hunter, Wilhelm, active in the Ruthenia (Red Rus') in 1628; G I, 10.

Innes (Ines), Alexander, noted in Lvov as a Pińczów merchant in 1630, 1642 and in 1644, active in the Red Rus'; G I, 10–12.

Jenent, George, together with the above-mentioned Peter Gordon, traded in the Ruthenia (Red Rus') in 1630; G I, 10.

Jonston, Ian (John), between 1635/36–1644 a Pińczów burgher dwelling temporarily in Chęciny. In 1636 he transferred his property in Chęciny to his brother Jakub; G I, 9.

Jonston (Ianston), Jacob, active at the Cracow market in 1617–1618. Probably the same Jacob residing in Pińczów in 1633–1651 and noted in Pińczów in 1633 and in the Lvov records in 1650. Maybe the same was married to Sophia and brought their daughter Margaret to be christened on 25 October 1634; G I, 9; K I, Table 2; noted in 1651; PS 24; Biblioteka Jagiellońska, Protocolum advocatiale Racoviæ, MS 145, 5ᵛ, 9ᵛ.

Jonston, Margaret, Jacob[?] Jonston's daughter, on 18 March 1646 stood godmother to a child of local burghers; ADK, A par P, 1643–1674, MS, f. 42.

Lewitt, Catherine, wife of Iylhian [Kilian?] the butcher, mother of Andrew, who was baptized on 4 April 1638; ADK, A par P, MS 635, f. 99[46].

Mer, William, active in the Ruthenia (Red Rus') in 1631; G I, 10.

Prengiel, Ian (John), in 1619 noted in Cracow; G I, 10.

Reu (Rheu), Ian, in 1627 in Lvov with his cousin John, traded in the Red Rus'; G I 12.

Ron, Ian, in 1615 bought stall merchandise worth 30 marks, in 1623 in Poznań (Posen), and in 1628 in Rzeszów (Red Rus'); G I 12.

Smet (Schmid, Smith?), Ian (John?), in 1619 noted in Cracow; G I, 10.

Thory, Richard, in 1631 active in the Ruthenia (Red Rus') together with William Mer, a Pińczów Scot; G I, 10.

Połaniec, *a royal town*

Kilian, carried stall merchandise from Cracow in 1600; G I, 8, 23.

Radom, *a royal town*

Anna, born to Ian and Hedvigis; christened on 6 July 1599; Archiwum parafii Nowego Miasta Radomia p.w. św. Jana Chrzciciela, Liber baptisatorum 1590–1649, sygn. 1 [hereafter ANR 1].

Dolarius (Dolary), Albert (Wojciech), a godfather, noted in 1631; *KMKR* 2, 574.

George, married to Anna; Peter was christened on 23 June 1604, Radom, the New Town's burghers; ANR 1, p. 34.

Ian 'Schotkowicz' [a Scot's son] from Gołębiów, a suburb of Radom; married to Regina, brought their son with an unknown name to be christened on 16 May, 1604; ANR 1, p. 33.

Ian, married to Hedvigis; Anna was baptised on 6 July 1599; ANR 1.

Lurens [Lawrence], Susanna, a godmother in 1622 and 1630; *KMKR* 2, nos. 87, 488.

Mathew [called 'Koszyk'—the Basket], married to Hedvigis, 'Szoti' [the Scots], with a daughter Regina, baptized on 17 March 1607; ANR 1, 59.

Mek, Thomas, carried stall merchandise from Cracow in 1603; G I, 8, 23.

Peter, born to George and Anna; baptized on 23 June 1604, ANR, 34.

Regina, born to Mathew and Hedvigis, 'Szoti' [the Scots]; christened on 17 March 1607; ANR 1, p. 59.

Russell, Andrew, Ph & MD, bought real estate in a suburb in 1608. He died before 24 March 1626, when his daughter Elisabeth was christened. His wife ('Ruslowa') was noted before 1606; it is not possible to say whether she was the Elisabeth noted below. *KMKR* 2, nos. 99, 167, 258; Józef Gacki, *Radom i jego kościoły do końca XVIII wieku* (Radom: Stanisław Zieliński, 1999), 158, 162.

Russell (Ruszelowa), Elisabeth, wife of Andrew, a medical doctor, noted from 1622 through to 1636; *KMKR* 2, *passim*.

Russell, Ian (John), a servant, mentioned in 1648, 1651; G I, 8, 23.

Russell, Kristin, a daughter of Andrew, the medical doctor, noted as a 'maiden' in 1629 and through to 1635; *KMKR* 2, *passim*.

Russell (Ruszel), Paul, a son of Andrew, the medical doctor, and his wife, Elisabeth; baptized on 30 June 1622; *KMKR* 2, no. 99.

Smus, Anna, Bartholomew's wife, noted in 1607; ANR 1, s. 62.

Smus, Bartholomew, from Dzierzków, a suburb of Radom, married to Anna; Regina baptized on 31 August 1607; ANR 1, s. 62.

Smus, Regina, Bartholomew's daughter, baptized on 31 August 1607; ANR 1, s. 62.

Raków, *a private town*

Alan, Alexander, a merchant, noted in 1664, Stanisław Malanowicz, 'Ludność miasta Rakowa w XVII i w XVIII wieku,' in *Raków—ognisko arianizmu*, ed. S. Cynarski (Kraków: PWN, 1968), 26.

Alan, Andrew, a merchant, noted in 1664; Malanowicz, 'Ludność,' 26.

Alan, Edward, a merchant, noted in 1664; Malanowicz, 'Ludność,' 26.

Guthrie (Gutry), Dorothy, mother of Anna who converted in Jedlińsk, in Raków, in 1642 a.q.; K II, 25.

Guthrie (Gutry), Peter, father of Anna who converted in Jedlińsk, in Raków, in 1642 a.q.; K II, 25.

Hayd, Simon; his wife was noted in 1633; BJ, MS 145, f. 14.

Łaszan (Larson?), Jacob, mentioned in the town records in 1633; BJ, MS 145, f. 5^v, 9^v, 10^v.

Russ, John, noted in the town council records in 1655; BSDS, Księga radziecka miasta Rakowa, no signature, f. 20^v.

Stameth, a mercer trading with Cracow in 1661–1665; Lech Stępkowski, 'Religia i gospodarka. Z dziejów gospodarczych Rakowa w drugiej połowie XVI I w XVII wieku,' in *Ojczyzna bliższa i dalsza. Studia historyczne ofiarowane Feliksowi Kirykowi w sześćdziesiątą rocznicę urodzin*, ed. J. Chrobaczyński, A. Jureczko & M. Śliwa (Kraków: Secesja, 1993), 225.

Wood, John, mentioned in the town records in 1691; Malanowicz, 'Ludność,' 26.

Sandomierz, a royal town

Afflak, Andrew, a burgher, noted in 1587; Zenon Guldon, Karol Krzystanek, 'Żydzi i Szkoci w Sandomierzu w XVI–XVIII wieku,' *Studia Historyczne* 31.4 (1988): 539–540.

Albertus, ran a stall with his wife, Magdalene, in 1587; Guldon, Krzystanek, 'Żydzi i Szkoci,' 540.

Brussius, Gulienus (William), enrolled in Cracow University in 1594; Feliks Kiryk, Franciszek Leśniak, 'Mieszkańcy,' in *Dzieje Sandomierza XVI–XVIII w.*, ed. H. Samsonowicz, vol. 1, pt. 1 (Warszawa: Polskie Towarzystwo Historyczne, 1993), 247.

Brysz, Christian, joined the local St. Anna Fraternity in 1627; Kiryk, Leśniak, 'Mieszkańcy,' 248; Guldon, Krzystanek, 'Żydzi i Szkoci,' 541.

Egry, Maciej, a house owner in 1607, married to Eva Jakuszkówna, with children Regina, Jadwiga and Elżbieta; Kiryk, Leśniak, 'Mieszkańcy,' 248.

Gordon, Agnes, sued the local cobblers' corporation in 1640; Guldon, Krzystanek, 'Żydzi i Szkoci,' 541.

Gordon, Alexander, in 1603 presented 'a letter of lawful birth' issued by Aberdeen city council. In 1614, Gordon was granted the right to build a stall at the market. In 1623 he was expelled from the city for 4 weeks for cohabitation and died the same or next year; Kiryk, Leśniak, 'Mieszkańcy,' 247–248.

Gordon, Kilian, noted as a Sandomierz burgher and merchant in 1626 and 1640, married to Agnes Łonakiewicz; Kiryk, Leśniak, 'Mieszkańcy,' 248.

Gordon, William, son of the above-mentioned Alexander, received citizenship in 1624; G I, 7.

Hannus (Hanusz), Ian, brought cloth and stall merchandise from Cracow in 1602; G I, 7–8; Kiryk, Leśniak, 'Mieszkańcy,' 247.

Jacob, lived in Sandomierz in 1601; Kiryk, Leśniak, 'Mieszkańcy,' 247.

Kilian, brought cloth and stall merchandise from Cracow in 1601; G I, 7–8.

Kinier, John, a merchant, noted in Sandomierz in 1657 and in Jarosław in 1663; Guldon, Krzystanek, 'Żydzi i Szkoci,' 541.

Miel, William, a merchant in 1626; Kiryk, Leśniak, 'Mieszkańcy,' 248; Guldon, Krzystanek, 'Żydzi i Szkoci,' 540.

Ramza (Rancza, Ramsey), Ian (John), a merchant, exported herring to Cracow; in 1598 transferred his building lots in Cracow, Lublin and Lvov to Kilian Barkl (Barclay?), a Cracow burgher. In 1602 Ramza owned a stall at the Sandomierz market; Kiryk, Leśniak, 'Mieszkańcy,' 247; Guldon, Krzystanek, 'Żydzi i Szkoci,' 540.

Sinkler (Szynkler, Sinclair), Albert, married to Magdalena; a real estate owner, brought cloth and stall merchandise from Cracow in 1587, 1600–1602; G I, 7–8; Kiryk, Leśniak, 'Mieszkańcy,' 247.

Wolkisson, Alexander, a son of John and Elizabeth at Edinburgh, received citizenship in 1676, in 1692 a rich burgher married to a gentry woman, Anna Bronikowska; G I, 7; Guldon, Krzystanek, 'Żydzi i Szkoci,' 541.

An unknown number of Scots, a few families at least, paid state tax in Sandomierz in 1578; G I, 7.

Secemin, *a private town*

Albert [Zins?], carried cloth and stall merchandise from the Cracow market in 1601; G I, 8, 22; G II, 16.

Alexander, carried stall merchandise from the Cracow market in 1601; G I, 8, 22.

Dun, Jacob, carried cloth from Cracow in 1604; G I, 8, 22.

Jarnge, Gregier, carried stall merchandise from the Cracow market in 1601; G I, 8, 22.

Nefel, Andrys, carried spicy goods from Cracow; G I, 8, 22.

Tum, Andrys, carried stall merchandise from the Cracow market in 1604 and 1605; G I, 8, 22; G II, 16.

Zins, Albert; in 1604 bought stall merchandise in Cracow to sell in Hungary; G I, 8, 22.

Skrzynno, *an ecclesiastical town*

Anson, died in 1625 in the time of pestilence, having left a donation for the local church; BSDS, MS G 925, f. [3].

Forbes (Forbesz), William, Thomas Siffert's servant c.1645; Wijaczka, 9.

Gifert, Agnes, Thomas's wife, noted in 1651; PS 23.

Gifert, Thomas, †1651 a.q.; PS 23.

Kutbernth, Alexander, noted in 1651; PS 23.

Sanxter, Andrew, Sophia Sanxter's (of Szydłowiec) brother, a Skrzynno burgher in 1642; Krzysztof Dumała, 'Studia z dziejów Szydłowca,' *Rocznik Muzeum Świętokrzyskiego* 4 (1967): 244.

Siffert, Thomas, a merchant, sued Peter Lesels in 1645 and appointed Daniel Mangwillian his court representative; G I, 24; Wijaczka, 9.

Szydłowiec, *a private town*

Chrzan, Thomas, a Szydłowiec[?] burgher in 1608; Dumała, 'Studia,' 245.

Donhey, John, appointed David Mangwillian's representative in Scotland in 1643; Wijaczka, 9.

Giffert, Thomas, a merchant, noted in 1639–1642; Dumała, 'Studia,' 245.

Lesels, Peter, a merchant, sued by Thomas Siffert in 1645; Wijaczka, 9.

Mangwillian, David; a son of John and Catherine Stretey (of Sterviling); before 1638, he married Dorothy Russell, Daniel's daughter; c.1640 town's bailiff; 9; Dumała, 'Studia,' 245.

Mutro, Alexander, Peter Lesels's servant c.1645; Wijaczka, 10.

Narn, John, see Nern, David

Nern, David, possessed a house 'in civitate Aberstinensi in Regno Scotiæ', bequeathed money and real estate to his daughter Sophia, son John and cousin Thomas Nern in 1639, died the same year; Wijaczka, 9; Dumała, 'Studia,' 245; G II, 17.

Nern, Sophia, see Nern, David

Nern, Thomas, see Nern, David

Russell, Alexander, a town councillor, married to Margaret Sanxter (†1620) and to Elżbieta, a daughter of Andrzej Lorek, a town councillor, and Zofia Czaplanka; Zenon Guldon, Wojciech Guldon, 'Saga szkockiego rodu Russellów w Szydłowcu w pierwszej połowie XVII wieku,' in *Szydłowiec. Z dziejów miasta*, ed. Jacek Wijaczka (Szydłowiec: Muzeum Ludowych Instrumentów Muzycznych, 1999), 37–46; Waldemar Kowalski, 'Szydłowiecka epigrafika doby Baroku,' in *Studia z historii Szydłowca*, ed. Zenon Guldon, Jacek Wijaczka (Szydłowiec: Burmistrz & Muzeum Ludowych Instrumentów Muzycznych, 1995), 30–31.

Russell, Anna, noted as Jacob (Sybaldt) Szybałt's wife in 1639 and 1640; Wijaczka, 9; Guldon, 'Saga,' 38, 40.

Russell, Daniel, Alexander's brother[?], noted in Szydłowiec town records from 1614 through to 1647, married Agnieszka Abrachamowska 1640 a.q.; Guldon, 'Saga,' 46–47.

Russell, Dorothy, Daniel's daughter and David Mangwillian's wife from 1638 a.q.; Wijaczka, 9; Guldon, 'Saga,' 47.

Russell, Kilian, a son of Alexander and his wife Margaret Sanxter; Guldon, 'Saga,' 38.

Russell, Margaret, Alexander's wife from 1599 a.q., died in 1620; Guldon, 'Saga,' 37–38; Kowalski, 'Szydłowiecka epigrafika,' 30.

Russell, Valentine, a son of Alexander and his wife Margaret Sanxter; Guldon, 'Saga,' 38.

Sanxter, Hanus, noted in the town records from 1598 through to 1602; Wijaczka, 8.

Sanxter, Margaret see Russell, Margaret

Sanxter, Sophia, Jacob Todt's wife, (†1643); G I, 13; Guldon, 'Saga,' 41; Wijaczka, 8.

Smus, Adam, Sophia Sanxter's neighbour; Wijaczka, 9.

Szybałt (Sybaldt), Jacob, married to Anna Russell, Alexander's daughter, c.1639–1651; Wijaczka, 11; Guldon, 'Saga,' passim.

Tempelton, Hanus, a Szydłowiec[?] burgher in 1607; Dumała, 'Studia,' 245.

Todt[?], Hedvigis (Jadwiga), Sophia Sanxter's daughter; wife of Zachary Szulc (Schulz), an apothecary; Wijaczka, 8.

Todt[?], Ian (John), Bachelor of Arts and Philosophy, a curate to St. Mary's Church in Cracow, Sophia Sanxter's son; Wijaczka, 8.

Todt, Jacob, a town councillor and mayor (1608) noted from 1604, married to Sophia Sanxter; wrote his last will in 1626; Wijaczka, 8; Dumała, 'Studia,' 244.

Todt[?], Olbrycht (Albert), a monk at the Cistercian cloister at Wąchock near Szydłowiec, Sophia Sanxter's son; Wijaczka, 8.

Walti, Anna, Christopher Walti's wife; Dumała, 'Studia,' 245.

Walti, Christopher, married to Anna, died before 21 October 1635; Dumała, 'Studia,' 245.

Walti, Nicholas, Christopher's son, noted in 1635; Dumała, 'Studia,' 245.

Walwad (Walwood?), Thomas, noted with his wife Marianna Gradkowicz in 1637 and 1639, as a real estate owner noted in 1640–1645; Wijaczka, 10; Guldon, 'Saga,' 43, 45; Dumała, 'Studia,' 245.

An unknown number of Scots settled in the town as early as 1576.

Tarnów, *a private town*

Aikindhend, David, a merchant, noted in Rzeszów in spring 1677; G I, 22.

Ardys, see Hardysz

Bala, Kilian, a merchant, active in the Cracow market in 1649; K I, Table 2.

Barton, Thomas, a burgher, noted in 1639; G I, 21. Probably the same mentioned by Stanisław Wróbel, 'Tarnów w XVII I XVIII wieku,' in *Tarnów. Dzieje miasta i regionu*, ed. F. Kiryk & Z. Ruta, vol. 1 (Tarnów: KAW Rzeszów, 1981), 361 as Bratran.

Bernath, Peter, a trader, noted in Cracow c.1602–1605, a servant of the town's owner; G I, 14; Feliks Kiryk, 'Miasta regionu tarnowskiego: Tarnów, Tuchów, Ciężkowice do końca XVI w.' in *Tarnów. Dzieje miasta i regionu*, 267.

Burnet, Robert, a merchant, active in the Cracow market in 1649; K I, Table 2.

Burneth, Albert, sued the brothers John and William Burns for a sequestration of merchandise in 1646; G I, 21.

Cesseron, William, in Lvov in 1613; G I, 14.

Chita, Jacob, noted in Lvov in 1621; G I, 39.

Cruikshank, David, a merchant in the 1620s; Sybill Bidwell-Hołdys, 'Kupcy w siedemnastowiecznym Tarnowie,' *Sobótka* 30.2 (1975): 228.

Delfeln, William, a burgher in the first half of the 17th century; Wróbel, 'Tarnów,' 361.

Dixon, Alexander, a trader active in the Red Rus' in the late 1640s–1650s; G I, 18.

Douglas, Albert, brother of Ian, in Lvov in 1644; G I, 12.

Douglas, Ian (John), brother of Albert, in Lvov in 1644; G I, 12.

Drusl (Russell?), Jacob, noted as a Tarnów burgher in Pińczów in 1634; ADK, Akta parafii Pińczów, MS, f. 52.

Dynn, John, a burgher, noted in Lvov in 1668; G I, 22.

Eles, John, a burgher in the first half of the 17th century; Wróbel, 'Tarnów,' 361.

Ennies, George, a merchant in the 1620s; Bidwell-Hołdys, 'Kupcy,' 226.

Erest, Alexander, a burgher and merchant, settled in 1605; Kiryk, 'Mieszczanie,' 267.

Eues (Eves?), George, a burgher from 1599 a.q., a trader noted in Cracow c.1599–1603; G I, 14; Kiryk, 'Mieszczanie,' 267.

Eves, Alexander, a trader, noted in Cracow c.1602–1605; G I, 14.

Farchwar, Henry, a trader, noted in Lvov in 1647; G I, 21.

Fayz (Feyz), Jacob, a trader active in the Red Rus' in the 1640s; G I, 18.

Forbes, Alexander, a trader, noted in Lvov in 1618; G I, 14.

Forbes, Jacob, a trader, noted in Lvov in 1620; G I, 14.

Forbes, William, a merchant active in the Cracow market in 1649; K I, Table 2.

Galbraicht (Galbraith?), John, a burgher in the first half of the 17th century; Wróbel, 'Tarnów,' 361.

Gordon, George, traded in Jarosław and Lvov c.1634; G I, 15.

Gordon, Peter, a trader, noted in Lvov in 1609, the same [?] noted in Rzeszów in 1628; G I, 14, 15.

Gordon, Władysław, a burgher in the 1680s; G I, 22.

Guthrie (Guttry), Alexander, a representative of merchants in other towns to the local council; G I, 21.

Hardysz (Ardys), William, (†1653) a trader active in the 1640s, moved to Brody at the end of the decade; G I, 17.

Henath, Peter, a burgher from 1601, noted as a trader in Cracow c.1602–1605; G I, 14; Kiryk, 'Mieszczanie,' 267.

Henderson (Hunderson, Enderson, Heterson), Jacob (†1621), noted in Lublin and in Lvov in 1620; G I, 14–15.

Henry, Jacob, a burgher in the first half of the 17th century; Wróbel, 'Tarnów,' 361.

Herioth, Andrew, a burgher from 1602, noted as a trader in Cracow c.1602–1605; G I, 14; Kiryk, 'Mieszczanie,' 267.

Ines, George, a trader, noted in Lvov in the 1640s; G I, 12, 19.

Jun, Jacob, a trader, noted in Cracow c.1602–1605, in Lvov in 1613; G I, 14; Kiryk, 'Miasta,' 256. Probably the same mentioned by Wróbel, 'Tarnów,' 361, as Jacob Schot.

Karsten (Karster), David, noted in Rzeszów in 1628 and in Lvov in 1647; G I, 15, 21.

Kieth (Keyth), William, a trader active in the 1620s, a representative of Lieutenant-Colonel Walter Butler and of Colonel Jacob Butler; G I, 15.

Kiier, John, a trader, noted in Lvov in 1632; G I, 16.

Kilo (Kilorn), John, (†1651 a.q.) a trader noted in Nuremberg and in Lvov in the 1640s, moved to Brody at the end of the decade; G I, 16.

Kirchwed, William, a burgher in the first half of the 17th century; Wróbel, 'Tarnów,' 361.

Korban, Jacob, noted in Rzeszów in 1628; G I, 15.

Korban, John, noted in Rzeszów in 1628; G I, 15.

Lunan, Albert, a trader, noted in Lvov in 1647, cooperated with William Thory of Cracow; G I, 21.

Morton, John, (†1649) a trader active in the Red Rus' in the 1640s, joined the army in 1647 p.q.; G I, 20–21.

Murray, John, corresponded with Arthur Forbes in Lvov in 1685–1686; G I, 22.

Nax, John, a trader, noted in Cracow c.1602–1605; G I, 14; Kiryk, 'Mieszczanie,' 267.

Nikelson, a burgher in the first half of the 17th century; Wróbel, 'Tarnów,' 361.

Ohans, John, traded in Lvov, bankrupted before 1626; G I, *passim*.

Olefant, Archibald, a trader, noted in Lvov in 1618; G I, 14.

Ostafi, a burgher in the first half of the 17th century; Wróbel, 'Tarnów,' 361.

Peterson, David, a trader, noted in Lvov in 1623; G I, 15.

Petray (Petry), George, a trader active in the 1640s; G I, 21; Bidwell-Hołdys, 'Kupcy,' *passim*. Probably the same mentioned by Wróbel, 'Tarnów,' 361, as Petrici.

Reyd (Ryd), Alexander, a hide trader active in the 1640s; G I, 17.

Rhonald, Jacob, a trader, noted in Lvov in 1627; G I, 15-16.

Ross, Andrew, a burgher from 1599 a.q., noted as a trader in Cracow c.1599–1603; G I, 14; Kiryk, 'Mieszczanie,' 267.

Ross, Henry, a merchant in the 1620s; Bidwell-Hołdys, 'Kupcy,' 226.

Ross, Jacob, a merchant in the 1620s; Bidwell-Hołdys, 'Kupcy,' 226–227.

Sethon, Erasmus, a trader, noted in Cracow c.1602–1605, bought citizenship in 1605; G I, 14; Kiryk, 'Mieszczanie,' 267.

Sterling, George, Thomas's brother, a trader active in Wrocław (Breslau) and in the Red Rus' in the late 1630s–1650s; G I, 19.

Sterling, Thomas, (†1649 a.q.), George's brother, a trader active in Wrocław (Breslau) and in the Red Rus' from the late 1630s; G I, 19.

Thomson, John, a trader, noted in Lvov in 1632; G I, 16.

Tywender, Robert, a burgher, noted in Lvov in 1668; G I, 22.

Vlax, John, a burgher in the first half of the 17th century; Wróbel, 'Tarnów,' 361.

Walwad (Walwood), Adam, Bartholomew Wodt's servant in the 1620s; Bidwell-Hołdys, 'Kupcy,' 225.

Wilkinsson, a burgher in the first half of the 17th century; Wróbel, 'Tarnów,' 361.

Wodt, Bartholomew, a merchant in the 1620s; Bidwell-Hołdys, 'Kupcy,' 225.

The Scots in other Little Poland settlements

Jędrzejów, *an ecclesiastical town*

Ian Szot, skipped the Holy Communion in 1618; Archiwum Kurii Metropolitalnej w Krakowie, Acta visitationis capitularis, MS AV Cap 38, f. 78.

APPENDIX TWO

ENGLISHMEN, IRISHMEN AND SCOTSMEN RAISED TO THE RANK OF NOBILITY OR CONFIRMED NOBILITY IN POLAND, SIXTEENTH–SEVENTEENTH CENTURIES

Primary source: Album armorum nobilium Regni Poloniae XV–XVIII saec., ed. Barbara Trelińska (Lublin: Wydawnictwo Uniwersytetu Marii Curie-Skłodowskiej, 2001) [hereafter *Album*]

Secondary sources and literature: Mirosław Nagielski, "Społeczny i narodowy skład gwardii królewskiej za dwóch ostatnich Wazów (1632–1668)," *Studia i Materiały do Historii Wojskowości* 30 (1988): 61–102 [hereafter Nagielski]; *Papers Relating to the Scots in Poland 1576–1793*, ed. A. Francis Steuart (Edinburgh: Scottish History Society, 1915)

Anderson, Peter Benedict, a captain, confirmed as a nobleman in Poland-Lithuania in 1673; *Album* 1031.

Bazalski, Kazimierz a Bosuel, of Scottish ancestry, born in Prussia, a royal infantry captain raised for valour in 1662; *Album* 349.

Bretyss see Pretis

Buthler (Buttler), Jacob, a nobleman from Ireland, confirmed as a nobleman in Poland-Lithuania in 1627. On 23 October 1623 commended to James Stuart by Sigismund III Vasa; *Album* 705; *Res Polonicae Iacobo I Angliae Regnante Conscriptae Ex Archivis Publicis Londoniarum*, ed. Carolus H. Talbot, *Elementa Ad Fontium Editiones*, Vol. VI (Romae: Institutum Historicum Polonicum, 1962), no. 242; Nagielski, 68, 74.

Chambers, James, a baron from England, a royal captain of horse, confirmed as a nobleman in Poland-Lithuania for valour in 1673; *Album* 1044.

Chambers, William, James's brother, confirmed as a nobleman in Poland-Lithuania in 1673; *Album* 1045.

Gordon, George, major, confirmed as a nobleman in Poland-Lithuania in 1673; *Album* 1070.

Gordon, 'Margrave de Huntley' (as in the source), Henry, the youngest son of George, second Marquis of Huntly, a royal lieutenant-colonel, came from Scotland, confirmed as a nobleman in Poland-Lithuania for valour in 1658; *Album* 796; *Papers*, xxvii–xxviii; Nagielski, 99.

Gress, Martin, a dragoon lieutenant, raised to the rank of nobility on 13 July 1663; *Album* 1012.

Guthrie (or Guttry, as in the source), George, major, confirmed as a nobleman in Poland-Lithuania in 1673; *Album* 1074. See also *Papers*, xxv.

O'Kelly, Hugo, colonel, confirmed as a nobleman in Poland-Lithuania for valour in 1673; *Album* 1110.

Koch (Cook?), George, an Englishman, confirmed as a nobleman in Poland-Lithuania in 1658; *Album* 803.

de Lausson (Laussen), Ian, an artillery lieutenant from Forfar, Angus, confirmed as a nobleman in Poland-Lithuania for valour in 1685; *Album* 1337.

Meyfland, John, captain, confirmed as a nobleman in Poland-Lithuania for valour in 1673; *Album* 1105.

Mirisson (Murisson), Alexander, captain, confirmed as nobleman in Poland-Lithuania for valour in 1676; *Album* 1244.

Mirisson (Murisson), William, Alexander's brother, captain, confirmed as a nobleman in Poland-Lithuania for valour in 1676; *Album* 1245.

Pelkyn, Nicholas, a soldier raised to the rank of nobility on 20 February 1663; *Album* 1015.

Philipson, Gerard, raised to the rank of nobility in 1676; *Album* 1258.

Poleman, Joshua, major of the Prince Marshall of the Grand Duchy of Lithuania, confirmed as a nobleman in Poland-Lithuania for valour in 1673; *Album* 1354.

Pretis (Bretyss), Ian, an infantry colonel, raised to the rank of nobility for valour on 20 February 1662; *Album* 99.

Ramz (Ramsay?), major, raised to the rank of nobility for valour in 1676; *Album* 1244.

Rokiey, Constantine, a soldier raised to the rank of nobility for valour in 1662; *Album* 994.

Russel, Martin, came from Germany, lived in Cracow, raised to the rank of nobility for valour, 12 June 1593; *Album* 586.

Contrary to A. Francis Steuart's supposition, no sources he refers to (see *Papers*, xxxii) either explicitly confirm or suggest the ennoblement of the Chalmers and the Ross families. He also mentions the following families who 'were added to the list of Polish nobles,' and are not listed in *Album*: Bonar, Forsyth, Fraser, Halyburton, Hayna, Karkettle, Lindesay, Macfarland, Mackay, Ogilvy, Patterson, Stodart, Watson.

SEVENTEENTH-CENTURY SCOTTISH COMMUNITIES IN THE AMERICAS[1]

David Dobson

The seventeenth century was a period of both continuity and change for the Scottish diaspora. For centuries Scotland had looked east towards the North Sea and the Baltic lands with which it had major economic and cultural contacts. Many emigrants had settled in communities from the Gulf of Bothnia to the Bay of Biscay. However, those seeking new opportunities to better their circumstances in the seventeenth century increasingly found them in lands west of Scotland. Existing contacts with Ireland were expanded as tens of thousands of Scots left their homeland to settle in Ulster, while at the same time others took the longer sea voyage to America.[2] At this time too, economic links with America were established which would lead to settlement in due course. The population of Scotland for this period has been estimated at just over a million people, and by the close of the seventeenth century it appears that a significant percentage had emigrated.[3] As Paddy Fitzgerald discusses in this volume, the total number of Scots who settled in Ulster during the seventeenth century is thought to have been nearly 100,000. Similarly, as discussed in Waldemar Kowalski's chapter, by the 1620s it was believed (though not proven) that the number of Scots settled in Poland-Lithuania may have reached 30,000, with lesser numbers elsewhere on the continent.[4] In contrast, those voyaging west to the

[1] I would like to thank Professor T. C. Smout and the editors of this collection for several useful suggestions and additional sources freely provided for this chapter.
[2] D. Dobson, *Scottish Emigration to Colonial America, 1607–1785* (Athens, Georgia: 1994), 38–73.
[3] Sir John Sinclair, *Analysis of the Statistical Accounts of Scotland*, vol. I, (Edinburgh: 1826), 148–149.
[4] See Waldemar Kowalski's chapter in this volume and S. Murdoch, 'Kith and Kin: John Durie and the Scottish community in Scandinavia and the Baltic, 1624–1634' in P. Salmon and T. Barrow, eds., *Britain and the Baltic: Studies in Commercial, Political and Cultural Relations, 1500–2000* (Sunderland: 2003), particularly 23–27.

Americas are estimated to number somewhere in the region of 7,000.[5]
Compared with emigrants from England and Spain this is a small
number, but still significant when compared to other European ethnic groups such as the French (10,000), Dutch (8,000), Swedes (400),
or the 1,000 Courlanders in Tobago (then known as New Walcheren).[6]

Scotland's geographical location, on the north-west periphery of
Europe, facilitated this growth in maritime and mercantile contact
with North America. Scottish mariners in both Scottish and foreign
service were found along the American coast from Labrador down
to Brazil from the earliest decades of the seventeenth century. The
earliest-known Scottish vessel in what is now Canada was the *Gift
of God* of Dundee, recorded as trading between Newfoundland and
Lisbon around 1600.[7] Elsewhere Scots worked for themselves in
trading missions to Virginia and the Caribbean.[8] Admiral John
Cunningham led a Danish exploration of Greenland's coast in 1606
as commander of *Den Røde Løve* and also made a landing on the
Labrador coast of modern Canada.[9] The collective activities of these
men led in due course to the settlement of small numbers of Scots
in areas as widely dispersed as Hudson Bay and Surinam. Often
these communities have been presented as failures because they are
only viewed through an historical lens focused on the successful estab-

---

[5] D. Dobson, *The Original Scots Colonists of Early America: Supplement 1607–1707*
(Baltimore: 1998); D. Dobson, *The Original Scots Colonists of Early America: Caribbean
Supplement, 1611–1707* (Baltimore: 1999). J. Horn also concluded that 7,000 Scots
emigrated to the Americas between 1601–1700 in 'British Diaspora: Emigration
from Britain 1680–1815' in P. J. Marshall, ed., *The Oxford History of the British Empire,
vol 2: The Eighteenth Century* (Oxford: 1998), 31.

[6] E. Anderson, *Senie Kurzewnieki Amerika un Tobago Kolonizacija* (Stockholm: 1970);
Jaap Jacobs, *Een Zegenrijk Gewest* (Leiden: 1999), 516.

[7] W. A. McNeill 'Papers of a Dundee Shipping Dispute, 1600–1604' in *Scottish
History Society*, 4th series, vol. 2, (Edinburgh: 1965), 80.

[8] The first Scottish ship known to have traded with the West Indies was the *Janet*
of Leith in 1611, and with Virginia, the *Golden Lion* of Dundee, recorded as bound
for the Chesapeake in 1628. For the *Janet* see NAS, Leith Port-book, E71.29.6/22.
For the *Golden Lion* see PRO, London Port-book, E190.21.1.

[9] Cunningham had earlier led the voyage of exploration to Greenland by the
Danish navy in 1605 and made landfall in Greenland at 67 degrees north at
'Danmarks Havn', south of a place known as 'Cunningham's Mount', now called
Qaqatsiaq. He was specifically appointed to this role due to his knowledge of the
area, signifying he had made the voyage before. See *Dictionary of Canadian Biography*
(Toronto: 1966), I, 243. For more on this remarkable man see R. Hagen, 'At the
Edge of Civilisation: John Cunningham, Lensmann of Finnmark, 1619–51' in A.
Mackillop and S. Murdoch, eds., *Military Governors and Imperial Frontiers, c.1600–1800:
A Study of Scotland and Empires* (Leiden: 2003), 29–51.

lishment and maintenance of a colony. As typified by the Darien 'Disaster', historians frequently neglect the success of many Scottish communities in the Americas by highlighting episodes such as the French takeover of Port Royal or the Spanish capture of Stuart's Town. Yet a colony, a plantation and a community are quite different things (though often conflated) and it is only by surveying the earlier attempts at Scottish plantation and community-building that the famous Darien 'Disaster' can really be understood.[10]

Colonial Failure and/or Community Success: Nova Scotia 1621–1637

The French, with their existing claim to the Canadian Maritimes, had attempted to settle on the shores of the Bay of Fundy and elsewhere in Acadia.[11] Their first settlements at the Bay of Fundy were at the mouth of the St Croix River and later, in 1605, they settled at Port Royal on the eastern shore. Port Royal was destroyed in 1613 by an English military expedition. In 1620, King James I (as King of England) granted all of Acadia, as far as 48 degrees north, to the Council of Plymouth, New England. In the following year the council resigned part of that grant, including an area lying to the north of the St Croix River.[12] In September 1621, King James (as James VI of Scotland), under the Great Seal of Scotland, granted this territory to Sir William Alexander of Menstrie, later Earl of Stirling, stretching from the St Croix to the St Lawrence rivers. From this date the land became known as Nova Scotia.[13] As a royal courtier

---

[10] M. Lynch, *Scotland: A New History* (Edinburgh: 1990), 308. In a section considering the rights of Scots to establish plantations, Lynch discusses attempts to found colonies in places like New Jersey. However, in 1682, the Scots could not and would not attempt to claim part of an existing English colony, though they were welcome to send planters to them.

[11] For further reading on the French settlements see J. C. Webster, *Acadia at the end of the 17th Century* (New Brunswick: 1934); M. Trundel, *The Beginnings of New France, 1524–1663* (Toronto: 1973).

[12] *CSP Colonial, 1574–1660* (London: 1860) 24.

[13] *RGSS*, VIII, 72, no. 226; W. Anderson, *The Scottish Nation* (3 vols., Edinburgh: 1866), I, 107; S. Murdoch, 'Cape Breton: Canada's 'Highland' Island?' in *Northern Scotland*, vol. 18, (1998), 32–34. The two best collections of original documents relative to this enterprise are D. Laing, ed., *The Royal Letters, Charters, and Tracts Relating to the Colonisation of New Scotland, 1621–1638* (Edinburgh: 1867); C. Rogers, ed., *The Earl of Stirling's Register of Royal Letters relative to the affairs of Scotland and Nova Scotia from 1615–1632* (2 vols., Edinburgh: 1885).

based mostly in London, Alexander had met Captain John Mason,
former Governor of Newfoundland, and it is assumed that he received
a good report of this land and the opportunities it could offer. In
May 1622, Sir Robert Gordon of Lochinvar was also granted land
by the king on Cape Breton.[14] In March 1622, Sir William Alexander
obtained a vessel in London and despatched it to Kirkcudbright for
the purpose of loading men and provisions for a reconnaissance voyage to Nova Scotia. Alexander may have arranged to embark emigrants from Lochinvar's estates in that neighbourhood or perhaps
recruit there, but in the event found it difficult to enrol volunteers.
It is probable that the area's proximity to Ulster meant the latter
region was more appealing to those who wished to widen their hori-
zons. The ship left Scottish shores late in the year, and as a consequence, passengers had to winter at St John's, Newfoundland, while
the ship returned to Scotland.[15] The following spring, another vessel sailed for Nova Scotia via St John's, returning home after having surveyed the territory. In his report, the skipper Robert Angus
described the coast, its flora and fauna, and that of neighbouring
New England.[16]

In 1624, William Alexander began to promote settlement in Nova
Scotia by means of a pamphlet entitled *An Encouragement to Colonies*.[17]
Interestingly, his pamphlet included a map showing geographical features bearing Scottish names, and in this the St Croix River had
become the River Tweed. Beginning in 1625, finance was raised for
the costs involved in establishing a settlement in Nova Scotia by
means of a sale of baronies in the new land. These new creations
of 'knyght barronett' were seen as fundamental by Charles I "as the
plantation of New Scotland doeth much depend therupoun".[18] The
cost of these baronies was 3,000 merks (£150) each for 6,000 acres,
and the new owners were required to settle the land and also send

---

[14] *RGSS*, VIII, 79, no. 233.
[15] N. E. S. Griffiths and J. G. Reid, 'New Evidence on New Scotland, 1629', in
The William and Mary Quarterly, vol. 49, no. 3 (July 1992), 496.
[16] NAS, Yule Collection, GD90/3/23, Letter of Robert Angus, undated, c.1623
[?].
[17] Laing, *Royal Letters, Charters and Tracts*, tract 4; Anderson, *The Scottish Nation*,
I, 107.
[18] Rogers, *Earl of Stirling's Register*, I, 30. Charles I to Laird of Wauchtan, 24
March 1626.

six fully-equipped men to stay for a minimum of two years.[19] By 1632 eighty five baronies had been created, which would have provided a total of 510 settlers; with their families they would have created a viable basis for a community, had one been given the chance to develop.

The settlement programme took on new life when British relations deteriorated with France throughout 1626, culminating in open war in 1627. Troops from the British Isles were assembled and took part in the campaign at La Rochelle.[20] With hostilities ongoing in Europe, some of the Scottish nobility saw an opportunity to exploit the situation to grab land from the French in their colonies and plant the Stuart standard on French soil. Charles was persuaded to create titles in Nova Scotia and passed the task of selecting suitable candidates onto William Keith, 6th Earl Marischal of Scotland. This, according to Charles, would enable the Earl of Stirling to proceed with a new expedition there in the spring.[21] Similar commissions for plantations in territories contested by European powers were also granted to several London-based merchants, such as the family of David Kirk (Kertk) of Dieppe who were well known for their enterprise in Canada.[22] In the late summer of 1627 Sir William Alexander's son, William, Lord Alexander, arrived in Nova Scotia on a reconnaissance visit and left an advance party of seventy men and two women in the vicinity, though probably in Newfoundland rather than Nova Scotia.[23] Two ships had sailed for Nova Scotia in 1627. In March the *Eagle*, master Ninian Barclay, sailed from the Thames to Dumbarton, and that August departed from the Clyde bound for Nova Scotia together with a 300–ton vessel, possibly the *Morning Star*.[24] A number of Sir William Alexander's servants, including the

---

[19] Anderson, *The Scottish Nation*, I, 108.

[20] Rogers, *Earl of Stirling's Register*, I, 200–201. Charles I to Scottish Privy Council, 22 August 1627; C. Petrie, ed., *The Letters, Speeches and Proclamations of King Charles I* (London: 1968), 50–51. Charles I to Duke of Buckingham, 13 August 1627.

[21] Rogers, *Earl of Stirling's Register*, I, 122–123. Charles I to Earl Marischal, 26 January 1627.

[22] Anderson, *The Scottish Nation*, I, 109.

[23] Griffiths and Reid, 'New Evidence on New Scotland', 497.

[24] An entry in the 'Dumbarton Common Good Account' for August 1627 records the cost of a 'bonevale' held prior to Sir William Alexander's expedition setting sail. See F. Roberts and I. M. M. MacPhail, eds., *Dumbarton Common Good Accounts, 1614–1660* (Dumbarton: 1972), 53.

above-mentioned Ninian Barclay, were admitted as burgesses of
Glasgow in August 1627.[25] Glasgow Burgh Council may have hoped
that by admitting these burgesses and giving them trading rights in
the burgh, the city would benefit in due course by cornering the
potential trade between Nova Scotia and Scotland.[26] It seems logi-
cal that the expanding and prosperous fur export trade carried on
by the French, English and Dutch colonists in America would have
encouraged the Scots to emulate these countries' economic success.[27]

By 1629, Charles I had endorsed Alexander's recruiting of some
clan chiefs and clansmen to settle in Nova Scotia. On 4 February
1629 the Crown granted a "Commission to Sir William Alexander
and others to make a voyage to the Gulf and River of Canada and
the parts adjacent for the sole trade of Beaver wools, Beaver skins,
Furrs, Hides and Skins of Wild Beasts".[28] The fur trade was an
increasingly important part of the colonial economies, and the means
by which essential imports could be financed. Charles pressed on
with his desire to create more titles in Nova Scotia and ordered the
Earl of Menteith, Sir William Alexander and Sir Archibald Achesone
to proceed with the new selection in May.[29] That same month, a
number of vessels sailed from the Thames bound via St John's,
Newfoundland, for Cape Breton and Lochinvar's proposed plantation of New Galloway. With Alexander, a fleet of four vessels carrying colonists made for Nova Scotia. The settlers built Fort Charles
and called their settlement Port Royal, both built on the site of what
is known today as Annapolis Royal on the shores of the Bay of
Fundy.[30] Sir Robert Gordon of Lochinvar sailed from London, and
it is likely that the majority of the passengers onboard his ships were
English. Under the leadership of Sir James Stewart of Killeith, Lord

---

[25] J. R. Anderson, *The Burgesses and Guildbrethren of Glasgow, 1573–1750* (Edinburgh:
1925), 67.

[26] The return of the *Eagle* to Dumbarton is indicated in the burgh records through
references to disputes among its crew when there in November 1627 and January
1628. See J. Irving, *History of Dunbartonshire* (Dumbarton: 1860), 486.

[27] It appears that Sir William Alexander the younger had returned to Scotland
by December 1627, from the evidence of a Kirk Session Record of Stirling showing his donation of £58 to the poor box in that month. See *Miscellany of the Maitland
Club*, vol. I (Edinburgh: 1834), 467.

[28] *CSP Colonial, 1574–1660* (London: 1860), 96.

[29] Rogers, *Earl of Stirling's Register*, I, 349. Undated letter of Charles I.

[30] For the argument that this took place in 1629 rather than the usually quoted
date of 1628 see Griffiths and Reid, 'New Evidence on New Scotland', 493, 497.

Ochiltree, passengers disembarked on the shores of Cape Breton on 1 July and settled on a site named Baleine.[31] Lochinvar had hoped to achieve religious uniformity among his emigrants to avoid later problems, and as a result all his passengers should have belonged to the Church of England. Indeed during most of the seventeenth century emigrants from England had to prove that they conformed to the Established Church. However, within days of landing on Cape Breton eight households revealed themselves to be of a Puritan sect and separated from the main body of colonists.[32] Despite this initial split, a fort was quickly erected and named Rosemarine, under the command of Captain Ogilvie.

The fleet departed after approximately two weeks for Port Royal, taking with it the main body of colonists under the leadership of William, Lord Alexander. He remained until September 1630, leaving Sir George Home in command of an apparently thriving colony. The remainder of the fleet sailed on for Quebec under the leadership of David Kirk.[33] On arrival, they drove the French from their fortress, and for a short period, held the territory. In the autumn of 1629, during the time of the English occupation, these adventurers were able to ship at least one cargo of beaver pelts and products as well as deerskins to London. But neither Kirk nor Ochiltree could keep their colonies. Only three months after its establishment the small community of Baleine was overrun by the French. The settlers were deported back across the Atlantic in a French vessel and put ashore near Falmouth. The one exception was Lord Ochiltree, who was imprisoned at Dieppe. Kirk held on to Quebec slightly longer, but eventually he too was made prisoner of the French.[34]

As was so often the case, political expediency left the settlers in an awkward position. The Treaty of Susa (April 1629) between Great Britain and France brought the Franco-British war to an end. As part of the treaty, Charles I agreed to formally cede Cape Breton

---

[31] This settlement was situated near the place where the French later built Louisburg. Charles I had prepared a precept worth £500 sterling in one Patrick Baxter's name for the use of Lord Ochiltree in this venture. See Rogers, *Earl of Stirling's Register*, I, 403. A Precept of Charles I, 10 December 1629.

[32] Griffiths and Reid, 'New Evidence on New Scotland', 498.

[33] Anderson, *The Scottish Nation*, I, 110; Griffiths and Reid, 'New Evidence on New Scotland', 496.

[34] Anderson, *The Scottish Nation*, I, 110.

to French control. Most of the settlers returned to Scotland in 1631, with only a handful remaining among the French or moving south to Boston. However, that treaty did not settle the situation for the rest of Nova Scotia, and even in November 1629, Charles was still pressing for more planters to prepare for transplantation to Port Royal.[35] He thanked Sir William Alexander for his good efforts in this regard "which may be a means to settle all that cuntrie in obedience".[36] However, no matter how successful the Port Royal plantation was, the community was simply not allowed to hold on to their possessions. The capture of David Kirk at Quebec led to the withholding of 400,000 crowns of Queen Henrietta Maria's dowry for the royal coffers, thus leading to new negotiations. The objection from the French was that the 'colony' did not actually become established until after the Franco-British treaty, thus breaching the treaty articles.[37] After agreeing to the Treaty of St Germains on 29 June 1631, Charles ordered the destruction of the fort, the buildings and all signs of habitation.[38] He also sought to protect the planters in such a way that he could quit his claim to the region without prejudice to those who had invested so much in it.[39] Indeed, he ordered that William Alexander should be allowed to convene the baronets to consider the options.[40] But the order to leave Port Royal came from the king himself "by our commanding him to remove his Colonie of Port Royall for fulfilling the Article of ane treatie betuixt our brother the French king and ws".[41] Fort Charles, under Captain Andrew Forrester, continued to operate until 1632 when

---

[35] Rogers, *Earl of Stirling's Register*, I, 394–395. Charles I to Scottish Privy Council, 17 November 1629. The king also wanted all the new baronets to be identified by ribbons "for thair better distinctione from the others freeholders and inhabitants thereof". See *ibid.*, 420–421. Charles I to Sir William Alexander, 4 February 1630.

[36] Rogers, *Earl of Stirling's Register*, II, 439. Charles I to Sir William Alexander, 13 May 1630.

[37] Rogers, *Earl of Stirling's Register*, II, 463, 547. Charles I to Scottish Privy Council, 3 July 1630 and to King of France, 28 July 1631; Anderson, *The Scottish Nation*, I, 110.

[38] Anderson, *The Scottish Nation*, I, 110.

[39] Rogers, *Earl of Stirling's Register*, II, 544. Warrant to Sir William Alexander, 10 July 1631.

[40] Rogers, *Earl of Stirling's Register*, II, 545. Charles I to Scottish Privy Council, 12 July 1631.

[41] Rogers, *Earl of Stirling's Register*, II, 664. Charles I to Scottish Privy Council, 24 April 1633.

the remaining forty six settlers were taken aboard a French ship, the *Saint Jean*, to sail for England.[42]

On their return to Britain, disputes arose between the various parties who had participated. The Scottish Adventurers, Captain Kirk, Mr Barkley, Mr Charleton and Mr Henry Wilson were all summoned before the English Privy Council to try to resolve their differences.[43] More important however, is the fact that the Nova Scotia scheme—often portrayed as both an independent Scottish venture and thus a total failure showing "that specifically Scottish interests were also likely to be sacrificed when broader issues of state were concerned"—overstates the Scottishness of the undertaking.[44] The involvement of so many Englishmen, and of the English Privy Council, alerts us to the fact that rather than being an attempted Scottish settlement, Nova Scotia was always meant to be an integrated 'British' affair. This in many ways reflected the realities for the attempted development of Scottish communities in the trans-Atlantic world for the duration of the century.[45] Moreover, Charles I insisted that, contrary to rumour, he had no intention of giving up the notion of planting Nova Scotia, or of giving up any title to it, but only of returning the area to the condition it was in before the Franco-British hostilities, as per the agreement.[46] He wrote to the Advocate of Scotland in June 1632 insisting that his observance of the treaty in regard to Port Royal was one thing, but that he

---

[42] *Dictionary of Canadian Biography*, vol. I (Toronto: 1966), 270; N. E. S. Griffiths and J. G. Reid, 'New Evidence on New Scotland, 1629' in *William and Mary Quarterly*, 3rd series, XLIX, 3 (1992), 492–508.

[43] The complaint of the suitors was that they did not get the sole trading rights in the Gulf of Canada. The parties roughly broke down as Kirk and Barkley v. Charleton and Wilson, the latter two claiming to have put in £700 and £300 respectively. The debt of the company was put at £1,100, which Charleton denied. The council ordered a commission to examine the evidence and report on it. On the same day the English Privy Council considered the patent desired by William Alexander, George Kirk (Master of H. M. Robes), David Kirk Esq., William Barkley and the rest. Secretary Coke found no objection or infringement against any allies. The Attorney General was ordered to prepare a bill for Charles I to sign and the Scottish Adventurers were to be encouraged to join in the said patent. See *APC Colonial*, I, 181–182, no. 300. 12 December 1632; *Ibid.*, no. 301, 12 December 1632; *APC Colonial*, I, 185, no. 308. 25 January 1633.

[44] T. M. Devine, *Scotland's Empire* (London: 2003), 3.

[45] Griffiths and Reid, 'New Evidence on New Scotland', 499 and Dr Steve Murdoch's introduction to this volume.

[46] Rogers, *Earl of Stirling's Register*, II, 664. Charles I to the Commissioners for the Plantation of New Scotland, 24 April 1633.

retained his intention to continue with plantation schemes led by
Stirling.[47] The following January, Captain Kirk successfully petitioned
the English Privy Council to add to the patent for money for another
settlement in the Americas.[48] Charles then ordered that the Earl of
Stirling "with all such as shall adventure with him, shall prosecute
the said work [of plantation], and be encouraged by all lawfull helps
thereunto".[49] The same mix of Scottish and English investors in Nova
Scotia were about to seek out new locations to settle in the Americas,
while the Justices of Ireland were also being asked to participate in
plantations near the Hudson River in Canada.[50] The Earl of Stirling
continued to issue baronetcies until the last of the territory he laid
claim to was overrun by the French in 1637.[51] The plantations in
Port Royal and elsewhere in Nova Scotia ceased to exist, but due
to the British Crown's failure to hold on to its territories (Scottish
and English) rather than through a failing in a community whose
resilience and success is now being recognised.[52]

Scottish Communities in 'English' America

Since the foundation of James' Town in Virginia in 1607, there had
been Scots settled on the Chesapeake, albeit in very small numbers.[53]
Yet just as the series of plantations in Nova Scotia were orchestrated
through a Scot, the Earl of Stirling, so too were some of the English
colonies. For instance, the Barbados plantations fell under the control of another Scot. Within a couple of years of the English colonisation of the island, James Hay, Earl of Carlisle, took up his proprietary
patent, issued by Charles I in 1625, but only confirmed after a
'patent war' was settled by royal intervention in 1628.[54] He was soon

---

[47] Rogers, *Earl of Stirling's Register*, II, 599. Charles I to The Advocate, 14 June
1632.
[48] *APC Colonial*, I, 185, no. 308. 25 January 1633.
[49] Rogers, *Earl of Stirling's Register*, II, 664. Charles I to the Commissioners for
the Plantation of New Scotland, 24 April 1633.
[50] Rogers, *Earl of Stirling's Register*, II, 513–514. Charles I to the Justices of Ireland,
19 April 1631.
[51] Anderson, *The Scottish Nation*, I, 111.
[52] Griffiths and Reid, 'New Evidence on New Scotland', 492–493, 500.
[53] Shipping links date from 1627 when the *Golden Lion* of Dundee sailed to the
Chesapeake on a trading voyage. See PRO, E190.31.1.
[54] H. McD. Beckles, 'The "Hub of Empire": The Caribbean and Britain in the

joined by several of his relatives and other Scots who were employed in the administration of the island. William Powrie, son of Richard Powrie of Dawyck (Peebleshire), was recruited as a planter by 1630 and remained in Barbados until his death in 1648; he was symptomatic of a string of Scots who arrived in English America at this time.[55] Elsewhere, other Scots also became involved in English colonies, some of whom could trace their interest back to the Nova Scotia plantations. In 1635 William, Lord Alexander, was given a land grant by the Council of New England which embraced much of what is today Maine, New Brunswick and Long Island. On 12 June 1639 James Forret, described as a gentleman on Long Island, acting as deputy for William, Lord Alexander, sold land lying between Peacooeck and the eastern point of Long Island to a group of English settlers for £400 sterling.[56] The attempted claim on Long Island in September 1647 by Andrew Forrester, the former commander of Fort Charles at Port Royal, was rejected by the Dutch colonial authorities who were now firmly in control of 'Nova Batavia'.[57] Many Scots had been encouraged to the English colonies by John Winthrop, who believed that "the survival of the godly could not be assured by English resources alone", while Scottish preachers such as Patrick Copeland took up duties elsewhere in the colonies.[58] Yet while such sentiments of brotherly affection in the 1640s saw some new Scottish

Seventeenth Century' in N. Canny, *The Oxford History of the British Empire: the Origins of Empire* (Oxford: 1998), 221; NAS GD34, Section 26, letters and commissions 1636–1650. For more on this renowned Stuart diplomat see his entry in the DNB.

[55] For William Powrie see Barbados Archives, probate 1649 Barbados, RB3/532. Archibald Hay, another planter, worked the island until his death in 1652. See PRO, London, probate 1652 Prerogative Court of Canterbury. James Watson, a Barbados planter from Dalkeith, was shipwrecked returning to the West Indies in 1655. See BM. Add. MS 34015.

[56] C. B. O'Callaghan, *Documents Relating to the Colonial History of the State of New York*, vol. III (Albany: 1856), 21.

[57] O'Callaghan, *Documents*, 286.

[58] For John Winthrop see N. Canny, 'The Origins of Empire' in Canny, *The Oxford History of the British Empire*, 18. Canny also mentions the Aberdonian Patrick Copeland on the same page but erroneously believed him to be English. Perhaps the full extent of the Scottish role in the 'English' colonies will not be understood until a full prosopography of Scots within them is compiled. For more on Copeland see E. D. Neill, *Memoir of Rev. Patrick Copland, rector elect of the first Projected College in the United States: A Chapter in the English Colonisation of America* (New York: 1871); Shona Vance, 'Mortifications (Bursaries and Endowments) for Education in Aberdeen, 1593–1660 and their Implementation in the Seventeenth Century', unpublished PhD thesis, University of Aberdeen, 2000, 54–90.

settlers arrive in New England, it was the deterioration of the Scottish-English partnership after the execution of Charles I that led to an even greater increase.

The swell in the number of people of Scots descent in the northern colonies was largely due to the arrival of over 6,000 prisoners of war captured by Cromwell after the battles of Preston, Dunbar and Worcester, and transported to the colonies as indentured servants.[59] Around 1,000 of these were sent to the northern English colonies in America.[60] Some 500 more were sent to Barbados and Jamaica.[61] On 19 October 1654 the English Council of State ordered that English, Scottish or Irish pirates, prisoners in Dorchester jail, were to be sent to Barbados, Bermuda, or other English plantations in America.[62] Also at this time, a steady trickle of English and Scottish indentured servants and others sent by employers as factors added to the Scottish populations of the colonies. One group of some sixty one indentured servants found work in the Sagas iron-works in New England in 1651.[63] After their period of indenture had expired, some chose to travel north to the Leeward and Windward Islands and on to Jamaica, islands which the English had captured from the Spanish. Others opted to become some of the early settlers of South Carolina.

---

[59] C. M. Andrews, *The Colonial Period of American History* (4 vols., New Haven: 1934), I, 64; Devine, *Scotland's Empire*, 28. Not all 6,000 intended for shipment to the colonies were sent, and indeed the Royalist conditions for laying down their arms after the Middleton/Glencairn uprising of 1654 included the promise not to ship to the colonies, and the release of many of those already taken. See S. Murdoch, *Britain, Denmark-Norway and the House of Stuart, 1603–1660: A Diplomatic and Military Analysis* (East Linton: 2003), 169–170.

[60] One such was James Adam, captured at the battle of Dunbar on 3 September 1650, transported from London to Boston on the *Unity* of Boston in November that year, later an indentured servant at the Lynn Iron Works who subsequently joined the Scots Charitable Society in 1657. Many of the names of Cromwell's transportees are to be found in New England records, such as those of the Scots Charitable Society in Boston. The Scots Charitable Society, the oldest of its kind in North America and still extant, lists around 350 men who were admitted to its ranks before 1707. These included individuals like John Spratt, a merchant from Wigtown, who was admitted in 1685, and John Borland, a merchant in Boston, admitted in 1684. See New England Historic Genealogical Society, Boston, SCS. BS36V6; Dobson, *The Original Scots Colonists of Early America: Supplement 1607–1707*, 1.

[61] Bodleian Library, Rawlinson MS328/46; NAS JC41/1, transportation warrant, 1653; M. Wood, *Extracts from the Records of the Burgh of Edinburgh, 1652–1655* (Edinburgh: 1962), 31; Canny, 'The Origins of Empire', 23; Murdoch, *Britain, Denmark-Norway*, 169–170.

[62] PRO, Interregnum Entry Book, vol. CIII, 586.

[63] T. C. Smout, *Scottish Trade on the Eve of Union* (Edinburgh: 1963), 94.

Yet while we can point to groups of individuals, even clusters of Scots, it would be inappropriate to separate them from their English neighbours and, for the most part, social superiors. However, it would be wrong to conclude that the only incarcerated Scots were those sent by Cromwell's English regime. From the 1660s onwards the newly re-established independent Scottish authorities also began sending criminals and political undesirables to American shores, including militant Presbyterian Covenanters and simple criminals. For example, in September 1678 Ralph Williamson was due to take fifty two Scottish convicts to Virginia. However, before he did so (and probably wisely), he applied to the English Privy Council to ensure that he would be allowed to land them once he arrived in the colony.[64] King Charles wrote to the Governor of Virginia on 17 December 1678 permitting the landing and disposal there of this 'cargo'.[65]

The Restoration brought several changes in the opportunities for settlement in the Americas. The English Navigation Acts of the 1660s had imposed restrictions on direct trade between Scotland and the English colonies. On 30 August 1661, the Scots petitioned against this prohibition on their taking part in colonial trade, and the Act of Prohibition against the Scots was lifted by the English Privy Council on 6 November until further notice.[66] However, the window of opportunity for Scots wishing to exploit this relaxation was short-lived. By 22 November the committee considering Scotland's position revoked the lifting of the prohibition and directed the Scots to take their case to the English Parliament.[67] Nonetheless, northern Carolina soon had a Scottish governor in the person of William Drummond, who remained in his position from 1664–1676. Little is known of him, or his career, other than the fact that he was hanged for being a rebel in 1677 by the governor of Virginia.[68] It is very probable that he helped establish many of his countrymen within his colony during his term of office, though the records simply do not survive to

---

[64] *APC Colonial*, I, 788. 27 September 1678.

[65] *CSP, America and the West Indies*, 1678, 850. See also Smout, *Scottish Trade on the Eve of Union*, 177.

[66] *APC Colonial*, I, 318. 6 November 1661.

[67] *APC Colonial*, I, 318–319, 22 November 1661.

[68] R. Cain, 'Governor Robert Dinwiddie and the Virginia Frontier, 1751–57' in A. Mackillop and S. Murdoch, eds., *Military Governors and Imperial Frontiers c.1600–1800: A Study of Scotland and Empires* (Leiden: 2003), 161.

tell us. But in spite of the implementation of the Navigation Acts and the demise of Drummond on the scaffold, much illicit commerce continued between the ports of Glasgow and Ayr and the colonies, while Scots residents used patronage to ensure their trade.[69] In 1663 Charles II authorised John Browne, who had a licence to establish a sugar works in Scotland, to send four ships annually to trade with the English colonies.[70] Browne's sugar-processing plant in Greenock depended on regular supplies of raw materials from the West Indies in order to function. Barbados was the single most important English colony of the time, with its economic base in tobacco and sugar creating more wealth than all the other American colonies combined.[71] The raw materials were used to feed the four sugar-refining factories established in Glasgow between 1667–1700.[72]

While Charles II supported Browne's venture and Drummond's gubernatorial appointment, his brother James, Duke of York (the future James VII & II), supported other Scots seeking opportunities in the plantations. In April 1669, he encouraged Scots to go to New York to take part in the fishing trade, as well as inviting them to transport "the growth and manufacture" of the colony to Barbados or other Royal Plantations in America.[73] In addition to this legally-sanctioned trade, there was no restriction on the immigration of servants coming from Scotland, which in fact was encouraged. As Nicholas Canny has observed, a combination of decreasing opportunities in Ireland coupled with fewer English wishing to engage in menial work facilitated this increase in Scottish movement to the region. Scottish and Irish entrepreneurs were to share in both the risks and the spoils and "fashion a British North Atlantic World that would rival New Spain".[74] As a result, two passes were issued, for a ship of 500 tons and one of 250 tons. These ships were to carry as many Scots as would settle there on condition they did not trade with any foreign prince. They were guaranteed that they could set-

[69] More evidence survives for these networks in the eighteenth century and they are discussed at length by many of the authors in Mackillop and Murdoch, *Military Governors and Imperial Frontiers, passim*.

[70] Dobson, *Scottish Emigration to Colonial America*, 73.

[71] J. A. Williamson, *A Short History of British Expansion* (London: 1965), 288.

[72] Devine, *Scotland's Empire*, 34.

[73] *APC Colonial*, I, 512, 5 April 1669.

[74] Canny, 'The Origins of Empire', 23; N. Canny, ''England's New World and the Old, 1480s–1630s' in Canny, *Origins of Empire*, 165.

tle without let or hindrance.[75] The two ships eventually chosen were the *Hope* (350 tons) and the *James* (150 tons), both of Leith. The masters were to carry 400 people from Scotland on their first voyage and it was again stipulated by the English Privy Council that they must be 'Scotch'. Not only that but all the crews of the vessels had to be 'Scotch men' and they were only allowed to freight goods from England, Ireland and Scotland.[76] This was to be strictly observed and there were fears and rumours in England that the Scots intended to use the pass to sail two ships from the Netherlands full of Dutchmen. However, it is possible that the so-called Dutch ships may have been Scots shipping Scots from the large Rotterdam community.[77] The planned voyage to New York turned to disaster when the *Hope* was wrecked off Buchan Ness on 9 October 1669 and all the passengers and crew drowned.[78]

This setback did not prevent other attempts at plantation within the English colonies, often through royal patronage. James, Duke of York, had held a number of influential appointments and in 1668 he became the Proprietor of New York, formerly Nova Batavia, recently captured from the Dutch. At the same time his cousin, Prince Rupert, engaged in a contract to establish a fur trading monopoly as part of the quest to establish a north-west passage. After the initial voyages of *Nonsuch* and *Eaglet* from 1668–1689, the Hudson's Bay Company was granted a charter on 2 May 1670, with Rupert named as Governor.[79] Both the Duke of York and Prince Rupert had one Scottish parent and both certainly used Scots in prominent positions to further their various enterprises and work in their respective territories.[80] The Hudson's Bay Company had a preference for Scottish, particularly Orcadian, employees and many were found in

---

[75] *APC Colonial*, I, 512, no. 841. 5 April 1669; *CSP America and the West Indies, 1669–1674* (London: 1889), 42; The Privy Council of Scotland was petitioned in 1669 for 'strong and idle beggars, egyptians, common and notorious whores, theeves and others dissolute and louse persons banished or stigmatised for gross crimes'. See *RPCS*, 1661–1691, 3rd series, vol. 3, 46.

[76] *APC Colonial*, I, 516, 5 May 1669.

[77] *APC Colonial*, I, 517, 7 May 1669.

[78] This project has been fully described by P. Goldesborough in his 'An Attempted Scottish Voyage to New York in 1669' in *Scottish Historical Review*, vol. 40, (1961), 56–59.

[79] P. Morrah, *Prince Rupert of the Rhine* (London: 1976), 384–386.

[80] For example see Mackillop and Murdoch, *Military Governors and Imperial Frontiers*, xxxvi.

the various settlements of the Company.[81] Indeed in 1682 the Company
specifically requested the recruitment of Scots due to their hardy disposition and the recruitment of Orcadians became 'systematic' thereafter.[82] The Duke of York based himself in Scotland on several
occasions between 1678–1682, and the extent to which he may have
encouraged the Scots to participate in transatlantic trade and settlement in America has never been fully investigated. Certainly towards
the end of the 1670s plans were drawn up for the settlement of
between 500–1,000 Scots on St Vincent island, but the project was
abandoned.[83] This was not the last time such a project was considered. On 8 February 1681, the Scottish Privy Council considered a
"memorial concerning the Scottish plantation to be erected in some
place in America" which, on close reading, was clearly drawn up
by people with experience of trade.[84] Indeed, as Tom Devine cor-
rectly argues, there was more to the plantation schemes of the 1680s
than historians usually give those who conceived them credit for.[85]
Among the places they considered were the Caribee Islands, Jamaica,
Florida and the Bahamas and it is unlikely that a scheme could have
been considered in the first place without the backing of the Duke
of York. In the end, the Scottish Carolina Company was founded
with the objective of forming a settlement, albeit on land still claimed
by the Crown of Spain.[86] The investors included many influential
Glasgow merchants and a settlement was duly established on a site
south of Charles' Town at a place named Stuart's Town. The Scottish
merchants under the leadership of Lord Cardross attracted a degree
of envy from their English neighbours, although the plantation itself
was short-lived.[87] Stuart's Town lasted for only a couple of years

---

[81] The following sources are replete with references to the Scots in the Company:
E. E. Rich and G. N. Clark, eds., *Minutes of the Hudson's Bay Company, vol. 9,
1679–1684* (London: 1945–1946); E. E. Rich, A. M. Johnson and K. G. Davies,
eds., *Hudson's Bay Copy Book, vol. 20, 1688–1696* (London: 1957).

[82] E. E. Rich, *The History of the Hudson's Bay Company, 1670–1870* (London: 1958),
82–83, 389; Mackillop and Murdoch, *Military Governors and Imperial Frontiers*, xxxvii;
Devine, *Scotland's Empire*, 7.

[83] NAS, GD103/2/4/42, Representations to Charles II for settling a Scots colony
in the Caribee Islands, particularly in St Vincent, 1660–1685.

[84] *RPCS*, 3rd Series, VIII, 664.

[85] Devine, *Scotland's Empire*, 38.

[86] A. Calder, *Revolutionary Empire: the Rise of the English-speaking Empires from the
fifteenth century to the 1780's* (London: 1981), 377. See also Fryer, 'Documents Relating
to the Formation of the Carolina Company', *passim*.

[87] Andrews, *The Colonial Period of American History*, III, 220.

before being reclaimed by the Spanish.[88] The surviving Scottish colonists joined their neighbouring English and other British settlers in nearby Charles' Town.[89]

There were many reasons why the English would accept these Scots, not least that they had a certain martial reputation.[90] A desire to hinder 'Irish rebels' also led to repeated requests from the Barbados authorities seeking Scots to bolster their militia between 1693–1696, after the Irish fell victim to reports of their involvement in the abortive slave revolt of 1692.[91] Elsewhere the two communities appear to have acted in unison to overcome prejudicial laws against them. This facilitated smuggling, much to the annoyance of the colonial authorities. For example, on 27 June 1692 Edward Randolph reported to the customs commissioners noting the problems he was encountering in Maryland. In Somerset County he found two vessels, the *Providence* of London and the *Catherine* of Londonderry, both loaded with goods manufactured in Scotland, contrary to the Navigation Acts. However, when he attempted to take legal action the local sheriff, a Scotch-Irishman, selected a jury formed of Scots and their friends who decided in favour of the smugglers. He also mentioned that in that county there were "hundreds of Scotch and Irish families" who had set up a linen factory there, and that Scottish and Irish vessels were illegally exporting cargoes of tobacco.[92] Scottish entrepreneurs, particularly from the Glasgow area, were early participants in the transportation of tobacco from the Chesapeake area, and in due course the profits they made were to become considerable. Scottish participation, however, was in direct contravention of the English Navigation Acts and could therefore only occur through smuggling, or at least through trade of dubious legality orchestrated by Englishmen in Scottish ports and Scots based in English ones.[93]

---

[88] G. P. Insh, *Scottish Colonial Schemes* (Glasgow: 1922), chapter 6; Andrews, *The Colonial Period of American History*, III, 205, 230; Devine, *Scotland's Empire*, 38.

[89] J. G. Dunlop, 'Spanish Depredations, 1686', in *South Carolina Historical and Genealogical Magazine*, vol. 30, (April 1929), 81.

[90] Devine, *Scotland's Empire*, 28.

[91] Beckles, 'The "Hub of Empire": The Caribbean and Britain', 230.

[92] *CSP, America and the West Indies*, 1692, 2295. The scale and degree to which smuggling had an effect on the economy of Scotland in the eighteenth century is discussed in Devine, *Scotland's Empire*, 75–76.

[93] Smout, *Scottish Trade on the Eve of Union*, 80, 144, 178; Devine, *Scotland's Empire*, 32–33.

While the exchange of colonial produce (mainly tobacco) for man-ufactured goods was of direct benefit to both the colonists and the 'entrepreneur', it was clearly contrary to government policy. In prac-tice, it was condoned by many in authority in the region and the Scots even established a factory and community in Newfoundland around 1700 to aid their activities.[94]

Religious Communities

Another facet of Scottish community-building lay in the fractious nature of the Scottish Kirk. In this volume, Ginny Gardner describes the establishment of a Scottish religious exile community in the Dutch Republic between 1660–1689. However, the same religious intoler-ance that sent those people to seek refuge among the Dutch also led to increased contact with New Jersey, New York and New England. A refugee example was William Kelso, a surgeon-apothe-cary from Ayr, who had fought as a Covenanter at Bothwell Bridge in 1679, and fled to Ulster where he was imprisoned in Lisburn. In 1680 he escaped and took passage to Boston on board the *Anne and Hester*.[95] Indeed, Daniel Defoe claimed some 1,700 Covenanters were transported at this time.[96] Some of those who initially formed part of the Dutch exile community also added to those who chose to join the community in the American colonies. John Livingston, minister of Ancrum, initially settled with his family in Rotterdam in 1663. In 1674 his son Robert left Rotterdam bound for Charles' Town, New England, and before 1684 he had settled in Albany, New York (formerly Fort Orange, New Netherlands). Livingston, fluent in both English and Dutch with a mercantile background, was well-qualified to be a colonial administrator among the Dutch settlers of New York.[97] He rose from being a fur trader in Albany to Speaker of

---

[94] Devine, *Scotland's Empire*, 32–33.

[95] R. M. Young, *News from Ireland; Being the Examination and Confession of William Kelso, 1679*, in *Ulster Journal of Archaeology* (Belfast: 1895), no. 2.1, 274; N. Landsman, 'The Middle Colonies: New Opportunities for Settlement, 1660–1700' in Canny, *The Oxford History of the British Empire*, 358.

[96] Calder, *Revolutionary Empire*, 377.

[97] D. Catterall, *Community without Borders: Scots Migrants and the Changing Face of Power in the Dutch Republic, 1600–1700* (Leiden: 2002), 344–345.

the New York Provincial Assembly. As a merchant, Livingston had links with John Borland, a Scots merchant in Boston, and with Andrew Russell (his brother-in-law), a leading Scots merchant in Rotterdam. In one letter to Russell, Livingston expressed regret at the loss of his father-in-law, "the best friend I had in America". He described him as a leading Protestant, which was important to him "since such a cloud of Popery hangs over our heads".[98] Importantly, Livingston's presence encouraged links with existing Scottish mercantile networks in Scotland and Europe. Thus it is not uncommon to find the likes of Richard Wharton in Boston drawing bills of exchange against Andrew Russell in Rotterdam within a few years of Livingston's arrival.[99] Livingston was also a major financial backer of William Kidd, the Dundee-born New York shipmaster and privateer. His investment in the cruise of the *Adventure* in a way extended the Scottish trading network as far as Madagascar and the Indian Ocean throughout 1697–99.[100]

While the Presbyterian and the Episcopalian factions within the Church of Scotland fought each other for control of the Kirk, they were united in opposing the Society of Friends, better known as Quakers. Quakerism had been introduced to Scotland by the Cromwellian Army of Occupation and had taken root in five main locations, mainly in the east. However, Quakers were subjected to persecution by both Presbyterians and Episcopalians, and also by local and central government. At this time William Penn, the leading English Quaker, was encouraging Quakers from England, Wales, Ireland and the Continent to leave these lands and settle in Pennsylvania.[101] The English government supported this, and encouraged Quaker settlement in East New Jersey. William Penn and Robert Barclay of Urie, the leading Scottish Friend, may have discussed the participation of Scots Quakers in the settlement of the Middle Colonies when they met in Rotterdam at the house of Arent Sonnemans, a Dutch Quaker, in 1677. Within a few years the Scots Quakers took advantage of the opportunity to escape from persecution and take

---

[98] NAS, RH15/106/494/30 & 31, Livingston to Russell, 23 and 25 July 1683.
[99] NAS, RH15/106/639/17 & 18. Wharton to Russell, 3 February 1686; Smout, *Scottish Trade on the Eve of Union*, 114.
[100] For more on this episode see Richard Zacks, *The Pirate Hunter* (New York: 2002).
[101] Landsman, 'The Middle Colonies', 351–374.

up the offer of free land grants in East New Jersey, with a quarter of the proprietorships devolving upon Scots, though not all were Quakers.[102] In 1683, 1684 and 1685 several ships, the *Thomas and Benjamin*, the *Exchange*, the *Henry and Francis*, and possibly the *America*, sailed from Leith, Montrose and Aberdeen with several hundred passengers who intended to settle East New Jersey.[103] Though these ships were chartered by Quakers, many others who did not share their faith were allowed to take passage. Berths on board were allotted to Covenanter prisoners and a few felons freed from Scottish tolbooths for the purpose of emigration. On arrival the latter generally worked as indentured servants in East New Jersey, receiving land grants on completion of their indenture. Peter Watson, a Quaker from Selkirk, emigrated with his wife and family from Leith to East New Jersey on board the *Exchange* of Stockton as an indentured servant to Robert Barclay in 1683, and after completing five years' service was granted headland rights.[104] Watson wrote from Perth Amboy in 1684 to his cousin in Selkirk "Poor men such as myself may live better here than in Scotland if they will but work".[105] The following year, George Keith arrived to work as a surveyor of the Scottish proprietors.[106] Though he quarrelled with his fellow Quakers and moved to Philadelphia, the larger Scottish community succeeded in taking root, unlike Port Royal or Stuart's Town, and has been well documented, although claims that Perth Amboy represented a Scottish 'colony' rather than a community are perhaps stretching a point.[107] Ned Landsman suggests as many as 700 Scottish settlers arrived with the four expeditions orchestrated by the Scottish proprietors in the mid-1680s.[108] Through the patronage of James Drummond, Earl of Perth, and his brother, these settlers sought to challenge the land patents of older English towns in the colony. This resulted in a chal-

---

[102] Andrews, *The Colonial Period of American History*, III, 154; Calder, *Revolutionary Empire*, 378; Landsman, 'The Middle Colonies', 358.

[103] For a prosopography of Scottish Quakers see D. Dobson, *Scottish Quakers and Early America, 1650–1700* (Baltimore: 1998).

[104] New Jersey State Archives, East Jersey Deeds, Liber B, f.403; Andrews, *The Colonial Period of American History*, III, 154–155, 160.

[105] Insh, *Scottish Colonial Schemes*, 247.

[106] Landsman, 'The Middle Colonies', 369.

[107] See for example N. Landsman, *Scotland and Its First American Colony 1683–1765* (Princeton: 1985).

[108] Landsman, 'The Middle Colonies', 358.

lenge to the legitimacy of their status, the 'Scotch yoak' after the introduction of the 1696 Navigation Acts. Landsman notes that it led to an end to proprietary rule, though not proprietary ownership in the region.[109] The governor of New Jersey since 1692, a Scotsman, was also temporarily deposed due to claims he was not a "natural born subject of England"; however, as he fell into the 'post-nati Scot' classification highlighted during the post-1603 Union debates, he was subsequently reinstated.[110] Despite such challenges, the Quakers and other Scots managed to network within the colonies and on both sides of the Atlantic.[111]

In 1689 the Kirk of Scotland finally adopted the Presbyterian mode of worship, and those ministers inclined to Episcopacy were sidelined. This led many Episcopalian ministers to look to America and the opportunities offered in the new parishes of Virginia. Often those who had trained in the ministry became teachers in this new land and one of these was James Blair, later to become the first Commissary of Virginia and the founder of the William and Mary College in Williamsburg.[112] The success of these Scots in integrating into the English colonies is worthy of note, as are the several other routes they took into the Americas.

Scots in Non-British Colonies

The Dutch connection with America dates from September 1609 when Henry Hudson, an English mariner in Dutch service, landed on Manhattan searching for a route to Asia. Dutch settlement officially commenced in 1614 and continued until 1664 when the English captured New Amsterdam. During that period of rule the colony of Nova Batavia (New Netherlands)—later renamed New York—attracted nearly 10,000 settlers, most of whom came from the Netherlands, but a significant minority, including a small number of Scots, were

---

[109] Landsman, 'The Middle Colonies', 367.

[110] Calder, *Revolutionary Empire*, 378; Murdoch, *Britain, Denmark-Norway*, 17.

[111] Landsman, 'The Middle Colonies', 362–363. The Scottish Quaker family, the Trents, were established in Leith, Inverness, Barbados and East New Jersey, and shiploads of servants and cargoes were despatched from Scotland to both colonies. At the same time inter-colonial trade continued while events in Scotland would lead to yet more religious exiles seeking refuge in the colonies.

[112] Dobson, *Scottish Emigration to Colonial America*, 59.

from elsewhere in north-west Europe. Among them were Sander Leendaertse Glen, alias Alexander Lindsay, born in Dysart, Fife, in 1605, and his wife Catalyn Donckers, alias Catherine Duncanson, from Ellon, Aberdeenshire, recruited in Amsterdam as 'free colonists' by Kiliaen van Rensselaer on 26 March 1639 and transported on the *Harinck* to the New Netherlands, later settling at Fort Oranje. Glen became an Indian trader at Beverswyck and later at Scotia near Schenectady.[113] The Scots in Dutch colonies seem to have arrived as individuals more often than in groups. They were often two-stage migrants who moved initially to the Netherlands and later from there to the Americas. For instance, Captain Nicholas Nicholson served the Dutch in Brazil in the mid-1640s and, though described as a 'native of Amsterdam', probably had Scottish origins.[114] More definitively, we can look to examples such as John Hamilton, a soldier from Hamilton, who sailed on the *Bonte Koe* in April 1660, or William Scott who sailed on *De Arent* in March 1663.[115] Scots could also be found among the Dutch colonies of Curacao, Saba and St Eustatia. When the English captured the Dutch island of Nevis in 1664, they found among its European inhabitants sixty four English, Scottish, and Irish settlers.[116] One member of the Scottish community on Nevis, John Hamilton, possibly the same man as the soldier just mentioned, became fundamental in developing Scottish trade on the island by acting as the Scottish factor there.[117] While small in number, the seepage of Scots into the fledgling Dutch community is indicative of similar movements elsewhere along the eastern coast of the Americas.

The Swedish colony of Nya Sverige (New Sweden) on the South River (Delaware River) was founded in 1638 and lasted until 1655

---

[113] *Year Book of the Holland Society of New York* (New York: 1896), 130.

[114] Nicholas Nicholson was captured by the Portuguese. From Dutch prisoners he assembled four companies of soldiers to serve them, but only so he could take them back into Dutch service at the first opportunity. This he did in 1645 when he marched them to fort Bruin. In consequence, the Portuguese disarmed all the other Dutch in their service in the region under the pretence of sending them to Babia. On the way they murdered them with their wives and families. See John Nieuhoff, 'Voyages and Travels into Brasil and the East Indies [. . .] Translated from the Dutch Original' in *A Collection of Voyages and Travels, some now first printed from original manuscripts, others now first published in English* (6 vols., London: 1746), II, 98.

[115] NY Colonial MS, vol. XIII, ff. 88, 106.

[116] *CSP, America and the West Indies, 1661–1668* (London: 1880), 320.

[117] Smout, *Scottish Trade on the Eve of Union*, 98.

when the settlements came under Dutch rule. The inhabitants were overwhelmingly Swedish, Finnish or Dutch but there were a handful of Scots involved in the project. Among those on the first expedition to Nya Sverige in 1638 was a Jacob Evertsen Sandelijn (James Sandeland), who was said to be a Scot. Later, in early 1646, Sandelijn left Amsterdam bound for Nya Sverige on his merchant ship *De Schotzen Duytsman* (The Scots Dutchman), and within months was recorded actively trading along the South River. Sander Clerck (Alexander Clark), a Scot, was one of the crew of the *Kalmar Nyckel*, which also sailed from Sweden to Nya Sverige in 1638.[118] The number of Scots living in Sweden (for example James Lyall and George Garden) as merchants distributing tobacco imported from the colony was probably greater than the small number who actually settled among the Swedish colonists. In 1655 the Swedish colony was absorbed into the New Netherlands, which in turn was taken over by the English in 1664.[119] However, there is evidence of Scots in Nya Sverige being absorbed into the Dutch community only to find themselves in the employ of their native sovereign by the 1670s, such as the notorious Jacob Young.[120]

This transfer of colonies from one European power to another repeated itself elsewhere. Surinam was established as a sugar-producing colony by the Dutch in the 1630s. By 1650 English colonists had arrived and by 1663 it had become subject to England's Crown.[121] In 1667, under the Treaty of Breda (the peace settlement following the Second Anglo-Dutch War), Surinam was returned to the Dutch while they relinquished their claim to the New Netherlands. The majority of the British colonists in Surinam then moved to the nearby

---

[118] N. Jacobsson, *Svenska öden vid Delaware, 1638–1831* (Stockholm: 1938), 30–49.

[119] A. Johnson, *The Swedish Settlements on the Delaware, 1638–1664* (Baltimore: 1969), vol. 1, 60, 107, 159, 160 and vol. 2, 388, 722, 758.

[120] A. Åberg, *Kvinnorna i Nya Sverige* (Stockholm: 2000), 102–104. James Young (Jacob Jung) traded with the indigenous population in Nya Sverige in the 1650s. He ran off with the wife of Lars Lock, a Lutheran pastor, from Upland on the Delaware in 1661. They sought refuge in New York where Young worked as a policeman until he returned from exile in the 1670s. He thereafter worked as a bell-ringer and school-teacher until his death in 1686. Thanks to Dr Alexia Grosjean for this reference. See also Andrews, *The Colonial Period of American History*, III, 293, where mention is made of Scots arriving along the Delaware, but without numbers or specifics on individuals.

[121] *CSP, America and West Indies*, 1663, 451.

English colony of Barbados, which was experiencing a rapid economic and population expansion based on its sugar industry. A handful of Scots are known to have been settled in contemporary Surinam,
such as Henry MacIntosh, who purchased a sugar plantation there
in 1674. In 1688 in New York he married Elizabeth Le Hunt of
Port Royal, Jamaica, before returning to Surinam where he died in
1690.[122] MacIntosh was one of a small number of Scots merchants
and planters in Surinam, all of whom seem to have had trading
links with Andrew Russell, the aforementioned leading Scots merchant in contemporary Rotterdam.[123] Russell had connections with
Scots merchants throughout north-west Europe from the Baltic to
the Bay of Biscay, as well as in London, Scotland, New England
and New York. The Scots presence in Surinam was minimal and
may have arisen through two-stage migration, firstly from Scotland
to the Netherlands and from there to Surinam, as had happened in
the New Netherlands. However, later in the century, two or perhaps three vessels are believed to have sailed from Scotland bound
for Surinam, for example the Dutch ships calling for horses from
Inverness or the *William and Mary* of Glasgow directly to Surinam
in 1693.[124] These trading voyages also provided opportunities for limited emigration, although they highlighted a Scottish trading network
rather than a settled Scottish community.

Conclusion

There were distinct waves of Scottish emigration to America before
the political union of Scotland and England in 1707. For the most
part these were to Nova Scotia, Barbados and the West Indies (beginning in the 1620s), New England and the Chesapeake in the mid-
seventeenth century, South Carolina and East New Jersey in the
1680s, and Hudson Bay from the 1680s onwards. What has also

---

[122] *CSP, America and West Indies*, 1675, 01; *CSP, America and West Indies*, 1675, 401;
CSP, America and West Indies, 1676, 943; NY State Archives, NY Wills, Liber 1–2,
f. 184–186.
[123] Smout, *Scottish Trade on the Eve of Union*, 114; NAS, Russell Papers, RH15/
106/683, *passim*.
[124] Smout, *Scottish Trade on the Eve of Union*, 214–215; Edinburgh University Library.
Laing II. 490/111.

been shown is that Scots also settled in plantations or parts of communities in colonies subject to the rule of other European powers. When they strayed into the territories of enemy monarchs, it was usually at the behest (or covert approval) of their sovereign who wished to make a truly 'colonial' statement by their presence. Thus, after Port Royal returned to French control, Charles I sought to ensure the planters were compensated. But that was not the case with Darien. The history of the scheme and the outcomes of it are well rehearsed in Scottish history, but looking briefly at the background to it, we find a familiar pattern emerging. Rather than representing "the disastrous apogee of a movement to found Scottish colonies and exotic Trades" as many historians have insisted, Darien was perhaps the only fully Scottish colonial scheme in the Americas.[125] Yet although that was how it ended, that had not been the intention at the outset. Indeed, the venture can be traced back to 1695 and the request from King William that the Scots Parliament:

> pass an Act for the encouragement of such as shall acquire and establish a plantation in Africa or America, or in any other part of the world where plantations be lawfully acquired, in which act you are to declare that we will grant to our subjects, such rights and privileges as we grant in the like cases to the subjects of our other dominions, the one not interfering with the other.[126]

The Company of Scotland established in May 1695 had to have been formed as a result of this prompting by King William. It is worthy of note that half of the £600,000 capital for the Company of Scotland was originally raised by English merchants, specifically those opposed to the existing East India Company, and thus it carried many of the hallmarks of earlier plantation schemes.[127] It was

---

[125] For the tendency to look back on the seventeenth century plantations noted above as purely colonial failures rather than equally 'British' failures, or even community successes, see (among others) Smout, *Scottish Trade on the Eve of Union*, 28; Lynch, *Scotland: A New History*, 308; Devine, *Scotland's Empire*, 4.

[126] *CSPD*, 1694–1695, 428. 17 April 1695. 'Instructions to the Marquis of Tweedale for holding the fifth session of the current Parliament of Scotland'. See also Calder, *Revolutionary Empire*, 378.

[127] D. Ogg, *England in the reigns of James II and William III* (Oxford: 1955), 277; Smout, *Scottish Trade on the Eve of Union*, 150, 251; Lynch, *Scotland: A New History*, 308; Calder, *Revolutionary Empire*, 378. P. E. H. Hair and R. Law, 'The English in western Africa to 1700' in Canny, *The Oxford History of the British Empire*, 258: The Company of Scotland "originated in part, in an attempt by a group of London-based merchants to find a legal basis for breaking into the monopolies of the English

the involvement of that London-based East India Company which led to intervention by the English Parliament, the impeachment of Paterson and the withdrawal of English subscriptions.[128] It was only once the Scots were stripped of this support that they pressed on alone and established their new colony on Spanish territory explicitly against the instructions issued by their king. Little wonder he described them as 'raging madmen' and withdrew his support.[129] Despite this, throughout 1698–1699, several shiploads of emigrants sailed from Scotland all bound for the isthmus of Darien. They established several settlements, and one English mariner observed that the Scottish colonies in Terreto Bay and Golden Island "may not be unworthy of regard".[130] It was not to be so for long. Added to the effects of disease, the colony was attacked by the Spanish, against whom they maintained an effective blockade despite losing on land. The English government, partly concerned about the threat to the East India Company's monopoly over the Asian trade, decreed that no assistance was to be given to the colony. However, even if they wanted to, the English authorities could not have intervened in a scheme the monarch viewed as going against his will—a point neglected by most Scottish studies of the venture. In just over a year the Darien settlement, which had attracted around 3,000 Scots, was abandoned. The few survivors either returned home, or settled in the West Indies or along the American coast as far north as Boston.[131] Observing that the survivors were allowed to settle in the other English colonies at the same time, it becomes abundantly clear that neither the king nor the English government were against Scottish settlers in the Americas *per se*. Indeed it is also obvious that many

---

Royal African company and the East Indian companies; but it was reformed in 1696 as a more genuinely Scottish venture".

[128] Calder, *Revolutionary Empire*, 375.

[129] Devine, *Scotland's Empire*, 45.

[130] 'M. W.', *The Mosqueto Indian and his Golden River* (1699), reprinted in *A Collection of Voyages and Travels, some now first printed from original manuscripts, others now first printed in English. In six volumes* (6 vols., third edition, London: 1746) VI, 299.

[131] Among the more notable of these was John Anderson, captain of the *Unicorn* on the Darien Expedition of 1698, who settled in New Jersey in 1699, later becoming a judge and then governor there. The Reverend Archibald Stobo immigrated to Darien aboard the *Rising Sun* in 1699, and after the abandonment of the colony moved to Charles' Town, where he settled, becoming the leading Presbyterian minister there, along with many other Scots colonists. See SCHM.99.2.110; Dobson, *The Original Scots Colonists of Early America, Supplement: 1607–1707*, 5 and 166.

of the English settlements survived very much due to the Scottish presence within them, as stated by the likes of John Winthrop, hence their desire to take elements from across the strata of Scottish society into the heart of their communities. Moreover, as noted above, other shiploads of Scots set off to plant English colonies at the same time as Darien without hindrance.

By the end of the seventeenth century thousands of Scots had crossed the Atlantic and settled in places as disparate as Hudson Bay and Rio de Janeiro. The communities they formed among the colonies of the English and other European powers facilitated new trading opportunities both legal and otherwise. The resulting economic growth and industrial development greatly raised living standards in Scotland. While maintaining its traditional trading links with Europe, the period saw a very significant growth in transatlantic trade and episodic periods of emigration to the Americas. Sustained Scottish communities, however, only really evolved as a result of the Union of Parliaments in 1707. Thus the largest Scottish communities to arise in the British colonies did so following on from the failure of the Scottish colonial scheme at Darien—indeed as a direct result of it given the scheme's impact on British history. The Treaty of Union which followed formalised the pan-British nature of Scottish settlement that had been in evidence in the Americas even as early as the establishment of Nova Scotia and which had, for the most part, been a feature of Scottish communities in the North American continent thereafter.

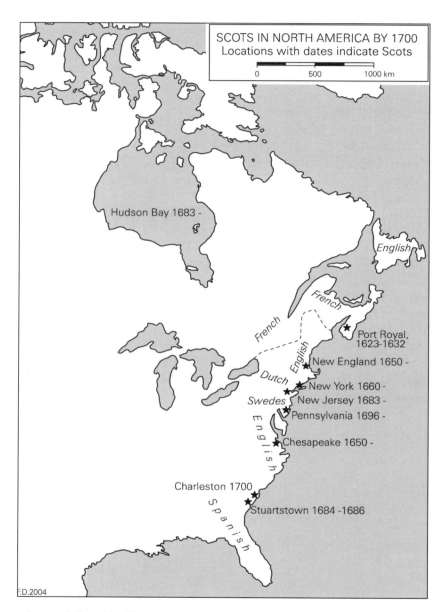

Located Scottish Communities in the North Sea Region in the Early
Modern Period

SECTION II

'LOCATED' COMMUNITIES

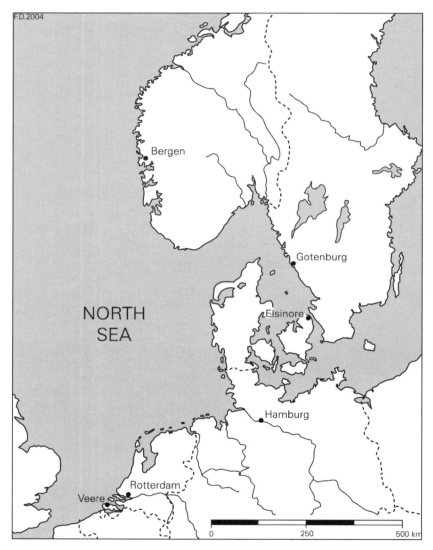

Key Scottish Communities in the Eastern North-Sea Region in the 17th Century

SCOTTISH IMMIGRATION TO BERGEN IN THE SIXTEENTH AND SEVENTEENTH CENTURIES

Nina Østby Pedersen

Bergen, situated on the western coast of Norway, was the largest city and commercial centre in Scandinavia in the early sixteenth century. It was already home to a multi-ethnic population and attracted Dutch, Danish, English and German immigrants. Scottish immigrants also constituted a distinct group, though not as numerous as the Germans, who were mainly Hansa merchants and mostly from the city of Lübeck, as well as some artisans from north German cities. During the course of the late Middle Ages, Bergen had become one of the most important cities for the Hanseatic League, and since the late thirteenth century significant settlements of Hansa merchants had dominated the city's economic life.[1]

Trade with northern Norway—importing grain from the Baltic and exporting stockfish to European markets—laid the foundation for the Hansa merchants' activities in Bergen. Through their trading privileges and their well-organised 'German Office', established around 1360, the merchants monopolised this trade for centuries.[2] German artisan guilds also enjoyed privileges in Bergen, and in the late Middle Ages they were dominant in the cobblers', goldsmiths', skinners' and tailors' trades in the city.[3] However, during the sixteenth century, the Hanseatic League's economic position in the

---

[1] Yngve Nedrebø, 'Fra Skandinavias største by til Strilane sin hovudstad', in *Frå Fjon til Fusa, Årbok for Hordamuseet og Nord- og Midthordland Sogelag* (1990/91), 36, 48 and Knut Helle, *Bergen bys historie I, Kongssete og kjøpstad, Fra opphavet til 1536* (Bergen: 1982), 385.

[2] The dominance of the Hansa merchants in the stockfish trade through Bergen can be traced back to 1278 and 1294 when they were given rights to conduct trade in Norwegian cities on equal terms with Norwegian citizens. Their position was further consolidated by their control of grain imports from the Baltic to Bergen, which gave them the upper hand in negotiations for exemption from civic burdens. For a further discussion on the Hansa merchants and the stockfish trade see Helle, *Bergen bys historie I*, 378–390, 773–788.

[3] The privileged position of the German artisan guilds dates from 1330 when German cobblers were given the monopoly on the manufacture of new shoes. For

North Sea area was significantly weakened, and this development also affected the position of *Det tyske kontor* (the German Office) in Bergen. By the end of the century the Hansa merchants and German artisans had lost ground to an expanding group of burgesses in Bergen. This left two competing commercial groups in the city: the domestic burgess class and the more or less independent German community.[4]

The division of the city's economic life was replicated in the pattern of settlement. While the Hansa merchants occupied the strategically-important wharf area, known as *Tyskebryggen* (the German wharf), the burgesses were located on the opposite side of the wharf, separated by a bay, on what is generally called *Strandsiden* (the Beachside). Although a burgess class had existed there throughout the late Middle Ages, it was not until the sixteenth century that it was able to pose any real challenge to the privileged German communities.[5] Increased immigration from other North Sea countries from the late fifteenth century onwards seems to have influenced this development. This paper will focus on the rise in Scottish immigration around the 1500s, highlighting the distinctive role this community played in the competitive environment of early sixteenth-century Bergen. The numerical importance of Scottish immigration throughout the sixteenth and seventeenth centuries will be discussed, along with its multi-dimensional character and an analysis of inter-Scottish relations in Bergen society.

The Bergen burgess-book reveals that burgesses originating from Scotland constituted a large group throughout the seventeenth century.[6] These records date back to the 1550s, but are less informative for the sixteenth century. However, there are other ways of determin-

---

further details on the German artisans in Bergen in the late Middle Ages see Helle, *Bergen bys historie I*, 485–487, 750–761.

[4] What the two German groups had in common was their detachment from the rest of the urban community. The German Office and the guilds managed to prevent integration and maintained strong links with Lübeck and other north German cities. The primary objective of their settlement in Bergen was to gain experience and assets before eventually returning to their home towns. For further details on the development of internal jurisdiction in the German communities, their exclusiveness and continued links with north German cities, see Helle, *Bergen bys historie I*, 473–75, 738–40, 746–47, 761.

[5] For a detailed survey of the development of the Bergen burgess-ship throughout the late Middle Ages see Helle, *Bergen bys historie I*, 820–824.

[6] N. Nicolaysen, *Bergen Borgerbog 1550–1751* (Christiania: 1878).

ing the size and significance of Bergen's sixteenth-century Scottish community. An incident which occurred in 1523, involving the city's Scottish burgesses, is a good starting point.

"The Scottish incident"

On the night of 9 November 1523, a woman called Marette Thomas-datter was pulled out of her bed by several Hansa merchants and German artisans who had broken into her home in Bergen. Marette was alone on this particular night. Her husband Duncan was away trading in skins to the coast of Agder in southern Norway. Although the intruders must have startled her, it seems she had some clue as to what they were after. At the sight of her assailants Marette said she didn't understand why they had broken in, importantly noting that her husband was not a Scot.[7]

Marette Thomasdatter was not the only one whose house was broken into on this particular night. At least twelve Scots, along with a few other burgesses, were attacked and robbed. One man was sup-posedly beaten to death, while others were brought back to *Tyskebryggen* where they were kept prisoner before being forced to flee the country.[8] This affair—attempts by members of the Hansa commu-nity and the German guilds to rid Bergen of some of its burgesses—soon came to be known as "the Scottish incident". A few months later a written complaint was sent from an unidentified location to the Danish-Norwegian King Fredrik I, mentioning twelve people who had been attacked, who "were all born in Scotland and the Northern Isles".[9] Marette's husband probably *was* Scottish, and her outburst is interesting. It could mean the intruders had asked for her Scottish husband, or simply that Marette thought they would leave her alone if she told them her husband was not Scottish. Either way, her response testifies to an ongoing conflict between burgesses—particu-larly those of Scottish origin—on one hand, and the Hansa com-munity and German guilds on the other. The idea that Scots not only constituted the majority of the victims, but were a targeted

---

[7] C. C. A. Lange, *Norske Samlinger II* (Christiania: 1860), 486–87.
[8] Lange, *Norske Samlinger II*, 482.
[9] Lange, *Norske Samlinger II*, 482.

group, is further substantiated in the correspondence between the
authorities and the victims following the incident. In their complaint
the Scottish burgesses explained that the Germans had threatened
to kill them if they didn't bind themselves to leave the country within
six months, abandoning their wives, children and personal belong-
ings. They had also been made to swear not to return to Scotland
or Denmark, but to find a new home in England or Holland. Whether
at the time of writing this letter the Scots were exiled in England
or Holland, or if they had found refuge elsewhere, remains uncertain. What is clear is that they were indeed separated from their
families and homes in Bergen when this letter was written. They
seem to have returned safely to Bergen a few years later, furthering
their case in what was to become a prolonged litigation process. In
the late 1520s a victim and burgess-councillor called John Thommessen
Scot recorded the damages he and his fellow countrymen had sustained in the attack, demanding satisfaction for their loss.[10] However,
they did not live to see restitution. Although numerous attempts were
made to reconcile the two communities in the 1530s, the case was
not brought to a close until 1604.[11]

Regarding the origins of the conflict, the fact that the assailants
didn't want the Scots to return to Scotland or seek refuge in Denmark
indicates that the incident had implications beyond the confines of
Bergen's urban community. Developments in mercantile policies during the early sixteenth century created a tense environment in the
city. The privileged commercial communities clearly resented the
new element of competition, and the fact that the authorities were
encouraging this development in an attempt to counterbalance Hansa
influence in the kingdom only made it more threatening. During the
reigns of King Hans and his son Christiern II, from 1481–1523, a
policy of establishing a strong burgess-ship in Bergen emerged. Indeed,
Christiern II is generally referred to as the burgess-king.[12] Through
a steady influx of immigrants eager to participate in Bergen's trade,
this community increased its competitiveness and, despite significant
opposition from the Hansa community, it was soon a force to be

---

[10] Lange, *Norske Samlinger II*, 485–87. Their loss was estimated to be around 38,142
marks.
[11] Lange, *Norske Samlinger II*, 481–492. In 1604 the German Office was ordered
to compensate the inheritors of John Thommessen Scot.
[12] S. Bagge and K. Mykland, *Norge i Dansketiden 1380–1814* (Oslo: 1992), 74–75.

reckoned with in the stockfish and other foreign trades.[13] The 1523 attackers also broke into the city council and stole the letters of privileges given to the burgesses, proving they believed that the latter posed a real threat to their monopoly.[14]

The question remains as to why Scottish settlers seem to have been particularly targeted. One obvious explanation is that they had a leading role in economic life on *Strandsiden* and thus stood out in the opposition to *Det tyske kontor* and the artisan guilds. As argued by Knut Helle, author of the history of Bergen in the Middle Ages, the list of stolen goods reported in John Thommessen Scot's letter indicates that several of these Scots were successfully engaged in a wide range of commercial activities. Apparently John Thommessen Scot, who was a tailor and merchant, and another prominent merchant called Sander Johnsen, sustained the heaviest losses in the attack. From their stalls the Germans had stolen spices, jewellery and expensive textiles of different origin. These Scots also had considerable stocks of other imported goods, such as Shetland and Scottish wool, down, and smaller amounts of English tin and German beer, in addition to Norwegian commodities such as timber, malt, skins, leather, furs and agricultural products. Sander Johnsen also had stocks of flowers and fish. Both of them lost a great deal of their foreign currency, and saw their smaller vessels and one ship damaged in the attack.[15]

Through these calculations of lost and damaged goods we can trace a considerable retail trade and wholesale buying of larger stocks of imported goods, as well as Norwegian country produce suitable for export. It's likely that the vessels were used to trade along the Norwegian coast, as in the case of the above-mentioned Duncan, Marette's husband. Being immigrants from the Northern Isles and Scotland, it is also possible that they undertook trips to their former home country to buy the Scottish goods mentioned above, or exported timber in their own ships to the huge markets there.[16] It proves that these particular burgesses were conducting trade in a progressive and successful manner, to an extent that would irritate the Hansa

---

[13] Helle, *Bergen bys historie I*, 788.
[14] Lange, *Norske Samlinger II*, 481.
[15] Helle, *Bergen bys historie I*, 815–816.
[16] Helle, *Bergen bys historie I*, 815–816.

merchants. Although the Hansa area of expertise was the stockfish trade, they sought to extend their monopoly to all aspects of Bergen's trade in the late Middle Ages. As Knut Helle argues, burgess activities didn't necessarily imply an economic setback for the Hanseatic community—but it did mean a shift from a progressive to a defensive approach to developments.[17]

Indeed, Sander Johnsen's stock of fish produce reveals his involvement in the stockfish trade. *Det tyske kontor* had a firmly-established position; not being allowed to travel north of Bergen themselves, the Hansa merchants had developed a relationship with the fishermen who brought stockfish and other fish produce to Bergen in exchange for grain. The fishermen were permanently indebted to the Hansa merchants, who furnished their expenses. This system helped to secure the Hansa merchants' position.[18] In order to increase the competitiveness of the burgess-class in this intensive trade, the authorities introduced certain privileges. In 1509 the burgesses were given an option on grain imported in English and Scottish ships, at the expense of the Hansa merchants.[19] Having access to grain, they then needed permission to travel north of Bergen to the fishing-grounds. This right was granted in 1528.[20] It remains unclear whether the privileges of 1528 actually created a new situation, or if they simply formalised administration of activities already taking place. In the case of Sander Johnsen it seems likely that he had made attempts to penetrate the Hansa monopoly and reap the profits of this lucrative trade.

Although less is known about the activities of the burgess artisans in this period, several of them seem to have been attacked; at least four tailors, including the aforementioned John Thommessen Scot,

---

[17] Helle, *Bergen bys historie I*, 778–787. Although adversaries in many respects, there was a degree of peaceful and co-dependant interaction between these two communities. For a detailed discussion of this relationship see Helle, *Bergen bys historie*, 761–773.

[18] For more details on this business relationship, see Helle, *Bergen bys historie*, 734–37, 738–40, 770–71.

[19] Helle, *Bergen bys historie I*, 708.

[20] A. B. Fossen, *Bergen bys historie II, Borgerskapets by 1536–1800* (Bergen: 1979), 15. Although Fredrik I chose to be on friendlier terms with Lübeck, he continued some of the policies introduced during Christiern II's reign. In addition to the privileges of 1528, he gave Scots and Dutch merchants extensive rights in the city's retail trade in 1524. See Helle, *Bergen bys historie*, 804.

who admittedly was predominantly a merchant, and one skinner were involved.[21] Many artisans of Scottish origin appear to have been employed at Bergen castle around 1520; this would have given them access to the local authorities, which was probably not well received in the privileged German guilds.[22] While the competition described here provides a probable background to the conflict, it doesn't really explain why the German assailants tried to prevent the Scots from returning to their native country. As will be shown below, the German community probably had other reasons for holding a grudge against Scots. At this time Scotland was an important ally of Denmark-Norway and this clearly contributed to increasing animosity between the two communities. In fact, the anti-Lübeck policies of the Danish-Norwegian authorities in Bergen in the early sixteenth century were determined by foreign policy issues rather than any real concern for the establishment of a national burgess-ship.[23] In a quest for control of the Baltic trade, the main adversaries of the Danish Crown were Sweden and the Hansa cities, and in this political climate, the alliance with the Scottish Crown was put to the test.

Political relations between Denmark-Norway and Scotland

Peaceful relations between Norway and Scotland were initiated by the Treaty of Perth in 1266. In addition to settling territorial differences, whereby the Norwegians had to surrender the Hebrides to the Scottish Crown, the treaty also laid the foundation for friendly interaction between the two parties. From the second ratification of the treaty in 1426, after the formation of the Scandinavian Kalmar Union, the parties agreed to surrender all claims to each others' territories, thereby allowing for peaceful intercourse and improved trading relations. During the reign of Christiern I the relations developed into a military alliance involving a third party, France. From a Danish-

---

[21] These artisans were Sander Tailor, William Tailor, Thomas Tailor and Henrik Skinder.

[22] Anton Espeland, *Skottene i Hordaland og Rogaland* (Nordheimsund: 1921), 51. They continued to be employed there for many years and included masons and stone-cutters who worked on the fenestration of the Rosenkrantz tower in the 1560s. See W. Douglas Simson, *The Castle of Bergen and the Bishop's Palace at Kirkwall* (Edinburgh: 1961), 57.

[23] Bagge and Mykland, *Norge i Dansketiden 1380–1814*, 75.

Norwegian point of view, mustering support against the Hanseatic League (and after 1521, against a newly-independent Sweden) seems to have been the main motivation. The alliance was consolidated through the marriage of Christiern's daughter Margaret to James III of Scotland in 1469. The best-remembered circumstance of this event, and probably the most important for Scotland, was the celebrated transfer of the Northern Isles from the kingdom of Norway to the Scottish Crown in pawn—a recurring thorn in the side of the alliance partners.[24]

The 1469 treaty was further ratified as a mutual defensive alliance in 1494 by kings Hans and James IV. As tensions increased between King Hans and Lübeck in 1509, James IV and the Scottish government were repeatedly asked to arrest and seize Lübeck ships in Scotland. In return Hans offered letters of marque to Scottish subjects and a quarter of the spoils to the Scottish king.[25] Correspondence between James IV and Maximilian I in August 1510 indicates that some Scots might have accommodated this request. However, in Hans' conflicts with Lübeck from 1510–12 he asked for more concrete help in accordance with the alliance, including military aid to Copenhagen and Marstrand in Norway. The Scottish government declined to comply, preferring diplomatic intervention.[26] Responding to Maximilian's complaints about Danish attacks on Lübeckers, the Scottish king claimed he was *not* helping Denmark, and that Lübeckers had attacked a Scottish ship, thus prompting the response of his privateers.[27] Yet some Scots seem to have continued to act in opposition to the Scottish authorities. During Albany's regency and the minority of James V, some Bergen merchants apparently complained of prejudicial Scottish privateering activities. In written instructions given to the herald Norge on his forthcoming journey to Copenhagen in 1515, he was to report to Christiern II that the Scots had been ordered under the heaviest penalties to refrain from injuring the Bergen merchants at sea; the goods of the Königsberg men, detained

---

[24] T. Riis, *Should Auld Acquaintance Be Forgot, Scottish-Danish Relations 1450–1707* (2 vols., Odense: 1988), I, 15–16, and S. Murdoch, *Britain, Denmark-Norway and the House of Stuart 1603–1660* (East Linton: 2003), 22.

[25] R. H. Brodie, ed., *Letters and Papers, Foreign and Domestic of the Reign of Henry VIII, Part I* (London: 1920), 117, 132. Thanks to Dr Davie Horsbroch for sharing his research notes on this subject with me.

[26] Riis, *Should Auld Acquaintance Be Forgot*, I, 83.

[27] Brodie, *Letters and Papers*, 323.

at St Andrews, had been restored.[28] The Bergen merchants referred to in this case were probably Hansa merchants and not burgesses, given that Scottish privateers would have been unwise to undermine the fragile position of several of their fellow countrymen in Bergen.[29]

Although probably motivated by the letters of marque, it is fairly certain that the privateers and the Danish king shared a common interest. Both Hans and Christiern II depended on Scots not only militarily, but also for mercantile expansion. The policy of making Norway less dependent on Lübeck shipping could not be achieved without Scottish, English and Dutch mercantile transport to and from the Baltic.[30] Undermining the position of the Hansa merchants in Bergen depended on immigration by experienced foreign traders who could raise the competitive level of the domestic burgess-ship and ultimately replace the privileged commercial groups altogether. Naturally the Danish-Norwegian Crown looked to their closest ally. Considering these circumstances, the influx of Scottish immigrants to Bergen in the early 1500s seems to have been not a fortunate coincidence, but a deliberate policy on the part of the Danish-Norwegian authorities. Thomas Riis further argues that continued Scottish support for Christiern II after his deposition in 1523, represented by the commercial establishment at Leith and merchants such as David Falconer, Robert Barton, and Robert Fogo, proves that the Norway trade was of the utmost importance to them. Evidently Christiern's supporters expected him to continue his policies if restored to power.[31]

The accession of Fredrik I in 1523 led to a resurgence of Hansa power in Bergen. In fact, the new political climate and the arrival of a new governor in Bergen on the very evening of 8 November 1523 triggered the attack on the burgesses. The assailants seem to have erroneously believed that they were acting in agreement with the new governor, Vincens Lunge, and in the interest of the new

---

[28] Robert Kerr Hannay, ed., *The Letters of James V* (Edinburgh: 1954), 25.

[29] Regarding Christiern II's conflict with Lübeck in 1522–23, we can only assume that he applied the same tactics as his father in calling upon Scottish privateering of Lübeck ships.

[30] T. C. Smout, *Scottish Trade on the Eve of Union, c.1660–1707* (Edinburgh: 1963), 210; Riis, *Should Auld Acquaintance Be Forgot*, I, 83.

[31] For a discussion of Scottish support for Christiern II's cause in the period from 1523–33, see Riis, *Should Auld Acquaintance Be Forgot*, I, 20–32.

king.[32] The idea that the Scottish burgesses in Bergen held the key
to the Danish-Norwegian authorities' anti-Lübeck policies is further
substantiated by correspondence between *Det tyske kontor* and their
head council in Lübeck following the 1523 attack. In an explanation dated 29 October 1529, the Hansa merchants claimed they were
only helping Vincens Lunge by making the Scots—who were on the
enemy side—surrender their goods and property to the Crown.[33]
Apparently the Scots' cooperation with Christiern II made them
unpopular with Fredrik I as well. Although supporting their claim
for satisfaction, he nevertheless proved indulgent to the Hansa when
they refused to comply with verdicts against them in the 1530 litigation process. In a letter written in 1530 to Eske Bille, governor of
Bergen castle, Fredrik I instructed him to make sure the Scots and
Germans in Bergen were reconciled, making the point that the Scots
had supported Christiern's cause and in that respect weren't really
his subjects at the time of the attack.[34]

To sum up, it was the competitiveness of the Scottish burgesses
and their significant role in the authorities' anti-Lübeck policies which
posed such a threat to the Hansa community and German artisan
guilds. The likelihood that some Scots took part in seizing Hansa
ships indicates that the 1523 attack was probably an act of revenge
on the part of the German community, carried out when the political climate was deemed more favourable towards their privileged
position. Considering the implications of the Danish-Norwegian alliance
with Scotland, it is not surprising that the Hansa community tried
to prevent the Scots from returning to their native country. The
prospect of seeing their evicted competitors hook up with Christiern
II's supporters in Scotland must have been undesirable.

Political relations between Denmark-Norway and Scotland remained
cool until the alliance was reconfirmed through James VI's marriage
to Princess Anna in 1589. This marriage initiated a long period of
flourishing relations between the two monarchies, enhanced by the
close friendship between James VI and his brother-in-law Christian
IV, who met in person on several occasions.[35] The Union of Crowns

---

[32] Helle, *Bergen bys historie I*, 768.
[33] Lange, *Norske Samlinger II*, 484.
[34] Lange, *Norske Samlinger II*, 484.
[35] Murdoch, *Britain, Denmark-Norway and the House of Stuart*, 24.

in 1603 did not bring about any significant changes in Stuart-Oldenburg relations. Scottish interests still dominated the agenda of the new British monarchy, demonstrated by King James' almost exclusively Scottish *corps diplomatique* in Denmark-Norway, Sweden and Poland-Lithuania.[36] During the reign of Charles I, however, Stuart-Oldenburg relations suffered significant setbacks. The alienation of the two allies was the result of contrasting interests and priorities during the wars of religion on the continent and was indicated by the withdrawal of resident court ambassadors.[37] In the late 1640s political circumstances led to the undermining of Scotland's role in Britain and abroad. In Scandinavia, this ultimately evolved into a Swedish-English agenda, which replaced the former Danish-Scottish dimension of Stuart northern diplomacy from the 1660s onwards.[38]

Judging from the significant number of Scotsmen serving as burgesses in Bergen in the first part of the seventeenth century, it seems obvious that the amicable political climate described above had a positive impact on migration. Indeed, Scottish citizens enjoyed the same status as Danes and Norwegians in Denmark-Norway, and vice versa, which must have encouraged potential emigrants.[39]

A numerically important Scottish community

A large percentage of the Bergen burgess-ship was of foreign descent in the sixteenth and seventeenth centuries. From 1613 onwards the council clerk made it common practice to write down the birthplace of new burgesses in the burgess-book. In the period from 1613–20, only about 16% of new burgesses were born in Norway,

---

[36] S. Murdoch, 'Diplomacy in Transition: Stuart-British Diplomacy in Northern Europe, 1603–1618' in A. I. Macinnes, T. Riis and F. G. Pedersen (eds.), *Ships, Guns and Bibles in the North Sea and the Baltic States, c.1350–c.1700* (East Linton: 2000), 92–107; Murdoch, *Britain, Denmark-Norway and the House of Stuart*, 2. For a detailed analysis of Stuart-Oldenburg relations in the period from 1589–1625, see pages 22–63.

[37] Murdoch, *Britain, Denmark-Norway and the House of Stuart*, 87–89.

[38] Murdoch, *Britain, Denmark-Norway and the House of Stuart*, 257–58.

[39] Murdoch, *Britain, Denmark-Norway and the House of Stuart*, 23. This became an issue during the negotiations leading to the marriage treaty of 1589. When Scottish envoys sought to ensure this status for Scots in Denmark-Norway, the Danes responded that such rights had been agreed in earlier treaties between the two monarchies.

and judging from their names quite a few of them were descendants of earlier immigrants.[40] As mentioned previously, burgesses born in Scotland were numerically important in the seventeenth century; 219 Scots served as burgesses from 1613–1711. Immigration was not spread evenly throughout the century; no less than 193 of these immigrants settled in Bergen before 1660, and more than three quarters of these before 1640.[41] The Scots constituted about 7–8% of the total group of new burgesses until 1640, but the number dropped to 2% in 1660.[42] Having remained insignificant for nearly thirty years, immigration from Scotland then rose again around the turn of century. In the period from 1692–1711, seventeen Scots became burgesses in Bergen.[43]

Interestingly, during this time burgesses born in England were numerically insignificant. From 1600–60 only ten Englishmen became burgesses.[44] The Swedes and Dutch both had a presence in the town, although both groups were far smaller than the Scots. Although the Scots were outnumbered by the large communities of burgesses from the German cities and princely states and Denmark, as a single national group they were probably equally important, given the complex origins of the Germans and Danes.[45]

Regarding the early sixteenth century, the numbers of Scottish immigrants compared to other ethnic groups is hard to determine. The Dutch element was probably strong at this point, as they had established themselves in foreign trade through Bergen some time before 1440.[46] The existence of a Dutch street in Bergen, *Hollenderstredet*, originating in the later Middle Ages, is also testimony to a considerable Dutch settlement.[47] Germans who had broken away from the Hansa community as well as immigrants from other parts of Germany were also an identifiable group in the burgess-ship at this time. Indeed, a few Dutch and German burgesses were among the vic-

---

[40] Nedrebø, 'Fra Skandinavias største by til Strilane sin hovudstad', 50.
[41] Nicolaysen, *Bergen Borgerbog*, 29–141.
[42] Nedrebø, 'Fra Skandinavias største by til Strilane sin hovudstad'.
[43] Nedrebø, 'Fra Skandinavias største by til Strilane sin hovudstad', 116–140.
[44] Murdoch, *Britain, Denmark-Norway and the House of Stuart*, 30.
[45] Nedrebø, 'Fra Skandinavias største by til Strilane sin hovudstad'. Some 677 Germans, 432 Danes, 54 Swedes and 46 Dutchmen became burgesses in the period 1613–1660.
[46] Erik Oppsal, *Norsk Innvandringshistorie, bind I, I Kongenes Tid* (Oslo: 2003), 186.
[47] Erik Oppsal, *I Kongenes Tid*, 186.

tims of the 1523 attack.[48] Nevertheless, in the sources that have survived from this period, Scots stand out from the various immigrant
communities. We can probably add another six Scottish burgesses
to the twelve attacked in 1523. These individuals appear in open
announcements from the late 1520s. When the Leith merchant David
Falconer had his ship arrested and its grain cargo despoiled by the
Norwegian archbishop's men in 1527, a prolonged process followed
until he finally received satisfaction in 1529. During this process his
agents, Thomas Gardener and Thomas Hutchensen of Leith, needed
witnesses to verify payments that had been made. The six witnesses
were all burgesses of Bergen and all had Scottish-sounding names.[49]
In records of expenses from Bergen castle around 1520, there are
also numerous references to Scots receiving payment for work done.
Mariners, artisans and workers with monikers like Scot and Hjelt
(for Shetland) attached to their names number at least eighteen other
individuals.[50] This evidence provides fairly certain documentation of
thirty six immigrants of Scottish descent in the years before the
Danish-Norwegian Reformation of 1536.

    In the second half of the sixteenth century the number of Scottish
burgesses seems to have increased. Although it was not common
practice in this period, fourteen Scots were listed with their birthplace in the burgess-book prior to 1613, and twenty eight new
burgesses were called either Skot or Hjelt. These forty two individuals must have been a fraction of the total group of Scottish immigrants in this period. Scottish surnames like Sinclair, Erskine, Guthrie
and Meen were common, and it is likely that a fair number of the
many Robertsens, Johnsens and Sandersens were Scots as well. A
German priest by the name of Sabinius throws light on this claim;
according to him there were far too many Scots in Bergen at this
time. In his allegory of Norwegian society written in 1587 he was
particularly concerned with Bergen, where he lived in the 1560s. He
was highly critical of Scots and those from the Northern Isles, whom
he compared to rats, claiming they contributed nothing but harm

---

[48] Lange, *Norske Samlinger II*, 482.
[49] C. R. Unger and H. J. Huitfeldt, *Diplomatarium Norvegicum VIII* (Christiania:
1874), nr. 569, 570, 571, 574, 575, 576, 578, 580, 581, 582, 591, 611. The six
individuals were: Anders Neskett, Rikert Johnsen, Peter Tailor, Peter Kawbrath,
Jan Baxster, Robert Carns.
[50] Espeland, *Skottene i Hordaland og Rogaland*, 8–9.

to the town.[51] Based on the names in the Bergen burgess-book, it can be shown that immigration from Scotland actually rose after Sabinius wrote his allegory.

From such evidence it is fair to conclude that the Scottish burgess community was significant in both the sixteenth and seventeenth centuries. Indeed, the influx of Scottish immigrants to Bergen seems to have been continuous from the early 1500s to about 1660, reaching a peak in the years around 1620, perhaps sooner. As pointed out by Steve Murdoch, a large burgess community is an indication of an even bigger trading community.[52] This was certainly the case for Bergen. The period studied here witnessed a steady and predictable arrival of Scottish ships at Bergen's harbour and at the timber trade areas south of the city.

Flourishing trade relations

Scattered customs accounts and other records measuring the foreign trade through Bergen provide evidence of the Scots' continued presence. The first reference to Scottish ships in Bergen in this period dates to 1509, when the burgess-ship was given the option on grain imported in English and Scottish ships. In the following years Scots seem to have outnumbered the English in Bergen's trade. Accounts kept from 1518–21 reveal that Scottish ships made nineteen visits to Bergen, compared to only three English.[53] During this period the Scots seem to have occupied a position as important as the Dutch. A 1524 decision to give Scottish and Dutch traders access to the city's retail trade supports this argument.[54]

The reconfirmation of the 1509 grain decision in 1541 shows the continued importance of Scottish trade.[55] However, it remains uncertain whether the Scots imported grain at this time, as they did in the seventeenth century. Scottish traders seem to have been mostly engaged in trades that were of marginal interest to the Hansa community in the early modern period. The export of timber and the

---

[51] N. Nicolaysen, *Norske Magasin II* (Christiania: 1858–1870), 19.
[52] Murdoch, *Britain, Denmark-Norway and the House of Stuart*, 30.
[53] Helle, *Bergen bys historie I*, 775.
[54] Helle, *Bergen bys historie I*, 804.
[55] Fossen, *Bergen bys historie II*, 25.

import of salt dominated Scottish trade through Bergen in this period. Scottish salt was a highly sought-after commodity in sixteenth-century Bergen. As the Lüneburg salt production gradually dried up in the 1500s, salt imports from Scotland and southern France became vital for the Bergen fish industry. For instance, in 1518 and 1519 the governor of Bergen castle, Jørgen Hanssøn, bought eleven lasts of salt from Scottish traders and in 1578, twenty four Scottish ships arrived with salt at Bergen harbour.[56] Regarding export of Bergen commodities, stockfish rarely reached the Scottish markets. However there was a strong demand for timber in Scotland, a commodity increasingly exported from Bergen throughout the early modern period. Until 1567 Bergen served as the customs port for the timber trade area of Sunnhordland, south of the city, where most Scottish skippers went to buy their timber. In 1567, thirty six Scottish ships paid customs for timber in Bergen, and apparently quite a few spent time in the city depositing goods before heading off to the Sunnhordland districts to load timber. According to these records several of the Scottish skippers "used their market in Bergen." One of them, by the name of Jørgen Villand from Leith, seems to have known the city well, making no less than three journeys to Bergen and Sunnhordland in that particular year.[57] The idea that Scottish traders had good knowledge of Bergen and sometimes even imposed on the city's hospitality is revealed in a 1629 complaint from the burgess-ship. Apparently quite a few foreigners had made a habit of storing their goods in the city, thereby trying to infiltrate the retail trade at the expense of the burgess-ship. Still, the Dutch seem to have been bolder than the Scots in this respect.[58]

Although the establishment of a local customs port at Eldøy in Sunnhordland in 1567 might have reduced Scottish trade to Bergen for a short period, this reorganisation did not bring about any drastic changes. In fact, the evidence shows that Scottish traders started

---

[56] Espeland, *Skottene i Hordaland og Rogaland*, 9, 21. Not until the early seventeenth century did better-quality French salt replace Scottish salt. See T. C. Smout, 'The Norwegian Timber Trade before 1700' in A. Lillehammer (ed.), *Timber and trade, articles on the timber export from the Ryfylke-area to Scotland and Holland in the 16th and 17th centuries* (Aksdal: 1999), 41.

[57] 'Toll av utenlandske skip som ladet på Bergen våg i 1567' in *Norske Lensregnskaper IV* (Oslo: 1941), 6–12; Fossen, *Bergen bys historie II*, 33.

[58] Fossen, *Bergen bys historie II*, 152.

buying deal and processed timber in the city around this time. The 1578 accounts also note that all the Scottish ships carried various processed timber products on their return to Scotland.[59] It is likely that some of these ships went further south to load bigger cargoes of unprocessed timber after stopping in Bergen, continuing the old trading-route shown above. Having been somewhat supplementary during the sixteenth century, the export of timber from Bergen increased significantly in the seventeenth century. Indeed, in an over-all Norwegian context Bergen became an important timber port from the 1600s onwards, a fact embraced by the huge Scottish markets. In 1629 about 35% of Bergen's timber export went to Scotland and England. Ten years later, no less than 47% of the total timber export was carried in Scottish, Orkney and English ships.[60] Probably most of them were bound for domestic markets.

Not surprisingly, even Bergen-registered ships seem to have taken part in exporting timber to Scotland. In the Aberdeen Shore Work Accounts there are seven references to ships coming from Bergen carrying deal in the period from 1642–62, and at least four seem to have been registered in Bergen.[61] Some may have been chartered by Scottish skippers and merchants, as the customs accounts for Sunnhordland in the first part of the seventeenth century reveal several instances of this.[62] As Scottish records like the Aberdeen Shore Work Accounts rarely differentiate between Norwegian ports and just record "coming from Norway" or "Norway ship," it is difficult to determine the extent of commercial contacts specifically between Aberdeen and Bergen at this time. Unfortunately there are no Aberdeen shore records from 1632. That year thirty one Scottish ships paid moorage at Bergen harbour, and no less than eleven of them came from Aberdeen.[63] Unless this year was exceptional we might assume that quite a few of the Norwegian references in the Aberdeen records actually mean Bergen.

The lack of references to Bergen in the Aberdeen Shore Work Accounts could also be explained by the emergence of triangular

[59] Espeland, *Skottene i Hordaland og Rogaland*, 21.
[60] Fossen, *Bergen bys historie II*, 209–212.
[61] Louise B. Taylor, ed., *Aberdeen Shore Work Accounts 1596–1670* (Aberdeen: 1972), 268, 311, 414, 418, 465, 489.
[62] Fossen, *Bergen bys historie II*, 212.
[63] NRA, Bergenhus lensregnskaper 1632.

trading routes. In the case of Andrew Mure, a Peterhead skipper trading through Aberdeen in 1634, Bergen seems to have been his first port of call. It is likely that he is the Anders Mejer of Aberdeen who turned up in Bergen twice that year.[64] In the Aberdeen records, however, he is registered as coming from Leith and Pomerania.[65] According to Christopher Smout, triangular trading routes involving Bergen and Norway in the seventeenth century were most often motivated by a lack of Scottish goods which could match the need for timber in the country. Although the demand for Scottish salt was a significant feature of trading links with Bergen in the sixteenth century, better-quality French salt seems to have replaced the Scottish product altogether in the seventeenth century. In the case of the timber trade, a triangular trade with the Netherlands, shipping cargoes of coal, cloth, skins and beer to Rotterdam in particular, and then bringing either Dutch goods or the financial proceeds of the trip to Norway was one way of solving the problem.[66] Importing grain was another way of accommodating this imbalance. Apparently Scottish traders often took grain from the Baltic ports to Bergen on their homeward journey. After depositing the grain, they loaded tar, which they shipped back to Scotland.[67] Thus in 1692, 25% of the tar export went to Scottish and English markets.[68] It is evident that it was the demand for Bergen's commodities in Scotland, rather than the other way around, which determined Scottish trade to the city in the later part of the period studied here. According to Christopher Smout, Bergen was indeed the "favourite" port in Norway.[69]

---

[64] NRA, Bergenhus lensregnskaper 1632–34.
[65] Taylor, *Aberdeen Shore Work Accounts 1596–1670*, 192, 194.
[66] Smout, 'The Norwegian Timber Trade before 1700', 41.
[67] Smout, *Scottish Trade on the Eve of Union*, 154, 157, 210.
[68] Fossen, *Bergen bys historie II*, 415. Aberdeen and Dundee are specifically mentioned by this author as significant import ports for tar.
[69] Smout, *Scottish Trade on the Eve of Union*, 154. For Aberdeen, Bergen apparently also served as an alternative port for the purchase of French salt, needed for salting fish, especially salmon. During the English occupation of Scotland in 1652, sanctions on Scottish trade were imposed. In a letter written in September that year, Aberdeen Council asked for permission to bring home French salt wherever it could be found, either in West Flanders or Bergen or anywhere else in good relations with England. (Louise B. Taylor, *Aberdeen Council Letters*, Volume III (London: 1952), 214).

The regions of Sunnhordland and Ryfylke, between the cities of Bergen and Stavanger, were important timber trade areas in the sixteenth and seventeenth centuries. Because such a high number of Scottish ships arrived every year, it has traditionally been called "the Scottish trade." Even the period from the 1550s to the early 1700s has been called "the Scottish period" in this part of the country. Judged by calls at the customs port of Eldøy in Sunnhordland from 1597–1642, Scottish ships (including those from the Northern Isles) made up 64–97% of all arrivals.[70] At Nedstrand, the customs port in Ryfylke, the equivalent figure for 1601–1647 is 43–83% of all visits.[71] Although skippers were not obliged to stop at Bergen or Stavanger to pay customs on timber, it is fair to assume that quite a few of them did. We can conclude that from the second half of the sixteenth century and throughout the seventeenth there was a close connection between western Norway and the destination ports for timber, namely the east-coast cities of mainland Scotland and the Northern Isles. Not surprisingly, the Scottish settlers in Bergen also came from these areas.

Immigrants from mainland Scotland came from towns such as Leith, St Andrews, Dysart, Dundee, Montrose, Aberdeen, Kirkcaldy and Fraserburgh. A significant proportion of burgesses were from the Orkney Islands. From 1613–72, ninety two individuals were admitted as burgesses, 39.5% of the total from Scotland.[72] According to the Bergen historian Yngve Nedrebø, this is evidence that the islands constituted part of the city's hinterland, equally as important as regions like Sunnfjord and Nordfjord, north of Bergen.[73] The 1469 transfer of the islands to the Scottish Crown probably had little immediate effect on how the islanders viewed themselves and their connections to Norway. The fact that they continued to enjoy privileges in their former home country, such as exemption from customs until the late sixteenth century, probably helped to maintain strong links. Indeed, the immigration documented above indicates

[70] A. Næss, 'Skottehandelen på Sunnhordland', in *Sunnhordland tidsskrift*, VII (1920), 33.

[71] A. Lillehammer: 'The Scottish Norwegian Timber Trade in the Stavanger Area in the Sixteenth and Seventeenth Centuries' in T. C. Smout (ed.) *Scotland and Europe 1200–1850* (Edinburgh: 1986), 110.

[72] Nicolaysen, *Bergen Borgerbog*, 29–100.

[73] Nedrebø, 'Fra Skandinavias største by til Strilane sin hovudstad', 52.

that Bergen continued to be a spiritual capital for these people. Although there appear to have been very few burgesses from the Shetlands (only eight from 1613–50)[74] this probably has to do with lack of urban tradition on these islands. As the following will show, Shetlanders were numerous among the lower levels of urban society.

Immigrants from all walks of life

Generally Norwegian historians have seen early modern immigration as elitist. Merchants were welcomed and given favourable terms. Towns needed experienced foreign merchants and mariners, and as we have seen in Bergen, they played an important role in establishing a strong burgess-ship.

However, the early sixteenth-century Scottish community was much more complex. Bergen was a huge labour market and it attracted many young unbound people besides Norwegians looking for work. There was no problem travelling on the ships sailing regularly between the islands and Bergen, and there seems to have been a significant influx of young people from the Shetlands, as the Northern Isles people were a sought-after workforce. A customs note from 1550 stated that although Shetland ships were exempt from customs, the skippers were obliged to send to the castle all the unemployed girls and boys they had brought with them, so that the regional governor could have first choice of workers.[75]

Scottish immigrants of low social standing also characterise later periods. In a 1657 tax list, assessed on the basis of property and other wealth, Scots with great fortunes are rare. There is an occasional skipper and merchant who must be seen as belonging to the upper layers of society, but they are exceptions. Among the top eighty burgesses there appears to be only one Scot, a skipper called Anders Joensen.[76] Other foreigners are better represented in this

---

[74] Nicolaysen, *Bergen Borgerbog*, 29–75.

[75] Næss, 'Skottehandelen på Sunnhordland', 28. It seems to have been a well-known fact that Bergen castle had access to such manpower. In 1530 the regional governor of Akershus, Magnus Gyldenstjerne, made a request to Eske Bille at Bergen castle for three or four of these workers from Shetland, seeing as he was in want of labour. Ludvig Daae, 'Om berøringer mellom Orknøerne og Hjaltland og moderlandet Norge efter 1468', in *Statsøkonomisk tidsskrift* (Christiania: 1896), 44.

[76] Fossen, *Bergen bys historie II*, 299. A Scot named Anders Joensen became a burgess in 1633. Nicolaysen, *Bergen Borgerbog*, 54.

group, which offers a different perspective on the claim of élitist immigration to Norway.

Artisan occupations were often noted in the burgess-book. From 1613–1700, thirty nine Scotsmen were registered, most as weavers or coopers. In the 1657 assessment these individuals rarely have "other fortune" and their houses are valued far below average. In 1604, three Scottish coopers—Sander Andersen, David Skott and Vilhelm Jacobsen—appealed to the Copenhagen authorities after being denied the right to practice their trade by the coopers' guild. The guild claimed there were too many coopers, but the authorities found in favour of the three Scots.[77] Several Scots, including Jacob Meell, Jacob Pettersen Mowat, Anders Joensen Skott and Mette Skott, appeared in a 1645 tax-census on poor peoples' houses. According to the assessor Mette Skott's house was in such a bad state that it was good for nothing but firewood. Quite a few of these people are listed as mariners, workers and artisans.[78]

At the other end of the social scale, pre-Reformation Scots also occupied high-profile positions in Bergen society. John Thommessen Scot and another 1523 victim known as Little Thomas were town councillors, a role which implies a certain degree of wealth and status. The industrious Scots continued to irritate the German community, to the extent that in 1544 the Hansa merchants officially complained about burgesses who kept permanent representation in northern Norway in order to buy stockfish. They made it clear that the complaint applied only to foreigners who had settled in Bergen: Scots, Danes, Dutchmen and former Hansa Germans.[79] In the 1560s another prominent figure called Jørgen Schotte was elected councillor. He was registered as the owner of two sloops and an 80-last ship for use in the northern traffic in a list of Bergen merchants drawn up by *Det tyske kontor* in 1571.[80] Like others, he seems not to have been on good terms with *Det tyske kontor*. The memoirs of

[77] O. G. Lindh, *Norske Riksregistranter IV* (Christiania: 1870), 204.

[78] A. M. Wiesener, 'Ringe og fattige folks hus i Bergen' in *Bergen Historiske Forenings Skrifter*, nr. 42 (Bergen: 1936).

[79] J. Schreiner, *Hanseatene og Norge* (Oslo: 1941), 151.

[80] Schreiner, *Hanseatene og Norge*, 357–59. Another Scot called Sander Schotte is also registered on this list as the owner of a ship large enough to be used for long-distance trading to the northern regions.

Absalon Pedersen Beyer, a Bergen priest, relate that Schotte didn't invite any Hansa representatives to the feast following his inauguration as a city councillor in 1567—according to the priest this had never happened before.[81]

Little is known about the lives and economic activities of the many Scotsmen serving as burgesses in the first part of the seventeenth century. Those who turn up in the 1645 and 1657 tax lists give an impression of low social standing, and few appear in other sources.[82] However, we must assume that some of these men continued to play an important commercial role on *Strandsiden*. Among the seventeen new Scottish burgesses admitted from 1692–1711, there were no less than nine skippers and six merchants,[83] some of whom were engaged in foreign trade. John Allen, a skipper originally from Queensferry in Scotland who became a burgess in 1692, was registered as the owner of the ship *Gregorius* in Bergen.[84] In 1694 he passed through the Sound on his return from Danzig with salt and stock goods. According to Patrick Leijel, the Scottish consul in Denmark, Allen traded between Bergen, Scotland and Danzig.[85] A year after his arrival in Bergen, John Allen was joined by another skipper from Queensferry, the burgess William Robbertsen.[86]

So far we have looked at Scottish immigration only from an economic viewpoint. But Bergen was also home to several high-ranking Scottish officers serving in the Danish-Norwegian army and navy in the sixteenth and seventeenth centuries. Andrew Mowatt and his son Axel, Alexander Durham and John Cunningham are some of these

---

[81] Fossen, *Bergen bys historie II*, 421.

[82] It remains unclear why so many Scottish burgesses are absent from the mid-seventeenth century tax-lists. Some of them may have taken up residence outside the city, as in the case of Peter Bell. He became a burgess in Bergen in 1672, but settled as a merchant on the island of Stord, south of the city. See Næss, 'Skottehandelen på Sunnhordland', 79. Some burgesses might also have found ways to circumvent the obligation to become lifelong, permanent residents. This was certainly true for Jacob Fortune, who became a burgess of Stavanger in 1665. By 1666 he apparently no longer thought it worth while to live in Stavanger and left for the Dutch Provinces. See A. E. Erichsen, *Samlinger til Stavangers historie I* (Stavanger: 1903), 330, 344.

[83] Nicolaysen, *Bergen Borgerbog*, 116–140.

[84] Fossen, *Bergen bys historie II*, 878.

[85] DRA, TKUA, England, AII. Patrick Leyel 1693–1698, 'Specification paa Danske og Norske skibe i januarii til 1. Decembris 1694'.

[86] Nicolaysen, *Bergen Borgerbog*, 118.

high-profile men.[87] Alexander Durham commanded the Bergen-based
North Sea fleet from 1587–89. Andrew Mowatt moved to Bergen
in 1587 and later married Else Trondsdatter Rustung, the daughter
of a landowner from south of Bergen. Both he and his sons Axel
and Christoffer had successful careers as admirals in the Danish-
Norwegian navy. Axel Mowatt inherited his parents' farm of Hovland,
but also kept a residence in Bergen. He was a considerable landowner
and, thanks to the timber trade, probably one of the richest men in
Norway in the 1640s. John Cunningham served as an admiral before
becoming regional governor of Finnmark in 1619.[88] However in 1624
he was given permission to winter in Bergen.[89] From 1644–49 five
Scots were commanding officers of the Bergenhus Regiment. John
Taylor became colonel and chief of the Bergenhus infantry in 1644,
and was later superseded by James Murray, Colonel Lawrence Blair
and Lt. Sir Thomas Gray. The latter also acted as governor of
Bergen castle when the commissioned governor Henrich Thott was
absent. When Thott finally left Bergen for good, Gray took over for
a short period before returning to Scotland. All these officers entered
the Danish-Norwegian army through Stuart patronage, although in
effect they were refugees from the Scottish Covenanting government.[90]

We can thus conclude that Scottish immigrants in Bergen formed
a highly heterogeneous community in the period studied. As well as
being simple artisans and traders, they could reach the highest ranks
of Norwegian society. Commercial traders, those sent by royal patronage and a few important military refugees all made up the fabric of
the Scottish Bergen community. An interesting feature of Scottish
settlements abroad is the tendency to form closed communities; to
some extent this could be said of the Scots in Bergen. The existence
of a Scottish quarter, *Skottebyen*, in the city provides evidence for this
claim.

[87] Murdoch, *Britain, Denmark-Norway and the House of Stuart*, 196–197; R. Hagen,
'At the Edge of Civilisation: John Cunningham, Lensmann of Finnmark, 1619–51'
in A. Mackillop and Steve Murdoch, ed., *Military Governors and Imperial Frontiers,
c.1600–1800: A Study of Scotland and Empires* (Leiden: 2003), 29–51.
[88] Murdoch, *Britain, Denmark-Norway and the House of Stuart*, 196–197.
[89] Murdoch, *Britain, Denmark-Norway and the House of Stuart*, 103.
[90] Murdoch, *Britain, Denmark-Norway and the House of Stuart*, 227, 236–237;
S. Murdoch, 'Scotsmen on the Danish-Norwegian frontiers, c.1580–1680', in A.
Mackillop and S. Murdoch (eds.), *Military Governors and Imperial Frontiers, c.1600–1800*
(Leiden: 2003), 17–22.

Relationships between the Bergen Scots

Two streets in present-day Bergen recall earlier Scottish settlements. *Skottestredet* (the Scottish street) and *Skottehallen* (the Scottish hall) on *Strandsiden* are probably located very close to the actual *Skottebyen*, a name which turns up in sixteenth- and seventeenth-century sources. In court books from the 1590s there is a reference to a woman called Karrine, widow of Jacob Bulder, who lived in *Skottebyen*.[91] The phrase also turns up almost half a century later; in a letter from 1637, reference is made to a man called Peder Michaelsen, also residing in *Skottebyen*.[92] Although this name was used by contemporaries it doesn't necessarily imply that the neighbourhood was inhabited by Scottish settlers throughout this period. Tax lists from 1645 and 1657 indicate that by this time Scottish immigrants were scattered around Bergen, co-existing with residents of many nationalities. Even though a majority still lived on *Strandsiden*, some appear to have settled very close to *Tyskebryggen*.[93] Given that by the mid-seventeenth century Bergen had witnessed a steady influx of Scottish immigrants for 150 years, this is unsurprising. Scots must have become a well-known element in the city and the need to 'stick together' became less important. This also testifies to a welcoming society. In the tense atmosphere of the early 1500s, settling in ethnically separate quarters probably appeared a much more reasonable and natural thing to do. In all probability the name stemmed from this period when Scots started to become a distinct group in the city.

There are few sources which provide accounts of the nature of the Scottish community from 1530–90. Nevertheless the court books from 1592–94 contain some interesting information on social networks and marriage patterns. An inheritance case brought before the city council in 1594 reveals details about several Scots and the relationships between them. Robert Guthrie and Anne Calendar both laid claim to the inheritance of a man named Petter Reffuen (Ruthven) who had died in Bergen in 1564. Guthrie, a merchant burgess

---

[91] Bergen rådstueprotokoll 1592–94, folio 88a. Thanks to Yngve Nedrebø at the Bergen archive for sending me a transcribed version of these records.

[92] Nedrebø, 'Fra Skandinavias største by til Strilane sin hovudstad', 48.

[93] A. M. Wiesener, 'Manntall over Bergen bys koppskatt for 1645' in *Bergen historiske forenings skrifter nr. 41* (Bergen: 1935) and 'Bergen byes huse of formue skatt, samt rentepenge og børnepenge' in NRA Bergenhus lensregnskap 1657–58.

originally from Perth, was Reffuen's half-brother. Because the deceased
had no children and had been born illegitimate, Guthrie had received
confirmation from James VI over his right to the inheritance. Anne
Calendar, on the other hand, was a friend of the now-dead widow
of Petter Reffuen, Marine Lagome. A few years previously she had
gone to Perth on her friend's behalf and purchased the inheritance
rights from Petter Reffuen's legal inheritor, the son of another half-
brother. Once Marine Lagome was dead, Anne Calendar laid claim
to the inheritance herself through her representative and son-in-law,
Thomes Thomessen.[94]

The outcome of the case has not survived, but the most interesting aspect is not the jurisdiction but the social network illustrated.
Both women involved had Scottish surnames. Additionally, Anne
Calendar's daughter was married to a man with a typical Scottish
name. This suggests that the case reveals at least one (maybe two)
Scottish marriages and connections between two Scottish families. It
remains unclear whether these documented inter-Scottish connections were a random or integral part of a larger Scottish network,
but we do have documentation of what presents itself as a more
extensive network from the mid-seventeenth century.

Genealogical data contained in the 'Sollied archive' in Bergen
reveals interesting details of the relationships between several Scottish
immigrants in the 1650s. This network seems to centre round the
figures of Henrich Guthrie and Andrew Davidson Christie, both originally from Montrose and burgesses from 1650 and 1654 respectively. When Andrew Christie came to Bergen in 1654 he married
Gisele Vernton, widow of Thomas Beeg and possibly the daughter
of Gilbert Wenton from Dundee who became a burgess in 1640.
Christie's second wife was Anna Henrichsdatter Guthrie, daughter
of the above-mentioned Henrich Guthrie. The latter also had a son
who was married to a woman named Anna Gillesdatter Meel; her
father was a burgess cooper. Another figure who could be associated with this network was Alexander Gordon, a burgess cooper
originally from Brusst or Banff, who settled in Bergen in 1631. He
married a woman called Elisabeth Venton, possibly another daughter of Gilbert Wenton.[95] These marriage patterns reveal connections

---

[94] Bergen rådstueprotokoller 1592–1594, folio 240a–242b.
[95] 'Sollied Archive', Stasarkivet i Bergen and SSNE Database.

between five, possibly six, burgesses of Scottish origin; Henrich Guthrie, Andrew Davidson Christie, Gilbert Wenton, Gilles Meel, Alexander Gordon and possibly Thomas Beeg.[96] We can only speculate on the implications of these relationships, but one obvious interpretation is that they benefited from a form of business cooperation. Andrew D. Christie married Gisele Vernton immediately after arriving in Bergen, implying pre-arrangement through networking. In the burgess book it is even noted that "he got Thomas Beeg's widow".[97]

For some, Bergen was simply a starting point for their career in Norway. Robert Fife, originally from Dundee, arrived in 1631 but left for the neighbouring town of Stavanger in 1642. There he immediately joined another Scottish network by marrying Giønette Willumsdatter Kay, daughter of the immigrant Scot William Kay. Apparently Giønette had previously been married to another second-generation Scot called Jørgen Johnsen Fife.[98] However, for Robert Fife, taking up residence in Stavanger didn't imply a complete break with Bergen. In 1666 he gave his son, Robert Robertson, permission to sell property there and to use the money to continue his studies.[99]

Some immigrants also seem to have maintained contact with their home country. If involved in foreign trade, continuing old trading links in familiar markets made a lot of sense. Although not documented, it is tempting to assume that Henrich Guthrie kept some business contacts in Montrose after settling in Bergen in 1650, and that knowledge of conditions in Bergen may have reached his future son-in-law Andrew Davidson Christie in this way, motivating him to emigrate as well. This could also have been the case for John Allen and William Robbertsen from Queensferry, and for William Vane or Mane who served as a burgess in Bergen in the 1580s. While visiting Scotland in 1587 he bound himself to a man called Robert Hay, burgess of Kirkcaldy, and noted that Mr. William Mylne, burgess of Bergen, was principal and Andrew Hay in Merkinsche

---

[96] Thomas Beeg is not mentioned as a burgess in the burgess-book. According to one expert, older derivations of the name Begg include Bege and Beig and the name was common in Edinburgh marriage records in the sixteenth and seventeenth centuries. See G. F. Black, *The Surnames of Scotland* (Birlinn edition, Edinburgh: 1999), 66.

[97] Nicolaysen, *Bergen Borgerbog*, 80.

[98] Axel Kielland, *Stavanger Borgerbok 1436–1850* (Stavanger: 1935).

[99] Erichsen, *Samlinger til Stavangers historie I*, 342.

was cautioner for surety and principle debtor for him.[100] This case not only proves continued links with Scotland, but that Scots in Bergen entered into business relationships with each other at home and abroad.

Not surprisingly, several immigrants appear to have been involved in the timber trade, linking them to their native country. In customs accounts for the Sunnhordland region south of the city, Bergen burgesses with Scottish-sounding names appear occasionally. In 1616 a burgess called Joenn Hay chartered a Lübeck-registered ship for timber cargo. Henry Watson did the same thing two years earlier; he chartered a Greifswald-registered ship, and according to the customs official, they were "off to Scotland".[101] It is likely that Henry Watson was familiar with the markets there.

For other Scots, it was not only business affairs which led them to keep contact with their native country. In 1541 an unnamed Scottish burgess in Bergen apparently abandoned his wife, went to Scotland and sailed back to Bergen with another Scottish woman who was still married to someone else. Although probably believing they could find a safe haven for their relationship in Bergen, this might not have been the case. The skipper of the ship, David Leslie, was imprisoned in Bergen for his involvement in the conspiracy.[102]

In the case of the admiral and landowner Axel Mowatt, visits to his father's home country also seem to have extended beyond taking care of his business there. When his nephew Christoffer Orning returned from a trip to Scotland in 1652, he wrote to his uncle saying there wasn't much to report except that Scottish ships had gone elsewhere this year, and probably wouldn't come to Sunnhordland to buy timber. At the end of the letter he extended greetings to his uncle from all his good friends in Scotland, particularly the Scottish ladies.[103] Knowledge of Axel Mowatt reached other levels of Scottish society as well. In the 1652 text *The Jewel* by Sir Thomas Urquhart of Cromarty, Admiral Axel Mowatt is mentioned in a comprehensive list of Scotsmen living abroad. Describing Mowatt, Urquhart

---

[100] National Archives of Scotland, RD 1/34, f. 117–118, 29 March 1587.
[101] NRA, Lensregnskaper for Bergenhus len, 1614–1615, 1616–1617.
[102] Hannay, *The Letters of James V*, 431.
[103] Næss, 'Skottehandelen på Sunnhordland', 43.

compares his position in Norway to that of a viceroy—which, although influential, Mowatt most certainly was not.[104]

Judging by the sheer number of Scots settling in Bergen in the early 1600s, the business opportunities presented by the town must have been common knowledge in Scotland. Bergen remained an important port of call for Scottish traders, providing a constant line of communication back home. There were fewer Scots in the neighbouring city of Stavanger, but due to the survival of seventeenth-century court books, we know more about their lives than those of their contemporaries in Bergen.[105] Jørgen Johnsen Pheiff (Fife), mentioned above, was involved in a fight in 1627 with a certain Gims Lindsay, and according to witnesses, not much could be understood of the disagreement which started the fight, since they were speaking in Scots.[106] Being a second-generation Scot, Jørgen's knowledge of the Scottish language was perhaps conditioned by these contacts with his father's countrymen. Jørgen's father-in-law William Kay seems to have been well-known in Scotland. When William Hunter visited Stavanger in 1622, he was summoned to court by William Kay for having spread the rumour that Kay had left Scotland after having killed a man.[107]

The existence of Scottish settlements in Norway may also have been important to Scots trading in the country. David Falconer, whose commercial interests in Norway and Bergen were revealed through his continued support for Christiern II's cause, apparently had contacts among the Scottish burgesses in Bergen. However we can only speculate whether this had any impact on the outcome of the case in which he finally gained satisfaction for his arrested ship *Peter* and its cargo in 1529.

Despite the evidence of continued links with Scotland and a degree of internal cooperation and intermarriage, the findings are nevertheless ambiguous. In terms of both marriage patterns and business

---

[104] Murdoch, *Britain, Denmark-Norway and the House of Stuart*, 29–30, and Murdoch, 'Scotsmen on the Danish-Norwegian frontiers', 1.

[105] From the late 1500s to the early 1700s we have fairly definite knowledge of twenty two Scottish immigrants in Stavanger. (Based on material from: Kielland, *Stavanger Borgerbok*, J. Elgvin, *En by i kamp, Stavanger bys historie 1536–1814* (Stavanger: 1956) and Erichsen, *Samlinger til Stavangers historie*.)

[106] Erichsen, *Samlinger til Stavangers historie I*, 219.

[107] Erichsen, *Samlinger til Stavangers historie I*, 100.

cooperation the sources also contain evidence of inter-ethnic relationships. Scottish immigrants in Bergen seem to have been an integral part of the urban community by the seventeenth century. When
the economic power of the Hansa was broken in the late sixteenth
century, the Scots entered a welcoming society in every respect, one
in which they were happy to integrate rather than challenge for
superiority.

Conclusion

Scottish contacts with Bergen and the surrounding timber-trade area
extend far beyond the time frame set for this study. Scottish traders
had arrived in the city from the end of the High Middle Ages,[108]
and throughout the eighteenth century British freight offered significant
competition to the city's own shipping. Timber exports were now
mainly to British markets. In 1760, no less than fifty seven out of
sixty nine ships carrying timber from Bergen were bound for Scotland
and England.[109] Regarding immigration, the occasional Scottish settler appears in sources before the sixteenth century,[110] and although
there was a definite decline after 1660, a new wave of Scottish skippers and merchants settled in Bergen around 1700. Throughout the
eighteenth century, new Scotsmen were admitted to the burgess-ship
every once in a while.[111]

Nevertheless the period from the early 1500s until 1660 stands
out in the history of Scottish immigration to Bergen. Throughout
this time, the number of Scotsmen at any level of Bergen society
was significant. Political ties between the Stuart and Oldenburg
monarchies provide one explanation for this influx. Based on the
burgess-policies of Christiern II, it is safe to say that Scots were
greatly welcomed, and as representatives of a close political ally,

---

[108] Helle, *Bergen bys historie I*, 378.

[109] Fossen, *Bergen bys historie II*, 579, 630. Although the 'Scottish timber-trade' is
associated with the period before 1700, Scotland also maintained a hegemony on
the export of timber from the Sunnhordland region south of Bergen until the 1750s.
(A. Næss, "Skottehandelen på Sunnhordland", 63–64).

[110] Helle, *Bergen bys historie I*, 804. In 1341 reference is made to a resident tailor
named Jon Skot, and a century later a figure named Jørgen Scot is mentioned as
a mariner trading with the north of Norway.

[111] Nedrebø, 'Fra Skandinavias største by til Strilane sin hovudstad', 50.

probably deliberately brought in to provide competition to the powerful Hansa merchants. John Thommessen Scot and his fellow countrymen certainly managed to make their presence felt among the privileged German communities. Despite insignificant political contact between Scotland and Denmark-Norway from 1530–80, the Scottish component of the Bergen population apparently remained strong. Once firmly established earlier in the century, their presence probably encouraged more immigrants who were tempted by the lucrative prospects offered by the deteriorating Hansa position. The Bergen burgess-book reveals numerous Scottish names in this period, and more following the confirmation of state relations by the 1589 alliance. This treaty doubtless boosted migration, as Scottish citizens were promised equal status to Danes and Norwegians in the Oldenburg empire. The overwhelming number of Scotsmen admitted as burgesses from 1613–30 (making them the third-largest foreign group in the burgess-ship) at a time when relations between the two monarchies were relatively good, does indeed suggest that the positive political climate had an impact on migration. However, the setback in Stuart-Oldenburg relations from the accession of Charles I onwards does not seem to have had an immediately adverse effect. Immigration had fallen to insignificant levels by the 1660s, by which time Steve Murdoch has concluded that the royal alliances of the Stuart and Oldenburg monarchies had come to an end. Scotland—and the rest of the British state—was in fact technically at war with Denmark-Norway after 1665, during the second Anglo-Dutch War (1664–1667).[112]

Trade seems to have been a much less vulnerable element of the relationship between Scotland and Denmark-Norway, and trade relations no doubt still influenced migration. At a time when Stuart-Oldenburg relations started to suffer, Scottish trade with Bergen was as important as ever. Handling 47% of the timber export with the English, Scottish traders were firmly established in Bergen, chartering ships and storing goods for the city's retail trade.

However, the background to the history of Scottish immigration to Bergen in this period is not entirely covered by Stuart-Oldenburg politics or trade relations. The considerable number of immigrants from the Northern Isles carried with them an identity of shared

---

[112] Murdoch, *Britain, Denmark-Norway and the House of Stuart*, 185–186.

history and cultural kinship with the Norwegian city, which separated them from mainland Scots. The fact that contemporaries denoted people from the Shetland isles as Hjelts rather than Scots proves this point. This background, coupled with the obvious advantage of geography, provides a likely explanation as to why so many Scots settled in Bergen at this time.

That immigration numbers never again reached early seventeenth-century levels can also be explained by the emergence of alternative destinations for Scottish emigration. According to Christopher Smout, Scottish emigration went increasingly southwards and westwards from the second half of the seventeenth century on, to destinations such as the Dutch Provinces, England, Northern Ireland and North America.[113] In the case of the Northern Isles, the migratory influence of cultural links with Norway must have become less important two centuries after the pledging of the islands to the Scottish Crown. However, the rather abrupt halt to immigration from the Northern Isles after 1660 is probably more accurately explained by the development of a new trading relationship with the Dutch Provinces, based on the rich herring fisheries beyond Shetland.[114]

Having discussed the issue of why Bergen was such an important destination for Scottish emigration, a few interesting points still need to be highlighted. There can be no doubt that Scottish immigrants had a decisive impact on the development of a competitive burgess-ship in Bergen in the early sixteenth century. The reaction of the privileged German communities show that these burgesses hit a nerve and the fact that the violence was directed against Scots in particular cannot be underestimated. In addition to their business enterprises, Scots also provided premises for some of these activities. Scottish trade was a continued feature of early sixteenth-century Bergen, and through the privileges of 1509 and 1541, the authorities ensured that the burgesses benefited from this trade. Clearly the Scots were a strong presence as the city entered a new economic era.

As noted, the privileged trading communities' attempt to strike at their competition was a complete failure. Throughout the sixteenth

---

[113] T. C. Smout, 'Scottish emigration in the seventeenth and eighteenth centuries', in Nicholas Canny, ed., *Europeans on the move* (Oxford: 1994), 86.

[114] L. Daae, "Om berøringer mellom Orknøerne og Hjaltland og moderlandet Norge efter 1468", 48–49.

century they witnessed a steady influx of immigrants to the Bergen burgess-ship, paralleled by a setback in their own position which led eventually to the phasing out of their hegemony altogether. Scottish immigrants nourished the burgess-ship through considerable recruitment. Although the Scots victims of the 1523 attack actually left the country for a while, their determination to gain compensation reveals that they were not prepared to back down. Nor were they weakened to the extent that they were forced to do so. On the contrary, the letters written to the authorities from the late 1520s on, when they were back in Bergen, indicate the strength of the community. The Scots appear firmly settled in the city and there is a pronounced sense of community among them. Although other victims were mentioned, the letters presented only the Scots' economic losses and were exclusively signed by them. As a distinct group who gained a secure foothold in urban society, their presence triggered a wave of immigration from Scotland. For a century and a half, this influx was to characterize the population of Bergen, less as a challenging phenomenon, and more and more as an integrated and harmonious part of the city's economic life.[115]

[115] I would like to extend my gratitude to Professor Sølvi Sogner at the University of Oslo and Dr Steve Murdoch at the University of St Andrews for their valuable contribution to my Masters degree on Scottish immigration to Norway in the early modern period.

Two views of the Rosenkrantz Tower in Bergen, completed by Scottish Masons in the 1560s. Photos© Reidun Østby Pedersen

SCOTS ALONG THE MAAS, C.1570–1750

Douglas Catterall

Between October 1493 and January 1494 Andrew Halyburton, Conservator and chief factor for the Scots staple in Middelburg, carried out a series of transactions for a group of merchants. Among them were the Scots Laurence Tailliefer, James of Towring, John of Twedy, John Quythed and James Comyng. Other Scots, such as the shipmaster James Makysson, helped make Halyburton's brokering for his fellow Scots possible, moving their goods from Scotland to Middelburg, where Halyburton sold them or forwarded them to the market in Bergen op Zoom. The buyers of the mainly woollen goods hailed from the Low Countries. They came from Tourcoing, Doornik, and the southern Dutch city of Rotterdam. Rotterdam had by the early sixteenth century established itself within the network of northern Low Countries towns trading with England, although it was by no means the most significant. However it figured far less in the world of Scots trade, the focal point of most Scots at that time being in Zeeland, due to the staple there.[1]

Some two hundred and fifty years after Halyburton's transactions had run their course, Rotterdam was tightly integrated into the economy of eastern Scotland. The propinquity books of the royal burgh of Aberdeen, for example, show that voyages between the city and Rotterdam were common. Moreover, the business connected to these voyages involved Scots at both ends. Scots residents were in fact a thriving group in eighteenth-century Rotterdam, and had been since at least the middle of the seventeenth century.[2]

---

[1] On Halyburton's putative position see J. Davidson and A. Gray, *The Scottish Staple at Veere: A Study in the Economic History of Scotland* (London: 1909), 390–391. For a summary of the transactions see *Bronnen tot de geschiedenis van den handel met Engeland, Schotland en Ierland, Tweede Deel, 1485–1585: Eerste Stuk, 1485–1558*, ed. H. Jakob Smit ('s-Gravenhage: 1942), 53.

[2] On Aberdeen's connections to Rotterdam in the eighteenth century, see for example Aberdeen City Archives, Old Town House, Propinquity Books, 2–4, 1706–1797.

Measuring the ebb and flow of economic transactions between the city on the Maas and the towns of Scotland's eastern coast is far beyond the scope of a limited work such as this. Instead some of the social structures that enabled the development of what can be called Scots Rotterdam will be explored. In particular it will be suggested that Scots Rotterdam was a fusion of medieval traditions of mercantile/maritime migration; Atlantic-world trade; and Scots and Dutch patterns of social ties that allowed Scots and Rotterdamers to flourish, even as the Dutch Republic and Scotland did not.

The Medieval Foundations of Scots Rotterdam

In the last decade or so scholars have recognized the importance of Scotland's medieval migration heritage.[3] One of the most striking things about Scotland's history is its fundamental dependence on migration at a number of levels, a dependence that scholars are now exploring in great detail and which no doubt has its parallels in other regions of Europe such as Livonia and Courland.[4] One early

---

[3] For incorporation of the medieval tradition of Scots migration into the succeeding era see *i.a.* D. Catterall, *Community without Borders: Scots Migrants and the Changing Face of Power in the Dutch Republic, c.1600–1700* (Boston and Leiden: 2002); N. C. Landsman, 'Nation, Migration, and the Province in the First British Empire: Scotland and the Americas, 1600–1800,' *American Historical Review* 104, no. 2 (1999): 464–468; Thomas Riis, *Should Auld Acquaintance Be Forgot: Scottish-Danish Relations, c.1450–1707*, 2 vols. (Odense: 1988); and T. C. Smout, N. C. Landsman, and T. M. Devine, 'Scottish Emigration in the Seventeenth and Eighteenth Centuries,' in *Scotland and the Sea*, ed. T. C. Smout (Edinburgh: 1992), 76–77. Medievalists have done the core work, some of which can be found in several volumes edited by Grant Simpson: G. G. Simpson ed., *Scotland and Scandinavia, 800–1800* (Edinburgh: 1992); G. G. Simpson ed., *The Scottish Soldier Abroad, 1247–1967* (Edinburgh: 1992); and G. G. Simpson ed., *Scotland and the Low Countries, 1124–1949* (East Linton: 1996). See also the work of David Ditchburn and Alexander Stevenson on medieval Scots trade: D. Ditchburn, 'Trade with Northern Europe, 1297–1540,' in *The Scottish Medieval Town*, eds., M. Lynch, M. Spearman, and G. Stell (Edinburgh: 1988), 161–179 and A. Stevenson, 'Trade with the South, 1070–1513,' in *The Scottish Medieval Town*, 180–206.

[4] Probably the best example of a comprehensive exploration of Scotland's international migration heritage during the pre-industrial era was the 2000–2003 research project at the Research Institute for Irish and Scottish Studies undertaken by Alexia Grosjean and Steve Murdoch. For an overview see S. Murdoch, 'The Database in Early Modern Scottish History: Scandinavia and Northern Europe, 1580–1707,' *Northern Studies: the Journal of the Scottish Society for Northern Studies* 32 (1997): 83–103. Internal migration in Scotland has been the subject of inquiry for some time. For

modernist, Ned Landsman, has even argued that Scots of all ranks both in and beyond Scotland had little attachment to specific places. Instead, he suggests that Scots participated in a more malleable concept of community, supported by their socio-professional networks that allowed easy transfer from one place to another.[5] To my knowledge the work has not yet been done to prove conclusively Landsman's contentions for migration within Scotland, which he applies even to the broad majority of Scottish rural society as well as urban society.[6] Nevertheless, his thesis is in keeping with work by other scholars that also points to the embedded nature of migration within Scots culture. It is the deep rooting of migration practices into Scots society that explains the spread of Scots communities in the Low Countries (and elsewhere) and which underlay the creation of Scots Rotterdam.

The Scots presence in the Low Countries rapidly took on an official profile, as readily-available primary and secondary sources reveal. The initial locus of Scots migration and settlement ran from northern Normandy (Artois) northward to Bruges and its port Damme. St Omer in southern Flanders and Arras in Artois were the first places to which Scots traders and wayfarers went. The city of Bruges, however, provides the first evidence of major Scots settlement.[7] Precisely when this community came into existence is hard to say, as a fire destroyed Bruges' earliest records in 1280.[8] Nevertheless, it

---

a good survey of work in the early 1990s see Ian D. Whyte, 'Migration in early-modern Scotland and England: A comparative perspective,' in *Migrants, Emigrants and Immigrant: A social history of migration*, eds. Colin G. Pooley and Ian D. Whyte (London and New York: 1991), 87–105. On this topic see also R. A. Houston, 'The Demographic Regime,' in *People and Society in Scotland, 1760–1830* vol. 1, eds. T. M. Devine and R. Mitchison (Edinburgh: 1988), 9–26. Unfortunately, this work has not yet been essentially linked with the international migration picture, partly as a result of the perception on the part of some historians that Scots who migrated abroad were a selective group. For a brief overview of the impact of migration on Livonia and Courland see A. Plakans, *The Latvians: A Short History* (Stanford, CA: 1995), 1–29.

[5] N. C. Landsman, 'Introduction: The Context and Functions of Scottish Involvement with the Americas,' in N. C. Landsman, ed., *Nation and Province in the First British Empire* (Lewisburg, PA: 2001), 21.

[6] While Landsman, for example, argues that the extensive powers of landlords in Scotland gave tenants "little permanence upon their lands," Ian Whyte has suggested that prior to the eighteenth century landlords actually had an interest in maintaining tenants on their lands. See Landsman, 'Introduction,' 21 and Whyte, 'Migration in early-modern Scotland,' 92–94.

[7] I. Flett and J. Cripps, 'Documentary Sources,' in *The Scottish Medieval Town*, 22.

[8] Flett and Cripps, 'Documentary Sources', 22.

is likely that it did not happen until after 1250. In any case, by the 1290s a portion of the main canal in Bruges was known as the '*Schottendyc*' (*i.e.* the dike of the Scots), and a nearby street was called 'Scotland.'[9] How large this community was is debatable, but the fact that the Scots were the only foreigners in Bruges to have their district so publicly recognized suggests that it was certainly important. The Scots community of the 1290s probably managed to weather the Wars of Independence, as relations with Bruges were maintained and even strengthened throughout this period, though not without friction.[10] In fact, Bruges' support for Scots resistance to English aggression (more than likely supported by the Scots community in Bruges) strengthened the relationship. The first staple contract between Scotland and Bruges probably stems from this trying time, most likely in the period from 1313–1321.[11] Indeed, Bruges was an important part of Scots trading activities in the Low Countries up to the end of the fifteenth century.

This continuity probably had much to do with the stability of Scots migration structures. It certainly cannot be said that political stability in the Low Countries was behind this enduring institutional uniformity. The alternating, interconnected conflicts between the English, the French, the Scots and the inhabitants of the Low Countries, which frequently disrupted trade throughout the fourteenth and fifteenth centuries, meant that the Low Countries were anything but stable. The inroads of English naval blockades at the end of the fourteenth century finally made locating the staple in Middelburg in Zeeland feasible. Although Middelburg was perennially vying for Scots custom, other towns in Zeeland and Holland also began to attract the attention of Scots merchants and political leaders. Veere, which ultimately won the contest for the Scots staple in the Low Countries, is first mentioned in the 1440s, when a sister of the Scots king married its patron. Bergen op Zoom and

---

[9] Stevenson, 'Trade with the South,' 187.

[10] Revolts in Flanders in 1303/4 and 1323/4 disturbed the generally good relations between the two nations; on both occasions the Flemings ordered the confiscation of Scots goods. See Stevenson, 'The Flemish Dimension of the Auld Alliance', 36–37.

[11] Stevenson, 'The Flemish Dimension of the Auld Alliance', 37. For a readily available collection of primary sources that suggest much of what I outline here using secondary literature, see H. J. Smit, ed., *Bronnen tot de geschiedenis van den handel met Engeland, Schotland en Ierland, 1150–1585* 4 vols., Rijksgeschiedkundige publicatiën, vols., 65, 66, 86, 91 ('s-Gravenhage: 1928–1950).

Antwerp (though not in Zeeland), which had emerged by the second half of the fifteenth century on the strength of their twice-yearly international fairs were also involved. Even expanding their range into more northerly portions of the Low Countries did not free Scots traders from the disruptions of conflict. The location of the Scots staple changed no fewer than nine times in the fifteenth century due to the outbreak of war. Even the idea of a staple was in flux, given the tendency for merchants from a particular royal burgh to build up their own 'staple' relationship with a town in Zeeland independently of other royal burghs. Thus, according to Ian Blanchard, Edinburgh wool merchants in the late fifteenth and early sixteenth centuries frequented Middelburg, while Veere attracted merchants from Aberdeen.[12]

Yet despite these vicissitudes, the evidence is that Scots became citizens in many of these towns. They established a network of Scots enclaves across the Low Countries region, in places such as Dieppe, Middelburg, Bergen op Zoom, and Veere. Thus, when Scots began settling in Rotterdam in appreciable numbers, they did not do so *de novo*, but were rather part of a long history of Scots settlement in the Low Countries. [13]

The Staple as Cultural Conduit for Scots Rotterdam

The central institution for understanding Scots trade during the medieval period in the Low Countries is the staple. It is by now well-established that the forms of rules and contracts discussed above guaranteed the monopoly of neither the royal burghs nor of the staple ports in the Dutch Republic in the early modern period.[14] In the medieval period the institution of the staple port was rarely even

---

[12] Flet and Cripps, 'Documentary Sources', 22; Davidson and Gray, *The Scottish Staple at Veere*, 115–165; Stevenson, 'Trade with the South,' esp. 192–199; Stevenson, 'The Flemish Dimension,' 33–42.

[13] For some evidence of Scots establishing citizenship in Low Countries towns in the medieval period see Flett and Cripps, 'Documentary Sources', 22; Stevenson, 'Trade with the South', 193, 199.

[14] I. D. Whyte, *Scotland before the Industrial Revolution: An Economic & Social History, c.1050–1750*, Longman Economic & Social History of Britain, ed. J. V. Beckett (London and New York: 1995), 284.

intended to guarantee a monopoly, but merely to safeguard and promote Scots trading interests.[15] But perhaps the staple port, and the
contracts and trading practices connected to it, served another, equally
important if unintended, function. Rather than focusing on the moribund economic potential of the staple in the early modern period,
it might be more useful to see it as one of the common sources for
Scots settlement and economic strategies in the Low Countries.
Viewed in this light, the staple in the early modern period was less
a throwback to medieval times and more a cultural conduit con-
necting the two eras.

By 1541 if not before, the Zeeland town of Veere had succeeded
in becoming the host of the Scots staple, a distinction it would never
again lose for any appreciable length of time. The driving force
behind the staple was the royal burghs' statutory if not always enforce-
able monopoly over Scotland's foreign trade, a concession first
confirmed in a 1364 charter from the reign of David II.[16] The
monopoly on foreign trade recognized the importance of the royal
burghs to state revenues and served as a recompense for the royal
burghs' contributions to David II's ransom payments from 1357–1373.
It was also a result of the higher political profile royal burghs began
to achieve in the first quarter of the fourteenth century, which saw
burgesses attending Parliament with regularity after 1357 and acquiring their own representative body, the Convention of Royal Burghs,
in 1487.[17]

Contracts that established a staple port were drawn up between
a local community and a community of foreigners, defined as a
nation or *natie* in Dutch. They were not in any way unique to the
Scots in the Low Countries but rather a product of mercantile and
political interests within the Low Countries on the one hand, and
politically and quasi-ethnically defined groups of merchants on the
other. In its ultimate form, the principle behind the staple was sim-

---

[15] See above for the effective existence of multiple 'staple' ports in the fifteenth
century, Middelburg for Edinburgh and Veere for Aberdeen.

[16] T. Keith, 'The Trading Privileges of the Royal Burghs of Scotland,' in *English
Historical Review*, vol. 28 (1913), 457–458.

[17] Whyte, *Scotland before*, 68–71; Davidson and Gray, *The Scottish Staple at Veere*,
142–166; and M. P. Rooseboom, *The Scottish Staple in the Netherlands: An Account of
the trade Relations between Scotland and the Low Countries from 1292 till 1676, with a
Calendar of Illustrative Documents* (The Hague: 1910), 28–85.

ply expressed. Scots merchants from all royal burghs who had staple wares (chief among them salmon, raw wool, hides and plaiding) to sell in the Low Countries were to have them conveyed to one port, the staple port. Here the wares would typically be sold at a common price by specified factors, who returned the proceeds to the originating merchant minus a commission. The staple also guaranteed the Scots certain legal rights, freedoms and privileges, and exemptions from duties, monetary and otherwise, in the staple port. Finally, the ideas behind the staple port supported a legally-defined sense of ethnicity.[18]

The Contractual Dimensions of the Scots Staple in the Low Countries

The contract signed between Dordrecht and the Convention, dated 7 July 1669, shows the staple privileges that Scots achieved in the Low Countries in the period of their fullest development, although the staple itself had been considerably weakened by that time. The relevance of this charter will become apparent as one of Dordrecht's competitors for the staple in the 1660s was Rotterdam, and adaptations of the staple concept evolved in the city on the Maas.

---

[18] Davidson and Gray, *The Scottish Staple at Veere*, 115–127, 142–210, 417–424, 390–404; Rooseboom, *The Scottish Staple in the Netherlands*, 5–85, V-C. The earliest contracts between Scots merchants and Low Countries polities stem from the fourteenth century, when Bruges and sometimes Middelburg served as hubs if not true staple ports. In the earliest extant charters of privileges for Scots merchants, usually between the Scots Crown speaking for the Scots mercantile community and the Count of Flanders with input from Bruges, one finds the broad outlines of the personal and commercial rights that would typify the more highly developed staple contracts. Scots received rights with regard to legal proceedings against them in civil and criminal causes; they received concessions with regard to securing debts from transactions; guarantees of security for person and property were given; and the right to sell wholesale and retail was conceded. It was with the early fifteenth century and the 1407 contract with Bruges that the Scots staple began to take on its more final form. This contract offered Scots merchants the right to have so-called commissaries who would defend their interests. It also offered Scots the same privileges, freedoms, immunities and amenities that other foreign merchants in Bruges received. Not until the sixteenth century, however, were firm commitments finally made to create a single and true staple port, and not until this time does the concept of the *natie* or nation make regular appearances in contracts. On the broader European context that made the Scots staple possible see R. Bartlett, *The Making of Europe: Conquest, Colonization, and Cultural Change, 950–1350* (Princeton, NJ: 1994), 182–196.

It is fairly easy to break down the 1669 contract with Dordrecht into three groups of clauses. One major category which the staple contract covered was infrastructure. The staple contract guaranteed housing at a fair price for all "marchants, factores, shipmasters, seamen, collectors, and others . . ." and contained a promise to provide housing gratis for the officers of the staple: the Conservator, the secretary, the treasurer and the Presbyterian minister.[19] Dordrecht's city fathers also agreed to assist in the provision of additional personnel, whether Scots or Dutch. There was also a provision for a hostel that was to be supplied only by arrangement with the Conservator. This was in addition to ample harbours and harbour facilities, financial facilities and many amenities, such as a recreation site and freedom to hunt and fish. A second group of clauses in the contract concerned the freedoms, rights and privileges accruing to each individual member of the staple and also the jurisdiction of the Lord Conservator as representative of the Scots nation in Dordrecht. The agreement promised security for the members of the staple, including safe transport out of the country in time of war. The personal incomes of the members of the staple were to be free from taxation. Moreover, members of the staple were to operate in a different legal environment. Disagreements and crimes among members were solely in the Lord Conservator's jurisdiction so long as both parties were Scots. *Dordtenaars* could choose to prosecute a Scot before the Conservator or Dordrecht's *schepenen* in the case of civil suits, but once begun a suit could not be transferred to the other jurisdiction. In civil suits, Scots and members of the staple could choose to prosecute *Dordtenaars* either before the Conservator or the Dordrecht courts; these latter courts were to keep a separate roll for expediting the causes involving members of the staple. In criminal prosecutions, except *ex officio* cases, the accused staple member if apprehended had the right to have his accuser apprehended also until the accuser had proven the justness of his case. Nor could any arrests for debt take place without notification to the Lord Conservator. Individual rights in the matters of bankruptcy, intestacy and indigence were

---

[19] *Extracts from the Records of the Convention of the Royal Burghs of Scotland, 1615–1676,* vol. 3 of *Records of the Convention of the Royal Burghs of Scotland: with extracts from other records relating to the affairs of the burghs of Scotland* 4 vols., ed. J. D. Marwick (Edinburgh: 1866–1880), 677–678.

also covered by the contract. Finally, the Dordrecht staple contract extended some economic privileges tied to transactions.[20] Staple goods were to be free from customs and the *Dordtenaars* promised to make an effort to free other key non-staple goods, such as 'Scots coall' and 'whyt Scotts salt' from imposts and dues.[21]

The staple also had a more punitive side for Scots and non-Scots who might wish to violate it or who did not want to adhere to the spirit of its rules. A sense of this dimension can be gained from a set of regulations passed by the Convention of Royal Burghs in 1649, at which time Veere was the staple port. It is not necessary to note here all those regulations pertaining to the conflicts that were then unfolding in the British Isles. The first two articles essentially forbade the shipping of staple wares by Scots or non-Scots shippers to any but the staple port in Veere. The Lord Conservator was to prosecute violators, whether merchants or shippers. Alternatively, transgressors could be prosecuted in the appropriate royal burgh, if the occasion should offer itself. Once staple goods had arrived in the Dutch Republic, the articles forbade their sale anywhere else but in the staple port and then only through the authorized channels. Factors were admonished to be present at all unloading and loading of vessels and were also commanded to meet at least twice a year to agree on the prices for staple goods. These prices, once agreed, were not to vary from merchant to merchant, for the factor was not to "play the marchand".[22] Moreover, there was to be no bargaining with those who would not accept bills of exchange from the factors or merchants of the staple. Finally, the Lord Conservator was to be considered the primary judge for all Scots tied to the staple. In addition, all persons wishing to have the goods of another arrested had to provide sufficient proof that he would be able to pay the damages to the innocent party if his cause should fail.[23]

---

[20] *Extracts from the Records of the Convention of the Royal Burghs of Scotland*, 677–686.
[21] *Extracts from the Records of the Convention of the Royal Burghs of Scotland*, 679.
[22] *Extracts from the Records of the Convention of the Royal Burghs of Scotland*, 349.
[23] *Extracts from the Records of the Convention of the Royal Burghs of Scotland*, 348–352.

Rotterdam as a 'Staple' Port in the Seventeenth Century

There is some striking overlap between the agreements and arrangements that the Scots reached with their Dutch hosts in Rotterdam and what Dordrecht and Veere respectively offered to members of the staple. This is worth noting, because these arrangements committed Rotterdam to changing its legal jurisdiction and to offering significant financial resources to a community of foreigners from whom it could expect no guaranteed profit, such as it could from the Sephardim, for example.[24] Nor was this solely down to religious affinity, since Rotterdam had English Presbyterians aplenty who never gained the same privileges as the Scots.[25]

The core institution around which Scots in Rotterdam eventually consolidated their presence was the Scots Church of Rotterdam. Too often historians have seen its foundation as the real beginning of the Scots community in Rotterdam, which is far from the case. A steady Scots military presence (begun in 1572 with the siege of Haarlem) as well as a strong mercantile/maritime component, typified the Scots settlement long before the Scots church came into existence. However, it is with the 1643 founding of the Scots Church of Rotterdam that the principles surrounding the Scots community's existence in Rotterdam became more clearly defined. Firstly, the church was founded in an agreement between the *Schotse natie* and the city fathers of Rotterdam, much as agreements that underlay the Scots staple

---

[24] On the Sephardim's economic role in the Dutch Republic's rise to mercantile prominence see J. de Vries and A. van der Woude, *The First Modern Economy: Success, Failure, and Perseverance of the Dutch Economy, 1500–1815* (Cambridge: 1995), 368. On the presence of the Sephardim in Rotterdam see Jonathan Israel, *The Dutch Republic: Its Rise, Greatness, and Fall, 1477–1806* (Oxford: 1995), 658, 1020, 1025; Daniel M. Swetschinski, *Reluctant Cosmopolitans: The Portuguese Jewry of Seventeenth-Century Amsterdam* (London & Portland, OR: The Littman Library of Jewish Civilization, 2000), 11, 33–40, 94–96.

[25] It is important to remember that the Merchant Adventurers certainly did extract significant privileges from Rotterdam, but this was far from being an institution run by Calvinists. The fundamental works on the Merchant Adventurers in Rotterdam are still R. Bijlsma, 'Rotterdams Handelsverkeer met Engeland tijdens het verblijf der Merchant Adventurers, 1635–1652,' *Bijdragen voor Vaderlandsche Geschiedenis en Oudheidkunde* 5th ser., 4 (1917): 81–107 and C. te Lintum, *De Merchant Adventurers in de Nederlanden* ('s-Gravenhage: 1905). On the English Independent and Presbyterian congregations in Rotterdam see K. Sprunger, *Dutch Puritanism: A History of English and Scottish Churches of the Netherlands in the Sixteenth and Seventeenth Centuries* (Leiden: 1982), 162–175, 428–431.

port in the Low Countries had been. Secondly, the Scots obtained some definite statutory privileges from Rotterdam's city fathers. By 1653, the material support on offer from the city fathers included a substantial poor relief subsidy backed by the promise of municipal poor relief for all Scots born in Rotterdam and salaries for the Scots minister and other personnel, as well as money for the church fabric. Finally, on the legal side, the city fathers, with the consistory of the Rotterdam Dutch Reformed congregation as their agents, created a sphere of legal influence for the Scots Church of Rotterdam's session, albeit not intentionally.[26]

On paper, none of these things may appear to resemble or even rival the types of privileges that the staple ports offered to their Scots 'nations'. A closer look at everyday practices, however, suggests otherwise, and the jurisdiction of the Rotterdam kirk session will be considered first. *De jure*, the session had no more power than the church councils of Rotterdam's Independent churches, whose governance the Scots Church of Rotterdam's first minister, Alexander Petrie, scathingly derided. First, Petrie and his session members were denied the right to sit in the Classis of Schieland, the equivalent of the presbytery in Rotterdam and environs. This effectively cut the Rotterdam session's discipline off at the knees. Moreover, the ecclesiastical authorities of Rotterdam went even further. They stated in effect that only those who chose to be bound by the session's jurisdiction could be subject to its discipline. In other words, only Scots who voluntarily joined the Scots Church of Rotterdam and agreed to be bound to it as full members were subject to the session's discipline.[27]

However, the reality of the Rotterdam session's jurisdiction was otherwise. It departed from both Dutch Reformed and Independent norms, resembling a kirk session in Scotland more than it did its many Rotterdam counterparts. For one thing, especially in its early

[26] See H. Dunthorne, 'Scots in the Wars of the Low Countries, 1572–1648,' in *Scotland and the Low Countries*, 104–121; J. MacLean, *De huwelijksintekeningen van Schotse militairen in Nederland, 1574–1665* (Zutphen: 1976), 226–257; *Bronnen tot de geschiedenis van den handel met Engeland, Schotland en Ierland, Tweede Deel, 1485–1585: Eeerste Stuk, 1485–1558*, ed., H. J. Smit ('s-Gravenhage: 1942), 1151; Gemeentearchief Rotterdam (hereafter GAR)/Oud Stadsarchief (hereafter OSA)/719, 890v, 918v–919r; GAR/OSA/721/480, 8-2-1653; Catterall, *Community without Borders*, 202–206; and Sprunger, *Dutch Puritanism*, 175–178.
[27] Catterall, *Community without Borders*, 243–248.

decades of operation, the Rotterdam session regularly threatened parishioners with fines for trespasses against its rules, a form of penalty that Dutch Reformed churches were never allowed to assess. Nor were the Dutch Reformed churches allowed to have parishioners imprisoned, corporally punished, or pursued at law. All of these are actions that the Rotterdam session took on a fairly regular basis throughout the mid-1660s, and continued to engage in sporadically even after that time in the seventeenth century.[28]

To carry out the disciplinary regime outlined above, the Rotterdam session members used their official status as a *natie* with a sanctioned presence to develop ties to the authorities in Rotterdam, effectively co-opting them in building their *de facto* jurisdiction. The bailie of Rotterdam, who acted as chief of police, chief prosecutor and sheriff all at once, worked fairly closely with the Rotterdam session members. In addition, the session members had no compunction about lending the session's support to the legal suits of parishioners whom it wanted to support, regardless of the implications of such partisanship for the purity of the Eucharist or the social stability of the Scots community. Even notarial agreements were employed to project the session's jurisdiction into Rotterdam's public sphere. Lack of official jurisdiction, then, did not ultimately mean that the Scots Church of Rotterdam lacked influence in Rotterdam's public sphere.[29]

Poor relief also underwent an important metamorphosis, again underwritten by the initial contract between the Scots *natie* and the Rotterdam city fathers. The shift in thinking with regard to poor relief came first from the Rotterdam authorities themselves. Seeing that there were several stranger churches in their midst, the city fathers and particularly the Dutch Reformed congregation sought to limit their responsibility for poor relief among the newcomers.[30] What was at first intended as a cost-saving measure, however, ultimately resulted in a fundamental shift in the way people in Rotterdam thought about poor relief. As Charles Parker among others has shown, poor relief in the Dutch Republic was often confessionally mediated. The Dutch Reformed congregations strove, whenever possible, to

---

[28] Catterall, *Community without Borders*, 194–230.
[29] Catterall, *Community without Borders*, 194–230, 253–292.
[30] Catterall, *Community without Borders*, 82–84 and Schoor, *Stad in aanwas*. 268–270.

care only for the poor of their own faith community. In many cities and communities of the Republic, however, imposing this degree of exclusivity was not possible because the city fathers demanded that the Dutch Reformed churches administer poor relief as a public trust. This meant caring for Reformed and non-Reformed alike, although not those who were openly members of other denominations with their own poor relief mechanisms.[31] The Rotterdam city fathers' policy of making stranger churches responsible for the poor of their fellow countrymen was a variation on this tendency among the less ardently Reformed patriciates in the province of Holland to make poor relief public. As a result of the city fathers' initiative, relief would be dispensed for reasons of ethnicity rather than belief or even merit. One might view this as an outgrowth of medieval concepts of corporatism, and there is a degree of accuracy in that point of view. In making ethnicity a criterion for relief, however, the city fathers also changed poor relief, making it possible to reformulate the city's membership in terms of the category of ethnicity, whereas previously the idea of the *gemeente* was more religious and communal in nature. Rotterdam's Scots *natie*, having established its official ties to Rotterdam through a contract, proceeded to deepen them through military service. In a 1653 resolution from the Rotterdam city council, the deaconry of the Scots Church of Rotterdam acquired official responsibility for all Scots-born Scots in Rotterdam apart from those who fought for the Dutch forces in the First Anglo-Dutch War.[32] Thus, those Scots who were 'Dutch' by birth or deeds received relief from the Dutch Reformed Church. Those who were Scots by birth and had not made the political commitment that military service represented received relief monies from the Scots Church of Rotterdam. Some of these monies were actually Rotterdam funds, as the 1653 resolution dedicated 1,200 guilders per year from the Rotterdam treasurer to the deaconry of the Scots Church of Rotterdam. Still, the Scots received these funds on the strength of their official status as a *natie* in Rotterdam.

We can even find the more punitive aspects of the staple contract having some influence on Scots in Rotterdam. Among the more

---

[31] C. H. Parker, *The Reformation of Community: Social Welfare and Calvinist Charity in the Six Great Cities of Holland, 1572–1620* (New York: 1998), esp. 155–190.

[32] Catterall, *Community without Borders*, 82–84; Van der Schoor, *Stad in aanwas*, 268–270; and GAR/Scots Church of Rotterdam Archive (hereafter SCR)/1, 8-3-1653.

frequently enunciated and thus probably more frequently flouted rules associated with Convention regulations governing the staples in the Low Countries was the prohibition on non-freemen working as traders or sailors in the overseas trade zones of the royal burghs. These regulations were rooted in the notion that only burgesses should have the right to trade, and in pre-industrial ideas about the correlation between status and physical appearance. Initially the rulings governing the staple ports were focused solely on mercantile issues and aimed chiefly at men who did not have merchant guild membership trying to pass themselves off as merchants. The medieval origins of these laws are clear in their resemblance to sumptuary legislation and indeed some regulations were effectively sumptuary laws. But in the sixteenth and seventeenth centuries the Convention of Royal Burghs began promulgating laws against other forms of 'unworthiness.' For example, Catholics and so-called scandalous persons wanting to go abroad were targeted. These same ideas of worthiness cropped up occasionally in Rotterdam, as in the cases of female servants who had left Scotland to escape the consequences of out-of-wedlock relationships that had resulted in pregnancy.[33]

Lastly, it is worth noting that the site of the first building for the Scots Church of Rotterdam, in the recently built south-western harbour districts of Rotterdam, became the locus for Scots settlement. The main dike in this district, which was then and is still called the *Schiedamsedijk*, was known in the seventeenth and eighteenth centuries as the *Schotse dijk*. Another alley in this district, the *Wartelaarsgang*, took its name directly from one of the Rotterdam Scots community's more prominent members, James Wardlaw, who was the *koster* of the Scots Church of Rotterdam in the 1640s and 1650s and also worked as a translator of the Scots language into the 1660s.[34]

---

[33] To trace the regulations of the royal burghs see *Records of the Convention of the Royal Burghs of Scotland, passim*. For an example of the application of standards that the royal burghs helped to set see GAR/SCR/1, 10–21–1643. Lest these developments seem limited to the Scots context I note here that Kathy Stuart found a strong concern among the respectable (and not so respectable) over the identification of individuals connected with so-called polluted trades in what is now south-western Germany. See K. Stuart, *Defiled Trades & Social Outcasts: Honor and Ritual Pollution in Early Modern Germany* (Cambridge: 1999).

[34] Catterall, *Community without Borders*, 99–102, 199.

Innovation in Rotterdam

Thus the concept of nation or *natie*, which defined the Scots as a group with particular legal privileges in Rotterdam, came to have other very specific, equally contractual meanings that very much resemble some of the clauses in the staple contracts. At the same time there is no doubt that these meanings also departed from the original intentions of the agreements made between the Scots and the Rotterdam city fathers and from the ideas embedded in staple port contracts. To take the example of poor relief, what at first appeared to be a cost-saving measure for the city government probably increased the city's migration intake and also created a more ethnically tinged definition of membership in Rotterdam's urban community. By making the city more attractive to Scots who did not have a guaranteed place before their arrival, the city fathers ensured that Rotterdam became the destination of choice for Scots bound to the Low Countries. In addition, by defining poor relief according to national birthplace and admitting Scottish-born Scots to relief on the basis of what was effectively national military service, the city fathers made membership of Rotterdam more a matter of ethnicity. In the case of groups targeted for monitoring, such as runaway servants, obviously ideas of unworthiness had been updated to include not just those who might contravene the rules of the staple in the Low Countries, but more generally those who were judged marginal and undesirable.

In the matter of economic arrangements, Rotterdam showed even more distinct departures from the standard practices found among the Scots enterprises in the Low Countries. Since it has been suggested that much of Scotland's trade with the Low Countries started to flow chiefly through Rotterdam in the 1600s, even as the city proved unable to attract the staple port, this is not surprising. Alternative economic arrangements were necessary to make Rotterdam viable without the advantages accruing to a staple port. The arrangements that seventeenth-century Scots Rotterdamers made regarding the coal and tobacco trades are perhaps the most helpful in understanding the changes to the economic dimensions of the medieval Scots legacy of Low Countries settlement.

As the work of C. A. Whatley has made clear, estate owners along Scotland's eastern coast, especially around the Firth of Forth, pursued the complementary production of coal and salt on their estates, beginning in the later 1500s and continuing vigorously into the later 1600s.[35] Coal was an important heating and industrial fuel in the rapidly developing Dutch Republic, and the port of Rotterdam was able to benefit from both its new links to Scotland and the Republic's demand by fostering the coal trade.[36]

Precisely when Scots coal became important to Rotterdam would be difficult to ascertain without a detailed study of the city's notarial archives, beginning with the last quarter of the sixteenth century. However, it is safe to say that by the 1620s Scots coal and Scots importers of this product were integral to Rotterdam's economy. Scots coal was commonly used in nearby Dordrecht's breweries by 1590, and by 1612 the presence of Scots coal in neighbouring Schiedam was sufficient to provoke legislation against its use at any season other than winter. By the 1620s the economic value of Scots coal to Rotterdam was such that the city council was lobbying the provincial States of Holland to prevent the taxation of its import, arguing that it would be a blow to Rotterdam's brewing industry if this fuel were subjected to an impost.[37]

Given the importance of this fuel to Rotterdam's emerging manufactories (*e.g.* beer and brandy breweries and sugar refineries), it is not surprising to find the city government interested in the trade in Scots coal as well. All wholesale transactions in Rotterdam were managed by municipal brokers who received a set amount of money per transaction as mandated by a list of fees set by the city authorities. As with many mid- and low-level municipal functions in Holland's towns, Rotterdam's brokers were organized in a guild. Both the official nature of the broker's duties and his links to a guild might suggest that outsiders would be unwelcome in such an organization. In the case of Scots coal, however, this was not true as there were both Dutch and Scots brokers in the trade. The reason for this is probably obvious enough. Scots knew and understood the Scots coal and carrying trades, both of which were important in bringing coal to Rotterdam. It was therefore good business to employ Scots as brokers.[38]

---

[35] *The Scottish Salt Industry, 1570–1850* (Aberdeen: 1987).

[36] On coal's importance to the Dutch Republic see Z. W. Sneller, *Geschiedenis van den steenkolen handel van Rotterdam* (Groningen: 1946), 62–72.

[37] See Sneller, *Geschiedenis*, 67–69.

[38] See GAR/KOF 1632–02 (Keure ende ordonnantie op 't stuck van de pontgaerders

There were, however, some important consequences that flowed from Rotterdam's employment of Scots brokers for Scots coal. Here we have a municipal office that, at least until the 1660s, employed Scots. This may not seem in any way contradictory, but it was potentially at odds with the purpose of the broker in Rotterdam. Brokers were meant to advocate for whoever employed them. Yet it is hard to imagine that if the Scots brokers employed in Rotterdam were there due to their 'insider' knowledge, this would not have resulted in 'insider' dealing on occasion. At the very least Scots brokers worked with Scots shipmasters, sailors and merchants, effectively constituting an official tie between Scots involved in the coal trade and their Rotterdam market. In much the same way that Scots factors in a staple port would have acted to regulate the market in staple goods, the presence of Scots brokers in Rotterdam helped fellow Scots involved in the trade to access the Rotterdam market. The possibilities and potential for Scots brokers in the Rotterdam coal trade having influence would seem to have been further increased by their serving as factors in the coal trade as well as sworn brokers for Rotterdam. For, in serving as factors, Rotterdam's Scots brokers would have been openly advertising their intention to work for a particular sub-group in one of Rotterdam's key trades, which was expressly against the regulations of the coal market. Finally, and in violation of their oaths, it seems likely that some of the men who were factors and brokers also operated as merchants. The same complaint was heard of the official factors of the Scots staple, so this should not be surprising, but it is still worth noting.[39]

---

ende makelaers binnen Rotterdam, 1632); Sneller, *Geschiedenis*, 94; and Catterall *Community without Borders*, 191–192, 199–200 for an overview of Rotterdam's brokers and Scots participation in their ranks.

[39] For examples of these developments see the following GAR/ONA/154/685, 5-18-1650; GAR/ONA/96/312, 5-21-1649; GAR/ONA/438/189, 11-10-1646; GAR/ONA/171/12, 3-3-1644; GAR/ONA/96/226, 11-18-1647; GAR/ONA/95/478, 11-18-1644; GAR/Weeskamer Archief Rotterdam/482/655-657, 12-15-1645; GAR/ONA/143/556, 8-10-1628; GAR/ONA/88/746, 3-22-1627; and GAR/ONA/89/72, 7-22-1630. The preceding acts concern three men: Thomas Woedhead, Robert Bord or Burt and, for the last three acts, John Forgan or Forgun. All were active some time in the period from 1625 to 1670 in various capacities and both Woedhead and Burt certainly worked as sworn brokers, factors, and merchants, while Forgun seems to have worked both as a factor and a merchant. For the complaints about factors to the Scots staple in Veere see Davidson and Gray, *The Scottish Staple at Veere*, 390–404.

The presence of Scots brokers in the Scots coal trade segmented the Rotterdam administration's governance of the coal market in the city, effectively giving it into the hands of the Scots newcomers to some extent. To what extent exactly is a matter that warrants further research, but I have identified several Scots brokers for the period from 1630–1660, and Z. W. Sneller suggested that there may have been three as early as 1626. Those governing Rotterdam's markets, both in Rotterdam and Scotland, viewed the activities of men like Robert Burt, Thomas Woedhead and John Forgun as violations of the law. Historians have viewed their activities chiefly as a sign that the concepts embodied in a staple contract were outmoded. However, another way to view the actions of such men is from the standpoint of innovation. They were combining Scots methods of regulating trade with Dutch methods in order to create a new approach to commerce whereby merchants could act in various capacities yet at the same time remain within a relatively controlled framework. This model worked especially well for Rotterdam, in my view, because it accounts for the presence of the many factors operating in the city, contrary to what one might have seen in earlier centuries or even in other parts of seventeenth-century northern Europe. A number of men were noted as factors or as brokers in the notarial acts that I have consulted in Rotterdam, which suggests that Scots Rotterdam's economic and social order was less strictly structured than that of Scotland.[40]

Another hallmark of the innovative trade structures that Scots Rotterdamers were constructing can be illustrated through the careers of the Forgun family. Working both within and yet outside the nascent colonial architecture that the Dutch Republic and England were erecting in the Caribbean, John Forgun and his brother Robert Forgun (and their children) were able to forge very successful careers in much the same way that the men Alan Karras has labelled as sojourners were to do in the eighteenth century. John Forgun, who reached the military rank of sergeant, had become a broker and cloth dealer by the later 1620s, perhaps on the strength of military

---

[40] On factors see T. C. Smout, *Scottish Trade on the Eve of Union, 1660–1707* (Edinburgh and London: 1963), 80–99. For a sample of those acting as factors beyond what has been given above, see GAR/ONA/668–677, the protocols of Balthasaer de Gruyter. See above for the acts concerning Burt, Forgun, and Woedhead.

contracts to help supply uniforms. Forgun's son and namesake John Forgun served as a mariner in the fledgling Dutch West India Company, while his son William became a doctor and appears to have ended his days in Scotland. John Forgun the elder's brother Robert, who served in the leadership of the Scots Church of Rotterdam, was a merchant in tobacco and also sponsored family members to set up shop in the West Indies, such as John Smith the son of his sister Aeghjen Forgun, who was living in 'West Indien' at the time of Forgun's death in 1654.[41]

Before bringing this survey of innovation in Rotterdam to an end, attention should also be drawn to those who really made Scots Rotterdam work, mariners and their families. They were the back-bone of Scots Rotterdam, although their contribution could not be included here. Moreover, they were no less inventive in making Scots Rotterdam their own. As in Bo'ness, a point of origin for many who migrated and eventually settled in Rotterdam, sailors and shipmasters succeeded in founding a friendly society in the 1670s that contributed money to the families of mariners who had died, and supported mariners and their families who had fallen on hard times. Perhaps even more impressive than this, however, was the manner in which mariners and their wives in particular were able to construct a system of mutual support whereby sailors who were not resident in Rotterdam could find shelter in Scots Rotterdam without fear of being exploited by a crimp.[42]

Conclusion: The Shadows of the Past in the Eighteenth Century

As Ned Landsman has noted, it has been very common for those focusing on Scots participation in the British Atlantic to ignore the

---

[41] For the above see i.a. GAR/ONA/82/act #78, 1–1–1640; GAR/ONA/150/1120, 4–6–1636; GAR/ONA/90/127, 8–23–1640; GAR/ONA/96/214, 9–6–1647; GAR/ONA/668/219–220, 10–23–1651; GAR/ONA/670/147–149, 8–7–1654 and Catterall, Community without Borders, 258–272.

[42] See Catterall, Community without Borders, 123–129, 145–169. Examples of the credit and boarding house network supporting Scots sailors can be found in the following notarial acts, although they should not by any means be seen as an exhaustive list of the available evidence: GAR/ONA/430/80–82, 86, 89, 90–91; GAR/ONA/431/4, 8–9, 14–16, 20–22, 27, 37, 45, 49; GAR/ONA/33–34/143–144; GAR/ONA/433/22.

long history of Scots migration in northern Europe.[43] In part I suspect this is because some scholars have worked from the assumption that Scotland prior to the 1707 Union was an impoverished
and peripheral place. I would like to argue that there is a need to
re-evaluate how we deal with countries/regions such as Scotland,
whose inhabitants were peripatetic and yet remained in touch with
the home country. Instead of trying to separate Scotland from Scots
communities overseas, it may be that for purposes such as calculat-
ing Scotland's economic and political impact it would make more
sense to consider Scotland together with these communities. One
Rotterdam-based example suggests the validity of this approach.

Shortly after the death in 1672 of his father, the Covenanting
minister John Livingston, Robert Livingston emigrated first from
Rotterdam to Scotland and from there to Boston and the new
province of New York. There he was to make a very successful
career for himself. His older brothers, William and James, had traditional careers as Scots merchants trading with Europe, returning
to Scotland after 1689 and participating in the failed Darien scheme.
As of late 1674 or early 1675 Livingston was in Albany, using his
mastery of the Dutch, Scots and English languages to carve out a
career for himself in New York. Typically, scholars have stressed the
extent to which Livingston ignored his Rotterdam connections.[44] In
one regard, however, he did not. He continued the Scots penchant
for close familial-based professional/social networks, marrying Alida
Schuyler in 1679, which tied him to three powerful Dutch New York
families: the Van Rensselaers, the Van Cortlandts and, of course,
the Schuylers. With these connections and his own drive, Livingston
became a successful trans-Atlantic merchant, politician, and landowner.
His descendants also did well. Even as they rooted themselves in
New York, however, Robert Livingston and his descendants maintained ties with Scotland and Rotterdam. It is even possible that the
New York Livingstons had direct ties to a Livingston family active
in Rotterdam that had a hand in the new developments unfolding
there for Scots involved in international trade. In 1755, the mer-

---

[43] Landsman, 'Nation, Migration, and the Province,' 464–468.
[44] As Professor Smout points out, however, the Russell papers reveal Livingston's
frequent correspondence with his sister and brother-in-law in Rotterdam, and his
attempts at trading with them.

chant John Forbes, a member of the board of directors of the ill-
fated Royal Prussian East India Company of Emden, went bank-
rupt. His failure also meant financial pain for many of Scots
Rotterdam's merchant houses, among them Symson and Livingston,
a firm that might have had connections to Robert Livingston's descendants. Whatever form their trans-Atlantic ties took, the continuing
interest of the New York Livingstons in Scotland and Europe suggests that the seemingly conservative, family-based structures that
Scots preferred through the end of the eighteenth century remained
relevant even as the scale of commerce changed. Moreover, if we
consider that but for their choice to join the American Revolution,
the New York Livingstons would likely have joined those refugees
who then settled in another part of Britain or its empire and continued to remain tied to Scotland, an analysis that integrally links
Scotland to Scots overseas seems even more reasonable.[45] Contacts
between families in Scotland and their relatives or peers in Scots
trading communities around the world were of importance then and
remain of importance to scholars now.

---

[45] For the early career of Robert Livingston see L. H. Leder, 'Robert Livingston
(1654–1728): Businessman of Colonial New York,' *Business History Review* (1956):
18–45; D. Merwick, *Death of a Notary: Conquest & Change in Colonial New York* (Ithaca
& London: 1999), 35–37; and Robert C. Ritchie, *The Duke's Province: A Study of New
York Politics and Society, 1664–1691* (Chapel Hill, NC: 1977), 103, 115, 138, 151,
160, 162, 185, 190, 217, 218, 223, 225. On the eighteenth-century history of the
New York Livingstons see C. A. Kierner, *Traders and Gentlefolk: The Livingstons of New
York, 1675–1790* (Ithaca: 1992) and E. G. Burrows and M. Wallace, *Gotham: A
History of New York City to 1898* (New York and Oxford: 1999). On the Rotterdam
bankruptcy of John Forbes and the firm of Symson and Livingston see GAR/ONA/
2703/112–115, 3–4–1756.

THE SCOTTISH COMMUNITY IN
SEVENTEENTH-CENTURY GOTHENBURG

Alexia Grosjean and Steve Murdoch

Early in November [1649] Montrose passed over to Gothenburg in Sweden. The port was full of long-settled Scots merchants, and one, John Maclear [Maclean], put his house and his wealth at his disposal.[1]

The principal merchants in Gothenburg are Scotsmen. In consequence of letters of introduction which we carried to several of them, we experienced from that liberal and respectable body a profusion of kindness and politeness which it was impossible to surpass, and which it would be very difficult to equal. The want of inns, and our ignorance of the Swedish language, would have made it very difficult for us to have procured dinner while we stayed at Gothenburg, but this difficulty was obviated [sic] by the merchants, with one or other of whom we dined every day during our stay in that city.[2]

As the above comments show, an identifiable and thriving Scottish community existed in Gothenburg by the mid-seventeenth century which survived through until at least 1812. The west coast Swedish port and town had been founded merely a quarter of a century earlier in 1621, to serve not only as Sweden's international trading port but also as an important fortification against her neighbours. This development arose from Sweden's need for unhindered access to the North Sea, bound as the kingdom was geographically by Denmark and Norway. There had long been ports and communities in the area, notably Lödöse, Nylöse and Älvsborg, and these had already seen the settlement of foreign migrants, amongst whom Scots also figured. From its very inception Gothenburg continued this multi-cultural pattern: when Gustav II Adolf (1611–1632) decreed that the town was to be administered by twelve town councillors, these included four Swedish, three German, three Dutch and two Scottish men.[3]

---

[1] J. Buchan, *Montrose* (London: 1928), 340.
[2] Thomas Thomson's 'Travels in Sweden', 1812, reproduced in J. Berg and B. Lagercrantz, *Scots in Sweden* (Stockholm: 1962), 76–78.
[3] H. Almquist, *Göteborgs historia. Grundläggningen och de första hundra åren. Förra delen. Från grundläggningen till enväldet* (Göteborg: 1929), 81.

In addition, the Swedish Crown granted fifteen years' tax exemption to foreigners who settled and became burgesses in Gothenburg, enticing incomers to the town. The seventeenth century was Sweden's 'golden age' (known in Swedish historiography as *stormaktstiden* or 'age of great power') during which time Swedish military and political aggression resulted in great territorial expansion, whilst an advanced system of administration was developed at home. Additionally, changes made to the economy saw progress in mining and manufacture which came to supersede the importance of agriculture.[4]

Previous studies

It has commonly been presumed that the Dutch and Germans were the only significant foreigners to establish communities in Gothenburg in the seventeenth century. This was probably due to their numerical majority over the Scots in the town council, giving them control over the regulation of privileges there. It has also been frequently stated that migrants from the British Isles did not begin to make an impact in the town until the next century.[5] There are several reasons for this, not least of which that Scottish, and some English, surnames were often Germanicised in Swedish sources, and that many of the British migrants functioned within German-speaking social groups, as will be highlighted later.[6] Added to this was the impact of secondary migration, namely that of the British migrants who came to Sweden from another place, such as the Netherlands or German states, where their names had already been altered. This was highly relevant given that trade with the Dutch and the northern German states was particularly important to Sweden's economy.

---

[4] J. Weibull, *Sveriges Historia* (Trelleborg: 1997), 68, 96.

[5] B. Andersson, *Från fästningsstad till handelsstad. Göteborgs historia. Näringsliv och samhällsutveckling* (Stockholm: 1966), I, 160: "Under 1700-talet kom två andra invandrargrupper att få stor betydelse för stadens utveckling. Det var dels britterna, inte minst de många invandrarna från Skottland". [During the 1700s two other immigrant groups became more significant for the development of the town. These were partly the British, not least the many immigrants from Scotland]. See also A. Attman, *D. Carnegie & Co. 1803–1953. En hundrafemtioårig merkantil och industriell verksamhet* (Göteborg: 1953), 5, for a similar reference.

[6] For example, James Ewan of Aberdeen appears as Jacob Jun in Gothenburg shipping lists at Göteborg Landsarkiv, Drätselkammare.

Indeed, when the first plans for Gothenburg were laid out as early as 1597, it is said that Duke Karl (later King Karl IX from 1599–1611) hoped to design Gothenburg as a Dutch colony in miniature.[7] However, the Dutch were not the only foreign nation of significance in Sweden, as migrants from Denmark, Franconia and Rostock also became burgesses in the 1620s. To understand how evident the British, or particularly Scottish, presence was in Gothenburg from the town's earliest history this essay will depict the actual military, political or economic influence that some Scots wielded in the town long before the eighteenth century.

Despite the range of published material on the subject of the Scots established in Gothenburg from 1621 onwards, there are only a handful of scholars of that British community, and their focus has been on quantitative rather than qualitative analysis. Göran Behre has attempted to establish a pattern of settlement among the mainly mercantile Scottish inhabitants of Gothenburg during the eighteenth century.[8] Elsa-Brita Grage prematurely concluded, in a brief survey of seventeenth-century Scottish mercantile activity in Gothenburg, that no Scots settled there between 1630 and 1670, and that no Scots were registered there between 1682 and 1720.[9] A reason for this conclusion perhaps lies within the debate of 'when did a resident Scot become a Swede?'. Usually the answer to this was only upon ennoblement, as a prerequisite for the privilege was that an individual held Swedish nationality. As ennoblement sometimes did not occur until the third generation, this implies that previous generations, even those born and raised in Sweden (often of one Swedish parent) were still considered foreign. Thus second- or third-generation Scots who obtained burgess-ship should then be viewed as Scots, and not as Swedes. Christina Dalhede has recently undertaken an investigation into trade between Gothenburg, Augsburg, Lübeck and Antwerp.[10] Dalhede's accompanying database of shipping relies, however, on the Germanic form of names and does not include

---

[7] Andersson, *Från Fästningsstad till handelsstad*, 25.

[8] G. Behre, 'Scots in "Little London". Scots settlers and cultural development in Gothenburg in the eighteenth century', in *Northern Scotland*, VII, nr 2, (1986), 133–150.

[9] E. Grage, 'Scottish merchants in Gothenburg, 1621–1850' in T. C. Smout, ed., *Scotland and Europe 1200–1850* (Edinburgh: 1986), 112–115.

[10] C. Dalhede, *Handelsfamiljer på Stormaktstidens Europamarknad* (3 vols., Partille: 2001).

nationality amongst its fields. Her appendix of Gothenburg councillors, presidents and burgesses from 1621–1700 contains only eleven
obviously British names. All of this has served to reconfirm the impression that the Scots were few and far between in Gothenburg
during the seventeenth century. However, many of these time-worn
perspectives on the apparently minor Scottish role in Sweden's 'golden
age' have recently been robustly challenged, to show that in fact the
period was one of unparalleled cooperation in political and economic
terms for the two nations.[11]

Church records provide an obvious source for determining the
size and strength of a community, but those of Christina Church—
the German church to which many of the Scots belonged—appear
to have been largely overlooked. Interestingly, although their presence was formalised in the Gothenburg town charter, no provision
was made for the Scots' spiritual needs.[12] Despite the lack of a separate 'Scots' church, the Christina Church records illuminate the
close-knit nature of the Gothenburg Scots, particularly with regard
to the attendees at baptisms and christenings.[13] From this source
alone, five families in particular emerge as strong and important
community members: the Macleans, the Spaldings, the Sinclairs, the
Hamiltons and the Belfrages. Individuals from these families, often
more than one, tended to serve as godparents to each other's and
other newborns (both Scottish and Swedish) in Gothenburg. Thus
even in the social sphere the Scottish influence can be shown to be
significant and will be discussed more fully below.

In terms of trade, the frequency of names appearing in the
Gothenburg shipping lists for the seventeenth century reveal a lot
about the mercantile community there. With the exception of Dalhede's
work, these records also appear to have been either neglected or not
systematically trawled for a Scottish or British presence. The records
appear to begin around 1638, and from 1641 onwards contain a

---

[11] A. Grosjean, *An Unofficial Alliance: Scotland and Sweden, 1569–1654* (Leiden: 2003).
See also J. R. Ashton, *Lives and livelihood in Little London* (Sävedalen: 2003) for a study
of British presence in Gothenburg.

[12] Grosjean, *An Unofficial Alliance*, 257. See also M. Roberts, *Gustavus Adolphus: a
history of Sweden, 1611–1632* (2 vols., London: 1953–1958), I, 370, who notes the
lack of active persecution against non-Lutheran Protestants in Sweden.

[13] W. Berg, *Samlingar till Göteborgs Historia. Christine Kyrkas Böcker för Vigda, Födda
och Döda*, vol. I (Göteborg: 1890).

large group of Scots shipping timber and iron products to many destinations, including the east coast of Scotland.[14] During the 1650s
and 1660s more Scots joined them, indicating that the mercantile
community was constantly expanding and not restricted to the better-
known Maclean and Spalding families.[15] Unfortunately, sometimes
all that is known of some of these merchants is that on a certain
date they shipped cargo to a given location. However, by placing
this information in context with the social information derived from
church records and the official records of mercantile activity a more
comprehensive history of Scottish settlement in Gothenburg will be
presented, with a focus on the community's identity during the largely
ignored period of 1621–1720.

Known Scottish burgesses of Gothenburg

As noted, Gothenburg's geographical situation made it an ideal location for a new town, with two main purposes of defensive capabilities and mercantile opportunities. The new fortification required a
permanent military presence, which at the same time offered a protected Swedish trading port.[16] This facilitated trade with the North
Sea countries as Swedish ships could avoid the Danish Sound, a
route often hostile for Swedes. Both these aspects were favourable
to migration from Scotland. From 1569 onwards Scottish troops—
companies and even entire regiments—had increasingly come to
Sweden to fight for the Swedish Crown, and perhaps as many as
25,000 served during 1630–48 alone.[17] This military movement did

---

[14] This group included William Jack, James Mercer, John Maclean, Andrew
Wishart, Alexander Young, John Spalding and Francis Barker.

[15] In the 1650s we find John Watson, William Black, David Brady, John Dun
and Robert Bruce appearing in records. From 1660 William Ballier, John Sinclair,
James Jack, Robert Law, Andrew Morisson, William Hardistie, William Guthrie,
Robert Clerck and Daniel Crocket occur. In the following decade Robert Weir,
Gabriel Spalding, John Kerr, Patrick Kenny and John Small joined the list.

[16] This role was strengthened in July 1628 when Gustav II Adolf, in response to
rumours of a Spanish fleet heading for the Sound, ordered defensive preparations
to be made in the town, see *Svenska Riksrådets Protokoll* (18 vols., Stockholm: 1878–1929),
I, 99.

[17] A. Grosjean, 'Scotland; Sweden's Closest Ally?' in S. Murdoch, ed., *Scotland
and the Thirty Years' War, 1618–1648* (Leiden: 2001), 151. For a more complete eval-
uation of Scottish military migration to Sweden see Grosjean, *An Unofficial Alliance*,
chapters 1–4.

not occur in isolation; at the same time an outward mercantile migration spread largely eastward from Scotland, often flaunting the government regulations of the host country for decades. Despite the passing of the *Handelsordination* in 1607 limiting non-burgess traders to an eight-week period of activity in Sweden per annum, in 1638 it was revealed that seventy merchants had undertaken trade for as long as twelve years without becoming burgesses.[18]

An obvious explanation for the first influx was the aforementioned tax privileges available, along with the initially relaxed approach to the usual requirement that foreign burgesses had to build a house in the town.[19] A 1618 proclamation describes the process of a foreigner becoming a Swedish burgess.[20] It was normally necessary for a foreigner to present a town council with a birthbrieve and in the presence of two guarantors make an official request to become a burgess. Upon payment of ten *daler* an oath was to be taken before the governor and council, and an agreement to live in the town for at least six years. The burgess's name was then to be inscribed in the town's citizen-list and the burgess would have full permission to undertake his trade. Despite the above proclamation, it did not become a legal obligation to seek burgess-ship from Gothenburg until 1668, which further explains the lack of evidence for many of the resident Scots in previously published sources.[21] However, through-

---

[18] Ashton, *Lives and Livelihoods*, 9. Information on those who settled in Sweden can be found in the *Scotland, Scandinavia and Northern Europe* database.

[19] Grage, 'Scottish merchants in Gothenburg, 1621–1850', in Smout, ed., *Scotland and Europe 1200–1850*, 112.

[20] As printed in E. Långström, *Göteborgs Stads Borgarelängd 1621–1864* (Gothenburg: 1926), 6: *'Är mannen å landet eller i staden eller ock utrikes född, och vill borgare varda, då skall han hafva med sig burbref af deras överhet, där han tillförene hafver varit, och det uti 2 bolfasta mäns närvaro, där för ordhafvande borgmästaren, gifvandes honom icke mindre tillkänna, hvarmed han vill sig nära: Och där ordhafvande borgmästaren hans burbref nöjaktigt finner, skall han förvisa honom till de 7 män att erlägga till staden till viderkänsel 10 Daler, och med deras kvittobref ställa sig in på rådstugan för ståthållare och rådet, och uti deras närvaro och åhöro göra sin borgerliga ed, och sätta borgen för sig, att han åtminstone i 6 år vill burman vara och allan stadsrätt uppehålla. När det är skedt, då skall borgarens namn i stadens mantalslängd inskrifvas, samt hans borgens namn, och den näring han aktar bruka, och därefter må han köpa och sälja, samt sin gärning och handtverk drifva efter sin förmåga . . .'*

[21] Långström, in *Göteborgs Stads Borgarelängd 1621–1864*, only notes the following Scottish/British citizens in the 1620s: John Young 1624, Francis Barker 1625, Thomas Hunter burgess and tailor 1624, James and John Lindsay (brothers) 1620s, Alexander Sandilands burgess 1628, James Garden 1639, George Scott 1639, Andrew Wishart 1639, William Jack 1639, George Ogilvie 1621, Anna Cummings 1625 and James Kinnaird 1628.

out we have collated information relating to at least twenty five burgesses of Scottish origin active in the town between the peak years of 1622 and 1629 alone, and a total of about fifty burgesses throughout the century. This not only far exceeds the eleven names found on Dalhede's published burgess list, but it also provides an indication of the permanence and success of this community.[22] What has not been considered previously is the role that the presence of already-established Scots in the area played in attracting new migrants.

A place for two Scots was officially enshrined in the Gothenburg town council from the moment of its foundation, and the first two such councillors involved, Thomas Stewart and John Young (Hans Jung), were not newcomers to the area.[23] Thomas Stewart had initially been a burgess in Nylöse, the forerunner to Gothenburg, and had served on the town council there in 1603. Although his colleague John Young was first noted as a burgess of Gothenburg in 1624—the same year he became a town councillor—his Germanicised name indicates that he was already established in the area. Indeed, Stewart was not an isolated example of long-term residents becoming Gothenburg burgesses as James Lindsay, a fellow burgess from the 1620s, had similarly been noted in Nylöse before moving to Gothenburg.[24] The presence of these people implies that at least the beginnings of a Scottish community had developed in that part of Sweden, and its origins probably dated from the 1570s, when James Reid and his wife Agnes Gibson lived at Nylöse.[25] Incidentally, it is at this time that an early Scottish community emerges in Stockholm, and indeed the Stockholm burgess James Maclean also spent time in Gothenburg during the 1620s. He has often been confused with John Maclean, perhaps the best-known of the Scots settled there, who will be discussed in greater detail later. As previous studies have already revealed Scottish links to Sweden in the 1500s–1600s, it would have been unusual for the established Scots not to be involved

---

[22] Dalhede, *Handelsfamiljer*, III, Burgess Appendix.

[23] Långström, *Göteborgs Stads Borgarelängd 1621–1864*; Grage, 'Scottish Merchants in Gothenburg, 1621–1850', 13; H. Fröding, *Berättelser ur Göteborgs äldsta Historia* (Göteborg: 1908), 61; H. Almquist, *Göteborgs Historia*, 320–321.

[24] Långström, *Göteborgs Stads Borgarelängd 1621–1864*; Fröding, *Berättelser ur Göteborgs äldsta Historia*; Almquist, *Göteborgs Historia*, 320–321.

[25] See her grave monument preserved in Göteborgs Stadsmuseum.

in the towns from the outset.[26] The *Aberdeen Shore Work Accounts* note a healthy trade between that town and Gothenburg as early as 1624. In April Alexander Murray received twelve lasts of imports from Gothenburg; the following month Alexander Reid not only paid for Thomas Book of Caithness's exports to Gothenburg, but also sent twelve lasts of exports himself, while Walter Rankin imported timber from the Swedish town.[27] Unfortunately shipping lists from Gothenburg do not survive from that date so this is the only official record of trade to Aberdeen from the town, and even where these records do survive they appear incomplete.[28]

The presence of these early 'Swedish-Scots' also facilitated and encouraged further Scottish migration to Gothenburg by those already settled in other parts of Scandinavia and the Baltic. For example, James Kinnaird had settled in the Danish town of Elsinore by 1616 with his wife Elizabeth Wedderburn. Kinnaird acted as a retailer and his estate was registered on 18 July 1628 on his removal to Sweden. He left Denmark to become a burgess of Gothenburg and lived there with his wife throughout the 1630s, although as yet no specific reason has emerged for this move. He appears to have become master of the mint in Sweden.[29] It was during this time that John Maclean (commonly called Hans Macklier) also arrived in Gothenburg from Germany. This suggests the Swedish-based Scottish community were quick to let their countrymen abroad elsewhere know about, and share in, the new opportunities offered by the town—particularly the tax breaks.[30] In 1629 John became a burgess of Gothenburg, trading mainly in iron bar and timber cargoes.[31] His

---

[26] J. Dow, 'Scottish trade with Sweden 1512–80', and 'Scottish trade with Sweden 1580–1622', both in *Scottish Historical Review*, 48, (1969), 64–79, 124–150; Grosjean, *An Unofficial Alliance*, particularly chapters 1 and 2.

[27] L. B. Taylor, ed., *Aberdeen Shore Work Accounts 1596–1670* (Aberdeen: 1972), 131, 132.

[28] Imports were also registered for 1625, 1628, 1639 and 1642. Taylor, ed., *Aberdeen Shore Work Accounts*, 137, 155, 241, 270. Similarly, although James Ewan's exports to Gothenburg in 1653 appear, his return imports in 1654 do not.

[29] Elgenstierna, *Svenska Adelns Ättartavlor*, VII, 370–372; T. Riis, *Should Auld Acquaintance Be Forgot* (2 vols., Odense: 1988), II, 228; Långström, *Göteborgs Stads Borgarelängd 1621–1864*, 18; T. Fischer, *The Scots in Sweden* (Edinburgh: 1907), 12.

[30] Originally from the Island of Mull and son of Hector Maclean 5th Baron Duart and Isabella Acheson, daughter of Sir Archibald Acheson of Gosford. Elgenstierna, *Svenska Adelns Ättartavlor*, V, 142, and Grosjean, *An Unofficial Alliance*, 141.

[31] Göteborg Landsarkiv, Drätselkammare: he frequently appears in these accounts, for example in 1638 as the owner of bar iron on Oluf Kotter's ship going to Anstruther, and later sending timber on Hans Adam's ship headed for Crail.

cargo also included livestock such as oxen, mainly to Amsterdam and Oostend, but also horses and sheep for the West Indies in 1655.[32] Maclean did not content himself with simply being a prominent merchant in Gothenburg. He was also a customs officer and his local business contacts included Alexander Young, Francis Barker and James Mercer (none of whom appear on the burgess list). His duties extended far beyond the confines of Gothenburg and he represented the town in 1632 and in 1649 at the Swedish parliament.[33] He was ennobled in Sweden under the name of Makeleer in 1649 and introduced to the Swedish House of Nobility in 1652. Maclean also owned land in Sweden, such as the estate of Hammerö on Lake Vänern in Värmland, which he bought from another Scot settled in Sweden, Colonel John Gordon—whose widow he would later marry. He also received three royal donations of land in Halland in 1658, indicating the extent of his integration in Sweden. In 1660 the Swedes further recognised his importance when he received the title of commissioner. He died on 7 July 1666 and was buried in Christina Church after forty years' service to both his native country and his adopted town. Maclean's contemporary, John Spalding, migrated to northern Europe, perhaps initially to Mecklenburg where his brother Andrew was based.[34] However, he eventually became a merchant in Gothenburg. Like Maclean, and concurrently with him in the 1640s, Spalding served as a town councillor. He also worked as President of Commerce for the town from 1658 until 1667, the year of his death. While the death of these two men brought to a close a significant building phase for the Scots in Gothenburg, they had sown the seeds of perhaps an even more crucial second phase as their children took over their fathers' mantles.

Thus the appearance—or lack—of names on the official burgess list does not necessarily reflect the extent of those individuals'

---

[32] For his Swedish business correspondence see SRA, Brev til Nils Börjesson Oxenstierna, 1639–1653; SRA, Adolf Johans arkiv i Stegeborgssamlingen, 1653–1660; SRA, Kommerskollegii underdåniga skrivelser, 1651–1840, 26/04/1665.

[33] A bundle of his official correspondence to Chancellor Axel Oxenstierna exists in SRA, Axel Oxenstiernas Brefvexling, E657 Makeleir.

[34] Born in Scotland c.1600, the son of George Spalding of "Grangaben" (Darngaber?) of "Milhauch" (Millheugh?) in Scotland, Elgenstierna, *Svenska Adelns Ättartavlor*, VII, 370–371, and Grosjean, *An Unofficial Alliance*, 141. The exact location in Scotland is still to be determined, but Professor Smout has suggested it could be Millheugh near Darngaber Castle.

involvement in Gothenburg society. John (Hans) Carnegie is mentioned in most sources as being a citizen of Gothenburg from the foundation of the town (1621) but a burgess only from 1634. However he had already been granted the use of four sawmills in 1627. This indicates either that holding a burgess-ship was not a prerequisite to running a business, or that the recorded date of his admission is simply erroneous.[35] Despite this, his trade appears to have been largely England-bound, particularly between May and August 1638, although the first shipment went to Spain and the last to Hamburg. The only record of direct trade to Scotland was when he sent cargo there on a fifty-eight-ton ship in 1641.[36] Carnegie's letters show that he was still alive in the late 1640s, during the peak of Scottish-Swedish relations. The same case can be argued for William Hunter who was recorded as a smith in Gothenburg soon after the town was founded. Being a skilled tradesman probably meant that he was a member of a guild and eligible for citizenship, but he only appears on Långström's list of Gothenburg citizens dated c. 1639.[37] Thomas Hunter (a relation?), well-known in sources as a tailor turned clergyman, is noted as a burgess but does not appear to have undertaken any foreign trade at all.

These burgesses varied in their mercantile activities. The majority were merchants trading abroad as well as with other Swedish towns. Francis Barker, listed as a furrier in Långström's citizen roll for 1639, only appears on the shipping lists for 1649, but during that year he freighted goods to Leith and Dumbarton in Scotland, and to Hull and King's Lynn in England. The information gathered by Dalhede in her database seems to confirm the perception that trade between Gothenburg and Scotland only really developed in the second half of the seventeenth century, and that the east coast, particularly Fife, was a frequent destination. Dundee appears by far

---

[35] SRA, Biographica Microcard, E01300 3/11, undated letter to Queen Kristina mentioning customs officer Henry (Henric) Sinclair, plus three further letters all on the same subject and one dated 19 January 1648. See also Almquist, *Göteborgs Historia*, 320–321; Fröding, *Berättelser ur Göteborgs äldsta historia*, 61, 197; Berg, *Samlingar till Göteborgs Historia*, I, 1624–1725.

[36] Dalhede, *Handelsfamiljer*, III, Database [henceforth Dalhede, Database, followed by identity number] [804].

[37] Långström, *Göteborgs Stads Borgarelängd 1621–1864*, 16; Almquist, *Göteborgs Historia*, 320–321.

the most popular port of origin and destination for cargo ships (albeit only after 1650), followed by Leith, Anstruther, Crail, Glasgow, Aberdeen, Ayr and Montrose. Anstruther and Crail first appear in 1638 and 1641, and Ayr in 1646, while the remainder only appeared after 1649. Irvine, Bo'ness, and Dumbarton appear three times, while Kirkcaldy and Edinburgh only appear twice, the former in 1657 and 1678, and the latter in 1670 and 1691. Pittenweem, Leven, Dumfries and Banff appear once each in 1652, 1660, 1686 and 1686 respectively.[38] While most of the other ports saw their heydays during the 1650–80 period, Glasgow proved popular from the 1670s to 1699. The demonstrably regular and widespread trade to Scotland seems to shift from east to west coast, and lessens in frequency by 1700.

A difficulty regarding many of the Scottish or British merchants based in Gothenburg is the lack of evidence revealing whether these men were first or second generation, or whether this even mattered. Even so, it is probable that many of the Scots noted in the first twenty years of the new town were first generation or had come directly from the two towns which Gothenburg replaced. In any case, birth abroad did not remove an individual's Scottish citizenship and many of the second- and third-generation Scots in Gothenburg had to apply for Swedish naturalisation despite their Swedish birth.[39] This combination of Scottish and foreign-born Scots enabled some of these Scots to form dynasties which effectively ran large sections of the civic, commercial and military apparatus of the town for the duration of the century. Two men in particular, the aforementioned John Maclean and John Spalding, were largely responsible for providing the Gothenburg-Scottish community with numerous motivated children. Family connections frequently extended beyond the town and even beyond the country. The Spaldings, for example, could be found in Gothenburg, Norrköping, and Stockholm as well as Mecklenburg, Dunkirk and London.[40] The Gardiners could be found

---

[38] Another as yet unidentified Scottish port "Erllian" appears on the Dalhede database as a destination in 1645; Professor Smout has suggested to us that it might be Elie in Fife.

[39] Grosjean, *An Unofficial Alliance*, 145–151, 153–155.

[40] E. Spalding, *Geschichtliches urkunden, stammtafeln der Spalding in Schottland, Deutschland und Schweden: während der letzten sechs jahrhunderte, speciell der deutsche zweig der familie* (Greifswald: 1898); Elgenstierna, *Svenska Adelns Ättartavlor*, VII, 370–371; Grosjean, *An Unofficial Alliance*, 141.

in Gothenburg, Stockholm and Åbo. The Macleans (through John and James), the Mercers and the Petries were all to be found both in Gothenburg and Stockholm.

Johan Maclean succeeded his father on 7 July 1666 at the age of thirty. Like him he began business life as a merchant, but from 20 February 1677 until 18 October 1695 he also served as President of Justice in Gothenburg, and as mayor from 18 October 1695 until his death in April 1696.[41] His fellow Gothenburg-born Scot, Gabriel Spalding, also became a merchant in the town, taking over much of his father's business after 1667. In a career pattern uncannily matching that of Johan Maclean, Gabriel became President of Commerce in 1677, a position he held for over ten years.[42] Other Scots, both native and foreign-born, joined in these civic duties well into the 1690s.[43] For instance, Gabriel Spalding's cousin Andrew Spalding later became a chancellor in the royal chancellery and a legal mayor in Gothenburg in 1696, though in some sources he is also described as civic mayor or *borgmästare*.[44] Thus he achieved high status in two capacities within the town. He was important enough to merit particular mention to Karl XII, who was informed of Spalding's death just four days after it happened, on 16 December 1698.[45]

The sources do not imply that any negative feeling was created by the success of some of the foreigners who held town council seats. However, it has not been determined just how long the divisions

---

[41] Göteborg Landsarkiv, Förteckning över Landshövdingens i Göteborg och Bohuslän—Skrivelser till Kungl. Maj:t 1657–1840—noted as the late 'justieborgmästeren i Göteborg' in correspondence relating to his widow, Anna Gordon, 5 April 1696.

[42] SRA, Biographica Microcard E01832 3/6; Brev till Magnus Gabriel de la Gardie a) från enskilda Afd, I:II 1677 (five letters); Göteborg Landsarkiv, Förteckning över Landshövdingens i Göteborg och Bohuslän—Skrivelser till Kungl. Maj:t 1657–1840—13 December 1687; Elgenstierna, *Svenska Adelns Ättartavlor*, VII, 371–372.

[43] See for example Göteborg Landsarkiv, Förteckning över Landshövdingens i Göteborg och Bohuslän— Skrivelser till Kungl. Maj:t 1657–1840—21 October 1690, 2 March 1691.

[44] Göteborg Landsarkiv, Förteckning över Landshövdingens i Göteborg och Bohuslän—Skrivelser till Kungl. Maj:t 1657–1840—noted as 'borgmästare' in correspondence dated 24 July 1696; SRA, Biographica Microcard E01832 2/6 and 3/6; Andersson *et al.*, *Uppsala Universitets Matrikel* (Uppsala: 1900–1911); Fisher, *The Scots in Sweden*, 215–267; Elgenstierna, *Svenska Adelns Ättartavlor*, VII, 371.

[45] Göteborg Landsarkiv, Förteckning över Landshövdingens i Göteborg och Bohuslän—Skrivelser till Kungl. Maj:t 1657–1840—20 December 1698. Mentioned as dead, and payment to be made to his widow, same collection, March 1699.

along lines of nationality for these seats lasted in Gothenburg. Thus it is unknown when the last Scots, Dutch and Germans, specified as such, took their places on Gothenburg council. It also remains to be clarified whether Gabriel Spalding and Johan Maclean sat on the Gothenburg council as Scots or as Swedes.

Gothenburg's missing burgesses and residents

The availability and reliability of source material are perhaps any historian's two greatest concerns. Not only are many of the surviving burgess lists for seventeenth-century Gothenburg incomplete, but many years are also missing in entirety.[46] The absence of surviving records goes a long way to explain the relatively small number of Scots commonly associated with Gothenburg in the second half of the century. For example, James Mercer, first noted in Gothenburg during the 1630s, was not only a citizen and burgess of the town from 1621, but also served as a town councillor from 1652–56. His name appears on shipping manifests between 1638 and 1655, often alongside other Scottish burgesses such as John Maclean, Alexander Young and Francis Barker. In 1645 and 1649 he dealt only with Scotland, exporting tar and bar-iron to Crail and Anstruther, as well as timber products to Crail, Anstruther, Dundee and Leith. In other years he also freighted goods to Amsterdam, Hamburg, Stockholm, Norrköping, Stralsund and Norway. Mercer had business dealings with other Gothenburg Scots such as John Spalding and William Jack.[47] One particular letter was co-signed by William Mercer, Jacob Gardiner, Ignatius Menner, Jurgen Garden junior, James Gardiner and Robert Smidt, some of whom are known to have been merchants, others of whom there is little trace.[48] This letter offers evidence of a community that both traded together and had a sense of itself as an entity. Not only are several of the signatories members of two particular families, Mercer and Gardiner, but the ethnic mix is virtually uniform except for Menner, who was presumably

---

[46] The incomplete years are: 1622–31, 1637, 1644, 1667 and 1670. The missing years are: 1632–6, 1638–43, 1645, 1648, 1657–61, 1663–4 and 1689.
[47] Göteborg Landsarkiv, Drätselkammare, volumes for 1638, 1641, 1645, 1649 and 1655.
[48] SRA, Biographica Microcard, E01412 4/7.

German. Further, in 1672 one Hans Merser (probably a relative, possibly a son of James') also became a Gothenburg burgess; his occupation was noted as 'merchant'.[49]

Another elusive Scot, Alexander Murray, is a perplexing case as his widow is noted in the citizens' roll for Gothenburg in 1639, yet he himself does not appear on the burgess list. There is also some confusion concerning James Maclean (Jakob Mackler). He is generally noted as a Stockholm burgess, but the Riksråd recorded him as a Gothenburg burgess as late as 1632 when they were discussing letters of reprisal for merchants who had lost goods to the Spanish, and other sources note that he had been a burgess of Nylöse from 1621–28.[50] Given James's close association with John Maclean and the wealth of information relating to the man, it is surprising that he does not appear on previously published lists.

Similar omissions exist for the following decades, such as Johan Sinclair, who served as a customs inspector at Lilla Edet from the early 1650s until the 1660s. In 1656 he became involved in a case against Anders Wetterman and the following year both were condemned by the Göta main court. Sinclair was later described as "*en av värsta kverulanter*" ("one of the most cantankerous persons") in Sweden. However, this did not prevent him from remaining as the customs inspector of small tolls in Bohuslän from 1665–72.[51] Another missing Gothenburg Scot is Johan Williamson Leyel. He signed a deposition to the Swedish resident in London in 1666 stating that the Swedish Trade Commissioner, Johan Bierman, helped him become a citizen of Gothenburg and also captain of his ship *St Johann*.[52] Like many others from his nation, there is no record of this in the secondary sources, but the fact that Bierman was an official of the Swedish Crown and the document was forwarded to the Swedish representative in London suggests it is authentic. Perhaps one of the most significant missing burgesses is the aforementioned John Spalding.

---

[49] Långström, *Göteborgs Stads Borgarelängd 1621–1864*, 40.

[50] *Svenska Riksrådets Protokoll*, II, 184, 28 July 1632; J. N. M. Maclean, *The Macleans of Sweden* (Edinburgh: 1971), 5.

[51] C. F. Corin, *Vänersborgs Historia. Bind I, Tiden till 1834* (Stockholm: 1944), 94, 132, 136–137, 154: SRA, Adolf Johans Arkiv i Stegeborgssamlingen, four letters from Johan Sinclaire, 1651–1652, Lilla Edet; SRA, Kommerskollegii Underdåniga Skrivelser 1651–1840—Johannes Sinclair, 'Inspector over småtullarna i Bohuslän 1665–1672'.

[52] SRA, Anglica, VII, 542, 1660–1670. 11 December 1667, 'Deposition by Johan Williamson Leyel'.

In 1672 a letter directed to his son, "a knowne merchand in Dunkirk", was found on board the Swedish ship *The Fortune* which had been taken prize in Scotland. The letter was from Henrie Browne at Gothenburg who, the Scottish Admiralty recorded, was married to one of Spalding's many sisters.[53] Johan certainly formed part of the Scottish community in the town as his birthbrieve shows, but his service abroad has led others to miss his significant contribution to Gothenburg.[54] Further, this familial relationship perhaps helped to obtain *The Fortune*'s release from Scottish captivity as both Johan and Gabriel Spalding were still Scottish citizens in 1672, despite having been born and raised in Sweden.[55]

Of course, one did not have to become a citizen of the town to become a part of the community. Grage argues for example that, "in 1689 the largest iron exporter was a Scottish factor, James Craig".[56] He is not to be found either in Långström's list or in numerous other sources on the subject of Gothenburg trade, including Dalhede's database.[57] As a Scottish factor, there was no reason for him to take citizenship. Evidence also exists identifying Scots like Hew Chartres as a "merchant, burgess of Edinburgh [and] residenter of Gottinberrie in Sweden".[58] Like Craig, he was probably a factor for a Scottish business concern lurking in historical obscurity in Gothenburg's commercial history. Similarly, many of the skippers undertaking shipments between Gothenburg and Sweden were resident elsewhere. But even without focusing on those settled Scottish merchants who did not receive citizenship, or did not need to, the

---

[53] This was probably Henrik Braunjohan who was married to Anna Spalding, but may have been a Briton called Henry Browne. The relationship is noted in NAS, AC7/3, Register of Decreets, 1672–1673, ff.202–221. 4 October 1672. Captain Patrick Gordon against Andreas Nielson of the Swedish ship *The Fortune*. See also S. Murdoch, A. Little and A. D. M. Forte, 'Scottish Privateering, Swedish Neutrality and Prize Law in the Third Anglo-Dutch War, 1672–1674' in *Forum Navale: Skrifter utgivna av Sjöhistoriska Samfundet*, no. 59, (2003), 52–53.

[54] *RPCS*, 3rd series, IV, 1673–1676, 306.

[55] For more on this argument see Murdoch, Little and Forte, 'Scottish Privateering, Swedish Neutrality and Prize Law', 52–53.

[56] Grage, 'Scottish merchants in Gothenburg' in Smout, *Scotland and Europe 1200–1850*, 115.

[57] For example he does not appear in any volume of Dalhede's *Handelsfamiljer på Stormaktstidens Europamarknad*.

[58] Edinburgh Commissary Court, CC8/8/61. Will of Hew Chartres, 16 May 1644.

number of Scots resident in the town appears larger than previous studies have suggested. This contention is supported by examples of other 'missing persons'—the English community, for instance. There would certainly have been significant communication between the Scots and English, both on trade and personal levels, particularly with highly placed individuals such as Anthony Knipe, though as his correspondence reveals, he and Maclean did not get along.[59] Indeed, Knipe was eventually forced into exile from Sweden and started a new life in Norway. Relations were not always so frosty. Catherine Spalding, a Scot, married an English preacher, Thomas Hacker, in Gothenburg in 1644. His countryman, Arthur Rose, was noted in 1664 by the Swedish resident in London as a carpenter who had been pressed into English naval service. Rose was described thus: "though an Englishman, he has been a citizen of Gottenburg for 14 years, has his wife & children there now, & is consequently a subject of Sweden".[60] Yet neither Rose nor Hacker appears in printed lists of Gothenburg citizens. The presence of Hacker, Rose, and Knipe indicates the existence of an English community of sorts, although the number of English burgesses appears low and represents a fraction of the Scottish statistic.[61] Nonetheless they are indicative of the incomplete nature of sources traditionally relied upon while compiling data on the city's mercantile community.

There is a tendency to impose an artificial division between the mercantile and military components of the Scottish community in Gothenburg. Not only did the families of each sector of society intermarry, but they also did so with members of the other resident communities, whether English, German, Dutch or Swedish. Indeed the spheres of trade and defence were interdependent as regards supply and protection. Some of the soldiers made an important contribution to the defence of the town. Most notably these included the likes of David Sinclair of Finnekumla in Älvsborg.[62] David came to

[59] SRA, AOSB, E636. This volume of undated correspondence to Axel Oxenstierna relates to 'Stadspresident Anthony Knipe' c.1635–1645. The complaint against Maclean is c.1640; Långström, *Göteborgs stads borgarelängd*, 13.

[60] *CSPD 1664–1665*, 123, 26 December 1664. Thanks to Andrew Little for providing this reference.

[61] Ashton discusses the presence of an 'English' Poor Box in Gothenburg during the second half of the seventeenth century, *Lives and Livelihoods*, 27.

[62] The Swedish peerage notes him as the son of William Sinclair of Seba and his wife Barbara Halcro, the daughter of Baron Hugo Halcro. Elgenstierna, *Svenska Adelns Ättartavlor*, VII, 273.

Sweden in 1630 or 1631 with his elder brother John and his father, and they all entered military service, serving the Swedish Crown during the Thirty Years' War.[63] From 1640 onwards he was involved in the Scottish, and later English, civil wars. However, after Charles I's execution, he reappeared in Swedish service and bought property in Älvsborg. In 1651 he married Catherine Maclean, a daughter of John Maclean, at one time the wealthiest man in Sweden. Sinclair did not just marry into Swedish nobility but was himself ennobled in 1655.[64] When the Cromwellian ambassador Bulstrode Whitelocke visited the city in 1653, Sinclair was one of several Scots who had regular meetings with him.[65] His son William became a Swedish general and a baron. Sinclair died in battle in 1656, but even his short involvement in the Scottish community in Gothenburg was at the highest level.

Although Sinclair had come directly from Scotland, several Scots arrived from other parts of the Scottish diaspora. Hugh Hamilton was born on 20 May 1655 in Ireland in Monea Castle, the son of John Hamilton of Balgally and Jane Sommerville. He seems to have arrived in Sweden in 1680, called by his older brother Malcolm.[66] He served in the Swedish army, where he swiftly climbed the military ladder, resulting in the ownership of huge tracts of land including those of his late uncle and namesake.[67] Hamilton's promotion to a captaincy in the Älvsborg regiment was achieved through the patronage of his brother-in-law, Colonel Gustav Maclean, one of

---

[63] His military career can be traced in KRA, Muster Rolls: MR 1633/16–22, 25; 1634/12–23; 1635/20–26, 29–31; 1636/17, 20–22; 1637/13–16; 1638/21; 1649/19; 1655/1; 1656/3, 9, 10.

[64] Elgenstierna, *Svenska Adelns Ättartavlor*, VII, 273; Grosjean, *An Unofficial Alliance*, 142; E. Furgol, *A Regimental History of the Covenanting Armies 1639–1651* (Edinburgh: 1990); Berg, *Samlingar till Göteborgs Historia*, I, 10 and 457.

[65] R. Spalding, ed., *The Diary of Bulstrode Whitelocke, 1605–1675* (Oxford: 1990), 301–302, 15 November 1653; Grosjean, *An Unofficial Alliance*, 247.

[66] Malcolm was born in Ireland in 1635 and called to Sweden by his uncle Hugh Hamilton of Deserf in 1654. This Hugh had been sent to Sweden by his father in 1624. Malcolm served in the Swedish army and married Catherine Maclean (her second marriage). He died in 1699 and was buried in the Gustavi Church in Gothenburg. Elgenstierna, *Svenska Adelns Ättartavlor*, III, 453; Lt. Colonel George Hamilton, *A History of the House of Hamilton* (Edinburgh: 1933), 1014–1015.

[67] KRA, 0035: 0418: Ö, Karl Viggo-Key Arkiv, Hugh Hamilton to Riksråd, 9 September 1670; SRA, Biographica 5, E01463 5/8—'Hugo Hamilton's Relation of Lord Glenawly's Estate in Ireland, Dublin', 3 November 1690. Dr Karin Friedrich kindly translated this very complex document.

John Maclean's sons.[68] Like Sinclair before him he maintained both an interest and active military participation in the Stuart kingdoms, serving at the Battle of the Boyne in Ireland as a private volunteer.[69] In 1689 both Hamilton and his brother Malcolm were made Swedish barons and in 1693 they were introduced to the Riddarhus as Hamilton of Hageby.[70] After many military campaigns Hamilton returned to Gothenburg and settled there, becoming Lieutenant-Colonel of the Älvsborg regiment in February 1703.[71]

The military commitment shown by these foreign-born men was echoed by sons of Scots already settled in Gothenburg. John Maclean's sons, including the aforementioned Gustav, Peter and David, all served in the Swedish army. With his brother Gustav in command of the Älvsborg regiment, David was put forward as a commandant of Gothenburg with Henrik Johan Belfrage (also a son of a Gothenburg Scot) as his vice-commandant.[72] This is a microcosm in military terms of the role of Scots in the civic sphere, as epitomised by Johan Maclean and Gabriel Spalding. Indeed, Henrik Johan had served as Lieutenant-Colonel of artillery in Gothenburg since 1679. David Maclean's father-in-law, Rutger von Ascheberg, governor-general of Skåne, Halland, Gothenburg and Bohuslän, placed David as com-

---

[68] Noted in the following letters as commandant and colonel of the city: Göteborg Landsarkiv, Förteckning över Landshövdingens i Göteborg och Bohuslän—Skrivelser till Kungl. Maj:t 1657–1840—3 July 1697 and 27 November 1698; P. Sørensson, *Generalfälttygmästaren Hugo Hamilton en karolinsk krigare och landshöfding* (Stockholm: 1915), 269.

[69] SRA, Reduktionskommission till Kung. Maj., vol. 14, 27 April 1689; Sørensson, *Generalfälttygmästaren Hugo Hamilton*, 4. For his Swedish military service see KRA, Muster Roll, 1683/8, 17, 19; 1684/1; 1685/13, 19, F. 164; 1687/7; 1689/8; 1690/1, 6, 8; 1691/6, 11; 1692/1; 1694/1, 2, 15; 1695/1–3; 1696/1; 1697/1; 1698/1; 1700/1.

[70] N. Bohman, *et al.*, eds., *Svenska Män och Kvinnor Biografisk Uppslagsbok* (8 vols., Stockholm: 1942–1955), III, 269; Elgenstierna, *Svenska Adelns Ättartavlor*, III, 453.

[71] Sørensson, *Generalfälttygmästaren Hugo Hamilton en karolinsk krigare och landshöfding*; Around 1715 Hamilton and his regiment served in Karl XII's unsuccessful Norwegian campaign, and the following year he served as commandant and vice-governor in Gothenburg.

[72] Göteborg Landsarkiv, Förteckning över Landshövdingens i Göteborg och Bohuslän—Skrivelser till Kungl. Maj:t 1657–1840—15 April 1684, 18 November 1684, 3 November 1685 and 22 June 1696. These letters note that Belfrage sought a commandant's position in Nya Älvsborg. He was the son of John Belfrage who was born in Kirkcaldy in Scotland in 1614. Corin, *Vänersborgs Historia. Bind I. Tiden till 1834*, 218–219; Elgenstierna, *Svenska Adelns Ättartavlor*, I, 266–267.

mandant in Malmö.[73] However, David returned at the end of 1693 when he was appointed regional governor of Älvsborg.[74] While predominantly soldiers, the military Macleans all engaged in some form of trade with Britain. None of them undertook direct trade with Scotland but all freighted ships to London at some point in their career, emphasising that city's important role for the Scottish diaspora's contact with Britain.

A final category of missing persons in the town is of course the women. Often little is known about most of them other than that they were there, perhaps married and produced children. However, deducing from the few examples we have, we can argue quite strongly that they played a more interesting role than historians have traditionally given them credit for. Alexander Murray's widow (neither her name nor her nationality are known) and Anna Cummings for instance were both listed as citizens of Gothenburg in their own right, though it is not clear whether either woman specialised in a particular trade.[75] The evidence of Lunetta Beata Hamilton's life in Gothenburg reveals that she lived all her life in or near Gothenburg, never married but was wealthy and well-versed in state affairs.[76] She was benevolent towards the poor and all her church involvement seems to have been as a communicant in Christina Church along with other Scots. We can also note that some women became members of the Riddarhus on their own merits, like the Spalding sisters.

---

[73] Göteborgs Landsarkiv, Förteckning över Landshövdingens i Göteborg och Bohuslän—Skrivelser till Kungl. Maj:t 1657–1840—10 July 1693; KRA, Muster Roll, 1669/6; 1670/5,6; 1671/1; 1672/5,11; 1677/7; 1678/9; 1679/17; 1680/3; 1681–2/1; 1682/1, 4; 1683/8, 12, 17, 19; 1684/1; 1685/1, 14; 1687/7, 9; 1689/6; 1690/1; 1691/4; 1694/1, 8; SRA, Eric Dahlbergs Arkiv, XXX, 13/04/1693.

[74] In 1708 he was raised to a baronetcy, and at this point he insisted his ennobled name was Maclean and not Mackleer; see Elgenstierna, *Svenska Adelns Ättartavlor*, V, 142.

[75] Långström, *Göteborgs stads borgarelängd*, 14, 23. These were not the only women burgesses in the town and this source is replete with the names of many others.

[76] Baroness Lunetta Beata Hamilton (1674–1761) died unmarried, but even Frederick I is said to have deeply respected her. This is recorded on her funeral monument in Christina Church which notes: "Feb 2 1762 begrub Dn. Muller die Baroness Lunetta Beata von Hamilton, geboren zu Gothenburg und hier getauft d. 28 Aug 1674, gestorben zu Roda auf ihrem Landguth im verwichenen jahr, da Sie d. 13 Nov herein gefuhret wurde. Sie war wohlerzogen u. eine gute Christin. Sie besas darneben eine grosse Einsicht u. statsklugheit, die der König Friederich I selbst bewundern mussen. Sie war sehr gutig gegen ihre Unterhanen, milde u. mitleidig gegen arme leute u freijebig gegen unsere Kirche". Elgenstierna, *Svenska Adelns Ättartavlor*, III, 453; Hamilton, *A History of the House of Hamilton*, 1083.

Finally we have to observe that rather than simply undertaking the household chores, many women actively engaged in freighting cargo. Often the most that is known of them is that they were daughters or wives of Gothenburg Scots and it is conceivable that shipments consisted of personal household goods rather than trade goods *per se*. Elisabeth Kinnaird undertook two shipments, one from Amsterdam in 1650 and another to Stockholm in 1652.[77] However, Catharina Fistulator entered into multiple shipments from 1651–8, largely to and from Amsterdam.[78] Catharina Sinclair received goods twice from Hamburg, in 1656 and 1657.[79] Annicka Fistulator shipped cargo in 1668 from Hamburg, Anna Spalding in 1672 from Hamburg, Catharina Maclean in 1678 from Hamburg, Annicka Sinclair in 1689 from Hamburg, Elsa Maclean in 1690 from Amsterdam, Anna Maclean in 1694 from Hamburg, Sara Maclean in 1694 from Amsterdam, and Anna Margaretha Hamilton in 1695 from Lübeck.[80] These women have several things in common: they all appear to have been solely engaged in single transactions, all of which occurred on Swedish-based ships with Swedish skippers. Further, they were all members of the most important Scottish families in Gothenburg. We should also note that the use of a woman as a named freighter of cargo was a cynical expedient for avoiding the confiscation of vessels during times of conflict. This was certainly the case with Margaret Kohl, whose brother Henry, a Dutch citizen, had registered the ship *Margaret of Arensburg* to her as a Swedish citizen. He did so in an unsuccessful bid to avoid the ship's confiscation by British privateers during the Third Dutch War (1672–1674).[81] Most notably, from the perspective of this essay, none of the women seem to have sent goods directly to Scotland. But where there may be an absence of information in one sphere, there is more in terms of the women's role as an anchor of the community.

---

[77] See Dalhede, Database [2228].

[78] See Dalhede, Database [1245].

[79] See Dalhede, Database [3800].

[80] See Dalhede, Database [1242], [3853], [2572], [3799], [2574], [2571], [2580] and [1511].

[81] This case is discussed in detail in Murdoch, Little and Forte, 'Scottish Privateering, Swedish Neutrality and Prize Law', 46–47. The case notes are to be found in NAS, Register of Decreets, AC7/3, ff.235–280; SRA, Anglica, Bihang Scotica II (unfoliated), numerous documents.

Marriage within the Gothenburg community

Several studies of the Scots abroad have featured analyses of marriage patterns.[82] What is clear from the Gothenburg community is that it is almost impossible to discuss a single 'pattern' as such, as the Scots within the community married Scots, Swedes and other foreigners. As most of the information available is derived from secondary sources, it is really only possible to highlight some examples to show the effects of marriage on the community rather than to derive definitive statements from them. There are almost as many combinations of marriage as there were Scots in the town at the time but they can be broken down roughly to show Scots marrying other Scots before they arrived in Sweden, those who married Scots in Sweden, and those who married other foreigners or Swedes once in the town.

Of the first group not much is known other than the wives' names. Thomas Hunter married a Scotswoman, Elisabeth Aberback. John Spalding married twice, first to Johanna Kinnaird, herself the daughter of the Gothenburg Scot, James Kinnaird. She was born in Dundee in 1609 but lived in Gothenburg and died there in 1646. Spalding's second wife was Ingeborg Danielsdotter, also in her second marriage; she was Swedish.[83] John Maclean similarly married both Scots and foreigners, though his first marriage, to James Maclean's sister-in-law Anna Gruber, was indicative of strengthening community bonds with another group settled in Sweden. John Maclean's second wife, Lilian Hamilton, was a first-generation Scottish woman, but their marriage only lasted from December 1655 until her death in 1658. That year John Maclean married his third wife, Anna Thomson, daughter of Colonel Thomas Thomson and Catherine Murray. Anna herself was the widow of another Scot, Colonel John Gordon.[84]

---

[82] M. Glozier, 'Scots in French and Dutch armies during the Thirty Years' War', in S. Murdoch, ed., *Scotland and the Thirty Years' War, 1618–1648* (Leiden: 2001), 131–137; M. Ailes, *State Formation and Military Migration: The British Community in Seventeenth Century Sweden* (Lincoln and London: 2002), 58–72; Grosjean, *An Unofficial Alliance*, 141–142.

[83] Elgenstierna, *Svenska Adelns Ättartavlor*, III, 410; IV, 98; VII, 370–371; Grosjean, *An Unofficial Alliance*, 142.

[84] Elgenstierna, *Svenska Adelns Ättartavlor*, V, 142 and VIII, 265; Maclean, *The Macleans of Sweden*, 26, 28; Berg, *Samlingar till Göteborgs historia*, I, 519.

The next generation showed similarly varied marriage patterns. Johan Maclean junior married Anna Margaretha Gordon in 1677; she was not only a Scot, but also his stepsister.[85] Johan's sister Catherine also married a fellow Scot, Colonel David Sinclair of Finnekumla in 1651. When he died she remarried within the community to Major-General Malcolm Hamilton of Hageby.[86] Her sister Maria Sofia did likewise when she married General James Duncan.[87] Two other sisters, however, married into Swedish military families. Lunetta married Colonel Joachim Cronman in 1657, while Elsa Beata married Major Mårten Christensson till Anckarhielm, on 1 July 1666.[88] David Maclean also married 'abroad' from the community when he wed Eleonora Elisabet von Ascheberg.[89] Thus a mix of intra- and extra-community marriages was already apparent within a generation.

However, even after the community had become firmly integrated into Gothenburg society, intra-Scottish marriages were not uncommon. Elisabeth Clerck, daughter of Robert Clerck merchant burgess of Gothenburg and his unnamed wife, was born early in 1674 and when she was baptised her godparents included Lieutenant-Colonel Malcolm Hamilton and Major Gustav Maclean. On 9 December 1690 she married William Kinnaird, a fellow Scot.[90] Thus, she is very illustrative of the bonds which held the Scottish community in Gothenburg together—born of at least one Scottish parent, with two of the most important Scots among her godparents, she later mar-

---

[85] Elgenstierna, *Svenska Adelns Ättartavlor*, V, 142–144; Fisher, *The Scots in Sweden*, 15; Maclean, *The Macleans of Sweden*, 29–30; Berg, *Samlingar till Göteborgs historia*, I, 519; Grosjean, *An Unofficial Alliance*, 142.

[86] Berg, *Christine Kyrkas böcker*, 10, 537; Hamilton, *A History of the House of Hamilton*, 1083; Elgenstierna, *Svenska Adelns Ättartavlor*, III, 454 and V, 143; Maclean, *The Macleans of Sweden*, 26; Berg, *Samlingar till Göteborgs Historia*, I, 10, 537. She died in 1709 and was buried in Gothenburg at Christina Church, leaving children by both husbands.

[87] S. Murdoch, 'Scotsmen on the Danish-Norwegian Frontier', in S. Murdoch and A. Mackillop, eds., *Military Governors and Imperial Frontiers: a Study of Scotland and Empires c.1600–1800* (Leiden: 2003), 24–25 and *Dansk Biografisk Leksikon*, IV, 363.

[88] Maclean, *The Macleans of Sweden*, 27; Elgenstierna, *Svenska Adelns Ättartavlor*, V, 143.

[89] Elgenstierna, *Svenska Adelns Ättartavlor*, V, 139–140. Von Ascheberg was an old noble family originally from Italy, but as early as 1296 they have been found in the dioceses of Paderborn and Münster in Westphalia.

[90] Berg, *Genealogiska anteckningar om Göteborgs historia*, ser.1, II, 62–63; Berg, *Samlingar till Göteborgs historia*, I, 30, 122, 143, 484.

ried a Scot herself. However, in other families, the Scottish link was not overtly apparent. The younger Hugh Hamilton, for instance, married Anna Margaretha Henriksdotter, daughter of councillor Henrik Arvidsson. It is only when we see the name of Anna's mother that we can identify a Scottish link, she being Margaretha Jacobsdotter Lintzai (Lindsay).[91] For other families it is as if there was no Scottish marriage link at all, despite continued trading associations. Gabriel Spalding married firstly Catharina Schmidt and secondly Catharina Wernl, a Swedish noblewoman.[92] His sisters Christina (sometimes Catharina) and Elisabeth also married outwith the Scottish community. Christina married the aforementioned English preacher, Thomas Hacker, himself born in Wismar sometime after 1642, while Elisabeth on the other hand married Nils Daniel Borgenström.[93] There were four more sisters in the extended Spalding family. Margareta Spalding married senior commissioner Per Larsson Gripenwaldt while Johanna Spalding married first Captain Johan Wilhemi and then commissioner Mårten Kanterberg.[94] Anna Spalding married war commissioner Henrik Braunjohan and Catharina married Mayor Hans von Gerdes in 1675.[95] Their cousin Jakob Spalding was the son of the Scot Andrew Spalding of Mecklenburg. Like his cousins he wed outwith the Scottish community both times he married. His first partner was Ingrid von Brobergen, from a family originating in the Rhine region, and his second wife was Dorotea Dreijer.[96] Some Scots married into the Gothenburg community, but did not initially live there, and the manner in which the families met is not yet clear. For

---

[91] Bohman, *Svenska Män och Kvinnor*, III, 269.

[92] The Wernle family originated from Nürnberg; Catharina was the third generation in Sweden. Elgenstierna, *Svenska Adelns Ättartavlor*, VIII, 745.

[93] Elgenstierna, *Svenska Adelns Ättartavlor*, III and VII, 370–372; H. Marryat, *One year in Sweden including a visit to the isle of Gotland* (London: 1862), 490.

[94] A noble family originating from Greifswald; he was born in Sweden in 1617. Elgenstierna, *Svenska Adelns Ättartavlor*, III, 158–159. Kanterberg came from a Swedish noble family and died in 1701. Elgenstierna, *Svenska Adelns Ättartavlor*, IV, 98.

[95] Henrik might have originated from the noble family of Braunjohan, originally from Spain. But before ending up in Sweden they passed through the Netherlands, Friesland and Westphalia. He is also probably the Henry Browne mentioned above. See Elgenstierna, *Svenska Adelns Ättartavlor*, VII, 371. Hans Gerdes was ennobled as von Gerdes. He was born in 1637 in Lübeck and became a merchant in Gothenburg, where he also became 'handels- och politieborgmästare' in 1687. Elgenstierna, *Svenska Adelns Ättartavlor*, III, 42.

[96] Elgenstierna, *Svenska Adelns Ättartavlor*, I, 617.

instance Kenneth Sutherland, Lord Duffus, married Charlotte Siöblad daughter of Admiral Erik Siöblad in 1711.[97] He did not move to Sweden until February 1716 after the failure of the 1715 Jacobite uprising.[98]

These few examples show that there was no single pattern for marriage, and it would be tiresome simply to relate every marriage that took place in the town. What can be said for certain is that while some Scots married closely within the Scottish community others moved beyond it, encompassing English, Swedish, Dutch and German partners to name but a few. It is similarly impossible to determine how many marriages were based on mercantile connections or whether other influences were at work. However the results show that links to Scotland were maintained while the family connections to the host community were strengthened through new family alliances, whether this was by accident or design. The marriages between Scots and Swedish members of the elite could serve as useful conduits to apply pressure in cases where covert and overt contact was required. An example of this is the "pillow diplomacy" applied by Scottish ladies in Sweden in 1649.[99]

Links to the Scottish community in Scotland and abroad

As has been adequately described elsewhere, political links with Scotland during her various upheavals were maintained by the more famous of the Gothenburg Scots. John Maclean in particular supplied the Scottish Covenanters with ships and weapons during the Bishops' Wars (1639–1641) that took place between the Presbyterian Scottish provisional government and the Royalist forces of Charles I.[100] He

---

[97] Elgenstierna, *Svenska Adelns Ättartavlor*, VII, 284. For his daughters Charlotte Regina and Anna Sutherland Duffus see V, 622 and IX, 60.

[98] Gothenburg Landsarkiv, Förteckning över landshövdingens i Göteborg och Bohuslän—Skrivelser till Kungl. Maj;t, 1657–1840. Letter to Karl XII, 28 February 1716; SRA, Kanslikollegiets—Skrivelser till Kungl. Maj:t 1656–1718, Robert Jackson's memorials on Scottish Jacobite refugees in Gothenburg, 10 March 1716 and 21 March 1716.

[99] This argument is expanded in Grosjean, *An Unofficial Alliance*, 157–159.

[100] Grosjean, *An Unofficial Alliance*, 165–190. See also A. Grosjean, 'General Alexander Leslie, the Scottish Covenanters and the Riksråd debates, 1638–1640; in Macinnes *et al.*, eds., *Ships, Guns and Bibles*, 115–138 for fuller discussion of these events.

also provided James Graham, Marquis of Montrose, with ships and weapons at his own expense when the Stuart Colonel John Cochrane was sent to Scandinavia in 1649 to obtain military support to restore Charles II.[101] Indeed the military college in Stockholm corresponded at length with Maclean regarding the delivery of ammunition and guns in April 1649.[102] In return for his help, the exiled Charles II created Maclean a baron on 13 April that year, though the Montrosian expedition which set out from Gothenburg was a fiasco which foundered to a great degree on Stuart duplicity.[103] The alleged Jacobite links of Hugh Hamilton and other Jacobite Scots have also been explored elsewhere.[104] However, these extraordinary events tend to overshadow the less overt, but perhaps more economically and socially significant links that the Gothenburg Scots maintained with their homeland, and with Scots elsewhere. Hew Chartres clearly maintained contact with Edinburgh, the city in which he gained his burgess status and the one in which he registered his will.[105] He is quite indicative of his countrymen. Like Chartres, other Gothenburg Scots traded extensively with their countrymen (though far from exclusively) and a review of the cargoes they shipped to and from Gothenburg shows Scotland as a frequent destination, even for Scots born in Gothenburg such as Gabriel Spalding. Interestingly Spalding, who married a foreigner, undertook more trade with Scotland than the Macleans, who married Scots, challenging any simple correlation between marriage patterns and business relationships.[106]

---

[101] See Grosjean, *An Unofficial Alliance*, 219–227.

[102] KRA, Krigskollegium Kancelliet B.1. Registratur. This archive contains eight letters to do with Maclean's gathering of arms for Stuart use.

[103] For Maclean's baronetcy see Maclean, *The Macleans of Sweden*, 20. For more on the Stuart duplicity during this period see S. Murdoch, *Britain, Denmark-Norway and the House of Stuart 1603–1660* (East Linton: 2003), 155–159.

[104] Behre has discussed how the Jacobites turned to Sweden for help in order to reinstate the Stuart king and he stated that "*Karl XII hade soldater, jakobiterna pengar*" ("Karl XII had the soldiers, the Jacobites the money") and that the interface between the two was the Scottish community in Gothenburg. See G. Behre, 'Från Högländerna till Älvdalen: Göteborg och Skottland 1621–1814', in *Personhistorisk tidskrift* (1993), 1718–19. See also S. Murdoch, 'The Scots and Ulster in the seventeenth century: a Scandinavian perspective' in W. Kelly and J. R. Young, *Ulster and Scotland 1600–2000: History, Language and Identity* (Dublin: 2004), 99–103.

[105] Edinburgh Commissary Court, CC8/8/61. Will of Hew Chartres, 16 May 1644.

[106] Deduced from Göteborg Landsarkiv, Drätselkammare and Dalhede, Database.

However, shipping was also undertaken to destinations other than Scotland. John Maclean, one of the most frequent freighters to Scottish ports, also traded heavily with Amsterdam, London, Spain and Hamburg. His last shipment to Scotland appears to have been in 1662, but he continued freighting until 1666. Similarly the rest of his family only appear to have sent goods to London, Hamburg, Stralsund and Amsterdam. Maclean's contemporary, John Spalding, traded extensively with Amsterdam, Hamburg, London, Spain and Portugal as well as Scottish ports. His son Gabriel did likewise. The Young family also sent goods intermittently to Scotland, but far more regularly to Hamburg, Amsterdam, Stralsund and London. Those who sent goods exclusively to Scotland were in the minority; most also dealt with English and other Dutch or Baltic ports. There was no single pattern as regards ships and skippers—sometimes they were Scottish ships with Scottish skippers, but they could just as frequently be Swedish ships with Swedish, German or Dutch skippers. Cargo freighted by Scots was often on board with that of other Swedish or German cargo-owners. The image that emerges is one of absorption into the wider mercantile community, which obviously served the Scottish merchants better than maintaining a distinct and potentially isolated trading community.

Even Hugh Hamilton, after serving in the Williamite army in Ireland and Britain in 1689–1690, took the opportunity to ship around eight consignments of goods between June 1691 and May 1697, mostly to London, but also to Hull and King's Lynn, as well as to Amsterdam and Hamburg.[107] Though not a registered burgess, this shows the importance of not discounting the trading aspect of the military community. Hugh was not alone in trading with Scots at home or in Ireland. John Maclean junior made shipments to Scotland through his kin network, and this even extended into Ireland where his relatives the Hamiltons (on his step-mother's side) had established themselves.[108]

As well as those who traded with home there were those who left Gothenburg either for short periods or for good to settle in the British Isles. In 1674 David Maclean, for example, accompanied the

---

[107] Dalhede, Database, Hugo Hamilton [1512].
[108] Hamilton, A History of the House of Hamilton, 1014–1015.

Swedish ambassador to Britain, and while there gained an M.A. at Oxford before returning.[109] Even members of the third and fourth generations would make the journey back to Britain from Gothenburg for a variety of reasons, like Michael Gabrielson Spalding who went to Britain and ended up serving aboard a British man-of-war.[110] Others left for good, such as Jacob Maclean in the 1650s: despite being Gothenburg-born, he chose to live out his life in Stuart service in Ireland.[111] They were to be followed by Ludovick Hamilton and his wife, Anna Catherina Grubbe-Stjernfelt in 1661, but Hamilton did not receive his final dismissal permit from Swedish service until 1662, along with a travel pass, and died before leaving Gothenburg, in May 1663. His wife made it to Ireland, where she was styled Anna Catherine, Lady Hamilton of Tullykeltyre, Co. Fermanagh.[112]

Conclusion

Seventeenth-century Gothenburg has been shown to have hosted a sizeable and specifically Scottish presence in terms of its mercantile community. The roles these men and women played in both Swedish and British domestic and economic developments cannot be ignored. The service to the Swedish Crown provided by these individuals was not only mercantile but also military, as demonstrated by the close connections between soldiers and merchants. Further, the networks created with Scots in other Swedish towns, most importantly Stockholm, formed an integral part of the success of the Gothenburg community. Initially the Maclean family seems to have dominated the social networks, not only within Gothenburg, but also in the wider Swedish context and in the three British kingdoms. However, the Spaldings, the Kinnairds, the Hamiltons and the Mercers were also heavily represented among the Gothenburg residents.

---

[109] Maclean, *The Macleans of Sweden*, 32; Elgenstierna, *Svenska Adelns Ättartavlor*, V, 139.

[110] SRA, Anglica 190, brev fran utlänningar, vol. 191, 'O'. C. Leijoncrona to Jean Oriot, 5 December 1704. Indeed, Spalding had been press-ganged into service, but released through Leijoncrona's intervention. This part of the future commander's naval service appears to have been omitted from his biographies.

[111] Maclean, *The Macleans of Sweden*, 27; Uppsala University Library, Palmskiöldiska Samlingen, vol. 225, 31; Elgenstierna, *Svenska Adelns Ättartavlor*, V, 139, 142–143.

[112] Hamilton, *A History of the House of Hamilton*, 1014–1015.

In the initial stages of Gothenburg's development its neighbouring towns were particularly significant in providing the source point for several of the Scots migrants. The influx of Scots directly from Scotland and other countries soon increased the community. The tax privileges for burgesses, valid for the first fifteen years of the new town, offered a substantial incentive to newcomers. Despite this, the number of seats for Scots on the town council was smaller than for other foreign nationals (Dutch and German). As yet, little information has emerged indicating that there were any difficulties between the various foreign communities at any time, as had happened in Bergen. This was probably due to the Scots' absorption into the wider community, as shown in the shipping records and marriage registers, leaving them less vulnerable to isolation.

Not all the Scottish migrants in Gothenburg took their new home country to their hearts. James Duncan was an example of this. He married Maria Sofia Maclean in Gothenburg and continued his military service in Sweden until 1671 when he transferred to Danish service. Under the Danish Crown he fought battles against Sweden, having entered the Danish army before the intra-Scandinavian conflict broke out in 1675. The Norwegians even named a part of the war after him, calling the campaign in Bohuslän 'Duncanskrig'.[113] These actions could imply that Duncan was a mercenary out for financial gain. However, he was already in Danish service at the outbreak of war and to desert would have been disloyal. In any case, his change in service cost him dearly as the Swedes confiscated his Swedish property.[114] Additionally he returned to Sweden within a few years of the peace treaty and spent his retirement years in Gothenburg.[115] For that to have happened, he must in some way have been able

---

[113] KRA, 0386, Krigshandlingar 1672–79, I, 'den skotske ryttmästaren Jacob Duncans adventyr i Bohuslän åren 1676–1679; Murdoch, 'Scotsmen on the Danish-Norwegian Frontiers', 24–25.

[114] S. Nygård, ed., *Fortegnelse over kongelige resolutioner gennem rentkammeret 1660–1719*, I, 1660–1679, nr 3005. 8 April 1676 "Det maa forblive ved forrige Resolution ang. det af General Major Duncan begjærede verderlag for hans konfiskerede gods i Sverige til 600 Rdl. Indkomst"

[115] Göteborgs Landsarkiv, Förteckning over Landshövdingens i Göteborg och Bohuslän—Skrivelser till Kungl. Maj:t 1657–1840, 28/03/1682 and 18/04/1682. Duncan died and was buried in the city on 13 March 1686. See Berg, *Samlingar till Göteborgs Historia*, I, 501.

to depend on the Scottish community in the town to protect him from the numerous Swedes harbouring grudges against him.[116]

Duncan's situation was clearly unusual. Most Scots within the Gothenburg community did more good service than harm and many in the Maclean family, including Duncan's brothers-in-law, did much to defend the town. Even though the main Scottish role in the town was transferred to Gothenburg-born Scots as the century wore on, it must still be remembered that until their naturalisation as Swedes in 1674, Gabriel and Johan Spalding both held their positions while being Scottish citizens. Similarly, the importance of their heritage was not lost on the Maclean children, some of whom moved to the British Isles, while David Maclean emphasised the point by re-adopting the Scottish version of his family name in 1708.

The influence of the Gothenburg-Scottish community extended to Britain as well as wider Scandinavia and northern Europe. This was not only seen in the trade undertaken by the merchants, but also during the Bishops' Wars in Scotland from 1639–41, or the Montrosian fiasco of 1649–1650, particularly evident in the activities of John Maclean.[117] This supports the impression that a form of political alliance, as highlighted recently, existed between Scotland and Sweden as early as the seventeenth century, as the emigrant community in Sweden was willing and able to provide this assistance when required. The influence of this community could be great or small, and admittedly was not restricted to the Gothenburg Scots. Indeed scrutiny of a variety of Stockholm's archival sources indicates that there were many more residents in the Swedish capital than the North Sea port. These communities were in constant communication with each other. Their combined support for both their new host country and their ancestral home continued into the eighteenth century during the Williamite Wars (through the Hamilton family) and in the well-documented Jacobite activity in the city following the 1707 Treaty of Union which restructured British politics. With the arrival of some

---

[116] Indeed his widow was invited to act as a godparent within the community after the couple returned to Gothenburg, even to Anna Maria Spalding and Sara Maria Crocket. See Berg, *Samlingar till Göteborgs Historia*, I, 212, 273.

[117] Murdoch, *Britain, Denmark-Norway and the House of Stuart*, 91, 96, 102, 105, 155; Grosjean, *An Unofficial Alliance*, 215–224.

twenty Jacobites accompanying Kenneth Sutherland, Lord Duffus, in 1716, a new phase for the Scots in Gothenburg unfolded. Despite the protestations of the Hanovarian representative, Robert Jackson, the Scottish community and their allies in Gothenburg were secure enough to resist attempts to dislodge them.[118] Having established the structure of the community, the presence and developments of it as discussed by Göran Behre in this later period can be better understood.[119] Over time there was bound to be more mixing with Swedish families, but new influxes of Scots after 1716 and on the establishment of the Swedish East India Company in 1731 ensured the community continued to flourish. Bearing in mind the letter of Thomas Thomson of 1812 quoted at the beginning of this chapter in combination with the other evidence presented, it is clear that Gothenburg's epithet of 'Little London' obscures the importance of the Scottish community for the city. Yet the full impact of this community on Scottish and British relations with Sweden will only be fully understood once the much older and larger Scottish presence in Stockholm receives serious scholarly attention.

---

[118] Gothenburg Landsarkiv, Förteckning över landshövdingens i Göteborg och Bohuslän—Skrivelser till Kungl. Maj;t, 1657–1840. Letter to Karl XII, 28 February 1716; SRA, Kanslikollegiets Skrivelser till Kungl. Maj:t 1656–1718, Robert Jackson's memorials on Scottish Jacobite refugees in Gothenburg, 10 March 1716 and 21 March 1716. Kanslikollegiets notes on Jackson's memorial, 11 April 1716; Steve Murdoch's review of Rebecca Wills, *The Jacobites and Russia 1715–1750* (East Linton: 2002) in *Aberdeen University Review*, LIX, no. 208, Autumn 2002, 344.

[119] G. Behre, *Sweden and the Rising of 1745* (Edinburgh: 1972); G. Behre, 'Göteborg, Skottland och vackre prinsen' in *Göteborg för och nu*, no 16, 1982.

APPENDIX A

KNOWN SCOTTISH BURGESSES AND RESIDENTS OF GOTHENBURG TO 1707[120]

Name	Year
John Carnegie	1619 (Nylöse)
James Mercer	1619 (Nylöse)
Andrew Young	1619 (Nylöse)
John "Bartsker"*	1619 (Nylöse)
Thomas "Smith"*	1619 (Nylöse)
John "Taylor"*	1619 (Nylöse)
Andrew "Weaver"*	1619 (Nylöse)
James Maclean	1621–28 (Nylöse)
James Lindsay	1621
Thomas Stewart	1621
Alexander Murray	1621
George Ogilvie	1621
John Young	1621
John Spalding	1621
Thomas Hunter	1624
Francis Barker	1625
James Garden	1625
Henry Sinclair	1627
John Maclean	1628
James Kinnaird	1628
Alexander Sandilands	1628
Anthony Kennedy	1629
William Petrie	1639
George Scott	1639
Andrew Wishart	1639
John Lindsay	1639
William Jack	1639
Anna Cummings	1639
George Spalding	1642
Hew Chartres	1644
(John) Hans Barker	1646

[120] The years noted here refer only to a probable date of burgess-ship. Several of these men had been in Sweden long before their date of becoming burgesses. The last two names have been included as their trading activities doubtless preceded their date of burgess-ship. The * refers to a trade given in place of a family name. The ‡ symbol indicates people whom Ashton notes as English, *Lives and Livelihood*, 22.

Appendix 1 (*cont.*)

Name	Year
Robert Bruce	1653
James Jack	1654
Gilbert Guthrie	1658
Gabriel Spalding	1666
Johan Spalding	1666
William Davidson	1666
Robert Beets	1666
John Parker	1666
Johan Williamson Leyel	1666
Thomas Bleckinhop	1666
Robert Clerck‡	1670
John Mercer	1672
Robert Guthrie	1672
Daniel Crocket‡	1673
John Small	1675
John Lindsay (Lentz?)	1681
Hugh Hamilton	1690
Colin Crocket‡	1691
Andrew Bruce	1694
Andrew Spalding	1696
David Kinnaird	1698
James Barclay	1701
James Galbraith	1705

APPENDIX B

LIST OF ENGLISH BURGESSES AND TRADERS OF GOTHENBURG IN THE SEVENTEENTH CENTURY[121]

Anthony Knipe	1621
Henry Hampton	1639
Thomas Hacker	1644
Arthur Rose	1650
Nathaniel Crispin?	1666
Maccabeus Thornton	1685
George Duck?	1686
John Rockes	1690
Joris (George) Pickerin	1691
Vincent Certain?	1693

---

[121] Those names with a '?' next to them are presumed English.

THE SCOTTISH COMMUNITY IN KĖDAINIAI
C.1630–C.1750

Rimantas Žirgulis[1]

This towne belongeth to the family of the Radzivills, where is the publick exercise of the Protestant religion, and, because of that, many Scotsmen here living, by one whereof wee lodged, and being welcomed by some of our countrymen with a hearty cup of strong meade.

Patrick Gordon, 1661[2]

Kėdainiai (*Kiejdany*) has been described as a centre for 'the propagation of the Reformation in the Grand Duchy of Lithuania' following the conversion of Anna Radziwill to the Protestant faith in 1549. Religious conflicts in Vilnius in 1611 and 1639 led to the expulsion of Protestants from the Lithuanian capital, and their troubles increased during the 1621 Livonia War, when Biržai (*Birze*), a Radziwill patrimony, was destroyed. Only Kėdainiai remained as a major Radziwill town, from where the family hoped to revive their fortunes.[3] With this goal in mind, they had to find like-minded people who shared their religious beliefs, and for this the family had to look beyond the borders of the predominantly Catholic commonwealth of Poland-Lithuania.

The Radziwill dukes were well-educated magnates who had studied in the Protestant universities of Altdorf, Leipzig, Heidelberg and Leiden. They visited several states and experienced a more progressive 'western' European way of life than that which they had known in Lithuania. They tried to replicate what they had seen in

[1] I would like to thank Dr Steve Murdoch and Dr Alexia Grosjean for inviting me to Aberdeen to present this paper and to learn so much useful information relating to it. I would also like to thank Dr Linas Eriksonas without whom these important links would never have been fostered, and to all again for their comments on my text.

[2] Spalding Club, *Passages from the Diary of General Patrick Gordon of Auchleuchries, A.D. 1635–A.D. 1699* (Aberdeen: 1859), 41.

[3] I. Lukšaitė, 'Kėdainių reikšmė Lietuvos reformacijoje', in *Mokslinės konferencijos "Kėdainių savivaldybei- 400" pranešimų tezės* (Kėdainiai: 1990), 10.

their own domains, initially in Kėdainiai. In 1627 Duke Krysztof
Radziwill (1585–1640) began reorganising Kėdainiai. He returned
the church of St George (occupied by the Reformers since 1549) to
the Catholics and confirmed the confessional equality of Catholics
and Protestants in the town.[4] He also re-confirmed the Magdeburg
Rights, which had been granted to the town as early as 1590, donated
a new coat of arms, and allowed free passage in and out of the
town to all.[5] The Radziwills considerably developed the town's government and its economic and religious life. But their influence
extended beyond the city. During the seventeenth century the main
institutions of the Protestant reformers in Lithuania were centred in
Kėdainiai. The most important of these, the 'Samogitian Superintendents', lived and worked in the city. Several Protestant churches
were built, one with a school attached which later developed into
an important Protestant college (*gymnasium*). The college masters were
renowned intellectuals. A printing-house was built beside the college,
where the reformers printed their religious books. Within a few
decades a strong Protestant infrastructure had developed in the city.

To encourage civic order and economic development, Krysztof
Radziwill invited people of various nations and confessions to settle
in Kėdainiai. In 1624 several Jews began to trade and settle there.[6]
Some local townspeople were initially hostile to the newcomers, whom
they viewed as commercial rivals. In 1628 this led to a complaint
from some of the townspeople to the king, Sigismund III Vasa, in
which they maintained that the newcomers impinged on their own
businesses. Here the Scots were mentioned among other foreigners:
Jews, Dutchmen and Germans. However, Sigismund III could not
help the locals as Kėdainiai was a private town belonging to Krysztof
Radziwill.[7] More foreigners were permitted to settle. The following

---

[4] J. Seredyka, 'Dzieje zatargów i ugody o kościół kiejdański w XVI–XVII w', in
Odrodzenie i reformacja w Polsce, XXI (1976), 100.
[5] A. Miškinis and H. Grinevičius, *Kėdainių urbanistinė raida//Architektūros paminklai*,
III (Vilnius: 1975), 160.
[6] A. Miškinis and H. Grinevičius, *Kėdainių urbanistinė raida//Architektūros paminklai*,
III (Vilnius: 1975), 160.
[7] L. Eriksonas, 'The Lost Colony of Scots: Unravelling Overseas Connections
in a Lithuanian Town' in A. I. Macinnes, T. Riis and F. G. Pedersen, eds.,
Ships, Guns and Bibles in the North Sea and the Baltic States, c.1350–c.1700 (East Linton:
2000), 178.

year, in 1629, German Lutherans arrived.[8] At this time Krysztof Radziwill was in touch with the Reformed Church of Elbing, which had Scottish members as well as a Scottish cleric, John Durie.[9] From 1628–29 Scottish Presbyterians also appeared in Kėdainiai, possibly from Elbing, although we do not know if there was an official invitation. Certainly the religious freedom encouraged in the town made Kėdainiai an attractive destination for Scots of the Reformed faith.[10] Their appearance is not surprising given the long-standing migrations to Poland-Lithuania from Scotland, as outlined by Professor Kowalski in this volume.[11]

It has previously been claimed that the main reason for Scottish migration to Kėdainiai was that it offered an escape from religious persecution at home.[12] However, given that the Scots in Kėdainiai were Calvinsts who were not persecuted until the second half of the century, other reasons must be found for their arrival in the 1630s. The two most likely are the economic and religious opportunities afforded by a move to Kėdainiai. These were well-known in Scotland; as early as 1537 Prussia had legislated against Scots who were trading there illegally in competition with local merchants.[13] The Scots then moved to Poland, where there was less animosity until they again settled and traded illegally and paid the subsequent penalties: expulsion from towns, confiscation of goods and other property,

---

[8] P. Šinkūnas, *Kėdainių miesto istorija* (Kaunas: 1928), 29.

[9] Eriksonas, 'The Lost Colony of Scots', 178; S. Murdoch, 'Kith and Kin: John Durie and the Scottish community in Scandinavia and the Baltic, 1624–34' in P. Salmon and T. Barrow, eds., *Britain and the Baltic* (Sunderland: 2003), 34.

[10] Anna Biegańska, 'In Search of Tolerance: Scottish Catholics and Presbyterians in Poland' in *Scottish Slavonic Review*, XVII, Autumn 1991, 39; A. Juknevicius and R. Žirgulis, 'Kėdainiai Region: Historical Review' in A. Juknevicius, A. Stanaitis and R. Žirgulis, *Kėdainiai and Environs* (Kėdainiai: 1998), 14; R. I. Frost, 'Confessionalization and the Army in the Polish-Lithuanian Commonwealth, 1550–1667' in J. Bahlcke and A. Strohmeyer (eds.), *Konfessionalisierung in Ostmitteleuropa* (Stuttgart: 1999), 142.

[11] G. Labuda and K. H. Ruffmann, 'Engländer und Schotten in des Seestäden Ost- und Westpreussens' in *Zeitschrift für Ostforschung*, Jg VII, (1958); *Rocznik Gdański*, XVII/XVIII, (1958/1959), 361; S. Murdoch, 'The Scots in Kėdainiai in their Scandinavian and Baltic Context' in *Almanach Historyczny* (2006); Murdoch, 'Kith and Kin', 36–45.

[12] J. Jaroszewicz, *Obraz Litwy pod względem jej cywilizacji od czasow najdawniejszych do konca wieku XVIII*, II (Wilno: 1844), 107; И. Пташкин, *Местечко Кейданы* (Ковна: 1899), 2; Šinkūnas, Kėdainių miesto istorija, 18.

[13] S. Tomkowicz, *Przyczynek do historii szkotow w Krakowie i w Polsce//Rocznik*, II (Krakowski: 1899), 157.

taxation with enormous additional contributions. Despite this, the solidarity of their communities led to an increase in illegal Scottish immigration. The sheer number of immigrants placed tensions on the relations between the Scots and their host communities, and in 1594 this led to an attempt by Sigismund III to curb the influx.[14] His measures had little effect, so the Scottish factor in Poland, Patrick Gordon, drew up a strict code in 1616 in a further attempt to solve the problem.[15] However, this measure also failed, compelling the Scottish community in Danzig to seek the intervention of King James VI and I of Great Britain in order to prevent any more of the "exorbitant numberis of zoung boyis and maidis vnable for any seruice, transported hier zierlie."[16] The Scottish community in Poland-Lithuania in the seventeenth century is already known to have been both large and influential.[17] So much so, that all the merchant consuls and diplomats sent out during the 'British' reign of James VI & I were in fact drawn from the Scottish nation.[18] Supposedly, there were between 30–50,000 Scots in the commonwealth at that time, although as Professor Kowalski shows elsewhere in this volume, that figure can be questioned. However, their numbers were still significant, and having encountered an unwelcoming attitude in Poland, the Scots looked to new territory—the Grand Duchy of Lithuania. This region actually proved harder to enter, as they were not allowed into the capital, Vilnius, and thus formed several small communities in Kaunas,

[14] *Edict against the Scots issued by Sigismund III*, 12 September 1594, reprinted in Th. Fischer, *The Scots in East and West Prussia* (Edinburgh: 1903), 158.

[15] *The eighty Articles drawn up by Patrick Gordon for the Scots in Prussia* (Königsberg: 1616), reproduced in Th. Fischer, *The Scots in East and West Prussia* (Edinburgh: 1903), 159–170; Seliga and Koczy, *Scotland and Poland*, 6–7.

[16] See 'Scottish subjects at Dantzic to King James VI, Dantzic, 30 August 1624' reprinted in the Abbotsford Club, *Letters and State Papers during the Reign of King James the Sixth, chiefly from the manuscript collections of Sir James Balfour of Denmyln* (Edinburgh: 1837), 367–368; *RPCS*, XIII, 702; Fischer, *The Scots in Germany*, 33–34.

[17] A. F. Steuart, ed., *Papers relating to the Scots in Poland, 1576–1793* (Edinburgh: 1915); Stanislaw Seliga and Leon Koczy, *Scotland and Poland. A Chapter of Forgotten History* (Scotland: 1969); A. Biegańska, 'Scottish merchants and traders in seventeenth and eighteenth century Warsaw', *Scottish Slavonic Review*, no. 5, (Autumn 1985); A. Biegańska, 'A note on the Scots in Poland, 1550–1800' in T. C. Smout, ed., *Scotland and Europe 1200–1850* (Edinburgh: 1986); A. Biegańska, 'In Search of Tolerance: Scottish Catholics and Presbyterians in Poland', *Scottish Slavonic Review*, no. 17 (Autumn 1991).

[18] S. Murdoch, 'Diplomacy in Transition: Stuart-British Diplomacy in Northern Europe, 1603–1618' in Macinnes, Riis and Pedersen, *Ships, Guns and Bibles*, 93–107.

Kelmė, Biržai, Tauragė and Skuodas. The largest and most influential Scottish community eventually emerged in Kėdainiai.[19]

Since most of the Kėdainiai magistrate books for the seventeenth century have been destroyed by fire, there is little official information on the Scots' arrival and their settlement in Kėdainiai. Many questions therefore remain unanswered. Almost no foreigners' surnames appear in the 'Kėdainiai Inventory' for the years 1604 and 1624, with the exception of a few German names.[20] However, an important source of information survives in a collection of financial documents belonging to the Reformed Church in Kėdainiai from the years 1628–63.[21] The first Scottish surnames do not appear in these documents until the 1630s, including Gilbert, Ogilvie (Ogilby), Gordon, Leonard (Lenart), Baldwin, Hendrie (Endrys); sometimes an entry consists simply of a name like 'Tomas Szot'.[22] Using these sources, we can be quite certain that the post-1628 period is an accurate date of arrival for the Scots. Throughout the decade, the number of Scottish names continues to rise. For example, the documents for the year 1637 contain some twenty four Scots who contributed money to the church. These individuals often adopted the local language and their names were usually noted in the Polish form: Jan, Jerzy, Wojciech, Katarzyna, etc., which makes it difficult to separate them from other citizens. Nonetheless we can establish that four of them rented the church's shops.[23]

Not all of these migrant Scots were mercantile traders. Some served as soldiers for the Radziwill dukes.[24] In 1629 two Scots doctors of theology, James Patterson and Alexander Nicholas, were noted among the first four lecturers of the Kėdainiai college.[25] Thus various motives

---

[19] Jaroszewicz, *Obraz Litwy*, 107; S. Z. Tworek, 'dziejów kalwinizmu w Wielkim Księstwe Litewskim w XVIII w', in *Annales Universitatis Mariae Curie—Skłodowska. Lublin—Polonia*, Vol. XXI: 8 (1966), 197; S. Aleksandrowicz, 'Zaludnenie miasteczek Litwy i Bialorusi w XVI i pierwszej połowie XVII wieku//Roczniki dziejów społecznych i gospodarczych' T.27 (1966), 48; E. Meilus, 'Žemaitijos kunigaikštystės miesteliai XVII a. II pusėje—XVIII a. (Vilnius: 1997), 47.

[20] Vilnius University Library (hereafter VUB), f. 4, A1723, '1604 Inventory of Kėdainiai'; VUB, f.4, A1724/'1624 Inventory of Kėdainiai'.

[21] *Collecta zboru Kiejdańskiego* (Wilno: 1939).

[22] *Collecta zboru Kiejdańskiego*, 8, 13, 16, 24, 32.

[23] *Collecta zboru Kiejdańskiego*, 35–38.

[24] Eriksonas, 'The Lost Colony of Scots', 179.

[25] Šinkūnas, *Kėdainių miesto istorija*, 22.

must be considered when studying the Scots' movement to Kėdainiai. The quest for a religious Utopia was undoubtedly behind the later presence of several theologians. During the Thirty Years' War in Europe, the Protestant ideologists Samuel Hartlib and John Durie created an ideal of 'the Promised Land' which they called 'Antilia'. It was to be a community of dedicated and faithful workers of the Lord, which would be founded in a place unhindered by religious and political oppression and ruinous warfare.[26] Krysztof Radziwill corresponded with various prominent European Protestants, and among his correspondents were the authors of the Utopian Antilia. In this way Kėdainiai—owned by a powerful patron of the Protestants—became the place in which to realise Antilia.[27]

An example of this movement is the military clergyman John Douglas, who served as a chaplain to the Scots-Dutch Brigade in the Dutch Republic after being ordained in Stirling in 1606. On leaving the military he served at the English Reformed Church of Amsterdam, before being accepted as a member of the Classis of Utrecht and subscribing to the Dutch Reformed confession. He had returned to St Andrews by 1621, and became a doctor of divinity the following year. In 1637 Douglas arrived in Kėdainiai, and although it is not known how long he remained there, it is recorded that he preached in both Scots and English, indicating the presence of both nations in the town.[28] It has also been observed that in the year Douglas arrived, some twenty two Scots were listed among his parishioners, an increase of twenty over the previous year. It is tempting to look to events in Scotland for the cause of their journey across Europe to Lithuania. However, an assumption that the Scots arrived as refugees in 1637 is flawed for two reasons; firstly, the National Covenant of Scotland was not drawn up until the following year, and secondly, hostilities against the Stuart regime did not begin until

---

[26] Eriksonas, 'The Lost Colony of Scots', 178. This article is an important contribution to our understanding of the Scots in the city. The title is somewhat misleading. The Scots had no intention of setting up a colony and had no imperial designs on the city. Rather they sought to form a community of like-minded souls from whatever ethnic background. As to it being a lost community, that is a matter of perspective. Certainly some of those who still live in the city are aware of it.

[27] Eriksonas, 'The Lost Colony of Scots', 178.

[28] A. C. Dow, *Ministers to the Soldiers of Scotland* (Edinburgh: 1962), 63; Juknevicius and Žirgulis, 'Kėdainiai Region: Historical Review', 16; Eriksonas, 'The Lost Colony of Scots', 176–177.

1639.[29] Even after war broke out, the serious fighting took place in the north of England, and the Calvinists held the upper hand until the mid-1640s. It is only during the late 1640s that we can really expect to find Calvinist refugees leaving the country, unless we wish to include Scottish settlers in Ireland escaping the Catholic uprising there at the end of 1641. The suggestion that the Kėdainiai Scots community was formed from existing members of the continental Scottish diaspora probably carries more weight, especially given the massive displacements which occurred elsewhere in Europe during the various phases of the Thirty Years' War.[30] Wherever they came from, the arrival of this particular wave of settlers reflected the beginning of a Scots community in Kėdainiai, rather than simply a group of Scottish individuals in a Lithuanian town.

The Scots in Kėdainiai were a privileged group, protected by Duke Krysztof Radziwill and his court as co-believers and important contributors to the town's economic life. In contrast with Poland, where most of the Scots were pedlars and petty traders, the Scots in Kėdainiai were integrated immediately into the town's elite, becoming prominent members and supporters of the main church.[31] Before the construction of the large Reformed church in the Main Market Square, the Scots Calvinists and the German Lutherans prayed in a Reformed church built next to the Radziwills' court (in the future district of Januszowo).[32] The perceived Scottish influence in the Reformed Church in Kėdainiai is reflected in the fact that in 1638 the church authority had to change the schedule of services. The Polish-speaking parishioners complained that after the Scottish service, which followed the Lithuanian one, there was little time left for a sermon in Polish. The new schedule put the Polish service ahead of the Scottish one.[33] This could have contributed to a deeper sense of separation felt by the Scots, and they certainly tried to maintain their distinctiveness. They often described themselves as being "*z naciej szkotskiej*" (of the Scottish nation) or "*ex gente scotica*" (from

---

[29] See A. I. Macinnes, *Charles I and the making of the Covenanting Movement* (Edinburgh: 1991).

[30] Macinnes, *Ships, Guns and Bibles*, xvi.

[31] Labuda and Ruffmann, 'Engländer und Schotten', 361.

[32] Пташкин, *Местечко Кейданы*, 11.

[33] *Collecta zboru Kiejdańskiego*, 43.

the Scottish race).[34] That they stuck together is evidenced by the fact that the godparents of a new-born child of a Scottish father tended to be Scots as well. Indeed the church authorities intervened to instruct them to communicate more with the townspeople, and not to celebrate the Lord's Supper or take the Holy Sacrament separately from non-Scots.[35] The integration policy did not succeed immediately; Eleazar Gilbert, author of a book published in London in 1641, described himself as preacher to the Kėdainiai Scots congregation rather than simply as the Calvinist minister in the town.[36]

The Scots overcame many of these cultural and linguistic differences by marrying into the local Protestant élite. But the process was not entirely straightforward. When a preacher of the Reformed Church, Jan Progulbicki, decided to marry a Scottish woman called Miss Chapman (Chapmanowa) in 1652, the local Scots complained to the church authorities that such a marriage could damage the Church. The authorities forbade the wedding, but after some time it transpired that Progulbicki was living with Miss Chapman despite their strictures. For this disobedience he was forcibly resettled to the Zawilejski district, although it is not clear if Miss Chapman accompanied him.[37] Neither is it known if the Scots objected because they wished Miss Chapman to marry someone else, but there may have been other reasons, given the response of the church authorities.

Despite this episode integration continued and within a couple of years Scottish surnames appeared among the members of the Kėdainiai assembly. On 3 June 1655, the Scottish parishioners of the Kėdainiai Reformed Church thanked the Vilnius Synod for sending them the Rev. Szydlowski, who held services in Polish. The Scots asked the synod to continue the minister's work in the office for the Scottish community, showing their further integration into the wider community.[38] It should be noted that at this time, the German Lutherans

---

[34] *Collecta zboru Kiejdańskiego*, 103; J. Lukaszewicz, *Dzieje kościolow wyznania helweckiego w Litwie*, I, (Poznan: 1842), 28.

[35] *Collecta zboru Kiejdańskiego*, 58.

[36] *Newes from Poland Wherein is declared the cruel practice of the Popish Clergie against the Protestants, and in particular against the Ministers of the City of Vilna, in the Great Dukedome of Lithuania, under the Governement of the most Illustrious Prince, Duke Radzivill. Faithfully set downe by Eleazar Gilbert, Minister to the foresaid Prince, and Preacher to the Scots Congregation in Keydon* (London: 1641).

[37] *Collecta zboru Kiejdańskiego*, 79, 82.

[38] Lithuanian National Library of Martynas Mažvydas (hereafter LNMMB), 3 June

were much more isolated: in Kėdainiai they had a specifically appointed residential district, and in Biržai, Krysztof Radziwill ordered them to use only their native German language, which reveals their lack of integration compared to the Scots.[39]

After the death of Krysztof Radziwill in 1640, the policy of supporting immigrants in Kėdainiai continued. His widow, Anna Kiszczanka Radziwillowa, exempted the Germans from taxation for ten years from 1643. Duke Janusz Radziwill (1612–1655), a son of the late Krysztof, inherited Kėdainiai and established another autonomous suburb in 1647 (Januszowo) for the German community. Quite why he wished to separate the Germans in this way is unclear. He regulated an order of election to the magistrates' court, indicating that neither the national nor religious orientation of candidates would be an obstacle to their election; this suggests the town was not to be a 'Germans only' preserve.[40] There is no doubt that this was a success for Janusz Radziwill—the town's economic life flourished, as did his personal income.

In contrast to his humble and moderate father Krysztof, Janusz enjoyed the high life and found himself continually in debt.[41] The Scot Jan Lauson (John Lawson), who contributed 2,000 zloty to the Kėdainiai Reformed Church, was among his creditors. Janusz Radziwill borrowed money in 1650 for a three-year term, with interest at 8%.[42] Although he spent money on the church, he also increased the trappings of his status. He reconstructed an old castle of his father's in Kėdainiai, in which 'Duke Ian Radzweill had a lyfe company, all or most Scottismen,' which even Catholic Scots like Patrick Gordon hoped to join.[43] Quite how many Scots there were in this company is unclear, yet their service is commemorated in the modern poetry

---

1655, Kėdainiai. Acknowledgment of Kėdainiai Reformed Church parishioners of the Scottish nation to Vilnius Synod for the appointed clergyman. f.93–558.

[39] Library of Lithuania Academy of Science, f. 1–259, 28 April 1648, Vilnius. 'A Privilege of Vladislaw IV Vasa to Kėdainiai'; H. Wisner, 'Kristupo Radvilos (1585–1640) požiūris į religijas', in *Protestantizmas Lietuvoje: istorija ir dabartis* (Vilnius: 1994), 40.

[40] A. Tyla, 'Jonušas ir Boguslavas Radvilos—Kėdainių miesto valdymo tvarkos kūrėjai', in *"Knyga nobažnystės krikščioniškos" (1653)—XVII a. Lietuvos kultūros paminklas* (Kėdainiai: 2001), 34.

[41] A. Paliušytė, *Dailė Biržų Radvilų dvare XVII a. pirmojoje pusėje// Kultūros istorijos tyrinėjimai*, IV (Vilnius: 1998), 33–38.

[42] *Collecta zboru Kiejdańskiego*, 68.

[43] *Diary of General Patrick Gordon*, 14.

of Vytautas Bloze.[44] These Scottish soldiers were soon to play a part in the hostilities between Poland-Lithuania, Sweden and Muscovy.

In 1655, the town had reached the height of its prosperity. There were about 500 houses with 4–5,000 residents, ten guilds, about 300 craftsmen and six market squares. Six religious confessions were recognised among the wider Kėdainiai community. The position of the town became more uncertain after Janusz Radziwill signed the Treaty of Kėdainiai with Sweden in August 1655 and Lithuania withdrew from the Polish-Lithuanian commonwealth on 20 October.[45] This resulted in the temporary formation of a new state, Sweden-Lithuania.[46] The war that followed the signing of this treaty raged for the duration of 1655–56 and the town suffered. Following the Swedish-Lithuanian union some Lithuanians turned against the Poles, while others joined the resistance to fight against the Swedes and Muscovites.[47] Janusz Radziwill led a small force of Lithuanian, Polish, German and Scottish soldiers against Jan Casimir after October 1655, perhaps, though not exclusively, because it became clear that Jan Casimir intended to fight the war on confessional issues.[48] The pro-Radziwill Scots supplemented large numbers of their countrymen in the Swedish army of Robert Douglas, attacking the Poles from Ingria. Other Scottish regiments undertook a diversionary attack from Narva.[49] Most of the townspeople deserted Kėdainiai and escaped to Prussia. Duke Janusz Radziwill died soon after and his property was forfeited for what was seen as his treachery. However, in 1657 Kėdainiai devolved upon his cousin and son-in-law Boguslaw Radziwill (1620–1669). The latter had saved his fortune by returning to the 'Polish'

---

[44] See the appendix.

[45] Frost, 'Confessionalization and the Army', 140.

[46] Juknevicius and Žirgulis, 'Kėdainiai Region: Historical Review', 18. A surprising role here for a 'Scot' arose through the participation of Bengt Skytte, one of the two Swedish signatories to the treaty. Skytte had a claim to call himself a Scot through his mother, Margaret Neave. The Skytte family maintained an interest in their Scottish lands, and Bengt himself had been knighted by Charles I in 1630 after travelling to the Stuart Court with the Scot, Sir James Spens of Wormiston. See Swedish Riksarkiv, Anglica V, Johan Skytte to James Spens, 4 September 1614; G. Elgenstierna, *Den Introducerade Svenska Adelns Ättartavlor* (9 vols., Stockholm: 1925–1936), VII, 319–320. I thank Dr Alexia Grosjean for this information.

[47] R. Frost, *The Northern Wars 1558–1721* (London: 2000), 168–177 and 254.

[48] Frost, 'Confessionalization and the Army', 139, 148.

[49] N. A. Kullberg, *et al.*, (eds.), *Svenska Riksrådets Protokoll, 1621–1658* (vols. 1–18, Stockholm: 1878–1959), XVI, 734. Riksråd minutes, 4/14 September 1656.

fold before the war ended. Thereafter, Majors Carstares (Caster) and Gardiner, and Captains Gordon, Maitland and Montgomery served the family well into the 1660s.[50] Possibly they recognized that to leave the security of this patronage could have been fatal in the increasingly anti-Calvinist commonwealth. They would certainly have wished to avoid the fate of their Jewish neighbours.

More than other ethnic groups, the Jews fell victim to the plague and wars that devastated the city in the 1650s and 1660s. In fact by 1663 many of the citizens of Kėdainiai had died or emigrated, including most of the Jews.[51] Some 25,000 had been resident in Lithuania, with many more living throughout the commonwealth.[52] Estimates for their population in the commonwealth suggest that from 100–180,000 Jews were killed or left Poland-Lithuania during this period.[53] The Scots fared better. They remained in positions of trust so that, under the patronage of Boguslaw Radziwill in the 1660s, they took over the town administration and occupied many other positions of authority.[54] It is obvious that the Scots were experienced merchants and understood finance as they were often mentioned as financiers of the church, tax-collectors, tenants of church shops and manorial estates.

One example is the manorial estate of Jodkiszki, which belonged to the Reformed Church and in 1659 was rented for a six-year period to the Kėdainiai burgess George (Jerzy) Anderson for 200 zloty. Another manorial estate was rented to James Cook (Jakub Kiuk) for 100 zloty.[55] Jerzy Anderson became the town's mayor and the majority of the court members were also Scots: William Cooper (Vilhelm Kuper), James Cook, George (Jerzy) Haliburton, Wojciech Livingston (Levingston), John (Jan) Davidson and George (Jerzy) Molleson.[56] The Scots also continued to appear in the personal guard of Duke Boguslaw Radziwill. In addition, throughout the period from 1660–90, the rectors of Kėdainiai College and the clergymen of the

---

[50] *Diary of General Patrick Gordon*, 41; Eriksonas, 'The Lost Colony of Scots', 179.

[51] Juknevicius and Žirgulis, 'Kėdainiai Region: Historical Review', 18.

[52] Z. Guldon and W. Kowalski, 'The Jewish Population of Polish Towns in the Second Half of the 17th Century' in A. Teller, ed., *Studies in the History of the Jews in Old Poland: In Honour of Jacob Goldberg* (Jerusalem: 1998), 67–68.

[53] Guldon and Kowalski, 'The Jewish Population of Polish Towns', 69.

[54] Eriksonas, 'The Lost Colony of Scots', 180.

[55] *Collecta zboru Kiejdańskiego*, 111–112.

[56] A. Tyla, 'Decemvyratas, arba Tertio ordo Communitatis, Kėdainių savivaldoje (XVII–XVIII a.)', in Lietuvos istorijos metraštis. 1999 metai (Vilnius: 2000), 73.

Reformed Church were also predominantly Scots. There were many Scottish academics and teachers on the continent, so the presence of James Patterson, Alexander Nicholas, John (Jan) Jordan and Thomas Ramsay in Kėdainiai is not unusual.[57] Naturally some of their students were Scots as well.[58]

Thus, in the second half of the seventeenth century a particularly Scottish oligarchy existed in Kėdainai. The situation can be illustrated by a drawing of the Main Market Square of 1661 and an inventory of 1663: eleven possessions out of nineteen in the main and prestigious town square belonged to Scots[59] (see appendix below). An inventory of 1666 mentions thirty one Scottish houses (two of which had been burnt down and three of which were uninhabited) and five additional properties. The Scots lived not just in the centre—the Main Market Square or the streets of Zamkowa, Konska and Skomgalska—but also in the German suburb of Januszowo in Roseynska Street, in the Jewish district in Zydowska and Poeismilgska streets, and even in the Catholic quarter on the left bank of the Nevėžis at Wilenska and Kowienska streets.[60]

Throughout the 1660s, Boguslaw Radziwill tried to reconstruct the war-ravaged town. In 1666 he added the 'Regulations of Kėdainiai' to the town's administration. In them he set about clarifying the civil jurisdiction. The 'Regulations' stated that "conversely to the will of Janusz Radziwill, foreigners are being prevented from becoming superintendents in civic society." Boguslaw therefore stipulated that:

> it is necessary, now and in the future, to ensure the equal right of all foreigners to participate in elections for the magistrates' court, together with the local residents. In addition, all vacant posts in future elections to the court of law, as well as in the magistrates' court, must be open to foreign citizens: 4 *decemvires*, 2 members of a bailiff court, 2 members of the magistracy and 1 burgomaster must be always elected from among them.[61]

---

[57] Eriksonas, 'The Lost Colony of Scots', 175; Akta synodow od roku 1676 do r. 1709, LNMMB, f. 93–20, p. 377; S. Tworek, 'Materiały do dziejów kalwinizmu w Wielkim Księstwie Litewskim w XVII wieku', in *Odrodzenie i reformacja w Polsce*, XIV (1969), 214; I. Lukšaitė, *Lietuvė kalba reformaciniame judėjime XVII a.* (Vilnius: 1970), 23.

[58] LNMMB, f. 93–541, l. 8^r., Acta sessialne zboru Kieydanskiego 1664–1717.

[59] J. Oksas, 'Kėdainių senamiesčio regeneracijos istoriniai tyrimai' (unpublished manuscript, Kaunas: 1990), 113–115.

[60] VUB, f. 4, A215, 16891, '1666, Inventory of Kėdainiai'.

[61] Šinkūnas, *Kėdainių miesto istorija*, 79.

Antanas Tyla gives information relating to the town officials from the years 1590–1795. For this period of the town's autonomous status, 225 officials' surnames were found in various documents. Some names were repeated, as several people held different posts at different times. Of the 225 officials, forty three were Scots (19.1%) and eighteen were Germans (8%). Thus sixty one surnames were of foreign origin, that is, 27.1% of the Kėdainiai officials' surnames. The rest were Lithuanians or Poles.[62] Foreigners did not completely dominate civic society in Kėdainiai, but the number of Scots is certainly significant, particularly in the second half of the century.

After the 1660s, Scottish numbers were perhaps bolstered by the arrival of new Scottish immigrants. The 'Protocol of the Extraordinary Church Session' on 25 February 1667 proclaimed that the Scots were an integral part of both the Reformed and the wider town communities, both of which lived under the same civic juristiction. It also noted that the Scots had nominated someone who, without permission from the church authority, held services in the community's native language. This in itself is probably indicative of new immigrants arriving directly from Scotland, as long-term residents would have adopted one of the local languages by this time. Nonetheless, until permission was obtained the Scots were asked not to hold private sermons and to accept sermons in Polish or Lithuanian. This would avoid upsetting the wider community and would maintain the same order as other Reformed churches in Lithuania. Thereby the Scots also avoided the censure the Anti-Trinitarians had attracted for holding private meetings.[63]

The list of Kėdainiai Reformed Church parishioners for 1679 recorded 253 people. Ninety-six of them were Scots or members of their families, that is, 37.9% of the total number of parishioners. This list noted Scottish family members, including wives, children and servants. Women's names and maiden names show that some Scottish families were of mixed ethnicity. Examples are Katarzyna Miszewiczówna-Mollison (Malleisson), Judyta Budrewiczówna-Gordon and Krystyna Boryszewska-Peterson (Petersonowa). In some families the wives were also of Scottish descent, such as Katarzyna Chrighton-

[62] Tyla, 'Decemvyratas', 73–75.
[63] 25 February 1667, Kėdainiai. A Protocol of Kėdainiai Reformed Church Extraordinary Session. LNMMB, f. 93–541, l. 15ʳ⁻ᵛ.

Livingston (Krechtonówna-Lewinston); Dorota Burnet-Davidson (Burnetówna-Dawidson); Zofia Bennet-Moncrieff (Bennetówna-Mongriff) and Katarzyna Helleb-Scharp. Examples of the community's sense of identity can be found in the adoption of Scottish orphans. For instance, the magistrate alderman Wojciech Livingston's family comprised his two sons and two daughters as well as two adopted orphans, Charles and Thomas Ramsay. George Mollison's family included a son and two adopted boys, Jan and Jozef Hey. The wealthy family of goldsmith Jerzy Makien had, in addition to his own son, three adopted Skromzer (Scrimgeour) children—Judyta, Katarzyna and Jan.[64]

The case of Thomas Ramsay shows that some Scots were firmly integrated into Kėdainiai society. Thomas grew up in Kėdainiai between 1692–97 and from 1700–02 he served as rector of Kėdainiai College. He was known in Lithuania as a Lithuanian preacher and called simply Tomas Ramza. From 1698–1701, together with his fellow Scot John (Jan) Paterson, he revised a translation of the New Testament into the Lithuanian language, which had been done by the Samogitian Superintendent, a clergyman of German descent named Samuel Bitner.[65] From the mid-seventeenth century, Kėdainiai was known in the Grand Duchy of Lithuania as a place where foreigners could specialise in Lithuanian philology. Apart from the above-mentioned Scots, the Poles Samuel Tamoszewski and Jan Borzymowski made considerable contributions to the largest Lithuanian book of the seventeenth century, '*Kniga nobažnystės krikščioniškos*' ('A Book of Christian Devotion'). The volume was published in the Kėdainiai printing house in 1653. Interestingly, the publication was supported by a Scottish soldier, Captain Jacob Mein.[66]

Despite being clearly willing to integrate into their host society, it is evident that the Scots also retained a strong sense of their cultural origins. At the end of the seventeenth century, when the Radziwill Dukes' Biržai Dubingiai branch died out, the Protestants of Lithuania

[64] Rejestr auditorow zboru Kiejdanskiego (1679). LNMMB, f. 93–541, l. 70–72; Tworek, 'Materiały do dziejów kalwinizmu', 213–215. The list also mentioned Tom and Jozef Skromzer who were perhaps already adults in the same family.
[65] Lukšaitė, *Lietuvių*, 23, 37, 40.
[66] I. Lukšaitė, 'Knygos nobažnystės (1653) parengimo kultūrinė aplinka', in *"Knyga nobažnystės krikščioniškos" (1653)—XVII a. Lietuvos kultūros paminklas* (Kėdainiai: 2001), 4, 9, 19.

lost their patrons, and after the plague epidemic which followed the Northern War, the Scots' situation in Kėdainiai greatly worsened. The community shrank, its economic power declined, and the 'Scots' started to seek aid from their ancestral homeland. In 1727, William Ross, Jacob Gray and Adolf Reinhold left for Great Britain to raise funds for the distressed Scots of Kėdainiai.[67] They described the town as follows:

> The district of the city of Kėdainiai in the Samogitian Duchy was granted these significant, even highest privileges from its luminous Radziwill Dukes, confirmed by the illustrious Kings of Poland: that the residents of British nationality were permitted not only their churches, religious rituals and schools, as well as the right to maintain these temples, and not only the right to earn their living by successful trading, to strengthen social and personal affairs, but also to pass all this to their successors and finally to teach their countrymen of the same faith who came from Great Britain, showing them how to get those things necessary to make a living and earn their bread, in order that they could, through permanent work, carry out the most important duties, arrange domestic affairs and rejoice peacefully in their well-deserved fruits, under the Lord's blessing; but also in order that this city itself might appear as a capital and a foundation of their holy Reformed faith, established in this land, as there is no such city in the whole Kingdom of Poland and Lithuania, where people of British nationality with full freedom of the faith also had full jurisdiction of civil and criminal rights and used this.[68]

It is unclear whether the mission was successful, as in 1730 the merchant Jacob Gray and a preacher, Jacob Gordon, left for London again. Their intention remained the same—to raise some much-needed financial support for their community. Great Britain was not chosen at random, as the country supported all European Protestants, especially those who lived in difficult conditions under a Catholic majority. When they came to London, a short report was published on the Kėdainiai Scots' situation and their goals, part of which read:

> These Protestants, during the last Wars between Sweden, Poland and *Muscovy*, which began in 1699 suffered such a Complication of Evils,

---

[67] W. Kriegseisen, *Ewangelicy Polscy i Litewcy w Epoce Saskiej* (Warszawa: 1996), 139.
[68] LNMMB, f. 93–568, l.1, 'Praeclarissimae Magnae Britanniae civibus omnium ordinum ac dignitatum honoratissimis, popularibus suis amantissimis, defensoribus fidei evangelicae strenuissimis', (1728).

as brought them at length almost to the Brink of Ruin. Besides the
common Calamities of War, it pleased God to visit this poor City in
1709 with a very sore *Famine*; and in the Year following with a most
terrible *Plague*, which swept away great Numbers, and raged through
the whole Country of *Samogitia*. It was likewise set on Fire by the
Soldiers three several Times, for the sake of Plunder, and forc'd to
pay very grievious *Contributions*, not only for themselves, but for other
Cities too; the principal Inhabitants of which, to avoid being plundered, having conveyed themselves, with the best of their Effects, to
other Places of greater Security. The more effectually to oblige this
unhappy City to pay such extraordinary Contributions, several of the
chief Inhabitants were clapt in Irons, and kept in Dungeons. These
severe Judgements occasioned the almost entire Loss of their Trade,
which was very considerable, in Flax, Hemp, Leather, Wax, Tallow,
and all sorts of Grain, with several other Commodities. The inhabitants of *Kieydan* had no less than twenty Sail of Vessels of an hundred
and twenty Tuns and upward, trading to *Conigsberg* in *Prussia*, most of
them belonging to Protestants, whereas there is now but one, and that
belongs to a Papist. The People who sell these several Goods, as well
as the Merchants from Conigsberg, would rather trade with the
Inhabitants of *Kieydan*, if they had a sufficient Stock, than with the *Jews*
and others they now deal with, both because they have the Reputation
of fair Trade, and in case of any ill Practise, can have a more easy
Relief. The Method proposed for employing this Charity, is to erect
a Company of Protestant Dealers at *Kieydan*, and to place out the
Money that has already, or may be farther be contributed, upon good
security, at Six *per Cent.* at *Dantzick*.[69]

Money for the Kėdainiai Scots was collected throughout England
and Scotland. As intended, it was used to buy iron, glass, lead, salt,
herrings and other goods popular in Königsberg. Part of the money
was allotted to the most distressed Scots and another part remained
in Danzig.[70] Mostly the collected funds were used for the promotion
of trade and the establishment of the merchants' company, *Societatis
Commerciorum*, on 7 July 1731.[71] The company founders were the
mayor of Kėdainiai, Alexander Cuthbert; the assessor Andrew Leith
(Andrzej Leityc); the bailiff George (Jerzy) Forsay; the aldermen
William Ross, Robert Livingston, David Anderson and Jacob Gray

---

[69] LNMMB, f. 93–568, l. 1, 'Praeclarissimae Magnae Britanniae'.
[70] S. Nishikawa, 'Across the Continent: The Protestant Network Between The
Society for Promoting Christian Knowledge (SPCK) and Kėdainiai', in *Kultūrų sankir-
tos* (Vilnius: 2000), 307.
[71] Tworek, 'Dziejów kalwinizmu', 195.

and the *decemvires* Daniel Mitchell and George Haliburton. In the company charter it was stated that its members were of '*nationis Magna Britannia*'—from Great Britain. The company's goals were to restore trade, support the Reformed Church, its clergy and buildings, and to endow families of distressed fellow countrymen and co-believers. Members of the company were officials of the Kėdainiai magistracy and seniors of the Reformed Church '*ex gente Magna Britannia*'. They undertook to allocate a part of their permanent income to the company's benefit. All members had to take an oath to carry this out and increase the company's funds. Links were established with merchants from Königsberg, Riga and Danzig—mostly Scots—in order to involve them in the company's future activities. This was probably the first stock company in Lithuania (formed in religious terms) and the first manifestation of 'Lithuanian' capitalism. The requirement of Scottish nationality or Protestant confession also limited the number of members and of course personal interests among members sometimes took precedence over social aims.[72] Unfortunately the company did not last long as it was short of circulating funds, while a fire in Jacob Gray's store in 1731 proved pivotal in the closure of the company.

Despite the efforts and the money collected from England and Scotland, the Kėdainiai Scots failed to noticeably improve their situation. Indeed the community had been in decline for a number of years. The counter-Reformation, religious intolerance, wars, disasters and economic crises markedly affected the life of the Scottish community in Kėdainiai. As early as 1686 Jews began to settle in Scottish houses. A Jew named Hirsz, who traded in alcohol, lived in a house belonging to Mayor Anderson in Zamkowa Street; a Jewish artisan lived in a house belonging to the magistrate assessor, George Haliburton; a Jew called Zelman, also an alcohol merchant, lived in Miss Gordon's (Gordonowa's) house in Konska Street; another Jew called Wigder lived in Miss Paterson's (Patersonowa's) house; and finally a Jew named Lewek, who was a pedlar, lived in Makienan's (Mackinnon's) house.[73] The recovery of the Jewish community in the town coincided with the decline of the Scots, and this trend continued

---

[72] Tworek, 'Dziejów kalwinizmu', 195–201.
[73] A list of Kėdainiai Jews of 1686, VUB, f. 4, A217, 17212, l. 1.

into the eighteenth century.[74] From 1695 to 1731, Kėdainiai was in the hands of the Catholic Duke of Neuburg, Karl Philip.[75] When it was passed on again, Kėdainiai—which had been a stronghold of the Reformation for more than a century—underwent re-Catholicisation in earnest.

The first major sign of the Catholic counter-Reformation was the settling of the Carmelite monks. Profiting from the chaos which followed the Northern War, the Carmelites obtained permission from the town's Catholic owner, Duke Karl, to erect a chapel, and started to build a church and monastery. They also seized houses and plots of land belonging to Kėdainiai residents. This caused great indignation among the Reformed community. The conflict later developed from the local confessional to the international arena. Among the property forcibly seized was William Cooper's (Wilim Kuper's) house in the Main Market Square, a property owned by Gray in Wielka Zamkowa Street, and a wineshop belonging to Miss Livingston (Livingstonowa). The Carmelites, when taken to court, returned the seized properties to the town, which immediately sold them: a wineshop beyond the Nevėžis river was sold to Livingstonowa for 200 tinfs, a house known as Kuperyszki in the Main Market Square was sold to Anna Summers (Anna Sumerowna-Kaneinowa) for 250 tinfs, and houses in Januszowo and Koyminy were sold to Forsay for 130 tinfs.[76] Unfortunately the Scots were unable to actually pay the sums demanded, and the houses were confiscated. In a twist of fate, it was apparently lack of money which forced the Scots to dispose of their wealth to the Catholics and the Carmelite monastery of Kėdainiai in 1731.

The decline in the Scottish community was reflected in the retail market. By 1735, out of eighteen shops which belonged to the Reformed Church, only eight were owned by Scots, while ten were in the possession of Kėdainiai Jews.[77] It is probable that the Scots

---

[74] Nishikawa, 'Across the Continent', 307.
[75] *Biržų dvaro teismo knygos 1620–1745.* T.1. (Vilnius: 1982), 11. Charles Philips had married Liudvika Karolina, a granddaughter of Jan Radziwill.
[76] R. Žirgulis, 'The Monastery of Kėdainiai Carmelites in the 18th and 19th centuries', Vilnius University, Faculty of History, unpublished Masters dissertation, Kėdainiai, (1993), 47–48.
[77] LNMMB, f. 93–95, l. 35ᵛ, 'Acts of Lithuania Reformed Church Samogitian district synod sessions, held in Kėdainiai in 1719–1744'.

deliberately passed their trade into capable hands; both Scots and Jews had proved themselves to be competent merchants, which had aroused jealousy and grudges among the local population. They may have been aware of a common struggle against growing local intolerance. It has been observed that "The Jews and Scots [in Poland-Lithuania] were frequently grouped together as people to tax, and to look down on."[78] The Scots were singled out for condemnation and often ridiculed by the Germans and the Poles. The word *Schotte* itself became a by-word for a 'pedlar' and gave rise to a Prussian idiom designed to scare children: *Warte bis der Schotte kommt*—'wait till the Scot comes to get you!'.[79] Jews suffered from the anti-Semitic propaganda which has dogged their people throughout history.[80] In Kėdainiai however, the two communities socialised to such an extent that the Scottish folksong 'Hame cam our Gudeman at E'en' was transformed into the Yiddish folksong 'I came to my stall'.[81] Cassel's explanation for this song passing from one community to the other is that many Jews had themselves arrived from Scotland as weavers, although this has yet to be verified from other sources.[82] Cassel admits that the song is perplexing as it has such a non-Jewish theme. This suggests that simple social acceptance and cultural osmosis accounts for its existence in Yiddish.[83] Yet despite evidence of good relations, the Jewish community was in the ascendant while the Scottish community had declined to such an extent that those with Scottish heritage were few and far between by the mid-eighteenth century.

---

[78] Kay, 'The Forgotten Scots Diaspora', 24.

[79] Tomkowicz, *Przyczynek do historii* szkotow, 166; Fischer, *The Scots in Eastern and Western Prussia*, 18.

[80] Cassel, *The City of Keidan*, X.

[81] This was apparently sung by Fraida Heisel of Kėdainiai in 1901 for Ginzburg and Marek for their collection *Yidishe folkslider in Rusland*. See B. C. Cassel, *The City of Keidan: An Historical Memoir* (New York: 1930), V. Cassel gives as his sources; *Lyric Gems of Scotland: A Collection of the Most Admired Scottish Songs* (London and Glasgow: 1856) and Sh. Ginzburg, and P. Marek, eds., *Yidishe folkslider in Rusland* (1901). The title of the song has become corrupted. I have not seen a copy of *Lyric Gems of Scotland*, but Dr Steve Murdoch kindly found it for me in another collection with the correct title as given above. See J. Fulcher, ed., *Lays and Lyrics of Scotland* (Glasgow: n.d.), 302–305. The song is now sung annually by children of the local Kėdainiai schools in its original Scots.

[82] Cassel, *The City of Keidan*, VI. Cassel goes as far as to call these people refugees, although from whom or what is unclear—Scotland has never had a pogrom against the Jews, at least not to this author's knowledge.

[83] Given that the Jews were so often tavern keepers, they may have simply learned the song from their customers.

After 1750 most Scottish surnames disappear from Kėdainiai documents, implying that the community itself had vanished. The German historian K. H. Ruffmann maintains that during the eighteenth and nineteenth centuries, the Scots moved their activities to Königsberg and Memel.[84] However, some Scottish surnames remained among the Reformers as late as the beginning of the nineteenth century (for example, Molleson). It is clear that most Scots who lived in the Grand Duchy of Lithuania were of Kėdainiai descent. For example, in 1763 a lieutenant in the army of the Grand Duchy of Lithuania, Jerzy Arnet, donated 21,600 zloty to the native Reformed Church of Kėdainiai.[85]

There are no estimates for how many Scots lived in Kėdainiai in the seventeenth and eighteenth centuries. According to Linas Eriksonas, the community could have numbered 2–300 people prior to 1655.[86] The present author has discovered about 125 Kėdainiai Scottish surnames, which suggests a much larger community—particularly as several households had the same family name. Indeed, when a group of Scottish soldiers passed through the town in 1661, the Catholic diarist among them noted that the Scots were there because of their Protestant religion. This did not prevent him from being welcomed by his fellow countrymen, with whom he lodged for several days. He appeared to get on particularly well with Major Carstares, with whom he exchanged gifts.[87] Archival destruction has probably ensured we will never know just how Scottish an atmosphere prevailed in the town that Gordon visited. But the Scots were there and they were influential. As Bloze and Kaminskas's poetry indicates, they have not been totally forgotten in the city they helped to create.[88]

---

[84] Labuda and Ruffmann, 'Engländer und Schotten', 362.

[85] 5 March 1763, A testament of George Arnott (Jerzy Arnet), lieutenant in the Grand Duchy of Lithuania's army. LNMMB, f. 93–579.

[86] Eriksonas, 'The Lost Colony of Scots', 180.

[87] *Diary of General Patrick Gordon*, 41.

[88] Both the Kėdainiai Regional Museum and the non-government organization 'Arnet's House' currently promote the multicultural and Scottish aspects of the town's history.

Conclusion

Did the Scots succeed in establishing the promised land of Antilia, or did they simply practise trade and maintain their religion in Kėdainiai? Did their activities lead to a so-called 'golden age' of Kėdainiai? In discussing the town, Professor Allan Macinnes commented, "Whether this community was a utopian experiment or simply a commercial venture patronised by the aristocratic Radziwill family remains an open question."[89] Given the favourable conditions and aristocratic support relating to confession of faith in Kėdainiai, it would have been more surprising if the Scots had not appeared there in the numbers they did. The size of the Scottish population in Kėdainiai indicates that the town was one of the most important communities of the diaspora in terms of settlement. Indeed it was the Samogitian centre for two confessions, Reformers and Jews. The significance of Kėdainiai for these two ethnic groups suggests that the town was of greater importance to Poland-Lithuania and the Baltic world in the late seventeenth and early eighteenth centuries than has been understood hitherto. Indeed the importance of the Scottish community in sustaining and developing the town in the late seventeenth century has been clearly demonstrated and can no longer be ignored by scholars studying Scottish communities in the early modern period.

---

[89] Macinnes, *Ships, Guns and Bibles*, xvi.

APPENDIX

In his poem *A letter from Mikas Kedainiskis to Himself*, Vytautas Bloze included the following stanza:

sliced, dried to tinder-fungus: carefully so they wouldn't break
I held the images in my hands: I see how
hungry children of Kėdainiai Scots climb from an old meat grinder
the Radvilas' future palace guard, yellowed and emaciated

He was not the only Lithuanian poet to address the arrival of Scots in the town. In a collection of poetry entitled *Kėdainiai Chronicles*, the former Kėdainiai resident Algimantas Kaminskas wrote:

Victims of injustice were searching here for a shelter.
They run from towns in the whole of Europe being pursued
by a black cross and treachery.
You had become beloved for everyone, for a Scot,
German, Pole and Dutchman.
Crafts flowered glorifying
a shoemaker and a tailor, a currier,
a potter and a weaver. The guilds joined
a competition of hands and neatness.
Mastership of a Lithuanian and a stranger
contended for the good of man and town.
[. . . . .]
The Scots are still arriving
and settle near the Big Market,
they settle for a long time, as walls of a house
are thick, strong and smell of stability.
And doors and windows as well as a roof
are heated with a colour of steadiness.
Thus, a house of Scottish merchants was born
and remained as if a relic, what came
to see us, it stays silent and even sorrowful,
as an untold grief between the merchant's
uproar and inner pain,
when homeland is recalled, disturbed even
merchants' trade. On Saturdays
—the days of market—Kėdainiai Scots
used to go across the square harbourwards,
hoping to meet a countryman,
or word, at least to relish
a smell of homeland, wafting
from packs, barrels and dusty clothes.
But time had already cut a mark for their settling.

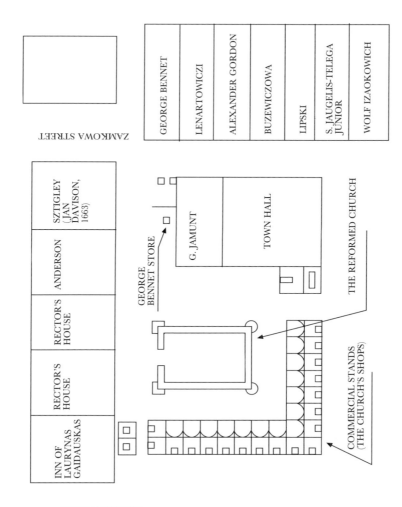

KĖDAINIAI BIG MARKET ACCORDING TO A DRAWING
OF THE TOWN ELDER WAWRYNIEC KOCHANSKI, 1661

ZAMKOWA STREET

GEORGE BENNET

LENARTOWICZI

ALEXANDER GORDON

BUZEWICZOWA

LIPSKI

S. JAUGELIS-TELEGA
JUNIOR

WOLF IZAOKOWICH

INN OF
LAURYNAS
GAIDAUSKAS

RECTOR'S
HOUSE

RECTOR'S
HOUSE

ANDERSON

SZTIGLEY
(JAN
DAVISON,
1663)

GEORGE
BENNET STORE

G. JAMUNT

TOWN HALL

THE REFORMED CHURCH

COMMERCIAL STANDS
(THE CHURCH'S SHOPS)

KONSKA STREET

ARNET
(JAN ARNET, 1663)

ARNET
(JAN KRUMZER, 1663)

KRUMZER
(WILLIAM COOPER,
1663)

ANDERSON
(JACOB PATERSON,
1663)

DIKSON
(THOMAS KRUMZER,
1663)

'BRITEANNIA IST MEIN PATRIA' SCOTSMEN AND THE 'BRITISH' COMMUNITY IN HAMBURG

Kathrin Zickermann[1]

Hamburg played an important role as a financial and political centre for the whole of northern Europe during the seventeenth century. Due to its geographical situation on the River Elbe and its shipping, the city was an economic powerhouse, its trading links stretching as far as the Iberian Peninsula and the New World.[2] Additionally, Hamburg's economic success and its relative openness towards religious minorities attracted a considerable number of Portuguese, Jewish, and Dutch merchants, who settled in the Lutheran city during the second half of the sixteenth century, strengthening the economy still further.[3] Yet surprisingly, given their celebrated mobility, Scotsmen fail to appear in the indexes of any literature about Hamburg during the seventeenth century.[4] Indeed, during the research for this chapter, the city's archivists were doubtful there would be anything relating to Scots in their documents. Yet, while no single corpus of material relating to the Scots in Hamburg survives, numerous individual records including personal memoirs, private letters and the marriage registers of churches in Hamburg reveal the presence of a number of Scots in the city at various times.[5] This

---

[1] I would like to thank Dr Steve Murdoch for co-supervising my Master's thesis and for the opportunity to present my findings in this collection. He has also provided me with numerous sources for this chapter for which I express my thanks.

[2] H. D. Loose, *Hamburg. Geschichte der Stadt und ihrer Bewohner* (Hamburg: 1982), I, 328.

[3] J. Whaley, *Religious Toleration and social change in Hamburg, 1529–1819* (Cambridge: 1985), 11.

[4] Loose, *Hamburg*; Whaley, *Religious Toleration*; W. R. Baumann, *The Merchant Adventurers and the Continental Cloth-trade (1560s–1620s)* (Berlin: 1990); E. Weise, 'Stader Fernhandelsplätze seit den Zeiten der Merchant Adventurers und ihre Beziehungen zu Hamburg', in *Hamburger Wirtschaftschronik* 1 (1950); Martin Knauer and Sven Tode, eds., *Der Krieg vor den Toren. Hamburg im Dreißigjährigen Krieg 1618–1648* (Hamburg: 2000).

[5] See for example Robert Monro, *His Expedition with the Worthy Scots Regiment called Mackeyes* (2 vols., London: 1637), I, 7, 10; James Turner, *Memoirs of his own Life and*

essay will investigate the arrival and status of Scotsmen in the city
and explain their presence where possible.

The search for a possible 'Scottish' community in Hamburg cannot, however, be undertaken without considering whether Scottish
networking was subsumed within a greater 'British' community. There
were many Englishmen permanently based in Hamburg, due to the
establishment of The Company of Merchant Adventurers there, making the city very different to places like Bergen, Gothenburg or
Danzig, where the presence of distinctly Scottish communities is
unambiguous. The role that Hamburg played in the wider seventeenth-century Scottish diplomatic and commercial network in Europe
must therefore be examined, whether as home to a specifically Scottish
community or as part of a larger British one—or indeed simply as
a transient base for Scottish interests.

Hamburg and the English Merchant Adventurers

As an economic centre, Hamburg was very attractive as a potential
market for the Company of Merchant Adventurers, who held a trade
monopoly in England's most important export, unfinished cloth. In
1567 the company wanted to make Hamburg its mart-town and was
first granted important privileges from the city council for a ten-year
period. When these privileges were not renewed, due to pressure
exerted by Lübeck and other Hanseatic towns, the Merchant Adventurers left Hamburg in 1604 and relocated themselves to Stade.[6]
However in 1611 the company re-established themselves in Hamburg,
and seven years later a definitive treaty between the firm and the
city was agreed, which granted important economic and political

---

Times (Edinburgh: 1829), 91; Franz Schubert, ed., *Trauregister aus den ältesten Kirchenbüchern Hamburgs. Von den Anfängen bis zum Jahre 1704. Hamburg Altstadt (6d) St. Nikolai, Deutsch-reform. Gde., Mennoneten, English Court, Röm.-kath. Gde., Hochzeiten Eidbuch des Amtes Bergedorf* (Göttingen: 1997); F. Schubert, ed., *Trauregister aus den ältesten Kirchenbüchern Hamburgs. Von den Anfängen bis zum Jahre 1707. Hamburg Altstadt (6c), St. Jacobi* (Göttingen: 1997); Franz Schubert, ed., *Trauregister aus den ältesten Kirchenbüchern Hamburgs. Von den Anfängen bis zum Jahre 1704. Hamburg vor den Mauern (2). St. Paulikirche auf dem Hamburger Berg* (Göttingen: 1994).

[6] Baumann, *The Merchants Adventurers*, 11; Weise, 'Stader Fernhandelsplätze seit den Zeiten der Merchant Adventurers', 14; S. Murdoch, *Britain, Denmark-Norway and the House of Stuart: A Diplomatic and Military Analysis* (East Linton: 2003), 32.

privileges to the Merchant Adventurers.[7] In addition to these the merchants also received a house in Hamburg, which they used mainly for meetings and as storage for goods. Part of the house was also used as a chapel, becoming known as 'the English church', where services were held under the Anglican confession of faith.[8]

However, Hamburg's importance during the seventeenth century was not reliant solely on its strong economy but also on the political circumstances of the time. With the help of other great powers, Hamburg defended itself successfully against the Danish kings, who claimed overlordship over the city.[9] More importantly, the city managed to remain untouched by the Thirty Years' War, which pushed much of the rest of Europe into turmoil, bringing destruction to many regions and towns. Hamburg avoided being besieged and occupied by the various fighting powers by providing a useful base where all opposing forces were able to buy arms and other supplies. As a consequence, Hamburg emerged as a pivotal wartime crossroads, becoming a key market not only for war supplies but also for information. All the great powers in the war had representatives in the city, expanding Hamburg's significance from an economic to a diplomatic focal point—a position it kept for the whole century.[10]

Early Scottish commercial links with Hamburg

Prior to the settlement of the Company of Merchant Adventurers, evidence of trading connections between Scotland and Hamburg can already be found from the late Middle Ages. Scotland's Guardian, Sir William Wallace, sent a message in 1297 to the provosts of Lübeck and Hamburg to inform them that his country had been freed from the English and its harbours were once again open to

---

[7] W. E. Lingelbach, 'The Merchant Adventurers at Hamburg', in *American Historical Review*, 4 (1904) (reprinted 1963), 270.

[8] H. Hitzigrath, 'Das englische Haus in der Grönigerstraße und der Boselhof an der englischen Planke', in *Hamburgischer Correspondent*, 460 (1 October 1901).

[9] H. D. Loose, *Hamburg und Christian IV. von Dänemark während des Dreißigjährigen Krieges. Ein Beitrag zur Geschichte der Reichsunmittelbarkeit* (Hamburg: 1963); J. Bracker, *Hamburg. Von den Anfängen bis zur Gegenwart. Wendemarken einer Stadtgeschichte* (Hamburg: 1987), 105–108.

[10] Knauer and Tode, *Der Krieg vor den Toren*, 21.

merchants from their cities.[11] By the seventeenth century, however, Scotland's trade with Hamburg was small-scale when compared to its much greater economic exchange with the Netherlands, Scandinavia and the Baltic.[12] The Company of Hamburg Merchants Trading to England did call at Scottish harbours—most often at the port of Leith.[13] The Hamburg merchants bought mainly coal in Scotland, while selling goods such as beer, ham and small quantities of iron, copper, *knapple* (cask staves), brandy, wine and aniseed.[14] However, the demand for these goods in Scotland was not high enough to balance the import of coal from Scottish mines. Conversely, Scottish merchants trading to northern Europe found it difficult to find suitable export goods for the Hamburg market. More important than trade with the Scottish mainland were the commercial links between Hamburg and the Shetland Islands. The Hamburg merchants, who were organised in their own company, were engaged in trade with Shetland from the second half of the sixteenth century onwards.[15] They bought cod and herring in exchange for specie or fishing equipment, providing the islands with an important source of revenue.[16]

It is this trade in particular which offers us a glimpse of a budding Scottish mercantile community in Hamburg at the end of the sixteenth century. The documents of the Hitland (Shetland) Company in Hamburg reveal that at least two Scotsmen—a man called Laurens Stinckler (almost certainly Sinclair) and another called Angus (Augustin/ Enghuß) Murray (Murer/Murre)—were not only its core members from as early as 1593, but also resident in the town.[17] In addition to these men, whose nationality is explicitly stated, there were three

---

[11] G. W. S. Barrow, *Robert Bruce & the Community of the Realm of Scotland* (3rd ed., Edinburgh: 1996), 10 and 90.

[12] T. C. Smout, *Scottish Trade on the Eve of Union, 1660–1707* (Edinburgh/London: 1963), 166.

[13] In the early 1680s four to five ships per annum arrived in Leith from Hamburg or Bremen.

[14] Smout, *Scottish Trade*, 166.

[15] Loose, *Hamburg* (Hamburg: 1982), I, 163.

[16] K. Friedland, 'Hanseatic Merchants and their Trade with Shetland', in D. J. Withrington, ed., *Shetland and the Outside World, 1469–1969* (Aberdeen: 1983), 91.

[17] Staatsarchiv Hamburg, *Verzeichnis der Hamburger Shetland- (Hitland-) Fahrer 1547–1646*, edited by P. Pipen, (Hamburg: 1988), 30, 116, 121, 158, 160–164. Laurens Stinckler is mentioned in a document from 1593 as giving 3 shillings for the poor. Angus Murer is mentioned as a member of the Hitland Company in 1617/1618 and 1624/1625.

other merchants who were probably relatives of the aforementioned Scotsmen. They were registered as Andreas Sinckler (Linckler, Senckler, Sinckeler, Synckeler), Thomas Senckler and Goen (Johan) Murer (Murre).[18] As members of a company which consisted of Hamburg merchants, these Scotsmen possessed citizens' rights in Hamburg, allowing them to trade in the city. Nevertheless, it is important to note that only the nationality of Laurens Stinckler and Angus Murer was explicitly mentioned, implying that the writer of the documents was aware of the fact they were not native to Hamburg. This raises the question of why this was not noted for Andreas Sinckler, Thomas Senckler and Goen Murer, if they too were Scotsmen. Either their nationality was unknown to the writer, or it would have appeared obvious to him given the context of the documents. In any case, there were certainly other Scots in Hamburg at the same time as these men. For example, the documents of the German Reformed (Calvinist) Church in Hamburg name at least three Scots among the congregation. Alexander Steffensen (Stevenson) from St Andrews married Barbara Cornelis in 1608. David Iansen (Johnson?) married the widow Anna Dirx in 1609 and John Thomessen from Carron wed the Hamburg-born Agatha Cornelis in 1636.[19] These men probably worked as merchants in the city, perhaps even for the Hamburg Company. However, an alternative route into Hamburg trade soon emerged after the Union of Crowns in 1603, and a handful of Scots found themselves with opportunities to trade with the English Merchant Adventurers in the city.

Attempting 'Britishness': Hamburg in Anglo-Scottish nation building

Hamburg's neutrality in the political machinations engulfing neighbouring states allowed it to serve as a diplomatic hub during the seventeenth century. This neutrality attracted representatives to the city from a number of political institutions in Britain, whether Scottish

---

[18] Staatsarchiv Hamburg, *Verzeichnis der Hamburger Shetland*, 71, 80, 97, 99, 179, 185, 161–165, 171. Andreas Sinckler appears in the records of the Hitland Company in 1607, 1609 and from 1613–16, whereas Thomas Senckler is mentioned in the documents of 1626. Goen Murer is registered as a member of the Hitland Company in 1624.

[19] Schubert, *Trauregister*, 32.

or English parliamentarians, privy councillors or envoys of the monarchy. This was particularly relevant during the souring of British relations with Denmark-Norway, and also during the various civil wars in the three Stuart kingdoms.[20] As the 1603 regal union had brought the three kingdoms of England, Ireland and Scotland under the rule of the same monarch, Scottish and English diplomats found themselves engaged on the same side on the wider political stage. This saw the evolution of a particularly Scottish-Stuart diplomatic corps operating in northern Europe, including Hamburg.[21] It is debatable whether all the Stuart diplomats working for King James VI and I evolved a 'British' consciousness and allowed their Scottish or English nationality to be subsumed by a common identity. However, there is evidence that in Hamburg some Scots and Englishmen appear to have done just that.

Initially the main point of contact between the Stuart Crown and the city of Hamburg was the secretary of the Merchant Adventurers. In 1612, the year after the company returned to Hamburg from Stade, Joseph Averie was elected to this position and remained in it until 1638. Thereafter he served as the company's court master from 1638–43, as well as acting as a diplomat for King Charles I. Naturally most of his contact was with fellow Englishmen among the Merchant Adventurers. Indeed, it is clear that initially he was quite suspicious of the Scots who were becoming more frequent visitors to the city.

One of these Scottish visitors, Robert Anstruther, served as senior British diplomat to Denmark-Norway and to the Hanseatic towns for both James VI and I and Charles I. He frequently used Hamburg as a base for his diplomatic missions from November 1627 onwards, and chose the city as his permanent residence in 1630.[22] This move

---

[20] For a review of the complexities of the various competing diplomatic missions leaving Britain at this time see Murdoch, *Britain, Denmark-Norway and the House of Stuart*, 20–21 and passim.

[21] S. Murdoch, 'Diplomacy in Transition: Stuart-British Diplomacy in Northern Europe, 1603–1618', in A. I. Macinnes, T. Riis and F. G. Pedersen, eds., *Ships, Guns and Bibles in the North Sea and the Baltic States, c. 1350–1700* (East Linton: 2000), 93–114.

[22] We do not know whether Anstruther had a permanent residence during his visits to the city before 1630 or if he was staying in different guest houses. Neither do we know exactly where his household was located in Hamburg after 1630, only that he was certainly based there.

was prompted by the signing of the 1629 Treaty of Lübeck between Christian IV of Denmark-Norway and Ferdinand II of Austria. Anstruther's mistrust was aroused by the generous terms of the treaty and the reserved behaviour of the Danish envoys toward him, as he viewed the treaty as signalling a convergence between Denmark and the Habsburg Empire.[23] He therefore left the Danish court in Copenhagen for Hamburg, where he continued to take care of diplomatic affairs between Charles I and Christian IV. Hamburg seemed an excellent base, allowing Anstruther to emphasise the now frosty British-Danish relationship by withdrawing from the Danish capital but remaining in close proximity to the Danish court. However, the arrival of a senior Stuart ambassador in Hamburg introduced a new dimension to the power politics among the British subjects resident in the city. From the moment of his arrival in town, English merchants were directed to Anstruther for advice, including the likes of Rowland Pittes, Charles I's 'Purveyor of Sea Fish' whom Anstruther helped to source sturgeon in Hamburg in April 1629.[24] As the senior British subject in the city, any disputes between the English Adventurers and the Hamburg authorities now fell under Anstruther's jurisdiction. The resulting impact on Averie, who was removed from the trading loop by a Scot, and was superseded in the social pecking order in a city where the English had long held the monopoly, naturally left him suspicious. Initially he made a clear distinction between himself [an Englishman] on one side and Anstruther and 'his countrymen' [the Scots] on the other.[25] He also noted that Anstruther and 'his countrymen' brought many more Scots to the city.

Anstruther's move to Hamburg in 1630 involved the transfer of his household as well, which comprised about twenty to thirty people (including servants) in total—most of whom were Scottish.[26] Some

---

[23] Murdoch, *Britain, Denmark-Norway and the House of Stuart*, 70.

[24] *APC*, July 1628–April 1629, pp. 93–94, 413–414.

[25] PRO SP 75/10, f. 346, Joseph Averie to ?, Hamburg, 25 November/5 December 1629.

[26] In 1626, Anstruther's wife received a passport in England for herself, her son William and about 18 servants to travel to the Netherlands. One would assume that they accompanied Anstruther from Copenhagen to Hamburg. Furthermore, the servants Clemat Messerve, George Rivers and Thomas Jones received passports in February 1627 to travel to Hamburg, along with another servant and a nanny, whose names we do not know. These would have been part of Anstruther's household when he moved to Hamburg. See *APC*, 1626, p. 30; *APC*, 1627, 65 and 198.

of them have been identified, such as his servants Clemat Messerve, George Rivers and Thomas Jones. His son William was also in the city, as was one Pinckney Steward, who substituted for Anstruther at a meeting with the treasurer in England, due to the advanced pregnancy of Anstruther's English wife, Catherine Swift.[27] Furthermore, it can be assumed that Anstruther's chaplain Sampson Johnson and his secretary Richard Hurst were living temporarily in his house in Hamburg.[28] In short, this one household expanded the Scottish presence in Hamburg considerably. These men were forced together with the existing residents to form an even larger 'British community,' allowing for a greater understanding between the Scots and English in the city. At least we know that Averie's personal aversion to Scotsmen did not appear to last long thereafter.

In addition to the groups of merchants and diplomats there was also a sizeable, if variable, military community, particularly after Sweden's entry into the Thirty Years' War, which brought a surge of new Scottish troops into the European arena.[29] Hamburg was already a focal point for armed forces, either in transit between different theatres of the war, or as a place to recuperate. Indeed the city served as the disembarkation point for Scottish troops who were sent to the continent in support of the rebel Bohemian monarchy in 1620.[30] One later meeting between soldiers and Hamburg merchants resulted in a number of the citizens—including English Adventurers—losing their goods to pillaging soldiers from the Swedish army. The Swedish king, Gustav II Adolf, insisted the pillaged items be brought to him under pain of death, and he thereafter restored them to the merchants in return for a small consideration towards feeding his army. The English did not pay anything, but had their goods returned anyway "by the request of the Cavaliers (who interceded for them to his Majesty) their country-men both *Scots &*

---

[27] PRO, SP 75/9, f. [smudged], Robert Anstruther to ?, Hamburg, 14 March 1628/29.

[28] *APC*, June 1630–June 1631, 263.

[29] For more on these Scots see A. Grosjean, *An Unofficial Alliance: Scotland and Sweden 1569–1651* (Leiden: 2003), 74–111.

[30] The Scottish Privy Council ordered the Leith skipper, Alexander Downing, to keep his ship ready for the transport of Scottish troops to Hamburg under the command of Colonel Andrew Gray to Hamburg in 1620. See *RPCS*, Vol. XII, 1619–1622, 257–258.

English".[31] Worthy of note is Lieutenant-Colonel Robert Monro's contention that both the Scots and the Englishmen were the countrymen of the English merchants. Monro was only one of several Scottish officers to spend time in Hamburg. Colonel Alexander Leslie corresponded with the Marquis of Hamilton from the city in 1631 and 1632.[32] During a later visit, in 1634, Leslie was accompanied by General Patrick Ruthven and several other Scottish officers, according to one of Averie's letters.[33] Monro himself was in the city along with Alexander Cunningham the same year, and remained until 1635 when he was present at the death of Hector Monro of Fowlis who died in the city.[34]

Many Scots officers called into Hamburg on their own military business while others arrived expressly to exchange information with Anstruther. In 1631 the Scot William Elphinstone reported to the Marquis of Hamilton that he had met Robert Anstruther and the Swedish diplomat Salvius in the city.[35] Such meetings led in turn to contact with Adventurers like Joseph Averie. Indeed, Averie himself received a considerable amount of intelligence from Scottish officers such as the aforementioned Alexander Leslie and Patrick Ruthven, Major David Drummond, and Major-General James King during their visits to Hamburg.[36] These men, already shown to have been pro-active in the formation of a pan-British military identity while serving in the Swedish army, would have influenced Averie's own views on concepts of 'Britishness'.[37] Indeed, by December 1634, Averie had become the main intermediary in a dispute between a group of Scottish privateers and the city of Hamburg, as a very

---

[31] Monro, *His Expedition*, II, 45.

[32] NAS, GD 406/1/9322, Alexander Leslie to Marquis of Hamilton, Hamburg, 12 May 1631; GD 406/1/277, Alexander Leslie to Marquis of Hamilton, Hamburg, 9 August 1632.

[33] PRO, SP 75/13, f.210, Averie to (Coke), Hamburg 15/25 July 1634.

[34] KRA, 0035: 0418: Ö. Karl Viggo Key Arkiv. Unfoliated letter, signed Robert Monro and Alexander Cunningham, Hamburg, 23 January 1634; C. T. Macinnes, ed., *Calendar of Writs of Monro of Fowlis, 1299–1823* (Edinburgh: 1940), 57–59.

[35] NAS, GD 406/1/9305. W. Elphinstone to Marquis of Hamilton, Hamburg, 27 March 1631.

[36] PRO, SP 75/13, f. 259, Averie to Coke, Hamburg 10./20 October 1635; PRO SP 75/13, f. 285, Averie to Coke, Hamburg, 31 December 1635.

[37] For a full argument see S. Murdoch, 'James VI and the Formation of a Scottish-British Military Identity' in S. Murdoch and A. Mackillop, eds., *Fighting for Identity: Scottish Military Experience c. 1550–1900* (Leiden: 2002), 3–31.

hostile relationship had developed between Scotland and Hamburg after 1629.[38] One of the main protagonists in the dispute, Captain David Robertson, arrived in Hamburg and found an ally in Averie, who wrote "A Scots gent arrived here lately and I will not fail to assist him with his business in the senate with al [sic] diligence and endeavour".[39] As has been noted elsewhere, Averie proceeded to act "on behalf of a Scottish Privateer, Captain Robertson, via an envoy of the Scottish Privy Council, Mr Colville, on the orders of the English Secretary of State" in a thoroughly British encounter.[40] Here Averie's change from being 'an Englishman' to sharing in a British identity is evident, probably as a result of contact with Anstruther, Colville and the Scottish soldiers, and he refers to the Scots as being of 'our nation', thereby mirroring Monro's contention that they were all countrymen.[41]

Subsequently, Averie acted as a contact in financial transactions and personal business for Scots in the city. One George Douglas died in a skirmish close to Hamburg, after which his body was brought into the city in 1636 by several British officers, among them some of his relatives. After the body had been laid out in one of the churches, Averie took care of Douglas's estate, deciding among other things to send his servants home to England or Scotland in order to avoid mounting costs which Averie was obliged to cover. Furthermore, Averie instructed Douglas's secretary, a man called Fowler, to send Douglas's remaining papers and letters to England.[42] We also learn from a later document written in 1639 that Averie

---

[38] This episode has been written up in S. Murdoch, 'Scotland, Denmark-Norway and the House of Stuart' unpublished PhD thesis, University of Aberdeen, 1998, 302–305, Appendix A 'Scotland and Hamburg in Stuart-Oldenburg Diplomacy'.

[39] PRO SP 75/13, ff. 233–235, Averie to Coke, 2/12 December 1634; See also Staatsarchiv Hamburg, 111–1, CL VI no. 2, vol. 1, fasc 1a, in vol. 5. Documents relating to Captain David Robertson, c. 1632–1633.

[40] Murdoch, Britain, Denmark-Norway and the House of Stuart, 19.

[41] For example in SP 75/13, f. 285, Averie to Coke, 31 December 1635. Averie wrote: '. . . And these particulars I have out of the army from Major General King, and another Colonel of our Nation, who were in action . . .' Since King is a Scot, the nation Averie was talking about must have been Great Britain. See Murdoch Britain, Denmark-Norway and the House of Stuart, 19.

[42] PRO, SP 75/13, f. 315, Averie to (Coke), Hamburg, 8/18 April 1636; PRO SP 75/13, f. 323, Averie to (Coke), Hamburg, 28 April/8 May 1636. Fowler is described as the 'Dutch secretary' of George Douglas indicating his role as interpreter or scribe for the German language.

received 500 Reichstaler from Count Warnke of Bremen on behalf of George Sinclair and Andrew Smith, which he transferred to a David Stirling in Scotland.[43]

The above details reveal that Averie, and by implication the Merchant Adventurers in Hamburg, had been drawn into close contact with a number of Scotsmen from the financial, mercantile, military and diplomatic spheres. The Scots, by their intervention in returning pillaged goods, had gained favour among several of the English merchants. More significantly, by getting Averie on their side, the Scots had won an important ally, which allowed their presence in the city to increase from the numerically inconsequential to a noticeable component of the larger British grouping.

The marriage registers of the English Church in Hamburg reveal another facet of the Anglo-Scottish interaction.[44] Before the advent of the Scottish National Covenant in 1638, both the English and Scottish churches had Episcopal government, and the presence of Scots at an English church is not surprising, particularly abroad. Indeed some of the names of members listed in the registers of the English Church in Hamburg, like George Stewart, James Murraye, Leonard Scott, Richard Lawton, George Hough, Hannah Baylie, and Charles Broughton, indicate a Scottish origin. James Murraye married a woman called Margaret Davidson, who was very likely Scottish herself. George Hough married a woman called Marie Young, who might also have been Scottish.[45] Other names, like Thomas Hammon (Hammond?), Henry Taylor, Richard and Thomas Young, could be either English or Scottish.[46] There does not seem to have been a need to stipulate exactly where people came from within the British Isles when their marriages were recorded in the English

---

[43] NAS, GD 3/151/3. Commercial Papers and Accounts relating to Patrick Smyth of Braco, 1629–1659, Hamburg, 29 November 1639.

[44] This source records 101 marriages in total between 1617 and 1701. See F. Schubert, ed., *Trauregister aus den ältesten Kirchenbüchern Hamburgs. Von den Anfängen bis zum Jahre 1704. Hamburg Altstadt (6d)*, 94–96.

[45] Schubert, *Trauregister*, 94–96. George Stewart married Magdelen Williames on 20 April 1624; James Murraye and Margaret Davidson married on 3 January 1626; Leonard Scott married Mary Lee on 21 July 1646; Richard Lawton married Sarah Medcaulf on the 27 May 1651; George Hough married Marie Young on 21 February 1656, Hannah Baylie married Jacob Coutons on 28 September 1663, and Charles Broughton married Mary Wolfenden on 7 May 1691.

[46] Schubert, ed., *Trauregister*, 94–96.

church. Nor was it felt necessary to record the status of the married couple within either the Adventurers' Company or the city. Despite this a glimpse of marriage patterns can be discerned from the church records.

To conduct business in Hamburg a merchant had to possess citizens' rights, which were available in limited form (without political rights) to members of Christian denominations other than Lutherans.[47] An exception to this was the Merchant Adventurers, who were able to undertake trade in Hamburg without citizens' rights, as a perk of the treaty agreed between the company and city in 1618. It is probable that the Scottish merchants who were resident in Hamburg were either citizens or members of the Merchant Adventurers themselves. The situation was thus different from Gothenburg or Danzig, where Scotsmen could purchase citizens' rights.[48] Those merchants who married women born in Hamburg or its surroundings probably did not belong to the Merchant Adventurers, who were dissociating themselves from the society of Hamburg citizens.[49] However, those Scottish men and women who married in the English Church of the Merchant Adventurers revealed that they were in contact with the company and possibly belonged to it themselves. There were even some Scots working to bring all the Protestant denominations closer together, and interestingly these negotiations were in part conducted from Hamburg by John Durie.

John Durie in Hamburg

The famous Scottish theologian, John Durie, attempted to appease the religious conflicts of his time and to unite all Protestant churches.[50] He established contacts with Hamburg in 1632, when he passed through the city on a journey from Amsterdam to the Baltic. Although his stay was short, this visit was of importance for Durie since he

---

[47] Loose, *Hamburg*, 266.
[48] M. Bogucka, 'Scots in Gdansk (Danzig) in the Seventeenth Century', in Macinnes, Riis and Pedersen, eds., *Ships, Guns and Bibles*, 40.
[49] Loose, *Hamburg*, I, 266.
[50] Thomas H. Rae, *John Dury and the Royal Road to Piety* (Frankfurt a.M./Berlin/Bern/New York: 1998), 17.

made the acquaintance of several Merchant Adventurers, including the secretary Joseph Averie and the minister Mr. Elborough.[51] He travelled throughout 1633 in the company of Sir Robert Anstruther and was himself a strong proponent of the 'British' project, styling himself *Ecclesiastae Scoto-Britanno*.[52] Durie's contacts with the Hamburg community were revived when he chose the city as his residence from 1638–40. His financial situation was at times desperate, and he received sums of money from his patron and friend Samuel Hartlib through members of the Merchant Adventurers such as Mr. Aldersee and Joseph Averie.[53] Furthermore, to earn some money of his own and to become accepted in the city, Durie became the co-adjutor of the minister of the English Church in Hamburg.[54]

Having already served as the minister for a combined Scottish-English congregation in Elbing from 1624–29, Durie's acceptance of this position is hardly surprising.[55] Nonetheless, this eased his integration into Hamburg society, a matter of great importance to him in order to gain the support of the city authorities in his discussions of his religious vision. Hamburg's toleration for interpretations of Christianity other than Lutheranism must have appealed to Durie. Unfortunately he does not comment on any results of his negotiations in Hamburg in his letters. That and the fact that he was not successful in any other city or duchy around Hamburg suggests his hopes were misplaced, as does the mention by Averie, who supported Durie's efforts, of the irreconcilable Lutherans in Hamburg in a letter to Hartlib in 1641.[56]

---

[51] HP 60/5/1A–8B, Durie to Hartlib, Narrative of his German Travels, 1632.

[52] S. Murdoch, 'Kith and Kin: John Durie and the Scottish Community in Scandinavia and the Baltic, 1624–34' in P. Salmon and T. Barrow, eds., *Britain and the Baltic* (Sunderland: 2003), 36–45.

[53] HP 2/2/22A–23B, Letter, John Durie to Hartlib, 12 June 1640.

[54] HP 5/12/13A–16B, Copy Letter in Hand?, John Durie to Bishop?, 30 June 1640; HP 6/4/68A–69B, Copy Letter in Hand?, John Durie to (Sir Thomas Roe), 3 July 1640.

[55] Murdoch, 'Kith and Kin', 34.

[56] HP, 45/3/3A–4B, Letter, Joseph Averie to Hartlib, 20 September 1641. Durie gives us some information on his bare accommodation, which cannot have been very comfortable as he informed Hartlib in one of his first letters from Hamburg that he was forced to study in a chamber without a fire, in cold winter weather. However, he probably changed his accommodation during his stay since he wrote to Hartlib in June 1640 that he had settled down in his residence and that his books and papers were in a better order than they had been for the last ten years. See HP, 2/6/12A–15B, John Durie to Hartlib, 30 November 1638; HP 6/4/56A–57B, Copy Letter, John Durie (to Sir Thomas Roe), 9 June 1640.

Contact between Durie, Averie and Elborough continued after the
Scottish theologian left the city in 1640, and he later returned to
the city several times.[57] However, events in the British Isles meant
that the vision of a united Britain had all but died except in the
minds of some of the intellectual and military elite still on the continent. One of these, General James King, declared in 1641 that:
"Briteannia ist mein patria, darin ich geborn sey", *i.e.* "Britannia is
my fatherland, where I was born".[58] His presence in the city along
with other Scottish officers informs us of the importance of Hamburg's
neutrality in the conflict in the British Isles.

Hamburg: Weapons Entrepôt, Neutral City and Safe Haven

In the 1630s tensions arose between the Scottish Covenanters and
Charles I, eventually leading to the Bishops' Wars (1639–1641), in
which the British monarch received a humiliating defeat at the hands
of the Scottish Covenanters. The Bishops' Wars contributed to the
destabilisation of the Stuart kingdoms, catalysing a series of civil wars
throughout the three kingdoms.[59] During this time of turmoil in the
British Isles, Hamburg continued to play an important role as a transit place for Scots, many of whom were quitting service in the
European armies to participate on their chosen side at home. For
example, we know that Captain James Lumsden, Captain David
Leslie, Captain George Monro and twenty other Scottish officers
(whose names are unknown) embarked in Hamburg to sail to Britain
in order to fight for the Covenanters.[60]

---

[57] HP 6/4/133A–134B, Copy Letter in Hand?, John Durie to Mr. Averie, 4
April 1642; HP 1/17/1A–2B, Copy Letter in Hand?, John Durie to Andrew Ramsay
& Alexander Henderson, Hamburg, 19 June 1643; HP 3/1/5A–6B, Letter, John
Durie to Hartlib, Hamburg, 12 June 1643. Durie let Hartlib know that he was
once again in financial trouble and therefore had to borrow 50 riksdollars in
Hamburg. However, since he did not want his friend Averie to think that he
intended him to bear the cost, he borrowed the money from someone else.
[58] *RAOSB*, Vol. IX, 959, James King to Axel Oxenstierna, Hamburg, July 1641;
Murdoch, 'James VI and the Formation of a Scottish-British Military Identity', 5.
[59] A. I. Macinnes, *Charles I and the Making of the Covenanting Movement, 1625–1641*
(Edinburgh: 1991), 206 and *passim*; J. Kenyon and J. Ohlmeyer, 'The Background
of the Civil Wars in the Stuart Kingdoms', in J. Kenyon and J. Ohlmeyer, eds.,
The Civil Wars. A Military History of England, Scotland and Ireland 1638–1660 (Oxford
and New York: 1998), 3–41.
[60] SRA, E 655. Undated letter of William Wimes to Axel Oxenstierna. Captain

Not all the Scottish officers involved in military affairs on the continent returned to Scotland, though they often participated in the conflict at some level. As a known weapons entrepôt, Hamburg obviously attracted those in search of arms. In 1638 Major-General James King arrived in Hamburg with his wife. He stayed for two years in order to gather political support and war supplies for Charles I from the city and neighbouring territories.[61] He and a group of other Scottish officers signed a document in 1639 in Hamburg, which confirmed that arms bought by Sir Thomas Roe were ready for the service of Charles I.[62]

It was not only the Royalists who were trying to purchase arms in Hamburg; the Scottish Covenanters were also attempting to secure munitions in the city. This led the Marquis of Hamilton to write to Charles I, making it clear that action should be taken to prevent any supplies of war goods reaching the king's enemies from the city.[63] Perhaps more interestingly, it can be shown that both Scottish Covenanters and Royalists were in the city at the same time without any hint of animosity between them. There is no evidence that the contesting groups of Scottish officers noted above actually met in the streets in the months from 1639–40. But it is known that important figures from both camps did meet and discuss the political situation at length. For example, the man who had done most to promote the cause of the Scottish Covenanters among the northern potentates and city-states was Colonel John Cochrane.[64] On 24 October 1640 the Royalist general and diplomat James King wrote of Cochrane:

James Lumsden even asked for his Swedish pension to be paid to him through Salvius, the Swedish resident in Hamburg.

[61] James King's wife gave birth to a daughter in Hamburg in 1640. *CSPD*, 1640–1641, 344, Letter of John Durie to Sir Thomas Roe, Hamburg, 3 July 1640.

[62] PRO, SP 81/47, f. 102, Certificate of General King upon arms sent to England, Hamburg, 28 June 1639. The other officers included Colonel Francis Ruthven, Lieutenant Colonel James King (a relative of the general), Colonel John Leslie, Lieutenant Colonel John Chamberlain, Colonel Henry Gladstone (Gladstein), Captain William Ogilvie, Captain Richard Shorland and Captain Bryan Stapleton. These may be some of the arms Roe bought in Hamburg from Albert Bernes including 1500 pikemen's arms, 700 arms for horsemen, 1500 muskets and bandoliers, 700 pistols and holsters and ammunition. See PRO SP 81/45. Manifest of Arms, Hamburg, 13 April 1639.

[63] NAS, GD 406/1/10491, Marquis of Hamilton to Charles I, Dalkeith, 24 June 1638.

[64] A. Grosjean, 'General Alexander Leslie, the Scottish Covenanters and the *Riksråd* Debates, 1638–1640' in Macinnes et al., *Ships, Guns and Bibles*, 115–130.

> Since my arrival heir at Hambourrie it was my fortune to encounter
> with a gentellman, a countryman and auld acquaintance of mine, cal-
> lit Colonell Cochrone a Gentellman who heath ben imployit by the
> Scotts to Establishe ther intelligence in the nichtbouring nations and
> to whom the wholl secreits of ther designs are committit.[65]

It is clear that this meeting had serious implications for future relations between the Royalists and the erstwhile Covenanter ambassador. Indeed it has been argued that it was during this meeting in
Hamburg that Cochrane 'turned' to the Stuart cause, albeit he kept
this secret until the following year.[66] But it does raise the question
of whether Hamburg was deliberately chosen as the place to meet,
being regarded as some kind of neutral venue.

After the conflicts between Charles I and the English Parliament
broke out, Hamburg was still targeted by contesting British factions
as a source of supplies and a place of retreat. In 1644, following the
battle of Marston Moor and the defeat of Royalist troops, a group
consisting of up to 180 Scottish and English Royalists arrived in
Hamburg, among them Lieutenant-General James King and Captain
Sir William Vavasour.[67] Those who remained in the city were joined
in 1646 by Sir John Cochrane, now firmly in the Royalist camp as
envoy to Denmark-Norway and various duchies since 1643. The aim
of his visit to Hamburg was to gather troops and arms for Charles
I. After negotiations with Christian IV of Denmark-Norway, Cochrane
received arms and ammunition from the Danish arsenal in Glückstadt
worth 29,300 *Reichstaler*, via the Berns & Marselis company.[68] Furthermore, Cochrane was mustering troops and organising ships for their
transport with the assistance of his old confederate James King.[69]

After the execution of Charles I in 1649, Cochrane returned again
to Hamburg, where the atmosphere among the Merchant Adventurers

[65] PRO SP 75/15 f. 475. James King to Charles I, Hamburg, 24 October 1640;
Murdoch, *Britain, Denmark-Norway and the House of Stuart*, 117–118.
[66] For more on the result of this meeting see Murdoch, *Britain, Denmark-Norway
and the House of Stuart*, 118–120.
[67] HP 3/2/45A–46B, John Durie to Hartlib, 28 July 1644; Peter Young, *Marston
Moor 1644. The Campaign and the Battle* (Kineton: 1970), 176.
[68] John T. Lauridsen, *Marselis Konsortiet* (Århus: 1987), 88 and 132; 'Scots Commissioners to the Committee of Estates in Edinburgh, 9 July 1646', in H. W. Meikle,
ed., *Correspondence of the Scots Commissioners in London 1644–1646* (Edinburgh: 1917),
199.
[69] 'Scots Commissioners to the Committee of Estates in Edinburgh, 7 July 1646',
in Meikle, ed., *Correspondence of the Scots Commissioners in London*, 198.

had become violent due to the splitting of company members into factions supporting either the Royalist cause or the English Parliament.[70] Cochrane became embroiled in clashes with the merchants, beating up some English republicans in the streets.[71] He also initiated an incident in which some Merchant Adventurers who supported the English Parliament were kidnapped with the help of Danish officers and soldiers and kept in a ship on the river Elbe. These merchants were subsequently freed by two men-of-war belonging to Hamburg.[72]

In November 1649 Colonel James Turner arrived in Hamburg, where he found a number of "Scottish gentlemen, who either had served the late King, or intended to serve the present one".[73] According to Turner, the Scotsmen were under the command of the Marquis of Montrose, awaiting their transport to Scotland from Hamburg.[74] The results of that shambolic enterprise are well known, and the ensuing destruction of the Royalist force left many of the Scottish participants destitute. But the paper trail they left does give us indications of who the Scottish officers had been trading with. A document from 1652 states that the Hamburg merchants W. Gryson, Leonhard Scott, James Harrington, Johan Staphorst, Thomas (Di?) Schirm, Johann Ward, Heinrich Lalmers, Johan Gilbertt, Paul Paulson and Daniell Krafft owed the Scottish officer Major Alexander Garden a considerable sum (over 6,000 dollars).[75] Some of their names— such as Scott, Gilbertt and Harrington—indicate a Scottish provenance. The origin of the other names is debatable though a Scottish origin cannot be excluded.[76]

---

[70] Joseph Averie wrote to Thomas Roe that although the majority of the merchants were loyal to the king they had been forced to join the Parliamentarians. See PRO SP 75/16, f. 178. Averie to Roe, Hamburg, 10/20 November 1643.

[71] J. N. M. Maclean, 'Montrose's preparations for the invasion of Scotland, and Royalist mission to Sweden, 1649–1651', in R. Hutton and M. Anderson, eds., *Studies in Diplomatic History* (London: 1970), 14; Murdoch, *Britain, Denmark-Norway and the House of Stuart*, 148.

[72] 'Sir John Cochrane's relations of the particulars that have occured in his negotiation since his coming to Hamborgh', in H. F. Morlund. Simpson, ed., *Civil War Papers 1643–1650* (Edinburgh: 1893), 183.

[73] Turner, *Memoirs*, 91.

[74] Turner, *Memoirs*, 91.

[75] NAS, Burnett & Reid Papers, GD 57/336/10, 'Notarial copy of obligations due to Major Alexander Garden, March 1651–April 1652'.

[76] For example, the name Krafft may well be a Germanised form of the Scottish name Crawford.

Garden's presence in the city in 1652 again highlights the role of Hamburg as a refuge. Another supporter of Charles II, William Cranstoun, sent a letter to the Swedish diplomat Peter Coyet from London, informing him that Charles II had promised him a payment through a diplomat in Hamburg called Mr. Cambro, who denied ever receiving such an order.[77] This is hardly surprising as Cranstoun's service in Sweden (an ally of Cromwell) was ambiguous at best and most Swedes wished to distance themselves, at least publicly, from any hint of support for Charles II.[78] Nonetheless, in 1657 Cranstoun himself was present in Hamburg, where he told Coyet of his huge financial problems, and asked him to send money to secure his passage to England.[79] Ten days later, however, Cranstoun informed Coyet that he had found another source of money in the city, and now had to travel as fast as possible from Hamburg to Scotland to sell his estates there in order to pay his officers, who were apparently threatening his wife at home.[80] For such a high-profile Royalist as Cranstoun, Hamburg proved to be a safe place in which to contemplate his future, even if it did not provide the financial support he required. But for other refugees from Cromwell and the troubles in the British Isles, Hamburg and her environs proved a very lucrative choice.

Hamburg and the wider Scottish community

After the Peace of Westphalia had been agreed, ending the Thirty Years' War in 1648/49, many Scottish officers remained in Germany and were joined by military refugees from the Cromwellian occupation throughout the 1650s. Some Scots found work, such as John Tommason, who was described as a Scottish captain belong-

---

[77] SRA, Coyetska Samlingen, 3398, Vol. 2, f. 4. Cranstoun to P. J. Coyet, London, 3 July [1656?].

[78] A. Grosjean, 'Royalist Soldiers and Cromwellian Allies': The Cranstoun Regiment in Sweden 1655–1658' in Murdoch and Mackillop, *Fighting for Identity*, 61–82.

[79] SRA, Coyetska Samlingen, 3398, Vol. 2, f. 130. Cranstoun to P. J. Coyet, Hamburg, 17 October 1657.

[80] SRA, Coyetska Samlingen, 3398, Vol. 2, f. 136. Cranstoun to P. J. Coyet, Hamburg, 28 October 1657.

ing to Hamburg in Sir Thomas Allen's naval journal of 1660.[81] Several even took over the command of towns surrounding Hamburg. Among them were Colonel Alexander Irving, governor of Stade between 1654–56 and Lieutenant-Colonel James Lundie, who commanded Bremervörde from 1649–57.[82] Another Scottish officer, Colonel William Forbes, was governor of Burg at Bremen-Verden, where he served the Swedish Crown from 1649–57.[83] On the Danish-Norwegian side Major Thomas Haliburton took over the command of Steinburg, north of Hamburg, in 1660.[84] General Patrick More served from 1646 until the 1670s as the commandant of Buxtehude, only a few miles west of Hamburg along the river Elbe.[85] General More frequently visited Hamburg during his time as governor, probably for commercial reasons as he was noted to have such interests in Buxtehude.[86] Another Scot, Colonel Andrew Melville, commanded the town of Gifhorn from 1677 to 1680. He too visited Hamburg, to secure feed for his horses, albeit the citizens (according to Melville) charged an outrageous price.[87]

Melville was a friend of Colonel John Mollison, who was made governor of the town of Lüneburg in 1674. Both men knew each other from their time in the Duke of Lorraine's army, in which they fought from 1647–50. They met again in Lüneburg in 1665, with Melville describing Mollison as his 'Scottish comrade' in his memoirs.[88]

---

[81] R. C. Anderson, ed., *Journals of Sir Thomas Allen*, Vol. 1, Naval Records Society 79, (London: 1993), 102. He was perhaps the same man, or more probably a relative of the John Thomessen married in the city 25 years previously.

[82] A. Grosjean, 'A Century of Scottish Governorship in the Swedish Empire' in A. Mackillop and S. Murdoch, eds., *Military Governors and Imperial Frontiers, c. 1600–1800: A Study of Scotland and Empires* (Leiden: 2003), 70, 73.

[83] Grosjean, 'A Century of Scottish Governorship', 61.

[84] S. Murdoch, 'Scotsmen on the Danish-Norwegian Frontiers, c. 1580–1680' in Mackillop and Murdoch, *Military Governors and Imperial Frontiers*, 22

[85] Grosjean, 'A Century of Scottish Governorship', 61; Grosjean, *An Unofficial Alliance*, 221.

[86] His presence in Hamburg is recorded in *RPCS*, 3rd Series, Vol. 1, 1661–1664, 355. The Council of Buxtehude noted on 10 May 1669 in a dispatch to Bremen Court that after 1650, Colonel More chose to live and trade in Buxtehude suggesting a retirement from service. Indeed, we know from the Buxtehude archives that More had accommodation near the Zwinger Tower and also paid taxes on a small farm near the town. See Stadtarchiv Buxtehude, StH. 38. M1 (1669). Documents detailing obligations and financial dealings between Patrick More and the Council and Mayor of Buxtehude.

[87] T. Ameer-Ali, ed., *Memoirs of Andrew Melville* (London: 1918), 214.

[88] Ameer-Ali, *Memoirs of Andrew Melville*, 153.

Although there is no evidence that Mollison was present in Hamburg as were More and Melville, it is hard to believe that he did not use the city as a market for supplies. The evidence comes from another comrade-in-arms. An intriguing letter from Sir James Johnstone of Elphinstone (who served as a captain in the Duke of Lüneburg's army) mentions his contact with a group of Scottish merchants in the city. He wrote to his brother-in-law stating that his equipment and status were as good as that of any other officer, a fact that any of the Scottish merchants who had seen him in Hamburg could confirm.[89] Unfortunately Johnstone does not name any of them. It is therefore unclear if these merchants were actually permanently resident in Hamburg or just there on a business trip. But the letter certainly suggests that those at home in Scotland would know who they were.

Andrew Russell, the Scottish factor in Rotterdam from 1660 to 1696, also had economic contacts in Hamburg, though it is uncertain whether he ever visited the city. On 11 November 1678, William Bogill (either a skipper or merchant) wrote a letter to Russell from Hamburg, letting him know that he had just arrived in the city from Bergen and that he had contacted his brother James. Furthermore, Bogill asked Russell for advice as to where he should sail with his goods from Hamburg.[90] Two years later, on 23 November 1680, James Campbell wrote to Russell from Hamburg informing him that James Bogill (William's brother) had arrived in the city.[91] In 1683 the Scottish merchant George Baillie of Jerviswood wrote a letter from Hamburg to his relative James Baillie promising to mind the recipient's business in the city.[92] He noted that it was possible to sell small quantities of herring in Hamburg, but apart from that, only fine stockings were in demand.[93] Nonetheless, Hamburg provided an

---

[89] NAS, GD 190/3/195, Misc. Correspondence (1639–1696), Sir James Johnstone to his brother-in-law, 24 April 1677.

[90] NAS, RH 15/106/305/6, William Bogill to Andrew Russell, Hamburg, 11 November 1678.

[91] NAS, RH 15/106/387/6, James Campbell to Andrew Russell, Hamburg, 23 November 1680. He also informed Russell about the loss of a vessel which had carried shipping equipment as cargo. The goods were secured and brought to the island of Ligoland—which seems certain to be a corruption of Helgoland.

[92] NAS, RH 15/49/7, George Baillie to James Baillie, Hamburg, 31 May 1683.

[93] NAS, RH 15/49/7, James Baillie, Captain of the Town Guard, Edinburgh, Correspondence, 1683–1698. Unfortunately the signature beneath the letter is destroyed and therefore we do not know the identity of the sender.

environment in which a network of Scottish traders could conduct their business.

From this evidence we can see that during the 1670s and 1680s there were numerous Scots in and around Hamburg. They were clearly in communication with each other and importantly, with Scots in communities elsewhere. Contact was not necessarily directly between Hamburg and Scotland, but between Hamburg and Scots elsewhere. For example, the city features in the commercial relations of the Gothenburg-Scottish families of Maclean and Spalding. Between 1666 and 1694 there were at least fifteen consignments of goods brought to or from Hamburg by members of the Maclean family, while another belonged to Anna Spalding.[94] Unfortunately we do not know who acted as contact for the Macleans or Anna Spalding in Hamburg, although it is fair to speculate that a Scottish factor in the city may have been involved, probably Nathaniel Watson who had commercial dealings with both the Scottish merchant in Stockholm, Alexander Waddell, and the Scottish and British diplomatic resident in Denmark, Sir John Paul.[95]

James Adie, the Scottish factor in Danzig, wrote to Andrew Russell from Danzig telling him that he had heard of the cheap prices for herring in Hamburg, and asking Russell to buy some herring there for him.[96] This proves that Adie knew about the trading contacts Russell enjoyed with Hamburg merchants. The same goes for George Melville, Earl of Leven, who asked Russell in a letter dated August 1686 to find a friend for him in Hamburg who would be able to vouch for him and so enable him to borrow 100 dollars in the town.[97] Indeed, Hamburg was a constant feature of Russell's postal network; the Hamburg postmaster knew to direct letters to and from Russell to particular places rather than where indicated. Thus in 1686, Patrick Thomson in Stockholm received and sent letters to

---

[94] Christina Dalhede, 'Göteborgs Tolagsjournaler 1638–1700', in *Handelsfamiljer pa Stormakttidens Europamarknad* (3 vols., Partille: 2001), III, CD-Rom appendix.

[95] H. Roseveare, ed., *Markets and Merchants of the Late Seventeenth Century: The Marescoe-David Letters, 1668–1680* (Oxford: 1987), 353–354. Alexander Waddell to Leonora Marscoe and Peter Joye, 24 July 1672; DRA, TKUA, England, A II 17, 'John Paul 1676–1679'. 'English' merchants to John Paul, 25 September 1674.

[96] NAS, RH 15/106/576/17, James Adie to Andrew Russell, Danzig, 6 July 1685.

[97] NAS, RH 15/106/609/16, George Melville, Earl of Leven to Andrew Russell, Helmstadt, 30 August 1686.

Russell via David Mollison in Elsinore, who in turn used the Hamburg postal service to get them to and from Rotterdam.[98]

In October 1689 three Scotsmen, Mungo English, Mr. Hume and Mr. Eliot, arrived in Hamburg on a tour through the Holy Roman Empire and Switzerland. Mungo English wrote from the city to Russell, informing him that they were contacting one of their countrymen there, a merchant called Robert Jolly, who loaned them money after they proved that they were friends of Russell.[99] A few months later Jolly sent a letter to Russell, in which he told him about the visit by the three Scotsmen and the money he had given to them.[100] Clearly the intention in writing was to make Russell pay back the money. However, these letters confirm both the significant economic relationship Russell had with Hamburg, and that Scottish merchants like Jolly were settled and trading there despite the presence of the English monopoly. The reason, as Jolly argued with the city magistrates, was that the monopoly only applied to subjects of the King of England, allowing Scots to trade freely without being confined by the England-Hamburg arrangement.[101] With that knowledge it is easier to comprehend that there were certainly more Scots operating in Hamburg in this period than simply those involved in Russell's network. One group of glassmakers (Englishmen as well as Scots) immigrated to Hamburg in 1690, including William Baily, William Blathes, Godfrey Brookes, Joseph Hosebury, Richard Smith and Thomas West.[102] Thomas Sysholms (Chisholm), a Scottish glovemaker, got married in 1696 in the St Pauli church, outside the city walls, to a woman called J. Elis, who was born in Altona.[103] Neither group of artisans has so far been shown to have had connections with Russell.

Another group of Scots arrived in the city soon after, this time

---

[98] NAS, RH 15/106/608/10, Patrick Thomson to Andrew Russell, 14 August 1686.
[99] NAS, RH 15/106/689/17, Mungo English to Andrew Russell, Hamburg, 26 October 1689.
[100] NAS, RH 15/106/689/18–19, Robert Jolly to Andrew Russell, 10 December 1689.
[101] *Records of the Convention of the Royal Burghs of Scotland*, III, 41, 5 July 1683 and 48, 4 July 1684.
[102] *CSPD*, 1689–1691, 516.
[103] Franz Schubert, ed., *Trauregister aus den ältesten Kirchenbüchern Hamburgs. Von den Anfängen bis zum Jahre 1704. Hamburg vor den Mauern (2)*, 82.

in search of investors. William Patterson and a delegation of agents from the newly-founded Scottish East India Company arrived in 1696. His attempts to gain financial support were obstructed by Sir Paul Rycaut, who had been instructed from England to oppose Patterson's endeavours. His stay was relatively brief, but gained the city some £30,000, which he spent there before moving on.[104] Patterson was not the last Scot to target Hamburg in a business venture. In the St Jacobi church in 1707, a Scotsman called Hans Morrha married a widow called Alheitd Stile; he was probably a resident merchant.[105] Another merchant, Arthur Nicolson, held shares in a vessel which had traded to Hamburg since 1699.[106] The same man sent letters from Hamburg in 1705–6 to a writer in Edinburgh called Charles Mitchell, highlighting his sustained interest in the city.[107] Mitchell received another letter from Robert Barclay, a Shetland merchant who was present in Hamburg in 1720, while correspondence from 1714 shows the involvement of George Pitcairn of Lerwick. All these letters concerned the ongoing trading links between Hamburg and Shetland.[108] In many ways this brought the story of the Scots in Hamburg full circle. As Scotland and England dissolved their independence within the unified British state in 1707, Scottish contacts returned to the status which they had held before the Union of Crowns in 1603—that is, a limited group of Scottish merchants trading herring to the city from the Shetland fishery.

Conclusion

From the trickle of merchants found at the opening of the seventeenth century it has been possible to trace a significant number of

---

[104] NAS, GD 26/7/113, Representation by the Council General of the Company of Scotland trading to Africa and the Indies to the Privy Council, 22 December 1697; *CSPD*, 1697, 189; David Ogg, *England in the reigns of James II and William III* (Oxford: 1955), 277–288.

[105] Franz Schubert, ed., *Trauregister aus den ältesten Kirchenbüchern Hamburgs. Von den Anfängen bis zum Jahre 1707. Hamburg Altstadt (6c)*, 2.

[106] NAS, RH 15/93/15 and 52, Papers relating to Shetland, 1693–1700. 5 December 1699 and 21 March 1702.

[107] NAS, RH 15/93/16/15, Papers relating to Shetland, 1705–1715. Various letters from Hamburg, 1705–1706.

[108] NAS, Russell Papers, RH 15/93/17/20 and RH 15/93/17/21, Papers relating to Shetland, 1714–1720.

Scots in Hamburg over the following hundred years. They came in a variety of capacities, including transient or resident diplomats, merchants, artisans and soldiers. However, the documents used for this essay do not reveal strong or consistent connections or contacts between the Scots they describe. Therefore it is not possible to say that there was a Scottish community in existence in Hamburg, comparable to others described elsewhere. Nonetheless, each episodic influx was like another building block in the Scottish presence in the city. And those Scots who were in Hamburg, particularly in the first half of the century, were incredibly influential. This raises the question as to whether their contact with the English in Hamburg allowed for the formation of a 'British community' in the city.

Some evidence points in this direction, particularly for the period during the 1630s. Members of the Merchant Adventurers, especially Joseph Averie, were in contact with influential Scots involved with the British experiment elsewhere. From an initial position of distance, Averie appeared to move to a 'British' position after the arrival of Anstruther to Hamburg. He certainly identified himself with fellow 'Britons' thereafter, while other Merchant Adventurers must have consented to this in some degree, as evidenced by Durie's role within their congregation. Certainly it cannot go unnoticed that James King uttered his declaration of Britishness in a city that also boasted John Durie 'Scoto-Britanno' as a resident at the same time. The acceptance of Scots among the Adventurers is given credence by the appearance of Scottish names in the marriage registers of the English Church. And while we do not have proof that other Scottish merchants and craftsmen were linked to the Merchant Adventurers, the lack of protest at their presence suggests that Scots were generally accepted by the English—even if the city magistrates could not comprehend why they were not considered by the Adventurers to be breaking the monopoly. The case for acceptance certainly appears to be confirmed by the example of David Melville, 3rd Earl of Leven, who arrived in the city in 1686.[109] A Scottish Presbyterian refugee in the aftermath of the 1685 Rye House Plot and Argyll uprisings, he lodged in the home of Mr Borick Taylor of the Merchant Adventurers.

---

[109] NAS, Russell Papers, RH 15/106/609. Numerous letters, Lord Leven to Andrew Russell, August–September 1686.

From the information scrutinised for this chapter it has been possible to show that, far from being a city devoid of Scottish connections, the Scots presence in Hamburg increased significantly during the century. It has been demonstrated that at various times important networks of influential Scots lived and traded in Hamburg, occasionally joined by transient colleagues. Some of these men were established motivators in the 'British' project begun by James VI and I, so to suggest tentatively the existence of a British rather than Scottish or English community in Hamburg is not unreasonable. Such contentions aside, this essay has shown that Hamburg continued as an important commercial hub for Scotsmen right into the incontrovertible 'British period' following the Treaty of Union of 1707.

SECTION III

COMMUNITIES OF MIND AND INTEREST

A HAVEN FOR INTRIGUE: THE SCOTTISH EXILE COMMUNITY IN THE NETHERLANDS, 1660–1690[1]

Ginny Gardner

Studies of the Scots abroad often cover long and settled periods of emigrant settlement. Links are established with host countries through a variety of means, such as trade, military service, religion or education, and reasons for emigration tend to focus on socio-economic trends. This is as true for the Scots' close relationship with the Netherlands as it is for their patterns of settlement across Europe and beyond. However, this chapter will concentrate on just one brief moment within that context—the exile community in the United Provinces during the second half of the seventeenth century. The exiles of course took advantage of long-established Scottish relationships with the Dutch merchant community, churches and universities. But, despite the strong bonds between exile and expatriate communities, there were differences—for example, their flight from Scotland, their pursuit whilst abroad by the British governments—that allow the exiles to be seen as a distinct society within the Scottish-Dutch community as a whole.

The exiles are worth considering within the wider theme of Scots abroad for two reasons: the temporary nature of the community, which lasted only thirty years in all; and the fact that the exiles maintained close links with Scotland and indeed expressed a continuing desire to be intimately involved in issues affecting their homeland. The exile community always aimed to return home and unlike many fellow expatriates did not become fully assimilated into Dutch society.[2] There were other exiles abroad during the Restoration

---

[1] Further information on the exile community can be found in G. Gardner, *The Scottish Exile Community in the Netherlands, 1660–1690* (East Linton: 2004).

[2] Virtually none, for example, appears to have established themselves by becoming a citizen of one of the Dutch towns: according to the extant registers for Amsterdam, Delft, Den Haag, Leiden and Utrecht, only one exile (Sir Duncan Campbell of Auchinbreck) was registered as a *burger*.

period, but those in the Netherlands are particularly significant because
the government to which they fled for shelter eventually authorised
an invasion of Britain and its prince became their king.

One peculiarity of the exile community—and the reason for its
impermanence and its continuing ties with Scotland—was that its
ebb and flow depended purely on religious and political discontent,
separating it from mainstream emigration in the period. This chapter therefore focuses on the subversive activities of the exiles and the
ways in which they sought to influence political and religious opinion at home (with varying degrees of success) from the 1660s onwards,
culminating in their participation in the indulgence debates of 1687
and the so-called Glorious Revolution of 1688. The chapter concludes with the successful outcome of such activity: the exiles' rein-
tegration into Scottish society and their considerable involvement in
the Scottish Revolution settlement in government and Church in
1689 and 1690.

The exile community

The community came into existence soon after the 1660 Restoration of Charles II. The catalyst for its inception was that king's religious intolerance, fired by his desire for vengeance on the staunch
Presbyterians who had humiliated him at his coronation in Scotland
in 1651.[3] The first known exiles were two ministers, James Simson
and Robert McWard, both of whom arrived in the Netherlands in
1661, soon after the reinstatement of Episcopalianism as the established religion in Scotland.[4] They and their compatriots were forced
to leave home because of their adherence to Presbyterianism and
their opposition to the Restoration regime's political and ecclesiastical
policies. Some, like Simson and McWard, were formally banished
from their homeland; others chose to leave before the government's
wrath was unleashed on them. A Dutch refuge was the obvious solu-

---

[3] S. Murdoch, *Britain, Denmark-Norway and the House of Stuart 1603–1660: a diplo-
matic and military analysis* (East Linton: 2003), 163. The subsequent execution of the
Marquis of Argyll in 1661 alarmed many Presbyterians and inspired them to flee
Scotland.

[4] Both enrolled at the University of Leiden in December. See *Album Studiosorum
Academiæ Lugduno Batavæ mdlxxv–mdccclxxv* (The Hague: 1875), 494.

tion—it was a Protestant country in the main sympathetic to Presbyterians, and close enough to Britain for the Scots to keep in touch with what was going on.

The community can be split into three groups: first, a core of Presbyterian ministers (there were sixty five in total), most of whom belonged to the older generation of exiles born in the first half of the seventeenth century. Next were the 'definite' exiles (over 170 in all), that is, those exiles who were not ministers but who could easily be classified as having left Scotland because of political or religious difficulties. As well as the ministers' family members, these were principally professional and landowning members of society, including some high-profile noblemen (such as Lord Melville and the Earl of Leven) and lairds (*e.g.* Andrew Fletcher of Saltoun, Sir Patrick Hume of Polwarth, or the lawyers Sir James Dalrymple of Stair and James Stewart of Goodtrees). The community was made more cohesive by the large number of relatives linked together by blood and marriage—for example, there were ten Stewarts and eight Humes.[5] Most exiles came from the traditionally strong Covenanting areas in southern Scotland and Fife; several had already participated in political protests against the Stuart monarchy, including the Pentland (1666) and Bothwell Bridge (1679) risings, before they joined the exile community.[6]

There were around 250 individuals in these two groups. This number swells to over 400 if the final group, the 'possible' exiles, is taken into account. These were individuals who appear to have been identified with the exile community but about whom sufficient doubt remains to prevent their classification as 'definite' exiles. One example is Andrew Russell, a prominent member of the Rotterdam kirk who operated as a merchant in the Netherlands for most of his adult life.[7] Russell was in Rotterdam by 1668, before the bulk of exiles arrived, and was certainly an established figure in the Scottish merchant

---

[5] This bond was strengthened when they returned home—when former exiles John Erskine of Carnock and Jean Mure of Caldwell married in 1690, their four witnesses were also fellow exiles. See W. Macleod, ed., *Journal of the Honourable John Erskine of Carnock 1683–87* (Edinburgh: 1893), xxviii.

[6] C. S. Terry, *The Pentland Rising and Rullion Green* (Glasgow: 1905); I. B. Cowan, *The Scottish Covenanters, 1660–88* (London: 1976), 64–72, 82–102.

[7] For Russell's trading activities, see T. C. Smout, *Scottish Trade on the Eve of Union 1660–1707* (Edinburgh: 1963), 185–94.

community there. Yet he was also strongly sympathetic to the
Presbyterian cause, may have attended conventicles in Scotland, was
married to the daughter of the exiled minister John Livingstone
and—not least—was considered subversive by the Scottish government.[8] Russell's extensive correspondence preserved in the National
Archives of Scotland demonstrates that the exile community trusted
him and relied on his judgement and discretion. The merchant's
generosity is constantly referred to in correspondence: for example,
James Stewart of Goodtrees described Russell's family as the "kind-
est I ever met with"[9] and when some of his compatriots were in
"great alarm" that the States "had consented to deliver them all
up", Russell was the one who tried to calm them and persuade them
that the rumours were false.[10] Goodtrees' brother, Thomas Stewart
of Coltness, even named one of his sons after the merchant in 1685.[11]

Although not as large a diaspora as the French Huguenots, the
exiles were nonetheless a significant group within the Scottish community in the Netherlands, and apparently of sufficient size for a
gallery to be built in the Rotterdam kirk to accommodate their
increasing numbers.[12] The profile of the community changed over
time, from a relatively small, clergy-dominated society in the 1660s
to a much larger, more diverse community in the 1680s. The lifetime of the clerical community drew to a close initially after several
ministers accepted the 1687 and 1688 indulgences offered by James
VII and II as a means of drawing moderate Presbyterians back to
the Church of Scotland. Greater numbers of the secular 'definite'
exiles had predominated from 1685 onwards, and their domination
was emphasised by the number of ministers who returned home to
benefit from the new king's religious concessions. When William of
Orange undertook the invasion of England in 1688 some of the
remaining clerics from the Dutch community joined him. Most of
those still left behind had returned home by 1690, the year which

---

[8] In 1683 Russell was charged with treason, his crimes including contact with
the murderers of Archbishop Sharp of St Andrews. See *RPCS*, 3rd series, VIII,
20–1, 455–6.
[9] NAS, RH15/106/638/15.
[10] NAS, RH15/106/483/26, November 1683.
[11] *The Coltness Collections mdcviii–mdcccxl* (Maitland Club: 1842), 84.
[12] J. Morrison, *Scots on the Dijk: the story of the Scots church, Rotterdam* (privately
printed: 1981), 20.

saw the re-establishment of Presbyterianism in Scotland and the decisive battle of the Boyne in Ireland, which signalled James VII and II's exile from the British Isles.

The exiles tended to congregate round the Scots churches and the universities, where they could easily meet up and exchange the latest gossip from home. The most popular residences were the port of Rotterdam, followed by the university towns of Utrecht and Leiden, where many exiles took the opportunity to study with illustrious professors in the colleges. The more extreme contingent of Cameronian sympathisers tended to settle in the northern towns of Leeuwarden and Groningen, thereby avoiding possible contamination by weaker Presbyterians elsewhere.[13]

Given that many of them had been banished, deprived of their livelihoods or in some cases had their estates forfeited, it is perhaps surprising that the evidence indicates that the community had a sufficient support network in place—whether through families at home, sea captains, or merchants in Scotland and abroad—to make life reasonably comfortable. Some wily landowners seem to have continued to receive rents from their confiscated estates. A marvellous pocketbook belonging to the Earl of Leven in the National Archives of Scotland shows that he spent much of his time seeking diversions from normal life, including visiting the opera, playing tennis, learning to dance and playing the viol. Leven even recorded the sums he lost when he was playing billiards.[14] Despite the hardships and uncertainty of being far from home, it is clear that most of the exiles had the leisure to involve themselves in plotting against the Stuart government and that the community as a whole provided the perfect haven in which to propagate ideas and develop intrigues.

---

[13] Robert Hamilton and his brother-in-law Sir Alexander Gordon of Earlston established links with Dutch ministers in the northern provinces to educate and ordain young Scottish Cameronians there—hence James Renwick was ordained at Groningen in April 1683. See M. Shields, ed., *Faithful Contendings displayed* (Glasgow: 1780), 29–45, 80–98.

[14] NAS, GD26/6/139. Other exiles survived by a variety of means—for example, ministers such as Robert McWard continued to preach; former merchants such as George Porterfield continued to trade; and young men like John Erskine of Carnock joined the Dutch army. Patrick Hume of Polwarth even seems to have passed himself off as a doctor in Bordeaux and Montpellier, while making his way back to the Netherlands after the Argyll rising in 1685. See NAS, GD158.

Influencing Scottish religious and political life

Throughout the lifetime of the community, the exiles remained concerned by what was happening at home and kept each other informed of the latest news.[15] However the first twenty years of the community, though no doubt a useful training ground for the future, witnessed only a few prepared to become involved in subversive activity. Before 1685 action was limited either to those who maintained links with the Dutch court and informed it of developments in Britain or to the handful of others who sought to influence British public opinion by publishing political and religious pamphlets. From 1683 onwards there were increasing numbers arriving in the Netherlands who were ever more willing to intervene in order to bring down the Stuart regime. There is no doubt that the governments both in Edinburgh and London considered the exiles a threat, even during the early years of the community. On a number of occasions they sought to harass the exiles in their new home, either through formal banishment orders or the more direct methods employed by the henchmen of the local English envoy.[16]

(i) *1660s and 1670s*

In the 1660s and 1670s activity centred round the exiled ministers who sought to influence Scottish attitudes to the indulgences, the series of measures introduced by Charles II with the aim of dividing Presbyterians by tempting moderates back to the established Church. Several ministers at home accepted the terms of the three indulgences published between 1669 and 1679, provoking Presbyterian splits that resembled the disputes between the 'Resolutioners' and 'Protesters' in the 1650s.[17]

---

[15] As well as contact through the churches and universities, the exiles kept in touch by clandestine correspondence (often using false names and disguised writing) sent through merchants such as Andrew Russell. Patrick Hume of Polwarth thus used a number of pseudonyms, including 'Peter St Clare', 'P. Pereson' and 'Peter Wallas'. See NAS, GD158/1016–1018.

[16] For example, Charles II persuaded the Dutch government to banish (albeit briefly) three exiles living in Holland in 1677. See ARA, 3.01.18; NLS, Wodrow MS Folio lx, nos. 64–83. The English envoy was foiled in his attempts to capture Robert Ferguson in Amsterdam in both 1685 and 1686. See Amsterdam Gemeentelijke Archief, 5028, 496B/uncat; British Library, Additional MSS 481812, ff. 195–200 & 41813, ff. 199–204.

[17] Cowan, *The Scottish Covenanters, 1660–88*, 17–34.

The attitudes of various sides were represented in manuscript and print and the exiled ministers, from the relative safety of the Netherlands, played a key role in such debates, stiffening the resistance of those who might otherwise have conformed. Robert McWard and John Brown's correspondence with John Dickson is said to have been particularly influential in persuading many Presbyterians against the indulgences and in encouraging divisions by its criticism of the indulged.[18] The two ministers published their views through a number of pamphlets attacking the Restoration Church, with stirring titles such as '*The Poor man's cup of cold water ministred to the Saints and sufferers for Christ in Scotland who are amidst the scorching flames of the fiery trial*' (McWard, 1678) and '*An Apologeticall Relation, Of the particular sufferings of the faithfull Ministers & professours of the Church of Scotland, since August 1660*' (Brown, 1665). The authors condemned several aspects of the post-1660 ecclesiastical order, including the king's supremacy in church matters, the tacit acceptance of prelacy by those who accepted the indulgences, and any attempt to divide and ruin the "poor remnant".

Not surprisingly, Brown and McWard's attitudes created acrimony both in Scotland and in Rotterdam. This reached a height in 1677 and 1678 and was bound up in the two ministers' support of the young extremist Richard Cameron. Commentators from Scotland reported that there was great dissatisfaction with Cameron and much criticism of Brown, who had "so exalted him".[19] Despite this censure, the two ministers ordained Cameron in Rotterdam in the summer of 1679.[20]

At the same time as these very public displays of interference, some exiles were also spying for the Dutch court and maintaining channels of communication in order to track political developments in Britain. McWard was involved in this too and in 1672 penned an anonymous political tract, entitled '*The English Ballance, Weighing the Reasons, of Englands present conjunction with France, against the Dutch.*

---

[18] T. McCrie, ed., *The Bass Rock* (Edinburgh: 1848), 341–2.

[19] NAS, RH15/106/128/13, Janet Fleming to Andrew Russell, Edinburgh, 20 May 1679.

[20] Morrison, *Scots on the Dijk*, 8–9. In the Rotterdam congregation, the kirk session was still confused about how to react to indulged ministers in 1685, well after the deaths of Brown and McWard. See Rotterdam Gemeentelijke Archief, Scots Church archive, MS 2, (2nd page numbering), 37, 40–3.

With some Observes upon his Majesties Declaration, of Liberty to Tender Consciences'. This document, with its anti-war emphasis on the Protestant links between the English and Dutch and its distrust of Louis XIV, in many ways paved the way for the more famous *'England's Appeal from the Private Cabal at White-Hall to The Great Council of the Nation, The Lords and Commons in Parliament Assembled'* which appeared in March 1673.[21]

Apart from overt and published resistance to the Stuart monarchy, the community also served the purposes of British-based undercover agents. The most notable Scottish spy was William Carstares, who began his political career as agent for the Dutch court during the third Anglo-Dutch war (1672–4).[22] The aim of the circle of spies set up in England was to provide intelligence and to persuade Charles II to withdraw from his alliance with Louis XIV. As with other agents, Carstares reported back on affairs in London. However, his correspondence was significant for its references to events in Scotland. It is clear from his letters that the Dutch were considering active encouragement of the opposition to the Duke of Lauderdale, the Scottish secretary of state at the time. Scotland was in as much turmoil as England: Lauderdale was almost universally disliked, an indulgence issued in 1672 had failed to attract many nonconformists, and there were continual disturbances against the government's measures to discourage Presbyterian gatherings. The parliament in Edinburgh, called like the English one to provide money for the war, was no less willing to publicise its grievances. Scotland thus entered the equation for the Dutch, for if pressure could be brought to bear there then they might achieve the same aim of inducing Charles II to retire from the war. The downfall of Lauderdale in Edinburgh could also serve to facilitate the speedier disintegration of the 'Cabal' administration in London.[23] A document headed 'Instructions for Mr W.C.s' and dated May 1674 in the National Archives in The Hague suggests that the Duke of Hamilton—leader of the opposition—was intriguing with the Dutch through Carstares, and that William of

---

[21] K. H. D. Haley, *William III and the English Opposition, 1672–4* (Oxford: 1953), 88–111.

[22] His correspondence can be found at ARA, 1.10.29, n. 547.

[23] The 'Cabal' was named after the initials of Charles II's five leading ministers between 1668 and 1673: Clifford, Arlington, Buckingham, Ashley and Lauderdale.

Orange was prepared to support action by Hamilton against Lauderdale if it became necessary.[24]

In the end negotiations did not progress to direct action, for the English government broke up the Dutch spy ring in the summer of 1674 and Hamilton and his opposition remained powerless to detach Lauderdale from the king's favour. Carstares himself was captured in London in September 1674 and held prisoner for nearly five years. Once released, the undaunted spy—along with fellow exiles Robert McWard, Lord Cardross and James Stewart of Goodtrees—became involved in political correspondence with the Dutch court and English opposition during the Exclusion Crisis in the late 1670s and early 1680s.[25] Carstares' capture did not prevent the flow of information reaching the exile network (and thus the Dutch authorities). Indeed in a witty and scathing letter, one Scottish agent in London was able to give detailed accounts of the goings-on in England with particularly harsh commentary on the Duke of Buckingham and the Earl of Anglesey, "formerly a Presbyterian—but now a corrupt Courtier".[26] The survival of such correspondence is crucial to our understanding of the continuous flow of information that allowed the community to remain abreast of information from home.

The period to 1680 demonstrates limited political achievement, though the evidence does reveal that William of Orange was prepared to rely on the Scots in his dealings with the government's chief opponents in both England and Scotland. A few individuals tested opinion at home and began to build up relationships with the Dutch court that were to prove advantageous after 1688. Most notably, the exiled ministers continued to take part in the church debates in Scotland and were able to influence and bolster negative attitudes to the indulgences in Scotland. Without this intervention, there can be little doubt that Presbyterian opposition to such measures would have been much weaker during Charles II's reign.

---

[24] ARA, 1.10.29, n. 556/2; Gardner, 'The Scottish exile community in the United Provinces', 182–6.

[25] NLS, Wodrow MS Folio lix; ARA, 1.10.29, n. 1982 & 3.01.18, n. 484.

[26] NAS, RH15/106/305. ? to Andrew Russell, 5 and 8 November 1678. The author writes in a Scots hand and details information pertaining to both Scottish and English affairs.

(ii) *1680–85*

The political temperature in Britain rose steadily in the first half of the 1680s. In the exile community too, where previous political involvement had depended on individuals such as William Carstares, there was an increasing influx of Scots from the early 1680s who were prepared actively to alter the government at home. This led to the Earl of Argyll's and the Duke of Monmouth's invasions of Scotland and England respectively in 1685.[27]

The background to the decision to invade lies in the various Whig plots of 1682 and 1683. Some of the Scottish exiles, led by the Earl of Argyll, had considered raising a rebellion in 1682; Stewart of Goodtrees had written letters aimed at identifying the extent of possible support, and in 1683 bundles of '*The case of the earl of Argyle*' were shipped to Britain.[28] But the plans then became mixed up with English Whig projects to exclude Charles II's brother James from the throne. After these were exposed through the 'Rye House' plotters, several more discontented Scots and Englishmen—including the Duke of Monmouth—headed for exile in the Netherlands.[29] The Earl of Argyll had himself been on the continent since his flight from a death sentence passed in Scotland in 1681.[30] Here were two noble leaders, able to attract the support of several other exiles and with the potential to draw the discontented at home to their side.

The accession of the Catholic James VII and II in February 1685 convinced many of the exiles that Protestantism was under threat in Europe and that they had a duty to defend it and the liberties of Britain. This belief culminated in plans to launch joint attacks on England and Scotland. Yet despite the enthusiasm, the enterprise was doomed from the start.[31] Jealousies existed between the two

---

[27] J. Willcock, *A Scots Earl in Covenanting Times: being life and times of Archibald 9th earl of Argyll (1629–1685)* (Edinburgh: 1907), 327–408; P. Earle, *Monmouth's Rebels: the road to Sedgemoor 1685* (London: 1977).

[28] *A Full Discovery of the Late Fanatical Plot in Scotland. or, The Deposition of Mr. William Carstares* (Edinburgh: 1685); F. A. Middlebush, ed., *The Dispatches of Thomas Plott (1681–2) and Thomas Chudleigh (1682–5) English Envoys at the Hague* (Rijks Geschiedkundige Publicatiën, Kleine Serie 22: 1926), 231.

[29] T. B. Macaulay, *The History of England*, ed. C. H. Firth (London: 1914), II, 520–35.

[30] *RPCS*, 3rd series, VII, 736.

[31] For Patrick Hume of Polwarth's account, G. H. Rose, *A Selection from the Papers of the Earls of Marchmont, in the possession of the Right Honourable Sir George Henry Rose. Illustrative of Events from 1685 to 1750* (London: 1831), III, 1–66.

leaders and there was discontent even among the main Scottish protagonists. The Scots leaders were worried that Argyll was exaggerating his claims about money, arms and support. Nevertheless, Argyll's three ships set sail from Amsterdam on 2 May 1685. Noticeably for once the rebels did not include William Carstares, who spent that summer travelling through Europe and thus distanced himself from a project of which he must have known his patron William of Orange disapproved.[32] After a disastrous landing on Orkney, the Scots headed for Argyll's own lands in the west but found little assistance from the mainland. By mid-June, Argyll had been captured and his rapidly diminishing force dissipated. Monmouth—delayed in leaving Amsterdam until 24 May—fared little better and was eventually defeated at Sedgemoor on 6 July.[33]

In the period up to 1686, whatever the exiles hoped to achieve, the opposition in Scotland remained too weak to be of much use to the Dutch. Hamilton and other nobles could do nothing to displace Lauderdale, his eventual overthrow being brought about by the Bothwell Bridge rising of 1679 and by events in England. The invasions of 1685 did show that there were many Scots willing to risk their lives, but the rising lacked decent leadership and, crucially, sufficient backing in Scotland to succeed. The correspondence maintained by the exiles in the 1670s and early 1680s may have been accurate in detail, but it was far too limited to establish a firm basis for revolt. This inadequate preparation, added to Argyll's inflated claims of support and the Cameronians' refusal to participate in the rebellion, suggests that the undertaking was bound to fail from the outset.[34]

Argyll's rising did however have a profound effect on the exile community, with the numbers of known exiles peaking in 1685 and 1686. For the moment, these exiles were beaten and demoralised, but from 1686 the momentum for change gathered pace. The disappointments of the first half of the 1680s were replaced by the

---

[32] R. H. Story, *William Carstares: a character and career of the revolutionary epoch (1649–1715)* (London: 1874), 107–11.

[33] Earle, *Monmouth's Rebels*, pp. 118–34.

[34] Argyll's vote in the privy council on the execution of Donald Cargill in 1681 did not endear him to the Cameronians. See *Historical Observes of Memorable Occurrences in Church and State, from October 1680 to April 1686 by Sir John Lauder of Fountainhall* (Bannatyne Club: 1840), 167; Willcock, *A Scots Earl in Covenanting Times*, 289.

concessions of the 1687 indulgences and an altogether more successful attempt to alter the British political scene in 1688.

(iii) *1685–88*

The increase in exile numbers also brought a shift in the nature of
the community's subversive activity. In the 1670s and early 1680s the
debate about indulgences had been mainly a theological one among
the exiled ministers, but in 1687 it came to be of more political significance. James VII's attempt to provide religious freedom for his
fellow Catholics was viewed by many as part of a 'Popish' plot to
subvert the liberties of Protestant Britons and appeared to confirm
their earlier misgivings when he had succeeded his brother to the
throne. The involvement of William of Orange and his advisers,
informed by exile intelligence, also brought a European dimension
to debates that had been exclusively Scottish in the 1670s.

The distinction between previous grants of indulgence and the
1687 indulgences was further demonstrated by the popularity of the
latter, especially the second one issued in July 1687. This had a
direct impact on the community as many Scottish dissenters accepted
freedom of conscience and several exiles returned home. Twenty one
of the exiled ministers were probably in Scotland in 1687 and 1688,
of whom eighteen seem to have returned directly as a result of the
second indulgence. Most notable of these was the respected James
Kirkton, a sixty-year-old who had been deprived in 1662 but who
was permitted to return and preach in a meeting house in Edinburgh.[35]
That so many of the exiles were prepared to return home as a result
of religious concessions granted by a Catholic monarch seems surprising, especially as Presbyterian attitudes to previous grants of indulgence had been less than lukewarm.[36]

Many of the conditions—such as reiteration of the king's supremacy
in ecclesiastical matters—censured by McWard and Brown in the

---

[35] H. Scott, *Fasti Ecclesiæ Scoticanæ* (New Edition, vol. I, Edinburgh: 1915), 119.

[36] The 1669 indulgence had been accepted by around forty ministers; the 1672
indulgence was extended to about forty more parishes, though many refused to take
up their appointment. J. Brown, *The History of the Indulgence Shewing its Rise, Conveyance,
Progress & Acceptance: Together with a Demonstration of the Unlawfulness thereof, And an
Answere to contrary Objections: As also a Vindication of such, as scruple to hear the Indulged*
(1678), 18–9, 25–6, 33–7; G. Burnet, *History of His Own Time* (London: 1857), I,
226.

1670s still applied to these proclamations and there was the added sin of association with Catholic and Quaker toleration. Of course, Brown and McWard and many of their Covenanting colleagues were dead by 1687 and it is certainly the case that their less tolerant views had been discredited by divisions at Bothwell Bridge, after which the first signs of a split between Covenanting and an "orthodox yet compromising" Presbyterianism had emerged.[37] General weariness over continuing the battle against the government (something Brown and McWard would have condemned as weakness and decay) must also have contributed to acceptance of the toleration.[38] William Carstares certainly believed that the "violence of extraordinarie and inhuman oppressions to which Dissenters . . . have for many years been exposed" had made "quiet sweet".[39] Fatigue would also have figured in the desire of several exiles to return home.

A key factor was the position of the returning exile James Stewart of Goodtrees, an unexpected convert to the government's side considering his previously strong Covenanting sympathies. Goodtrees played a significant role in convincing exile ministers and other Presbyterians of the indulgence's merits. He also tried to persuade William of Orange of the sincerity of James' intentions and his interference proved to be crucial in bringing the opposing views of William and the king out into the open.

The 1687 Indulgences

The first indulgence in February 1687 was still quite restrictive for Presbyterians; it allowed 'moderates' to meet in private houses and to hear any minister willing to accept the indulgence. However, they could not build special meeting houses and were not even permitted to use outhouses or barns. In comparison, Quakers and Catholics were allowed to congregate in places licensed for their worship.[40]

---

[37] C. Kidd, 'Religious Realignment between the Restoration and Union', in J. Robertson, ed., *A Union for Empire: political thought and the union of 1707* (Cambridge: 1995), 157–8.

[38] T. McCrie, *The Story of the Scottish Church. From the Reformation to the Disruption* (Glasgow: 1988), 372–376; R. Wodrow, *The History of the Sufferings of the Church of Scotland, from the Restauration to the Revolution* (Edinburgh: 1721–2), II, 615.

[39] PRO, SP 8/1, pt 2, ff. 141–2.

[40] NLS, L. C. Fol. 75, f. 114, *His Majesty's royal letter to his Privy Council of Scotland, concerning his Indulgence* (Edinburgh: 1687).

Not surprisingly, the exile response was cautious. There was extensive communication about it among the Scottish exiles and between them and the Dutch court.[41] James Stewart of Goodtrees, Patrick Hume of Polwarth and others were agreed that Protestantism was under threat and that James intended to bring about the establishment of Catholicism. This project was to be accomplished both by law and by armed force. As a consequence of this attack on their religion, the Scots expected action by the Dutch, particularly as they believed that the king might also try to prevent his heirs, the Protestant William of Orange and his wife Mary, from succeeding to the throne. There were a variety of suggestions about how the exiles could assist the Dutch, from merely influencing the political nation in Britain to the more drastic employment of military action.

In the first half of 1687, the exiles were extremely worried by James's interventions; the Dutch court was likewise perplexed.[42] However, although there was general agreement that the policy of indulgence could prove to be a real threat to Protestantism and to the prospect of a Protestant succession, there was as yet little evidence of direct involvement in the British political scene. The next phase of debate, from July 1687 to the first half of 1688, saw the Dutch and many exiles taking an ever firmer stance over the indulgences.

The second Scottish indulgence in July brought much wider benefits to the Presbyterians. Services could be held in private houses or public chapels, provided that officials were informed of the address and of the preacher's name, and all "penal and sanguinary" laws against nonconformists were suspended with immediate effect.[43] As mentioned above, the most public *volte-face* was that of the exiled Presbyterian propagandist James Stewart of Goodtrees, who was persuaded to return to Britain to promote the new religious policy. The move was in direct contrast to his entire political career during the Restoration and was a clean break from his viewpoint in the first half of 1687.

---

[41] See NLS, Wodrow MS Octavo xxx, ff. 37–42; N. Japikse, ed., *Correspondentie van Willem III en van Hans Willem Bentinck, eersten graaf van Portland* (Rijks Geschiedkundige Publicatiën, Kleine Serie 23–4 and 27–8, 1927–37), pt 1, vol. II, 13–21.

[42] In May, William Carstares informed Polwarth that the addresses of thanks sent to the king by English dissenters were "litle pleasing to the greatest". See NAS, GD158/1033, letters to 'Monsieur Walton'.

[43] *Historical Notices of Scottish Affairs, Selected from the Manuscripts of Sir John Lauder of Fountainhall* (Bannatyne Club: 1848), 806.

Stewart's importance lay in his correspondence with his old friend, William Carstares, who remained in exile in Leiden.[44] In reality, the correspondence was from James VII and II to the Dutch court and was a new attempt at persuading William of Orange to support the indulgences—a matter in which Stewart not only failed miserably but in which he ended up being highly embarrassed by the publication of 'Fagel's letter' defending the prince's position.[45]

Despite its success, the second indulgence did not solve James VII's problems in Scotland and, if anything, served only to alienate more of his subjects. Those (like the Anglicans in England) most offended by the toleration were members of the Episcopalian and royalist establishment. Worries over the direction of government policy had induced the resignation of Sir George Mackenzie of Rosehaugh in 1686 and then his successor Sir George Lockhart, as well as the removal from office of two bishops. Criticism of Catholic toleration from the pulpit led to a proclamation against seditious sermons, which upset many parish clergy.[46] James' problem was that these former supporters were not replaced by loyal Presbyterians: although Dundonald accepted a position in the privy council after a dispensation from taking the Test in 1686, many saw this as merely a precedent for allowing Catholics the same privilege (the Earl of Traquair was thus admitted three months later) and there was concern that similar terms for other Presbyterians would serve to strengthen the king's power to dispense with laws against Catholics.[47]

Within the exile community, the whole episode revealed a division between those who preferred to remain tied to William and those who were prepared to return home under James' favour. As in the period before 1686, the evidence demonstrates considerable contact between the exiles and William's top officials, as well as detailed debates amongst the exiles themselves. The second indulgence was the turning point. Polwarth and Stewart of Goodtrees,

---

[44] Goodtrees sent at least fifteen letters between July 1687 and April 1688. See NLS, Wodrow MS Octavo xxx, ff. 37–53 (copies by Wodrow) and PRO, MSS SP 8/1 and 8/2.

[45] *A Letter Writ by Mijn Heer Fagel, Pensioner of Holland, To Mr. James Stewart, Advocate; Giving an Account of the Prince and Princess of Orange's Thoughts concerning the Repeal of the Test, and the Penal Laws* (London: 1688).

[46] *Historical Notices of Scottish Affairs*, 739–40, 755, 773.

[47] *Historical Notices of Scottish Affairs*, 740–1, 748, 750, 775.

leaders of exile opposition to the first indulgence, now followed quite opposite courses. Though humiliated in public, Stewart's well-intended attempts to influence the political situation did not end in complete failure. He had been unlikely to alter the opinion of the Dutch court, for William had already expressed opinions in 1686 that conformed to moderate Protestant views and he maintained these throughout 1687. However, in Scotland many Presbyterians did accept the second indulgence and, though old friends remained deeply suspicious of Stewart's motives and of those of the king, its success can in part be attributed to Stewart's influence. He also probably did much to persuade exiled ministers to return home and, at the very least, can be regarded as articulating the views of these and other Presbyterians who, since the acrimonious divisions at Bothwell Bridge, had been increasingly eager to distance themselves from the actions of the extremists.

In a more pragmatic and compromising spirit compared to that of Charles II's reign, the Presbyterians accepted the second indulgence "without scruple" and sent addresses of thanks to James VII. Yet they remained stubborn in their refusal to agree to the abolition of the 1681 'Test', which in effect prevented Catholics from holding public office.[48] Arguably it was James' unwillingness to back down on this issue, publicised through the printing of 'Fagel's letter' and Stewart's correspondence, which "made the invasion of England inevitable and cost him his throne".[49]

1688 invasion

Acceptance of the indulgences did not translate into active defence of the government when William invaded. In fact, there was considerable activity in the country as the invasion neared and evidence that the prince and his supporters were still considering a diversion in Scotland late in 1688.[50] While the Scots exiles had a relatively minor part to play in Dutch preparations for the invasion, some of

---

[48] Burnet, *History of His Own Time*, I, 453.

[49] J. Carswell, *The Descent on England: a study of the English Revolution of 1688 and its European background* (London: 1969), 109.

[50] *Correspondentie van Willem III en van Hans Willem Bentinck*, pt 1, vol. ii, 612.

them did maintain close links with William and his court and one can imagine that they often discussed the details of the military plans, particularly as they related to Scotland. There is evidence that some exiles were also working in Scotland to propagate support and that parts of the population were primed for action on the eve of the invasion.[51] All of this modifies the traditional view that Scots were merely passive participants in the Revolution.

The invasion army itself included a number of exile volunteers and professional soldiers. The Scots-Dutch Brigade was part of the invasion force and included officers who had been exiles—for example, Sir Duncan Campbell of Auchinbreck and Henry Erskine, 3rd Lord Cardross, both of whom had been appointed captain apparently thanks to William of Orange.[52] Throughout the march towards London in November and December, the exiles continued to serve William of Orange. William Carstares led the service of thanksgiving when the invasion force landed, and the 3rd Earl of Leven headed the band of refugees that accepted the surrender of the significant naval port of Plymouth.[53]

In Scotland, the remnant of the privy council had already urged William to call a free parliament on 24 December, but it had to be repeated by the Scots nobles and gentlemen who were in London and were called together on 7 January 1689.[54] After two days of deliberation under Hamilton's presidency, an address was presented to William on 10 January asking him to call a meeting of the Estates in order to safeguard Protestantism and to restore the laws and liberties of the kingdom. It was signed by thirty lords and around eighty

---

[51] At least five Scots associated with the exile community: George Pringle of Torwoodlee, William Denham of Westshields and Dr William Blackadder among others appear to have been active in Scotland in 1687 and 1688. Some of the ministers who returned after James VII's indulgence may also have been involved. See *Correspondentie van Willem III en van Hans Willem Bentinck*, pt 1, vol. II, 13–5; NAS, GD158/1033/2 & GD158/1035; PRO, SP 8/2, pt 2, ff. 109–112A).

[52] PRO, SP 8/2, pt 2, ff. 109–112A; J. Ferguson, ed., *Papers illustrating the History of the Scots Brigade in the Service of the United Netherlands 1572–1782* (3 vols., Edinburgh: 1899), I, 518.

[53] J. McCormick, ed., *State-Papers and Letters addressed to William Carstares* (Edinburgh: 1774), 34; Carswell, *The Descent on England*, 194.

[54] R. Beddard, *A Kingdom without a King. The Journal of the Provisional Government in the Revolution of 1688* (Oxford: 1988), 166–7; I. B. Cowan, 'Church & state reformed? The Revolution of 1688–9 in Scotland', in J. I. Israel, ed., *The Anglo-Dutch Moment: essays on the Glorious Revolution and its world impact* (Cambridge: 1991), 164.

gentlemen. Given the fact that the exiles were in London as part of
William's army, and their later prominence in his Scottish government, it must be assumed that the most prominent exiles were surely
present at this crucial meeting.

It was certainly at this point that the years of intrigue in exile
began to pay off for those associated with William's court. There
were already indications that the exiles were being sized up as potential holders of power. The 2nd Earl of Tweeddale, whose son Lord
Yester was in London and reported all proceedings to his father,
was anxious that the family maintained every possible advantageous
connection. The earl obviously knew some of the exiles from previous acquaintanceship and urged his son to remain close to Gilbert
Burnet and Sir James Dalrymple of Stair, among others.[55] The
Presbyterian Church itself was also clearly aware of the need to have
an advocate among the exiles: a general meeting of the Church had
unanimously decided to ask Patrick Hume of Polwarth to act as one
of their commissioners in their quest to persuade William to re-estab-
lish Presbyterianism and restore 'outed' ministers.[56]

The Revolution Settlement, 1689–90

In the early months of 1689 the exiles were well-placed in London
with access to William, and soon their families who had been left
behind were returning to celebrate their good fortune. Their remaining political goal was to influence Scotland's future. To this end,
several exiles became involved in their country's Revolution settlement in government and Church. For most of the remainder, there
was a satisfactory return to estates and position in society—a tri-
umphant finale that would have been hard to predict after the ill-
fated Argyll/Monmouth invasions only four years earlier.

However, unlike the smooth progress of the invasion army towards
London, events in Scotland were leading to chaos. With troops sent
to England on the first news of the invasion, there were few soldiers
left to keep the peace. The government of the country broke down
as most of the privy councillors deserted their posts and hastened to

---

[55] NLS, MS 7026, f. 106.
[56] HMC, *Report XIV, Appendix, Part III* (London: 1894), 117.

London and all business in the law courts and elsewhere was suspended. In the south-west, the practice of 'rabbling' the curates out
of their parishes became a popular pastime of the Cameronians, one
of the few armed forces remaining in the country, led by the former
exile Daniel Ker of Kersland.[57] Regular troops—the Scots-Dutch
Brigade under the command of Major-General Hugh Mackay of
Scourie—did not arrive in Leith until midway through March 1689.[58]

The country was thus in a state of high disorder when the Convention of Estates met in March. Its foremost consideration was the
constitutional ramifications of James' flight: resolution of this matter,
along with a close monitoring of the military situation, was essential
for the recovery of government control. William and Mary were offered
the English crown in February 1689; the decision by the Scottish
Convention to follow suit came in the Claim of Right two months
later. Jacobite resistance rumbled on but became less of a threat
after the death of Viscount Dundee at Killiecrankie in July 1689.[59]

The task thereafter was to establish a new Williamite government
and to decide on the system of ecclesiastical government. Certain
prominent exiles took important parts in these military and constitutional affairs and many enjoyed substantial rewards as a result.
The Earl of Leven became governor of Edinburgh castle; Argyll's
son, confirmed as the new earl, became colonel of a regiment of
Highlanders; Lord Cardross's brothers also remained in the military,
John Erskine of Carnock becoming lieutenant-governor of Stirling
Castle in 1690. In parliament, seven lords and six shire and burgh
commissioners who had been exiles sat in the 1689 session; in the
1690 session, which established Presbyterianism, a further three were
involved.[60]

---

[57] J. Ker, *The Memoirs of John Ker of Kersland, in North Britain, Esq., Relating to Politicks,
Trade, & History* (3rd edition, pt 1, London: 1727), 10.

[58] Ferguson, *History of the Scots Brigade*, I, 482.

[59] While there had been no military invasion in November 1688, the resistance
of the Jacobites led (as in Ireland) to a more violent outcome in Scotland. The
Jacobite remnants were not finally defeated on the mainland until the clash at
Cromdale on 1 May 1690, and they held the Bass Rock until 1694.

[60] Lords: Sutherland, Leven, Forfar, Elphingston, Cardross, Melville and Argyll;
other commissioners: Patrick Hume of Polwarth, George Pringle of Torwoodlee, Sir
Duncan Campbell of Auchinbreck, Sir Robert Sinclair of Stevenson, Thomas Stewart
of Coltness and Sir William Scott, Younger of Harden. New members in 1690: Sir
William Denham of Westshields, Sir James Dalrymple (Viscount Stair) and Andrew
Fletcher of Saltoun.

The Convention set up a committee to consider the state of the government at the beginning of April 1689. Of the thirteen exiles sitting in parliament, six were chosen to sit on this 'Grand Committee'. Polwarth seems to have been particularly diligent and was one of a sub-committee of four asked to prepare reasons for the throne's vacancy and to draw up a list of grievances. In June, he claimed he had taken a 'principal share' in promoting the act declaring the throne vacant.[61] Five exiles (including Polwarth, Cardross and Dalrymple of Stair) were also on the committee for settling church government in May 1690. Prelacy had been ended without too much trouble in July 1689, but the re-establishment of Presbyterianism proceeded slowly and the final form of the established Church did not take shape until the abolition of lay patronage in July 1690. That the settlement ended up being such a moderate form of Presbyterianism and that the General Assembly proved to be less dogmatic than it might have been probably owed more than anything else to the influence of the former spy William Carstares, who retained both the king's and the ministers' respect.[62]

With the advent of the reign of William II in Scotland, former exiles in the main found life returning to the normality of the years before they had fled. Fines and forfeiture of family estates were reviewed by a committee of parliament and many exiles finally had their forfeitures rescinded in July 1690. The most obvious way in which the former exiles benefited from adherence to William's cause was in the attainment of high office. Of these, George, Lord Melville, was the most impressive beneficiary. He was appointed sole secretary of state for Scotland in May 1689 and, along with the Duke of Hamilton (Lord High Commissioner), was entrusted with the management of political affairs. Created earl in April 1690, he replaced Hamilton as commissioner in that year. Exiles and their relatives also constituted about one quarter of the privy council created in May 1689.[63]

---

[61] E. W. M. Balfour-Melville, ed., An *Account of the Proceedings of the Estates in Scotland 1689–90*, vol. II (Edinburgh: 1954), 19–20, 24; HMC, *Report XIV, Appendix, Part III*, 117–8.

[62] Carstares' 'Hints' to William in *State-papers and Letters addressed to William Carstares*, 38–42; Kidd, 'Religious Realignment between the Restoration and Union', 158–9.

[63] *RPCS*, 3rd series, XIV, 378–9. Lord Melville and his sons the Master of Melville and the Earl of Leven, Argyll, Sutherland, Cardross, Stair and his son Sir John, Polwarth, and Sir Robert Sinclair of Stevenson.

Although a member of the 'Club' opposition in parliament, in autumn 1689 Patrick Hume of Polwarth was persuaded to support the government position and in the 1690s obtained a number of key posts and honours, including Lord Chancellor 1696–1702; Lord High Commissioner 1698; and commissioner to the General Assembly of 1702. Having been created Lord Polwarth in 1691, six years later he became Earl of Marchmont and was granted the king's orange symbol as part of his coat of arms. He was also awarded an annual pension of four hundred pounds sterling to help defray part of the "considerable debts" brought about by his "former trouble".[64] In legal office, Sir James Dalrymple of Stair regained his former post as president of the Court of Session.

There was a great deal of patronage at work in 1689 and the exiles were not forgotten in the hunt for reliable supporters. Polwarth certainly remembered those who had suffered with him. In correspondence with his son in 1709, he wrote that his inclination led him to deal with those "with whom I was in the furnace" and he admitted that he was still "much addicted to those who were shaken together with me in the bag of affliction".[65] This reference to a mutual torment shared is perhaps the closest definition of the ties that bound the transient community together.

William Carstares did not obtain any official government position, but he was appointed royal chaplain for Scotland with the revenue from the chapel-royal for life and was granted apartments in one of the palaces. On several occasions, Carstares accompanied William on campaign in Ireland and Europe. There can be no doubt that he enjoyed the privilege of influence with the king about Scottish affairs, his power earning him the nickname 'Cardinal Carstares' and a description as the "jewel in [the king's] ear" in 1694.[66] At the Revolution, Carstares' main concern was with the Church and, as mentioned above, he is generally accredited with the orchestration of the moderate Presbyterian settlement of 1690. His later offices included Moderator of the General Assembly on several occasions and principal of Edinburgh University in Queen Anne's reign. He

---

[64] NAS, RH15/15/16/uncat.
[65] NAS, RH15/15/16/uncat.
[66] Story, *William Carstares*, 204, 270; A. I. Dunlop, *William Carstares and the Kirk by Law established* (Edinburgh: 1967), 89.

also ensured that the Church of Scotland broadly supported the Treaty of Union in 1707.[67]

Of the ministers who returned home from 1687 onwards, almost all are known to have filled positions in the renewed Church of Scotland. Although none rose as high as William Carstares, at least four (George Campbell, Gilbert Rule, Thomas Forrester and Alexander Pitcairn) later became professors or principals at the universities in Edinburgh and St Andrews; another two (Thomas Hog and David Blair) were appointed king's chaplains.

Conclusion

The most telling defining characteristic of the exile community is precisely their 'exile': these were people who had been forced abroad, against their wills, and who were hardly seeking to create a foreign community. However, the fact that when pressed they did unite to form a community, as transient as it may have been, perhaps indicates that a certain kind of 'clannishness' is endemic in the Scottish experience—particularly as the bonds of even this community was shown to be re-exported into Scotland. The exiles used their privileged position in the Netherlands to continue the political and religious intriguing that had begun at home and which had led to their exile in the first place. In the early period of the community, this role was left to individuals—ministers who constantly wrote against both the church regime and those who accepted it by taking indulgences, and other concerned individuals who risked their lives by spying or carrying intelligence back to the Dutch court.

In the 1680s the mood changed and more exiles were willing to take an active part in subversive activity. Although the early plotting and the Argyll rebellion in 1685 achieved little, the stage was set for the more successful attempts to influence Scottish affairs through the 1687 indulgences and the 1688 Dutch invasion of England. The exiles were therefore in an ideal position when William became king in 1689. They were deeply involved in the Revolution settlement in Church and government and their quality of life improved

---

[67] For details of his later career, see *State-papers and Letters addressed to William Carstares*; Story, *William Carstares*; Dunlop, *William Carstares and the Kirk by Law established*.

with the return of their estates, the attainment of public office and, in some cases, positions of considerable power. Most seem to have been happily incorporated back into Scottish society and few would have disagreed with Lord Cardross, who wrote in 1689 that "God hath wonderfully appired for us since we parted from Holland".[68] Indeed the community that had formed in the Netherlands generally (though far from universally) continued to operate as a community on their return to Scotland.

Meanwhile it is ironic but symptomatic of the accommodating nature of the Dutch people that some of the exiles' Jacobite enemies, driven out of Scotland after 1688, themselves settled for a time in the Netherlands. But that is another side to the story.

---

[68] NAS, RH15/106/690/22.

SCOTTISH STUDENTS IN THE NETHERLANDS, 1680–1730

Esther Mijers

In the middle of the seventeenth century, the author Thomas Fuller summed up the appeal of the United Provinces as "Minerva, Mars and Mercury, learning, war and traffic".[1] Although Fuller was referring to the attraction of the Netherlands in general, his definition seems particularly appropriate to Scottish-Dutch relations in the early modern period. Between 1650 and 1750, thousands of Scottish students, soldiers and merchants visited the Dutch Provinces. An average of 5,000 Scots per year seems to be a safe estimate.[2] As a result the Scottish community which developed in the United Provinces was a very diverse, predominantly male, grouping. It was divided into four distinct yet overlapping categories: the business community, made up of bankers, merchants, skippers and sailors; soldiers and officers of the Scots Brigade; exiles, including ministers of the Scottish churches in the Netherlands; and students. The merchant, exile and maritime communities will be addressed by other authors in this volume.[3] They will only be discussed here insofar as they relate to the student body, which they did to a large extent. Due to the distinct Scottish communities in the Netherlands, a sophisticated and increasingly Scottish infrastructure developed, upon which its members came to rely and which greatly benefited intellectual and educational exchanges. As such, Ginny Gardner's description of the

---

[1] Thomas Fuller, *The Holy State and the Profane State* (London: 1840, 1st ed. 1642), 128.

[2] Between 1650–1750 around 1,500 students matriculated at the four main Dutch universities, although the real number may very well have been up to four times higher. Annually there were some 3,600 soldiers and probably between 12–1500 members of the merchant community in the Netherlands. In addition there were exiles, ministers, shopkeepers and innkeepers, servants and Grand tourists.

[3] The Rotterdam merchant community is described by Douglas Catterall; the exiles by Ginny Gardner and the sailors by Andrew Little in this volume.

Scottish exiles as a "community within a community" can also be applied to the student body, particularly after 1700.[4]

Of all the Scots in the Netherlands, students are possibly the easiest group to trace as they left behind a fair number and variety of records. That said, the exact numbers will probably never be known. Although there is no doubt that they formed a 'community' in the Netherlands, it must be recognised that they differed from other groups of Scots in that they were voluntary and often only temporary migrants. In the following quantitative analysis of the Scottish student community in the United Provinces between 1680 and 1730, the numbers therefore need to be seen as indicative rather than exhaustive. As complete a picture as possible will be given, based on specific primary sources such as the matriculation lists and university registers of the four main Dutch universities: Leiden, Franeker, Groningen and Utrecht.[5] An attempt will be made to refine these numbers where possible through the use of additional sources, such as diaries, private and business correspondence and the so-called 'Zwolse Bible', which contains many signatures from British, especially Scottish, visitors. In relation to the notoriously incomplete matriculation list of the University of Utrecht, this proved to be a very successful exercise. Scottish student numbers will be analysed in detail and illustrated by several graphs, followed by a brief description of the purpose and composition of the Scottish student community.[6]

Student Numbers

When the University of Leiden, the first university in the Northern Netherlands, opened its doors in 1575, Scottish students were among

---

[4] Georgina Gardner, 'The Exile Community in the United Provinces, 1660–1690', D.Phil., University of Oxford, 1998, 11.

[5] Previous analyses concentrated either on Leiden, or on law students. See for instance: H. T. Colenbrander, 'De Herkomst der Leidsche Studenten', in: *Pallas Leidensis* (Leiden: 1925), 275–303; Robert Feenstra, 'Scottish-Dutch Legal Relations in the Seventeenth and Eighteenth Centuries', in: T. C. Smout, *Scotland and Europe 1200–1850* (Edinburgh: 1986), 128–142; R. W. Smith, *English-Speaking Students of Medicine at the University of Leiden* (Edinburgh and London: 1935).

[6] It should be noted that the student community in the years 1681–89 in particular overlapped with the exile community. For reasons of convenience these exiles will not be treated as a separate group, but instead will also be referred to as students.

the earliest foreigners to arrive. Between May 1582—only seven years after its foundation—and May 1642, some seventy nine Scottish students matriculated at Leiden.[7] Throughout the seventeenth century, Leiden and the other Dutch universities became increasingly popular with Scottish students, who were either forced to or simply preferred to study on the continent. As part of the same Protestant realm, the Scots felt at home among the Calvinist Dutch and their universities. Moreover, the large existing Scottish community and its networks greatly facilitated both their crossing and their stay. Existing trade and credit relations meant that travel to the United Provinces was reasonably cheap and easy. Scottish students made use of infrastructures which ensured relatively inexpensive and safe methods of sending money abroad, making the financing of their studies in the Netherlands easier than in many other countries.[8] Lastly, the presence of so many fellow countrymen encouraged and reassured both students and their parents. Indeed, tradition was to become one of the overriding reasons for attending a Dutch university. These factors, combined with the Dutch policy of religious toleration, the absence of an oath of allegiance for university students, and the growing international reputation for excellence of the Dutch universities and their scholars and scientists, made these institutions highly attractive to the Scots in the later seventeenth and early eighteenth centuries.

The Scottish presence at the Dutch universities reached its peak between 1681 and 1730. Some 1,027 Scots matriculated officially at the four main Dutch universities of Leiden, Franeker, Groningen and Utrecht. When compared to the number of matriculations at the five Scottish universities—Edinburgh, Glasgow, St Andrews, King's College and Marischal College—around the same time, it can be seen that the Dutch universities served effectively as a sixth Scottish university, particularly as many more Scots studied at the Dutch

---

[7] James K. Cameron, 'Some Scottish Students and Teachers at the University of Leiden in the late Sixteenth and Early Seventeenth Centuries' in: Grant G. Simpson ed., *Scotland and the Low Countries 1124–1994* (East Linton: 1996), 122–136, 124. See also: Daniella Proegler, 'English Students at Leiden', forthcoming D.Phil., Oxford. This dissertation will also include references to Scotland.

[8] John W. Cairns, 'Importing Our Lawyers from Holland: Netherlands' Influences on Scots Law and Lawyers in the Eighteenth Century', Simpson, *Scotland and the Low Countries*, 136–153, 144–145.

universities than matriculated. The matriculation lists of the Scottish
universities give the following numbers for the period 1681–1730.
The Aberdeen colleges, Marischal and King's, had approximately
2,230 and 550 students each, the combined colleges of St Andrews
had around 1,000 students, and Edinburgh and Glasgow had around
6,500 and 5,000 students respectively.[9] At the same time, Scottish
students formed a significant part of the total student body at the
Dutch universities and were recognized as such by the universities'
officials.[10] For example, at Leiden, Scottish students officially numbered 11.5% of all foreign students between 1676 and 1700. Between
1701 and 1725 this increased to almost 13%, and even after numbers started to fall in the period 1726–50 they still made up almost
10% of all foreign students.[11]

The source material on which these student numbers are based
does not do justice to the real number of Scots who were educated
in the Netherlands. Despite the fact that the published matriculation
lists of the Dutch universities, the *Alba Scholasticum* and the *Alba
Promotorum*, offer the most complete record we are likely to find of
student names and numbers, in most cases the lists only provide a
sample. They give the students' names, nationality, the faculty in
which they entered and their date of matriculation. They are partly
based on the *Alba Rectorum*, in which the *rector* (principal) of the university registered the student's name, and partly based on the *Alba
Minor*, in which the student wrote his own name, but they are far
from accurate.[12] Apart from obvious errors in spelling, dates, nation-

---

[9] Peter John Anderson, ed., *Fasti Academiae Mariscallanae Aberdonensis II. Officers,
Graduates, and Alumni* (Aberdeen: 1898); *Idem, Officers and Graduates of University and
King's College 1450–1860* (Aberdeen: 1893); 'Records of the University of St Andrews'
[typescript, St Andrews University]; *A Catalogue of the Graduates in the Faculties of Arts,
Divinity, and Law, of the University of Edinburgh* (Edinburgh: 1858); *List of Graduates in
Medicine in the University of Edinburgh, from 1705–1866* (Edinburgh: 1867); *Munimenta
Alme Universitatis Glasguensis III. List of Members* (Glasgow: 1865).

[10] There are several references to Scottish students, either as individuals or as a
group, in the records of both Leiden and Utrecht. See below.

[11] For a comprehensive, if slightly flawed, breakdown of foreign students at Leiden
around this time, see H. T. Colenbrander, 'De Herkomst der Leidsche Studenten',
in: *Pallas Leidensis* (Leiden: 1925), 265–303, 295, 299, 303. According to Colebrander,
just under half of all students at Leiden between 1676–1750 came from abroad.

[12] *Album Scholasticum Academiae Lugduno-Batavae* MDLXXV–MCMXL (Leiden: 1941);
P. C. Molhuysen ed., *Bronnen tot de Geschiedenis der Leidsche Universiteit*, III–V (1647–1682;
1682–1725; 1725–1765) (Den Haag: s. a.); *Album Studiosorum Academiae Rheno-Trajectina*
MDCXXXVI–MDCCCLXXXVI (Utrecht: 1886); *Album Promotorum Academiae Rheno-*

ality and faculty, which are to be expected, they are also likely to be incomplete, as many Scottish students never matriculated. On the other hand, some students matriculated twice, either at the same university in different years, or at different universities. The former problem should in theory not have occurred, as returning students were entered into the *recessie* books. However, these appear to have suffered from the same errors as the matriculation lists. If a student did not matriculate in the first place, the likelihood of his being entered in the *recessie* books later on was extremely slim. Students were frequently enrolled in these registers by a Latinized or 'Dutchified' first name, often omitting their nationality, which made the registers even more prone to errors than the matriculation lists.[13] However, despite inaccuracies, the matriculation lists do provide important information on the nature, geographical location and academic disciplines of the Scottish student community in the United Provinces. The following analysis reveals a number of trends, although it is more indicative than definitive. Moreover, by testing these hard figures against 'soft' data from additional sources, some important peculiarities are revealed and explained.

Figure 1 (below) confirms the notion that the number of Scottish students in the Netherlands peaked in the period 1681–1730.[14] The steady rise from the 1650s onwards can be explained by a number of factors, both external and internal. Politically, the late seventeenth and early eighteenth centuries was a period of great unease for Scotland. Civil war, the interregnum and, crucially, the Restoration of the Stuart monarchy caused an increase in students who had been

---

Trajectina 1636–1815 (Utrecht: 1936); *Album Studiosorum Academiae Franekerensis* (Franeker: 1968); *Album Promotorum Academiae Franekerensis* (1591–1811) (Franeker: 1972); *Album Studiosorum Academiae Groninganae* (Groningen: 1915); *Album Studiosorum Academiae Groninganae* (Groningen: 1915).

[13] Only the *recessie* books of the University of Leiden actually survive. RUL, Cur. 245–294, Registers van op Kamerswonende Studenten. These have not been used for the stated numbers as they do not actually add many names, as a systematic check of these lists has shown. The marginal returns from analysis of these books would not justify this extremely labour-intensive task. However they could be very useful for a social-historical study of individual students, as has been done by Van Strien, as they provide details of the student's address and housing. See also GAL, Stadsarchief II.7284 e.v., Recensierollen. C. D. Van Strien, 'Schotse Studenten in Leiden Omstreeks 1700', *Leids Jaarboekje* (1994, 1996), 133–148.

[14] The following figures are all based on the tables in E. Mijers, 'Scotland and the United Provinces: A Study in Educational and Intellectual Relations, 1680–1730', unpublished Ph.D., University of St Andrews, reproduced below, 327–331.

forced into exile or who left temporarily to escape the religious upheaval.[15] Although many exiles returned in the late 1680s, Scottish student numbers at the Dutch universities remained high. William of Orange's wars with France throughout the 1690s, which closed the country off to visitors from across the Channel, no doubt contributed to this. As a result, students were diverted to the Dutch universities.[16] Harsh economic conditions in Scotland also contributed to this peak in Scottish student numbers. Despite a marked drop in the early 1700s, which may be explained by the parliamentary Union of 1707 and the following Jacobite unrest, the reputation of the Dutch universities continued to attract large numbers of Scots into the eighteenth century. Individual professors, such as the medical professor Herman Boerhaave at Leiden and the legalist Jean Barbeyrac at Groningen, began to attract large groups of students in the 1720s and 1730s. Prestige and status became increasingly important factors in the choice of a Dutch education. In 1699, the minutes of the Faculty of Advocates recorded a complaint about the number of students claiming to hold a degree from abroad (*i.e.* the United Provinces) when in fact they did not.[17] Nevertheless, following the reform of the Scottish universities on the Dutch model, the Dutch stranglehold over Scottish education began to tail off in the later 1730s and the 1740s. Indeed, hardly any Scots appear in the matriculation lists after 1750.

As noted above, many more Scots were educated in the United Provinces than officially matriculated, although their numbers are virtually impossible to ascertain. These students attended public lectures, private classes, anatomical dissections and experiments in chemistry and physics without matriculating, for a variety of reasons. They may have been exiles, suffering financial hardship or wishing to keep a low profile for political reasons.[18] Other students visited a Dutch

---

[15] The 1680s in particular saw many high-profile Scots (professionals and politicians) leave, who subsequently found refuge at the Dutch universities, such as William Carstares and Sir James Dalrymple, Viscount Stair.

[16] Cairns, 'Importing Our Lawyers from Holland', in: Simpson, *Scotland and the Low Countries*, 144–145.

[17] John Macpherson Pinkerton ed., *Minute Book of the Faculty of Advocates I 1661–1712* (Edinburgh: 1976), 195–196.

[18] A number of exiles matriculated on purpose as the Dutch universities guaranteed their students protection from persecution. Once again Carstares and Stair are good examples.

university—or sometimes several—for a brief period, maybe only for one term, as part of their Small or Grand Tour of Europe. Others learned skills such as banking or trading, engineering, land surveying or military tactics either at the 'Illustrious Schools' or in apprenticeships, and therefore do not appear in the matriculation lists.[19]

The position of the University of Utrecht in the late seventeenth century provides an interesting example of how the reading of misleading matriculation numbers can be improved by the use of additional source material.[20] The university's incomplete matriculation list gives only forty six Scottish students for the period 1681–1700.[21] However, the Acts of Senate of 1693 mention an incident concerning the English Church and refer to seventy to eighty Scottish and English students resident in Utrecht that year.[22] Compared to the numbers in the matriculation list, this suggests four or five times more students than matriculations.[23] For the period 1681–90, this would increase numbers dramatically to at least 200 Scottish students at Utrecht.[24] In his journal, the Scottish student and exile John Erskine of Carnock mentioned twelve Scots who studied with him at Utrecht in the late 1680s; their names do not appear in the matriculation lists.[25] The English Dissenter Edmund Calamy also referred in his memoirs to the large number of Scottish students at Utrecht.[26]

---

[19] The Illustrious Schools were non-degree granting institutions which often offered a more vocational training. Their matriculation lists do not mention any Scots, although correspondence shows evidence of education at these and other institutions.

[20] The unique situation in Utrecht will be discussed further below. Cf. Gardner, 'The Exile Community in the United Provinces'.

[21] It does not list subjects. *Album Studiosorum Academiae Rheno-Trajectina*; *Album Promotorum Academiae Rheno-Trajectina*.

[22] 'LXX vel LXXX studiosorum Scotorum et Anglorum'. G. W. Kernkamp, *Acta et Decreta Senatus. Vroedschapsresolutiën en Andere Bescheiden Betreffende de Utrechtse Academie II* (Utrecht: 1938), 128.

[23] Based entirely on student correspondence, Van Strien and Ahsmann have come to a factor of four. Kees Van Strien and Margreet Ahsmann, 'Scottish Law Students in Leiden at the End of the Seventeenth Century. The Correspondence of John Clerk, 1694–1697', *Lias*, 19, 20 (1992, 1993), 27–330; 1–65, 280–281.

[24] Utrecht's matriculation list for the period 1689–1693, assuming a degree would take no more than five years to complete, only listed seventeen Scottish and English students. More realistically, these students would have stayed for only two years, in which case we are looking at a factor of eight, or 400 students.

[25] W. Macleod ed., *Journal of the Hon. John Erskine of Carnock 1683–1687* (Edinburgh: 1893).

[26] E. Calamy, *An Historical Account of My Own Life, with Some Reflections on the Times I have lived in (1671–1731)* (London: 1829), 172.

A further source which confirms a much larger student population
than that suggested by the matriculation list is the so-called 'Zwolse
Bible'.[27] This seven-volume folio bible was on permanent display in
the Mariakerk, the church used by the 'English' congregation throughout the seventeenth and eighteenth centuries. Visitors to the church
would sign this bible; at one time it contained over three hundred
names until one of the keepers in the first half of this century had
most of the signatures removed.[28] It still lists some eighty Scots, however, most of whom signed in the last decade of the seventeenth
century. These examples increase the ratio of students to matriculations to well over five to one. It is clear that we are dealing with
the tip of a substantial iceberg.

It must be stressed that the position of Utrecht in the late seventeenth century was by no means typical. It can be explained both
by the comparatively high number of exiles at the university, and
by the Duchess of Hamilton's bursary, which allowed Glasgow theology students to spend a year at Utrecht and Leiden. As the Grand
Tour increased in popularity in the early eighteenth century, an
increasing number of students appear to have visited more than one
Dutch university. Leiden and Groningen became a favourite combination in the 1720s and 1730s, and at least six students matriculated at both during this time, while others only matriculated once
or not at all.[29] Similarly a number of medical students are documented as having attended both Leiden and Utrecht. As a result,
the figure of four to five students to every matriculation would seem
not to apply for the period 1721–30: one and a half to two would
be more likely.

Bearing this shift in mind, an analysis of the numbers of Scottish
matriculated students per university for the period 1681–1730, as
shown in Figure 2, suggests several trends. The most important university by far was Leiden, where 867 Scots registered as students in

---

[27] UU, *Zwolse Bijbel*. Permission to consult this bible was obtained from the Keeper
of Manuscripts, Dr Koert van der Horst.
[28] A. Hulshoff, 'Britsche en Amerikaansche Studenten op Bezoek of voor Studie
te Utrecht', *Historia*, 12 (1947), 185–190; 229–239, 187.
[29] George Waddel, John and Alexander Udney, Alexander Boswell, Thomas and
James Dundas all matriculated at Leiden and Groningen, and, atypically, Alexander
Hume, Lord Polwarth registered at Franeker and Utrecht. At least once, a Scottish
tutor, George Waddel, was responsible for a double matriculation.

the period 1681–1730. This is not surprising, as Leiden was in many respects the heart of the Dutch academic world. The most cosmopolitan of all Dutch universities, it welcomed students from all over Protestant Europe in its classrooms, as well as many born in the various European colonies. Compared to Leiden, the other three universities seem to have attracted only small numbers of Scottish students. The universities of Utrecht, Franeker and Groningen respectively registered 118, twenty five and twenty seven Scots between 1681 and 1730. It is safe to assume that these students chose these universities for specific reasons. In the late seventeenth century the universities of Franeker and, especially, Utrecht were recognised for their theology faculties. In the early eighteenth century Franeker's reputation declined, but Utrecht reinvented itself as a medical centre. Nevertheless, Utrecht was unable to keep up with Leiden and rapidly began to lose its appeal after 1700, if not earlier. In fact, the increase in matriculations in the last decade of the seventeenth century could very well be deceptive; although more students made the effort to matriculate, actual student numbers probably decreased. An entry from the Acts of Senate confirms this. Concerned with the success of its rival, Leiden, the Senate of Utrecht considered in 1707 a number of measures to attract more students, including the appointment of a professor 'juris publici Romano-Germanici' and a new riding school.[30] Scots were specifically mentioned, alongside German, English and Dutch students. Yet Utrecht continued to lag behind Leiden, despite the Senate's efforts.[31] Moreover, the law faculty of Groningen began to gain international recognition in the 1720s, causing an important geographical shift of aristocratic students, who would have attended Leiden or Utrecht previously. As at Utrecht, the matriculation list does not reflect actual student numbers.

Overall, Scottish student numbers appear to have peaked in the 1680s and 1690s, and again after the Union in the 1710s and 1720s.[32]

---

[30] Kernkamp, *Acta et Decreta*, 213–216.

[31] Utrecht was the most conservative of the Dutch universities for most of seventeenth century. This was mainly due to the influence of Gijsbert Voet or Voetius, who was both professor of theology and minister of the Dutch Reformed Church. While this had been Utrecht's appeal for Scottish students in the seventeenth century, it became the reason for its decline in the first quarter of the eighteenth century.

[32] It should be noted that this figure is distorted by Leiden. Utrecht and Groningen did not follow this trend.

These trends are confirmed by the number of Scottish doctoral students, as is shown in Figure 3. The reason these numbers dropped slightly later can be explained by the duration of their degree. The increase in doctoral students at Leiden between 1711 and 1730 can be explained by the presence of the famous Professor of Medicine Herman Boerhaave, who taught at the university between 1701 and 1738. Very few Scots actually obtained a doctoral degree from a Dutch university. This has been confirmed by the absence of Scottish doctoral theses in the *Alba Promotorum*.

Which subjects did these Scottish students study? Figures 4–7 show the four Dutch universities, broken down by subject. Law was undoubtedly the most popular subject, followed closely by medicine. Of the 449 Scots who studied law at a Dutch university between 1681 and 1730, around 180 subsequently entered the Faculty of Advocates.[33] The majority appear to have studied at Leiden. However, although Utrecht's inaccurate matriculation list does not mention any Scottish law students, a fair number may be expected to have studied there. Edmund Calamy mentioned "several gentlemen from that country [Scotland] that studied the civil law [. . .]."[34] Robert Feenstra has identified twenty five Scots as having studied law in Utrecht between 1681 and 1730.[35] There was a steady rise in the number of Scots studying law until the first quarter of the eighteenth century. Interestingly, there was a drop in the number of law students at Leiden, but not of medical or other students, in the years around the Anglo-Scottish Union. In 1707 only nine Scots matriculated, whereas in both 1706 and 1708 the total was thirteen. Overall, however, domestic politics do not seem to have had a significant effect on the numbers of Scots who came over to study law. In the 1730s Scottish student numbers in the law faculty, as in all other faculties, began

---

[33] Based on the data in: Mijers, 'Scotland and the United Provinces', and Francis J. Grant, *The Faculty of Advocates in Scotland 1532–1943* (Edinburgh: 1944). Robert Feenstra has come up with slightly different numbers. For the period 1681–1730 he has found 490 Scottish law students of which 225 entered the Faculty of Advocates. The difference of around forty students can be explained by the fact that Feenstra identified the students who matriculated more than once (20) and the law students at Utrecht (20). Robert Feenstra, 'Scottish-Dutch Legal Relations in the Seventeenth and Eighteenth Centuries', in: Smout, *Scotland and Europe*, 128–142, 132.

[34] Calamy, *Historical Account*, 172.

[35] Feenstra, 'Scottish-Dutch Legal Relations', 132.

to decline dramatically. As noted, in Groningen Scottish student numbers peaked in the period 1721–30, but as at Utrecht, the matriculation list is incomplete. None of the eight Scottish students who matriculated in this period were registered with their subject. Personal correspondence, however, has shown that all eight studied law.[36] The presence of several prominent French professors, most famously the legal commentator Jean Barbeyrac, who taught at Groningen between 1717 and 1744, appears to explain this increase in numbers.

Students of medicine followed the law students in terms of numbers and trends, at least at Leiden and Utrecht. A total of 361 Scots studied medicine at Dutch universities between 1681 and 1730, most of whom would have subsequently entered the medical profession. Both Leiden and Utrecht boasted excellent medical faculties, and in the early eighteenth centuries many Scottish medical students attended both.[37] There was a particularly long-standing tradition of Scottish medical students attending Leiden.[38] Analogous to its earlier importance in the later seventeenth century, Leiden fulfilled a similar role in the 1720s when the Edinburgh medical school was founded after its model.[39] The number of doctoral students, as shown in Figures 8 and 9, confirms this trend. Attracted by the reputation of Herman Boerhaave, an entire generation of Scottish physicians received their education at this university and subsequently went on to found the Edinburgh school of medicine.[40]

---

[36] EUL, Mackie Papers, La.II.90, 91.

[37] This is where we find most 'double' matriculations. See also: R. W. Innes-Smith, *English-speaking students of medicine at the University of Leiden* (Edinburgh and London: 1935). Innes-Smith has identified 95% of all Leiden students, unfortunately without any sort of analysis.

[38] The Leiden medical school in particular benefited from the effects of the Counter-Reformation, as Protestant medical students and professors started to look for alternatives to the Italian universities of Bologna and Padua. Ole Grell, 'The Attraction of Leiden University for English Students of Medicine and Theology, 1590–1642', *Studia Historica Gandensia*, 273 (1989), 83–104.

[39] A number of virtuoso physicians, most famously Sir Robert Sibbald of Kipps, had been educated at Leiden in the 1660s, and ten of the twenty one original Fellows of the Royal College of Physicians in Edinburgh have been identified as having studied in the United Provinces. The first three professors of medicine at the University of Edinburgh also had close ties with the University of Leiden, as did several members of the Gregory dynasty. See also: 'List of the original fellows as they appear on the Patent of 1681', in: W. S. Craig, *History of the Royal College of Physicians of Edinburgh* (Oxford: 1976) 65–6.

[40] Only thirteen Scots actually received their doctorate from him. They are known

Unlike law and medical students, students of theology followed a pattern of their own. As many Scottish theologians were also exiles, the revolution of 1688–9 and the subsequent Presbyterian settlement had a profound effect on their numbers.[41] Here the matriculation lists are a particularly poor indicator, as many religious exiles never registered at a university. All four of the Dutch universities attracted larger numbers of theology students than the actual student figures show, especially in the late seventeenth century, although by this period the heyday of the faculties for the Scots had long since passed.[42] The overall decline of the University of Franeker can be explained in this way. The peak in student numbers in the 1680s, particularly in theology, was the tail-end of the university's former glory. To solve the puzzle of the 'invisible' theology students, we need to look at some of the trends in the faculties of law and medicine. A comparison between Scottish student numbers at Leiden and Utrecht can shed some light on the situation. In the 1680s and 90s Utrecht had a particularly high number of student exiles. Their concern with religion translated into a higher number of students in theology and related subjects such as ecclesiastical history, Greek, Hebrew and Oriental languages, than was found at any other university for the period 1681–1700. If the forty six matriculated Scots are taken as representative of all Scottish students at Utrecht between 1681 and 1700, the division into faculties appears as follows: at least seventeen Scots entered the law faculty, at least eleven took medicine and the remaining eighteen probably studied theology.[43] In percentage terms, 37% of Scottish students at Utrecht studied law, compared to almost 60% at Leiden. At Leiden around a third of all Scots

as 'Boerhaave's men'. They have been the topic of extensive research; see for instance: E. Ashworth Underwood, *Boerhaave's Men at Leiden and After* (Edinburgh: 1977).

[41] Gardner, 'The Exile Community in the United Provinces.'

[42] NLS, Wodrow Papers, Wod. Q. XXVIII, vii/92, 'Some Latin Notes on Human Reason, with Draft Testimonials for Glasgow Divinity Students Studying Abroad, 1696'. Robert Wodrow's correspondence shows that at least some Scottish students studied theology in the Netherlands as late as 1701–02. L. W. Sharp, *Early Letters of Robert Wodrow 1698–1709* (Edinburgh: 1937).

[43] As the Utrecht matriculation list does not mention subjects, these numbers have been established otherwise. The numbers of law students is based on: Robert Feenstra, 'Scottish-Dutch Legal Relations in the Seventeenth and Eighteenth Centuries', *Studia Historica Gandensia*, 273, (1989), 25–45, 34; Medical students at Utrecht usually obtained an M.D. as well: *Album Promotorum Academiae Rheno-Trajectina*.

studied medicine, whereas in Utrecht only a quarter did so; however at Utrecht, many more Scots studied theology: 39% versus Leiden's 4%.[44] The observations by Edmund Calamy, who knew "a great number of Scottish students [. . .] that applied to divinity", appear to confirm that Utrecht was the preferred university for Scottish theology students.[45] After 1700, however, they seem to have disappeared altogether, which confirms the strong links between Utrecht, student exiles and the Glasgow bursaries.[46] The slight increase at Leiden in the early eighteenth century could be explained by the fact that theology students were no longer exiles, and no longer inclined to forego matriculation. Moreover, the Hamilton bursaries appear to have ended by the early eighteenth century. The correspondents of Robert Wodrow, the librarian of Glasgow, most of whom were bursary students, confirm the decline in numbers of Scottish theology students at Utrecht and the increasing popularity of Leiden around 1700.[47]

The last faculty to consider is that of philosophy. Although almost all Scottish students in the United Provinces attended one or more colleges in this faculty, very few actually matriculated, as few took their first degree at a Dutch university, with the exception of a small number of exiles.[48] After 1690, the number of Scottish students in the philosophy faculties declined even further. This can be partly explained by the return of exiles and their families. It may also have something to do with the curricular reforms which took place at the Scottish universities at the end of the seventeenth century, offering the Scots a better and more interesting arts curriculum, which was the preparatory programme for the three higher faculties. At the same time a tendency towards specialization began to appear in the Dutch universities, separating the humanities from the mathematics and science courses, which were partly taken over by the medical faculties. As a result, an increasing number of students dropped the philosophy faculty altogether.[49]

---

[44] At Leiden, students were registered with their subject. Between 1681–1700, twenty two Scots matriculated in the arts faculty; 198 in law; 116 in medicine and fifteen in theology.

[45] Calamy, *Historical Account*, 172.

[46] References in private papers also stop completely after 1700.

[47] Sharp, *Early Letters of Robert Wodrow*, xl–xlii.

[48] Such small numbers do not justify a separate graph.

[49] A similar development took place at the University of Edinburgh after the reforms by William Carstares in the early eighteenth century.

Although these Scots were keen to study in the Netherlands, it is interesting to note how few of them obtained a degree there, with the exception of some of the medical men. The majority already held an M.A. from one of the Scottish universities or had at least spent several years at one before continuing their studies abroad. This offers an additional explanation as to why many Scots did not matriculate. For most students, a visit to one of the Dutch universities was not much more than that. For some, a Dutch doctorate would have been too expensive. They chose to finish their studies in France or Italy, where degrees were usually much cheaper and sometimes easier to obtain. Moreover, these degrees were universally recognized whereas Dutch graduates continued to have problems well into the late seventeenth century due to the United Provinces' political predicament.[50] Between 1681 and 1730, only one Scottish law student obtained a Dutch doctorate, and this was at Leiden. As the Faculty of Advocates had its own entrance exam, a doctorate would have been an unnecessary expense. In the same period, twenty four medical students graduated from Leiden, very few considering that some 303 Scots matriculated in the faculty of medicine. At Utrecht, however, thirty four medical students obtained their doctorate out of the eighty four matriculated Scots. Utrecht thus appears to have been more capable of keeping its medical students, despite the complaints in 1707 that Leiden was more successful in attracting large student numbers.[51] Scottish theologians also failed to obtain Dutch doctorates, although some were ordained in the United Provinces. Like the lawyers, future ministers did not need a doctorate as the Kirk had its own entrance requirements. This appears to confirm the notion that it was more important to spend some time at a Dutch university than to obtain a Dutch degree.

Identity

Who were these students, where did they come from and where did they go after their stay in the Netherlands? Unfortunately, in the

---

[50] See P. C. Molhuysen, *Bronnen tot de Geschiedenis der Leidsche Universiteit* IV (The Hague: n.d.), Resolutions of the Curates, 1682. The Curates specifically mention Denmark, Saxony and the Spanish Netherlands.
[51] Kernkamp ed., *Acta et Decreta Senatus*, 213–216.

case of the majority this will never be known.[52] It was those students who became Scotland's new intellectual and political elite after the revolution of 1688–9 who generally left most evidence behind. Working backwards from Scottish sources, it has been possible to establish the identity of some 300 such Scots. Data from institutional and private papers has been combined with the names found in the matriculation lists and entered into a database.[53] Although biographical data are still scarce, it is now possible to say something about the Scottish student community in the United Provinces as a whole. Its members were, with the exception of some of the exiles, mostly young men from landed or professional families who had a long-standing tradition of sending their sons abroad. Aristocratic families from the Edinburgh and Glasgow areas and the Borders, but also merchants from Dundee and the east coast of Fife, Stirling and Aberdeen, and even Highland lairds, all sent their sons abroad to study.[54] Some went with their tutor, some with other family members, but even if they travelled alone they soon found themselves in the company of their countrymen. During the 1680s, many Scottish students were more or less forced to go to the continent, whereas after 1688–9 a visit to the Netherlands became more a matter of tradition and prestige, and a visit to one or more Dutch universities became the start of a European tour.[55] Upon their arrival in the United Provinces, these factors were translated into geographical 'divisions'. Exiles and theology students seem to have favoured Franeker and especially Utrecht, whereas the students with no religious associations preferred Leiden. It seems that religion was only an issue if it had been so in Scotland.[56] After 1688, the United Provinces ceased

---

[52] As this article is part of a larger intellectual rather than a social study, this group is, to a large extent, self-selecting.

[53] The matriculation lists, records and muniments of the Scottish universities; the membership lists of professional institutions such as the Faculty of Advocates, the Royal College of Physicians in Edinburgh and the Glasgow Faculty of Physicians and Surgeons; the *Fasti* of the Kirk; the papers of the Scots Brigade; and membership lists of different improving and cultural clubs and societies.

[54] Nicholas Phillipson has suggested to me that almost every landed family in the late seventeenth and eighteenth centuries aimed to send at least one son to the Netherlands.

[55] It must be noted that in the 1680s the two were often combined, as many Scots took advantage of the opportunity to travel.

[56] There are at least two examples of cases where the university senate refused to get caught up in the politico/religious affairs of the students Duncan Cumming

to serve as a haven for Scottish refugees. The Jacobites who followed James VII and II into exile favoured the Catholic Southern
Netherlands, or France and Italy. For aristocratic students, Utrecht
remained the university of choice in the 1690s, but in the late 1720s
this role was usurped by the University of Groningen. Prestige and
social status frequently seem to have outweighed academic excellence. Moreover, on their return to Scotland, these students took on
different roles in society. When they returned with William of Orange,
former exiles became members of the new Presbyterian establishment, and as such were highly involved in the tumultuous politics
of the 1690s. The 'post-Revolution' students, on the other hand,
showed much less religious zeal and usually became professionals
and academics.[57] This is confirmed by the high number of returning students who entered such professional institutions as the Faculty
of Advocates, the Royal College of Physicians of Edinburgh and the
Glasgow Faculty of Physicians and Surgeons.

The full impact of these Dutch-educated men on Scottish society
can only be appreciated when we look beyond the legal and medical professions to the offices they held. Most of the Presbyterian
exiles who returned to Scotland in 1688 held political office. Probably
around a quarter of the Members of Parliament mentioned by
P. W. J. Riley had been in the Dutch Republic.[58] As such they were
involved in different projects during the 1690s, including the Darien

---

(at Leiden, 1684) and James Kidt (at Utrecht, 1693). See also: Kernkamp, *Acta et
Decreta Senatus* II (11–9 1693) and Molhuysen, *Bronnen der Leidsche Universiteit* IV (23–6
1693). Cf. Gardner, 'The Exile Community in the United Provinces'.

[57] In this context, it is worth pointing out that the institutional infrastructure of
the professions had been created in the 1680s, when scholarship and learning had
benefited from the patronage of the Duke of York, the future James VII and II.
Several of the virtuosi responsible for founding these institutions were also educated
in the United Provinces. Although the universities came under severe attack from
the new Presbyterian establishment, the professional bodies were left alone. It would
seem that educationally and institutionally, there was a definite continuity from the
1680s–1690s, even if governmentally there was none. The Duke of York's patronage has been explored in two extremely interesting articles: Hugh Ouston, 'York
in Edinburgh: James VII and the Patronage of Learning in Scotland, 1679–1688',
in: John Dwyer, R. A. Mason and Alexander Murdoch ed., *New Perspectives on the
Politics and Culture of Early Modern Scotland* (Edinburgh: 1982), 133–155; *Idem*, 'Cultural
Life from the Restoration to the Union', in: A. Hook ed., *The History of Scottish
Literature. II 1660–1800* (Aberdeen: 1987), 11–31.

[58] P. W. J. Riley, *King William and the Scottish Politicians* (Edinburgh: 1979), Appendix A.

venture and the reform of the universities and their curricula. William
Paterson, the architect of the Darien venture, almost certainly spent
time in the Netherlands, as had many of the venture's subscribers.[59]
By 1707, however, the Scottish Parliament had lost many of its
Dutch-educated members. Of the 114 participants in the Union
debate in the early eighteenth century, only nineteen had been to
the Netherlands, and not all of them were Scots.[60] By the time of
William of Orange's death in 1702, most emigré politicians had been
replaced by a younger generation. The focus of many returning students also began to shift as their involvement in the university reforms
of William Carstares, principal of the University of Edinburgh, reveals.
Nevertheless, some of the most prominent Scottish politicians continued to be educated at Dutch universities well into the eighteenth
century. Archibald Campbell, first Earl of Ilay and third Duke of
Argyll, one of Scotland's most important political managers, his political successor the Earl of Bute, and Bute's brother Stuart Mackenzie,
the Lord Privy Seal, as well as Andrew Fletcher of Saltoun—Lord
Milton, Sir Robert Walpole's agent in Edinburgh—had all been educated in the Netherlands. The study of civil law in the United
Provinces was still considered "a useful part of political education."[61]
Dutch-educated Scots were also found in many fields other than pol-
itics and education. Many judges had studied at a Dutch university,
as had a significant number of the members of the Faculty of
Advocates between 1681 and 1730.[62] In the Scottish Kirk, former
students of the Dutch universities played roles of major importance.
Half of the Kirk's Moderators in the 1690s had been in the Dutch
Republic.[63]

[59] Saxe Bannister, *William Paterson, the Merchant Statesman, and Founder of the Bank of England: His Life and Trials* (Edinburgh: 1858).

[60] W. R. McLeod and V. B. McLeod, *Anglo-Scottish Tracts. A Descriptive Checklist, 1701–1714* (n.p.: 1979).

[61] J. W. Cairns, 'William Crosse, Regius Professor of Civil Law in the University of Glasgow, 1746–1749: A Failure of Enlightened Patronage', *History of Universities*, XII (1993), 159–196, 161.

[62] The political importance of the Faculty of Advocates after 1707 is well known and has been extensively described by N. T. Phillipson.

[63] J. Warrick, *The Moderators of the Church of Scotland from 1690 to 1740* (Edinburgh and London: 1913).

The Mechanics of the Scottish Student Community

Interaction with the Scottish community in the Netherlands was a fundamental part of the students' experience. Despite their connections with the English and French expatriate communities around them, Scottish students relied on an almost exclusively Scottish network of sailors, merchants and bankers for their daily business. Further, they also had access to a wider network of Scottish, Dutch and, increasingly, French contacts, which to a large extent shaped the Scottish-Dutch experience. Fellow students and tutors, but also landlords and booksellers, made substantial contributions to the intellectual development of Scottish students in the United Provinces, outside the institutional confines of the universities.

The first aspect which must be considered is the crossing from Leith to Leiden. Although Leith was not the only place from which the Scots sailed for the Dutch Republic, it was by far the most important. It was the port of choice for both traders and soldiers of the Scots Brigade, and as such it had long-standing links with its Dutch counterparts.[64] Throughout the late seventeenth and early eighteenth centuries, ships sailed from Leith to the United Provinces on an almost daily basis.[65] Many of the smaller towns along the east coast of Fife, east Lothian and the Borders, as well as towns such as Glasgow, Ayr and Dumfries on the west coast, also regularly sent ships across the North Sea.[66] This active trade ensured a relatively safe and easy crossing to the United Provinces as travellers and cargo shared ships. It took less time to reach a Dutch port from Leith by ship than it took to reach London from Edinburgh by carriage. In good weather the voyage to one of the Dutch ports took only five days. However, as the academic year started in February, many Scottish students travelled during the winter months and frequently experienced rough conditions. As bad weather seems to have been more the rule than the exception, eight to ten days appears to have

---

[64] H. Dunthorne, 'Scots in the Wars of the Low Countries, 1572–1648', in: Simpson, *Scotland and the Low Countries*, 104–122, 109.

[65] P. G. B. McNeill ed., *Atlas of Scottish History to 1707* (Edinburgh: 1996), 280–281. For example, between 1680–86, more than 1,500 ships sailed from Scotland to the Dutch provinces, particularly to Rotterdam in Holland.

[66] T. C. Smout, *A History of the Scottish people 1560–1830* (London: 1985), 155.

been the average time for the crossing.[67] In addition it might take a student considerable time to travel from his home to the port of departure. In the eighteenth century Scots increasingly departed from London or Newcastle rather than from Leith.

Most Scottish students arrived in one of the ports of Holland and Zeeland, while others, particularly soldiers and later on Jacobites, sailed for the Southern Netherlands.[68] Rotterdam's importance as a port had grown in the seventeenth century, overtaking the staple port at Veere in the process. It was closer to the university towns of Leiden and Utrecht and to the capital Amsterdam, and was host to a large Scottish community. Some of the most important Scottish merchants were based in Rotterdam, such as Andrew Russell, Alexander Carstares (who was related to William Carstares), John Gordon, and the bookseller Thomas Johnson, who moved there from The Hague in 1728.[69] These merchants provided a first introduction to the Netherlands and its inhabitants for many students. Many Scottish travellers went straight to Rotterdam, as it had become the centre for all Scottish business affairs by the last quarter of the seventeenth century. At the heart of this lay the Scots Church, which maintained a central position within the Scottish community, despite losing most of its active members after 1688. In the early eighteenth century, this function was partly taken over by The Hague, the residence of both Alexander Cunningham, the famous book collector and tutor to a number of aristocratic Scottish students, and—until 1728—Thomas Johnson.

Scottish students and other visitors could count on a network of merchants and bankers, who provided them with credit; skippers and

---

[67] In particularly bad weather the crossing could take up to two weeks. C. D. van Strien, *British Travellers in Holland during the Stuart Period. Edward Browne and John Locke in the United Provinces* (Leiden: 1993), 68.

[68] In the course of the eighteenth century the Southern Netherlands gained popularity not only with Jacobites, but also with Protestants. The end of the Franco-Dutch wars opened the country up to travellers who visited Antwerp, Brussels, Ghent and Bruges and the bathing resort of Spa. The University of Louvain became popular with Jacobite students.

[69] Smout, *Scottish Trade on the Eve of Union*, 98. Smout mentions several other merchants, but these did not appear in the students' papers and correspondence. The main merchant house in Amsterdam for the Scots seems to have been Drummond and Van der Heyden, an apparently Scottish-Dutch company of which very little is known.

sailors, who took care of their letters and the goods they sent and
received from home; innkeepers and landlords, with whom they
stayed; and friends, political allies and fellow students with whom
they shared their lodgings, travelled, took classes, exchanged news
from home, wined, dined and went to church. Many students were
in fact warned against too much involvement with their fellow countrymen. Nevertheless, the student community relied heavily on the
two pillars of the Scottish presence in the Dutch Republic, the merchants and the Church. Merchants were of crucial importance to
the Scottish student community in the United Provinces, as they
were a direct link with home. They provided a fairly reliable postal
service, but also accounts and credit. Correspondence was important
to the Scottish traveller abroad. Letters brought news from home
and provided introductions, but were also necessary to financiers.
There were two ways of obtaining money, either through bills, sent
across directly from Scotland, or through letters of credit, which
allowed the recipient to cash money whenever he wanted to. Both
bills and letters of credit could be cashed with a specific merchant
who subsequently charged his correspondent in Scotland, with whom
the issuer, usually a family member, had an account.[70] This was
rather expensive, due to the unfavourable exchange rate and the
commission charged by the merchants.[71] The United Provinces were
an expensive place to live for the Scots, as the frequent requests for
money in the students' correspondence confirm.[72] Apart from their
financial importance, merchants were also the immigrants most integrated into Dutch society. Traders, goods, ships, captains and crew

---

[70] A letter from Patrick Hume of Polwarth to his mother, Lady Polwarth, dated
The Hague, 7 May, 1687, illustrates this rather complicated financial system. In
his letter Hume asked his mother to repay Alexander Baird, one of Andrew Russell's
correspondents in Edinburgh, for the sum he had drawn from Russel. NAS, Russel
Papers, RH 15/106/622/20.
[71] Van Strien and Ahsmann, 'Scottish Students in Leiden', 275.
[72] Van Strien's work gives an excellent indication of the cost of living for British
visitors in the United Provinces. Van Strien, *British Travellers in Holland*, Kees van
Strien, *De Ontdekking van de Nederlanden. Britse en Franse Reizigers in Holland en Vlaanderen,
1750–1795* (Utrecht: 2001). The Russell papers, RH 15, in the NAS contain a
large number of accounts and bills. An intensive study of these papers would provide a worthwhile insight into the world of Scottish travellers to the United Provinces.
For the frequent requests for money, see for instance the correspondence between
William Clerk and his father, NAS, Penicuik Papers, GD 18/2307. Over the course
of two years Clerk asked his father for more money in every letter but one.

commissioned by Scottish merchants were often Dutch. The merchants also usually spoke Dutch, which was essential for the students' day to day life outside the learned circles of exiled intellectuals, aristocrats, clergymen and the universities themselves. Merchants often acted as mediators between students and their guardians, providing advice on books, tutors and which university to attend.[73]

After their arrival, and having taken care of their finances, most Scottish travellers took up residence in more permanent lodgings. Students went on to their university; merchants and exiles stayed in their port of arrival or went on to Amsterdam or Rotterdam, and soldiers left to join their regiment along the southern or eastern borders.[74] Travel within the United Provinces was relatively easy and comfortable, if somewhat slow. As the country was home to the most extensive canal network in Europe, the *trekschuit*, a horse-drawn barge, was the most common way to travel. The trip from Rotterdam to Leiden took only a few hours, but travel to Amsterdam or Utrecht took two or three times as long.[75] The journey to Franeker and Groningen took longer; to get to the latter, travellers had to take a boat across the Zuiderzee. Travellers usually had lodgings already organized for them once they reached their final destination. They stayed in inns or with landlords, who were often Scots or English themselves. Indeed, students and travellers heard of the best English or Scottish 'houses' from their fellow countrymen. French boarding houses were also very popular with students who wanted to learn the language. By the eighteenth century, some of the most well-known inns featured in travel guides. Sometimes university professors also took students in to supplement their salary.[76] Many Scots

---

[73] Sir George Mackenzie of Delvine met the book collector Alexander Cunningham, who was also his tutor, in 1707, who 'friendly recommended me to Vout as my Professor [. . .], neither did he fail to inform me what books were necessary for me.' NLS, Mackenzie of Delvine Papers, MS 1118/59.

[74] The Scots Brigade was traditionally stationed in the provinces of Brabant and Gelders, close to the border with the Southern Netherlands. During the War of Spanish Succession a combined British army was stationed near Brussels. See also: Joseph Taylor, *The Relation of a Voyage to the Army. In Several Letters from a Gentleman to his Friend in the Year 1707*, C. D. van Strien ed. (Leiden: 1997).

[75] Van Strien provides a useful table of distances and cost of transport. Van Strien, *British Travellers in Holland*, 81.

[76] I have been unable to find any examples of Scottish students who stayed with their professors, although, as it was such common practice, some of them must have done so.

stayed in the same boarding houses as their relatives or friends, or shared their lodgings with their countrymen, whether fellow students or their tutor. Thus to some extent the student community was 'ready-made' in terms of well-established travel routes and living environments.

As noted, Scottish students also mixed with members of the English and, increasingly after 1685, the French communities.[77] The university towns of Leiden, Franeker, Groningen and Utrecht were host to large groups of foreigners, who provided a range of services to both the Dutch and the international students. Innkeepers, landlords, tutors, language teachers and fencing and riding instructors from many different countries offered the Scots a type of polite, rather than academic, continental education which they came to expect from their stay in the United Provinces. The Scottish students' contacts with the Dutch, however, were surprisingly limited. Unlike the exiles and other Scottish expatriates, whose stay in the Netherlands was of a more permanent character, few students bothered to learn Dutch. Exiles, on the other hand, had often learned the language and mingled with members of the Dutch elite. However these integrated Scots were more typical of the seventeenth century. By the early eighteenth century the 'Scottish network' consisting almost entirely of Scots and Dutch contacts had become quite rare. One notable exception was the small number of Scottish ministers and soldiers who had settled permanently in the United Provinces and taken Dutch nationality, while continuing to play their traditional roles in the Scottish Church, staple and army regiments.[78]

Purpose and Nature of the Scottish Student Community

The Scottish student community in the Netherlands was prone to change over time in both identity and geographical location. Its nature and purpose was defined by its members' different motivations for attending one or more Dutch universities. A necessarily

---

[77] Cf. Gardner, 'The Scottish Exile Community' for the increase in Franco-Dutch contact in the period 1680–1730.

[78] The authorities in Scotland and the community in the Netherlands were both aware of the problems caused by this 'Dutchification'.

artificial distinction can be made between students in exile, regular students and aristocrats on the Grand Tour. The motives of these three groups for choosing one university over another deserve special attention.

Students in exile preferred the University of Utrecht, which had a long tradition of orthodox Protestantism, personified in the figure of Gijsbert Voet, or Voetius, professor of theology and minister of the Dutch Reformed Church in Utrecht. His influence not only dominated the university but also the city of Utrecht, including the church and the town council. As a result Calvinism and conservatism were part and parcel of late seventeenth-century Utrecht politics. Moreover, the University of Utrecht, unlike Leiden in Holland, did not fall under the provincial States but under the direct rule of the town elders and their policy of staunch Calvinism. The particular appeal of Utrecht around the time of the Revolution of 1688 can thus be explained. As the political and psychological forces which had driven many Scots into exile in the late seventeenth century were gradually replaced by the pull of the continent and Scottish student numbers began to rise, Leiden and Utrecht gained reputations for progressiveness and conservatism respectively and, as a result, attracted very different student populations. Utrecht continued to attract aristocratic students in particular until well into the late 1690s, out of tradition more than anything else. Yet gradually its conservatism began to appear as a drawback rather than an attraction. Despite the university's attempts to catch up with Leiden by offering a more progressive curriculum and plans for a new riding school, it failed to capitalize on the increase in Scottish students. The result was a geographical move of the core of the Scottish student community, first to Leiden and later to Groningen.

The majority of Scottish students had always preferred the University of Leiden. Progressiveness and scholarly excellence were its great appeal. The university building itself, the botanical garden, the anatomical theatre and the library were further attractions.[79] The city was also host to a large number of Dutch and French booksellers and printers, most famously the internationally-renowned house of Elsevier,

---

[79] E. Hulshoff Pol, 'What about the library? Travellers' Comments on the Leiden library in the 17th and 18th Centuries', *Quaerendo*, VII (1977), 39–51, 39.

the university printer.[80] Leiden was situated conveniently for any students arriving from the British Isles; it was only a short journey by *trekschuit* from Rotterdam and was close to the stadholderly court in The Hague and the Dutch capital of Amsterdam. As such it was also a convenient starting point for travel to other Dutch provinces and the rest of Europe. In addition Leiden, like Utrecht in the 1680s, traditionally had a prominent expatriate community, among which were a number of permanently-resident English-speaking Puritans.[81] This latter group worked as tradesmen, merchants, shopkeepers and innkeepers. The presence of this network, although not strictly Scottish, often played an important part in Scottish students' choice of university. Even after 1688–9, they were not necessarily motivated by academic reasons. Instead, tradition, family connections, geographical location and prestige mattered as much, if not more, as is illustrated by the example of Groningen.

The University of Groningen had its heyday in the 1720s and 1730s, when a host of young aristocrats, both Scottish and English, chose this university over Leiden. Those who went to Groningen were almost all law students, attracted by the famous Huguenot legalist Jean Barbeyrac and his French colleagues Michael Rossal, Pierre De Toullieu and Jean Pierre Crousaz. Moreover, they were encouraged in their choice of Groningen by Charles Mackie, professor of history at the University of Edinburgh, who himself had studied at Groningen in the late 1700s. Prestige was also attached to a 'French' education. These aristocratic Scots attended colleges with the French professors, but also learned fencing, riding and French from French masters and stayed in French boarding houses. In their vacations, they visited the Frisian stadholderly court when it came to Groningen, or went to Leeuwarden, the political centre in the north of the United Provinces, or travelled to Leiden, Franeker and Utrecht.[82] The presence of so many French and other sophisticated influences

---

[80] Leiden had a large French-speaking population made up of Walloon exiles from the Southern Netherlands and Huguenots from France.

[81] Different groups of pilgrims, Puritans and Presbyterians had all settled in Leiden at some point during the seventeenth century. Cf. Keith L. Sprunger, *Dutch Puritanism. A History of English and Scottish Churches of the Netherlands in the Sixteenth and Seventeenth Centuries* (Leiden: 1982), Tammel, *Pilgrims and Other People*, 5, 7. Tammel estimates that by 1629 two thirds of the inhabitants of Leiden were foreigners.

[82] NAS, Leven and Melville Muniments, GD 26/13/613/3, EUL, La.II.91c.

made Groningen a centre of polite learning for the Scottish aristocracy, comparable to Utrecht in the 1690s. Significantly, many of these young nobles immediately travelled on to France after their stay in Groningen.[83]

Conclusion

The Scottish student community in the Netherlands between 1681 and 1730 was a complex, fluid and extensive entity. Although they shared an infrastructure with the other Scottish communities of merchants, soldiers and exiles, and to a large extent depended upon it, the students formed a separate community in the university towns, and were recognized as such by the university authorities. This must be largely explained by their number, rather than by their behaviour or their various motives. The different groups of students—exiles, Grand tourists, and 'serious' students—all attended the Dutch universities for particular reasons. Their behaviour seems to have been dictated by their reasons for going abroad and their status. Some were attracted to the conservative Voetianism of Utrecht, while others preferred Leiden's scientific progressiveness or Groningen's politeness. As a result there was a geographical shift of the core of 'high profile' students—exiles and aristocrats—from Utrecht via Leiden to Groningen, which has hitherto not been sufficiently appreciated. The Scottish students then were in effect a community by default, with no geographical centre and a constantly changing identity.

Scottish students were ambivalent about their stay in the Netherlands. Individual experiences were not always positive. Many were disappointed, sometimes even decidedly unhappy, with the Dutch and their universities. The laxness in the observation of the Sabbath and church attendance, the poor quality of teaching and the frequent absences of some of the professors, the large number of fellow-Scots and the expense of daily life were some of the most common complaints. Moreover, many Scots, perhaps even the majority, saw their stay in the Netherlands as the first stage of a larger tour of Europe, and the Dutch universities merely as the gateway to a polite continental

---

[83] EUL, La.II.91c.

education. In the course of the eighteenth century the many international, mainly French, influences both inside and outside the universities, coupled with their increasing prestige, proved irresistible,
even if the formal curriculum was no longer of much interest.
Nevertheless, the Dutch education had a profound impact on Scotland.
Between 1680 and 1730, a substantial part of the Scottish intellectual and political establishment had spent some time at a Dutch university and introduced and implemented at home what they had
learned abroad.

The importance and extent of the United Provinces as a 'sixth
Scottish university' and an educational entrepôt for Scotland in the
seventeenth and eighteenth centuries is not new. Although certain
aspects of the Scots-Dutch educational and intellectual exchange have
been examined already, an overview of the entire period and all
four Dutch universities is still lacking. By comparing the Universities
of Leiden, Franeker, Groningen and Utrecht, and the subjects they
offered, it is possible to uncover new trends and correct some of the
existing facts relating to this Scots-Dutch exchange. Clearly, the Dutch
education of many Scots in the late seventeenth and early eighteenth
centuries can no longer be seen as unequivocally positive, progressive, exclusively Dutch and inspired by Leiden. A much more nuanced
and complex approach will be required in future.

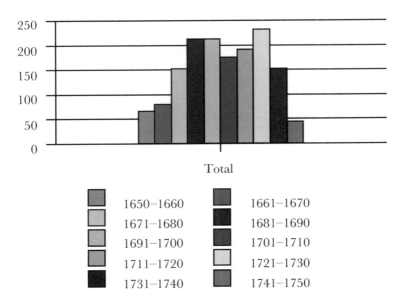

Figure 1. Total Scottish matriculated students, 1650–1750

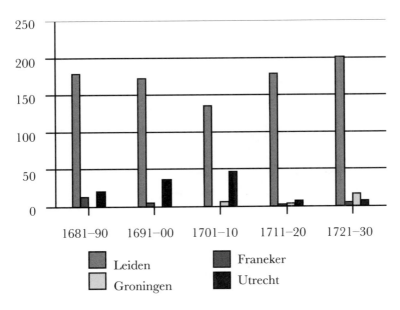

Figure 2. Scottish students per university, 1681–1730

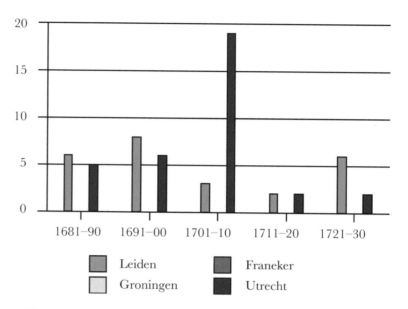

Figure 3. Scottish doctoral students per university, 1681–1730

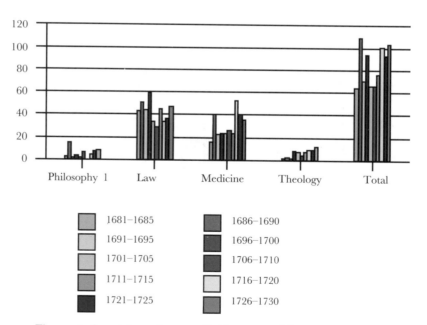

Figure 4. Scottish students at Leiden per subject, 1681–1730

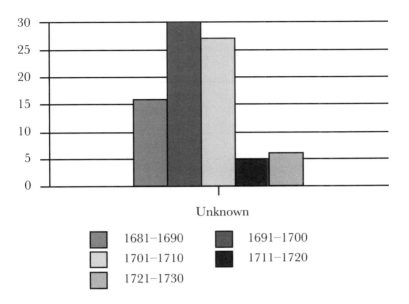

Figure 5. Scottish students at Utrecht, without subjects, 1681–1730

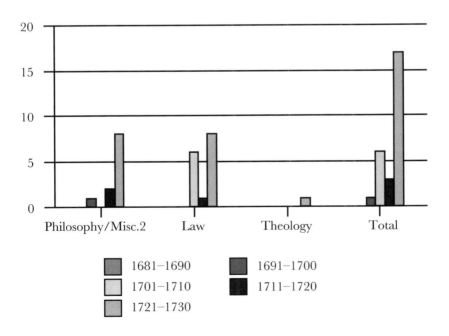

Figure 6. Scottish students at Groningen per subject, 1681–1730

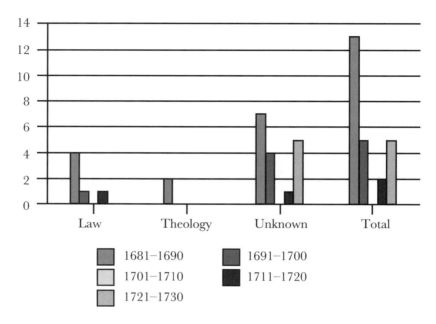

Figure 7. Scottish students at Franeker per subject, 1681–1730

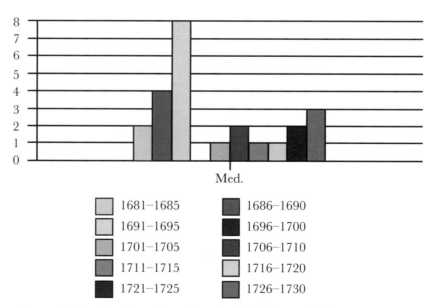

Figure 8. Scottish doctoral students in Medicine at Leiden, 1681–1730

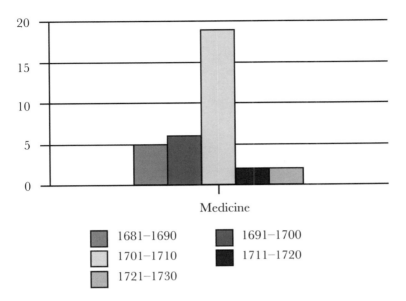

Figure 9. Scottish doctoral students in Medicine at Utrecht, 1681–1730

A COMPARATIVE SURVEY OF SCOTTISH SERVICE IN THE ENGLISH AND DUTCH MARITIME COMMUNITIES C.1650–1707[1]

Andrew R. Little

Two of Scotland's most powerful neighbours, England and the Dutch Republic, at various times supported Scottish communities of diverse sizes and duration in their naval forces. These might be as small as a proportion of a crew or number several hundred souls at a time. Prominent individuals have often been brought to the attention of historians; examples include James Johnson, the skipper of the Dutch West India Company (W.I.C.) warship *Gouden Lyon/Walcheren* off the Guinea Coast in the 1660s, and Admiral James Couper of the Dutch East India Company (V.O.C.) in the 1680s.[2] These were individuals in service rather than members of a community, but occasionally identifiable communities can be shown to have evolved. Consider that in 1649 a ship left Dutch service to join Prince Rupert's squadron at Ireland. The captain and entire crew of the ship were all reported to be Scots.[3] How long they had been in Dutch service is not made clear, but their further transfer to Royalist service suggests very strongly that political motivation was a major factor, at least among the officers. This in turn indicates that perhaps they had previously left Scotland as political refugees.

In examining the formation of Scottish maritime communities in foreign service a number of factors must be considered. For instance,

[1] My especial thanks are particularly due to Dr Steve Murdoch for his extensive help with this chapter, and also to Dr J. David Davies who suggested many improvements and additional sources. I am also very grateful to Professor N. A. M. Rodger, my new supervisor, who made many important suggestions at the last stage of writing. Any errors remain my responsibility alone.
[2] R. L. Ollard, *Man of War: Sir Robert Holmes and the Restoration Navy* (London: 1969), 87; S. Murdoch, 'The Good, the Bad and the Anonymous: A Preliminary Survey of Scots in the Dutch East Indies, 1612–1707' in *Northern Scotland*, vol. 22 (2002), 64. Johnson's gunner was also a Scot.
[3] R. C. Anderson, ed., *The Journals of Sir Thomas Allin, 1660–1678* (2 vols., London: 1939–40), II, 214.

the political situation of Scotland, her neighbours and her allies could all conceivably have a bearing on whether a community could spontaneously evolve, was encouraged to form or indeed was prevented from doing so. Sometimes such service in a 'friendly' country was simply not possible for many. During the Cromwellian period, Scots were often pressed into the Commonwealth Navy. They were, however, forbidden from serving more than six to a ship, because of the threat of unrest or mutiny against those who had both pressed them (on a personal level) and occupied their country (on a political level). This meant that throughout the 1650s there were very limited opportunities for any kind of Scottish community to form in a navy that was then more 'English' than at any other time after 1603. Therefore the chances of finding communities of Scots aboard Dutch vessels at this time was much higher—one reason being that Dutch service offered an opportunity for those who wished to fight the Cromwellian regime.[4] Further, the very action of joining Dutch service prevented some Scottish merchantmen from being pressed into the service of the occupying forces.[5] In contrast, a decade later the Scots were not only encouraged to join the Royal Navy (R.N.) as volunteers, but there were also no restrictions placed on the numbers who could serve on a given ship. This was certainly true in the Second and Third Dutch Wars of the 1660s and 1670s: in the former war, numbers on board given ships could and did exceed 100 Scots at a time. These figures imply both the Scots' willingness to serve their monarch and the trust the R.N. had in their service in such concentrated numbers. Yet, as discussed below, evidence remains to show that, while willing to serve in their king's navy, they did not wish to be scattered throughout the fleet; they preferred to stick together, although their opinion on the matter was seldom sought.

Later on it is possible to show examples of clusters of Scots in the Dutch marine who not only shared the same nationality, but also came from the same town, such as Queensferry in Scotland.[6]

---

[4] Douglas Catterall pointed out in his chapter the different entitlement to poor relief in Rotterdam of Scots serving in the Dutch forces during the First Anglo-Dutch War as opposed to those who had not.

[5] Murdoch, 'The Good, the Bad and the Anonymous', 67.

[6] Nationaal Archief, 1.01.47.01, Admiraliteitscolleges, 1111, Muster-roll of *Hollandt* (Rotterdam admiralty), 24 November 1702. The Scots in this case comprised 2.1% of the crew (and six of the eleven Scots came from Queensferry); this was the largest single component within the foreign nationals from a total foreign element of 9.1%.

That these men served concurrently in the same ship, *Hollandt*, could be interpreted as an attempt to remain among friends in foreign service. It was certainly not unusual practice for the age. On one contemporary British warship in 1689 many of the crew were drawn from Bo'ness.[7] Nonetheless, there is certainly strong evidence that when the Scots either placed themselves in the international maritime labour market, or were pressed into service, they hoped to be kept together with those of their own nation. In this chapter, the place of Scots in the R.N. is preliminarily charted throughout the complex period from the Restoration of Charles II in 1660 to the Parliamentary Union in 1707. In order to gain a better perspective on how the Scots viewed their service in the perceived 'English' navy, a comparative analysis of their service in Dutch (and other foreign service) has also been undertaken.

Scots Seamen in the British Navy

The Union of the Crowns of Scotland and England in 1603 brought change to the way the fabric of monarchically sponsored institutions such as the diplomatic corps and the military were organised. By 1604 James sought the complete union of his two British kingdoms and strove to get his officers, agents, civil servants and parliamentarians to accept his new vision of Great Britain. In the end he failed: by 1608 the union debates were over and Scotland and England remained two distinct kingdoms. Despite this the notion of 'Britishness' filtered through to the Stuart elite and impacted on such bodies crucial to the Jacobean infrastructure as the diplomatic corps and the fledgling 'British' military officer corps.[8] It is unsurprising,

---

[7] NAS, GD406/M1/19, f. 8. 'Petition to the Duke of Hamilton by the poor seamen of Bo'ness and the kin of such of them as are dead'. 13 January 1701. Also f. 9, Enclosure to previous. 'List of Bo'ness seamen on the ships of captain's Hamilton and Broun'. 13 January 1701. For other crew on the two ships, see also *RPCS 1689*, 42, 54, 81, 232, 277, 278, 324, 379, 381, 416, 417, 423, 439, 442. These two ships, hired merchantmen, comprised the main combat strength of what has been termed the 'Scots navy', funded by the Scottish Parliament. For our purpose here they may be compared to Stuart royal warships.

[8] S. Murdoch, 'Diplomacy in Transition: Stuart-British Diplomacy in Northern Europe, 1603–1618' in A. I. Macinnes, T. Riis and F. G. Pedersen, eds., *Ships, Guns and Bibles in the North Sea and the Baltic States, c.1350–1700* (East Linton: 2000),

then, that the navy underwent a similar restructuring. Under King James, Scotland had a commitment to supply men (and a small number of ships) to the R.N. for the defence of the British coasts.[9] Scots entered the British navy by a variety of routes: through a general press, pressing out of foreign merchantmen, a levy of seamen, and as volunteers. The regal levy was begun at least as early as 1626.[10] Other measures to facilitate recruitment included the removal of the merchant employment option by trade embargo, and State recalls of all British seamen in foreign service; Scots seamen were specifically recalled from abroad, and forbidden to take such service in the future.[11] The very nature of these orders reveals that the idea of foreign service for British seamen was accepted as a fact of the international maritime community, if sometimes challenged by royal edict.[12] That the number of Scots in Royal Naval service increased during

---

93–114; S. Murdoch, 'James VI and the formation of a Scottish-British Military Identity' in S. Murdoch and A. Mackillop, eds., *Fighting for Identity: Scottish Military Experience, c.1550–1900* (Leiden: 2002), 3–31.

[9] The works in print give an unsatisfactory account of the Scottish commitment to the Royal Navy. See J. Grant, ed., *The Old Scots Navy: from 1689–1710* (London: 1912), xix; Eric Graham, *Maritime History of Scotland, 1650–1790* (East Linton: 2002), 75; J. D. Davies, *Gentlemen and Tarpaulins: The Officers and Men of the Restoration Navy*, (Oxford: 1991), 75. For a more methodical approach see S. Murdoch and A. Grosjean, 'Scottish Naval Presence in the North Sea and the Baltic, 1603–1660' in A. I. Macinnes, S. Murdoch and A. Grosjean, eds., *Pirates, Capitalists and Imperialists from the North Sea and Baltic States c.1200–1939* (forthcoming, 2006).

[10] *RPCS*, 2nd series, I, Order of the Privy Council, 11 July 1626.

[11] J. F. Larkin, ed., *Stuart Royal Proclamations, 2, Royal proclamations of King Charles I, 1625–1646* (Oxford: 1983), 417–418. 'A Proclamation commanding all Our Subjects, being seamen and Shipwrights, in the service of any foreign Prince or State to return home within a certain time', Greenwich, 5 May 1634.

[12] Ehrman pointed out that this internationalisation of maritime labour was "too widespread and deep-rooted a custom to be prevented by an occasional proclamation". See J. Ehrman, *The Navy in the War of William III, 1689–1697: its state and direction* (Cambridge: 1953), 115. For overviews of the maritime labour markets see especially Paul C. van Royen, 'The "National" Maritime Labour Market: looking for common characteristics', & Jan Lucassen, 'The International Maritime Labour Market (Sixteenth–Nineteenth Centuries)', in Paul C. van Royen, J. R. Bruijn & J. Lucassen, eds., *"Those Emblems of Hell"? European Sailors and the Maritime Labour Market, 1570–1870*, Research in Maritime History, No. 13 (St John's: 1997), 1–9, 11–23. For an overview of British seamen in the Dutch Republic, with brief discussion of recalls and returns, see also A. R. Little, 'British seamen in the United Provinces during the seventeenth century Anglo-Dutch wars: the Dutch navy—a preliminary survey', in, A. J. Brand and D. E. H. de Boer, eds., *Trade, diplomacy and cultural exchange in the North Sea and Baltic region, ca. 1350–1750* (forthcoming, 2005).

the Jacobean and early Carolinian reigns is unsurprising. Both James and Charles were born Scots, and the desire to serve a Scottish monarch in his navy was a natural avenue for a Scottish seaman. Benedict Brone, for example, served thirteen years on many of Charles' warships. During his career he developed an evident personal attachment to Captain Plumleigh on *Antelope*, 1631 (following him into the latter's new commands *Assurance*, *Bonadventure* and *Leopard*), before a leg injury prematurely ended his service on Sir John Pennington's flagship *Rainbow* (56 guns) in 1639.[13] However, the Cromwellian occupation that followed the Battle of Worcester resulted in a shift in attitude towards Scots in the navy.

The Interregnum

The Interregnum created an obvious hiatus in the regal levy, and traditional English measures were applied instead. During the First Anglo-Dutch War, Scots could fall victim to the press in a way that was illegal under the independent Scottish regime.[14] Direct obstruction of the press by local authorities in Scotland was similar to that which took place in English ports. Indeed, the magistrates of "the several port towns allege they have no seamen, [though] we are assured to the contrary, which argues disaffection to the service".[15] The unpopularity of the press with the burghs was manifest. Seamen too dreaded it. At Leith in May 1653 the appearance of *Falcon* and another warship "so frightened the men that is impossible to procure any": the local seamen immediately went into hiding, but were expected to reappear the moment the ships withdrew to re-victual at Newcastle.[16] This reluctance, though possibly fuelled by some resentment at the English occupation, actually mirrors the actions of

---

[13] NAS GD406/M1/19 f. 12. Petition of Brone, 1639 & List of ships on which Brone served.

[14] Davies, *Gentlemen and Tarpaulins*, 75, citing PRO, ADM 1/5138, 266; Grant, *Old Scots Navy*, xix.

[15] *CSPD 1652–1653*, 241. Richard Saltonstall, Commissioner in Scotland, to Sir Henry Vane jnr., 29 March 1653.

[16] *CSPD 1652–1653*, 323. Edward Syler & Richard Saltonstall, Commissioners in Scotland, to Admiralty Committee, 12 May 1653; Captain Bartholomew Yate to Admiralty Committee, 12 May 1653.

contemporary English sailors. They too regularly hid from the press, gathered in large groups and forcefully resisted the press gangs, and rioted in London. At this time some Scots not only refused to join the navy, but also actively fought against it through service—along with Englishmen—in the Dutch marine. Their service, coupled with the Dutch flying of the "King of Scots" colours (see below) would certainly have fuelled Commonwealth fear and distrust. Little wonder then that under the Cromwellian regime, sailors pressed in Scotland were carefully divided among the fleet with no more than six allowed to serve together at any one time.[17] Further, it is likely that the end of the First Dutch War in 1654 did not see a return to Britain of many Scots sailors who had fought against Cromwell. Indeed, through their service, their continued exile seemed assured; many would go on to serve the Dutch Republic for many years to come and the exiled Scottish (and wider British) maritime community in Dutch service can be traced back to this very political conflict. However, the Restoration of Charles II also had major implications for the Scots in Royal Naval service.

Restoration, Revolution and Union

On his return to his British kingdoms, Charles II inherited a navy whose officer corps had undergone a thorough purge for political reliability—'new modelled'—during the Interregnum, and in which Scots had been pressed in to serve at the lowest level. Charles wished to reassert his authority over the navy and thus ensured that all his vessels flew the Union Flag, just as they had done in the Jacobean and early Carolinian periods. His officers were insistent on maintaining the dignity of the foreign salute to that British flag.[18] Sweeping changes in the composition of the officer corps were also made.[19] The need to crew these royal ships with at least some Scots came through the outbreak of the Second Dutch War. Scottish seamen

---

[17] *CSPD 1652–1653*, 565; Capp, *Cromwell's Navy*, 122.

[18] *The Journals of Sir Thomas Allin, 1660–1668*, II, xii, xviii, xxiv.

[19] For developments in the officers' corps see Capp, *Cromwell's Navy, passim*; Davies, *Gentlemen and Tarpaulins, passim*.

were found aboard British warships in large numbers, forming appreciable portions of the crews, with many later attaining senior rank. Indeed, in late 1664, some 106 Scots were put aboard *Henry* (74 guns), while 107 more served aboard Sir William Penn's flagship *Royal James* (82 guns).[20] Others were landed at Yarmouth although they never made it into service, opting instead to desert for higher merchant wages.[21] According to Robert Mein, the postmaster at Edinburgh, most of this first 500-strong levy out of Scotland were aboard *London* (80 guns) and therefore formed the bulk of her crew. Three hundred and thirty two men were lost in March 1665 when she blew up by accident in the Hope *en route* from Chatham to serve as Sir John Lawson's flagship.[22] This Scottish service in such large concentrations in two flagships reveals that they were no longer regarded as politically suspect. The administration now discounted the possibility of mutiny or of the crew's seizing control and carrying these prestigious and immensely powerful ships over to the enemy.

These men had found their way into Royal Naval service through a variety of means. The order for the first levy of Scots after the Restoration was accompanied by an order for the registration of seamen, a specifically separate recall of Scots seamen in foreign service, and a royal proclamation encouraging their entry into the R.N.[23] Two special characteristics mark out Scotland within the British polity. First, the levy was raised by means of a compulsory register of seamen, in marked contrast to England, where a voluntary register was tried much later (1696) and quickly abandoned. Second, the men actually supplied through the levy had to be the prime

---

[20] *CSPD 1664–1665*, 75. Sir William Penn to Sir William Coventry, 16 November 1664.

[21] *CSPD 1664–1665*, 79. Coventry to Bennet, 19 November 1664.

[22] *CSPD 1664–1665*, 256. Robert Mein to Williamson, 16 March 1665. The Dutch Ambassador recorded the casualties in detail; only nineteen men were saved. See *ibid.*, 249, Van Gogh to States General, 10/20 March 1665. The casualties are given elsewhere as 300. See R. Hainsworth and C. Churches, *The Anglo-Dutch Naval Wars, 1652–1674* (Stroud: 1998), 111. Twenty one of the crew were kinsmen of Lawson (a native of Scarborough). See Davies, *Gentlemen and Tarpaulins*, 70, citing BL, Add MS 10117, ff. 134–5.

[23] *RPCS 1661–1664*, 600–601, 620, 641–643. Charles II to Treasurer of Scotland, 8 September 1664; 'His Majesties Declaration for encouragment of seamen and mariners imployed in the present service', reprinted and published 10 November 1664; Missive to sheriffs, 27 December 1664. 1664 Recall and prohibition of foreign service, *ibid.*, xix, 538–539.

seamen specified under penalty of heavy fines on the burghs.[24] In effect this meant that only local magistrates managed Scottish compulsory recruitment (according to a system of lists and quotas), instead of the arbitrary methods by naval personnel (press officers and press gangs) that supplemented or overrode the magistrates in England. Nonetheless, the practical differences between the methods used in the levy and in impressment probably meant little to the seamen and their families. Andrew Hutton of Queensferry, for instance, was considered to have been "*pressed* furth" into the R.N. during the second levy of the Second Dutch War.[25]

Local magistrates were torn between protecting their burgh interests and obeying the monarch if that was their normal inclination. The loss of experienced seamen to the navy for an indeterminate wartime period was damaging to local trade interests but a burgh could potentially be fined 500 merks for each man they failed to provide for the R.N.[26] When sixty seamen were ordered to be raised from Kincardineshire the local authorities petitioned the Scottish Privy Council to reduce their quota of the levy: "there is not in the said shyre almost any seamen except poor miserable fishermen amongst whom it will be impossible to find the half of that proportion of able seamen".[27] Despite this the petition was refused and the full quota was ordered to be transported to Leith at local expense. How far at this time the Privy Council responded to the demands of more prosperous centres by foisting extra quotas on the less well-off and

---

[24] *RPCS 1665–1669*, 2–3. Missive and Proclamation of the Privy Council of Scotland, 12 January 1665. An insight into the structure of Scottish trade may be gathered from the proportions of the 500 seamen required from each of the various towns and shires: *RPCS 1669–1672*, 501–502. Act of the Privy Council of Scotland, 2 April 1672.

[25] *RPCS 1669–1672*, 202–203. Petition of Hutton's mother to the Scottish Privy Council, 1670 [my italics]. On demobilisation after the 1667 Treaty of Breda he transferred into the English merchant marine, working on an "Inglish pink" until captured and enslaved by the Barbary Corsairs in late 1669. The council recommended a collection for his ransom in the dioceses of Glasgow and Edinburgh.

[26] For example, Aberdeen had difficulty in raising fourteen men in 1665 as the seamen absented themselves during the call for service. This resulted in threats to withdraw brewing privileges for their wives should they fail to register themselves. See J. Stuart, ed., *Extracts from the Council Register of the Burgh of Aberdeen, 1643–1747* (Edinburgh: 1872), 215. 15 March 1665; T. C. Smout, *Scottish Trade on the Eve of Union, 1660–1707* (Edinburgh: 1963), 64.

[27] *RPCS 1665–1669*, 30. 'Supplication of sheriff depute and heritors of the shire of Kincardine', 16 February 1665.

less influential is unknown, but it seems that Kincardineshire would have had to make up the quota with whatever manpower was available or considered expendable. Corruption doubtless also played a part, similar to the way that administrators were often bought off by the seamen in England, and with the same results: inexperienced seamen or landsmen of various fitness and capabilities were sent instead of the more experienced mariners. Thus the quality of the first Scots levy of the Second Dutch War fell below the standard required.[28]

Perhaps due to this, the R.N. decided it would implement a small press in Scotland: the exact nature of the arrangement with the Scottish authorities at this time with regard to the press and its legality remain obscure. It also had chaotic effects on fleet supplies—pressing out of the navy's own victualling ships seriously disrupted ration supplies in the Second Dutch War. It further had direct effects on Scottish seamen and R.N. stores of materials when the crew of Captain George Strachan's privately-owned supply ship was pressed in the winter of 1666/7. His relative, Captain John Strachan, repeatedly asked for fresh protections to be issued for Scots seamen and for the restitution of those men already pressed. Otherwise the seamen's trust would be lost; protections having been promised for Scots trade to London, it was now extremely difficult to get men.[29] But the pressing continued on a small scale. In 1667 James instructed Sir Jeremy Smith to press from Scotland (as well as Hull and Newcastle) for his North Sea squadron.[30] On arrival at the Forth in May the squadron pressed two Scots privateers (ships and crews), whilst a shore party backed by eighty marines pressed most of the seamen at Anstruther. A company of Linlithgow's regiment challenged their authority to do so without commissions from either Lauderdale or the Scottish Privy Council. "The English told them they had none" and left with the seamen but without further challenge

---

[28] *CSPD 1664–1665*, 256. Robert Mein to Williamson, 16 March 1665.

[29] *CSPD 1666–1667*, 455, 477, 497. Captain John Strachan to Navy Commissioners, 15 and 29 January 1667, 5 February 1667. Unfortunately, all protection certificates—Scottish and English—exempting the holder from the press could be revoked if required, *i.e.* if the manning situation was serious enough (as it so often was). See *CSPD 1671–1672*, 288. Charles II to James, Duke of York, 6 April 1672.

[30] *CSPD 1667*, 101. Sir Jeremy Smith to Navy Commissioners, 15 May 1667.

or trouble.[31] In any case, the need to press was perhaps overstated. As Robert Mein said: "The people here take it ill that any are pressed, because some will go voluntarily, if Sir Jeremy Smith want men".[32] The willingness of Scots seamen to volunteer for the R.N. may of course have been Mein's wishful thinking. Thus a bounty of forty shillings (sterling) per man for volunteers was introduced in 1664, creating an appreciable inducement to sign on, especially for skilled seamen who were likely to be pressed or levied anyway. Nonetheless, the situation was aggravated in June when a Scot pressed from Kirkcaldy was given shore leave under guard to go home for his essentials. He was shot dead whilst attempting to desert. The captain of the frigate concerned was seized by "the rabble" ashore in retaliation, but later rescued. What enraged the local people appears to have been the killing of their neighbour, rather than the press itself. The Scots administrator, however, placed a portion of the blame on opposition to impressment, so we may conclude that whatever resentment there was blew up when ignited by the killing. How far the attitudes of Scots and English seamen to the press really differed is beyond the scope of this chapter, but the English experience ranged from downright opposition to tacit acceptance depending on the circumstances. In Scotland the case for returning to levies appears to have won through. During a particularly vigorous press in England in 1672, Charles II instructed that Scots seamen were not to be pressed, but instead "raised in an orderly fashion".[33]

The Scottish contribution expanded greatly after the Williamite Revolution, reflecting the growth of the R.N. and the consequent increased demand for manpower. In the spring of 1690 "several" warships arrived in Scotland to take on the seamen raised for them, and again the press became an issue. Although theoretical freedom from impressment for Scots was again granted, the Scottish Privy Council soon had cause to complain to William about the continu-

---

[31] *CSPD 1667*, 85–86. John Strachan to Navy Commissioners, 9 May 1667. Some naval historians confuse the press and the levy so that one has ventured that "Scots seamen were pressed in some numbers during the second and third Dutch wars, continuing a practice begun in 1626, but the administration was reluctant to follow this course, and on the rare occasions when pressing was contemplated in peacetime Scots were specifically exempted". See Davies, *Gentlemen and Tarpaulins*, 75, citing PRO, ADM 1/5138, 266.

[32] *CSPD 1667*, 161. Robert Mein to Williamson, 8 June 1667.

[33] *RPCS 1669–1672*, 499–504. Charles II to Privy Council, 28 March 1672.

ing press of Scots in the winter of 1691/2. William assured them that this would stop if compensated for by an increase in the number of Scots to be levied, stressing that the war "concerns not only England and Scotland but almost all Christendom".[34] In his requests to the Scottish Privy Council in 1692 and 1693, William gave them the choice of using "the same methods as formerly", or of finding their own "most speedy and effectual means" to raise "what seamen you are able to levy", reminding them of the forty-shilling signing-on bounty for the seamen's "encouragement".[35] The result was an increase from 500 to 1,000 seamen in the 1692 Scottish levy.[36] When asking for a new levy in February 1693, William (with one eye on the "security and encouragement of the free trade of Scotland") again specifically exempted Scottish merchantmen from the press.[37] That same month the English Admiralty discussed Scottish recruitment as an integral component in their plans for manning the R.N.[38] The old Stuart levy (previously thought to have been discontinued on the accession of William and Mary) therefore continued.[39] But again, in May 1702, four Scots ships in the Thames were almost completely stripped of their men. The Secretary of State for Scotland, James Ogilvie, Earl of Seafield, reminded Anne of the Scots' privileges and complained of "an injury to the merchants and a manifest contempt of authority".[40] The matter was dealt with swiftly and by December Prince George of Denmark, the Lord High Admiral, again requested the Scottish Privy Council to supervise fresh recruitment "as was done in 1691".[41] Whether this represented the clout of Scots politicians

---

[34] *CSPD 1691–1692*, 104–105. William III to Privy Council of Scotland, 19 January 1692; Graham, *Maritime History of Scotland*, 75.

[35] *CSPD 1691–1692*, 104–105. William III to Privy Council of Scotland, 19 January 1692; *CSPD 1693*, 47. William III to Privy Council of Scotland, 28 February 1693. In 1692 the council were to notify when 'competent numbers' were ready at Leith. In 1693 the levy was to be assembled in the Forth by 30 April. See *ibid.*

[36] *CSPD 1690–1691*, 1; *CSPD 1691–1692*, 104–105. William III to Privy Council of Scotland, 19 January 1692; Smout, *Scottish Trade on the Eve of Union*, 64.

[37] *CSPD 1693*, 47. William III to Privy Council of Scotland, 28 February 1693.

[38] *The Manuscripts of the House of Lords, 1693–1695*, 147. Admiralty Letter Book, Admirals to Admiralty, 6 February 1693.

[39] Graham, *Maritime History of Scotland*, 75.

[40] *CSPD 1702–1703*, 51, 53. Seafield's memorial to Anne, 6 May and Nottingham to Seafield, 8 May 1702.

[41] *CSPD 1702–1703*, 352. Minute of Order in Council, 31 December 1702. The request originated from a memorial from George, 12 December 1702. See also PRO, PC 1/1, f. 201. Admiralty memorial for an order for recruiting seamen in

or the political expediency of the English-dominated administration
is unclear, as unfortunately a general trade embargo was laid almost
immediately afterwards and the Scots seamen, like their English counterparts, must have been left with little choice but to enlist in order
to subsist, despite the Scots' protection certificates. The press in
Scotland remained a recurring theme and even a feature fit for consideration of inclusion in the Treaty of Union of 1707.[42] The final
irony in the story of the press in the Second Dutch War is that
many of the press gangs operating in London were themselves Scots—
in a rather unwise expedient, Scots soldiers were used when seamen
objected strongly to being pressed by any others than their own.
While some Scots wished to opt out of the practice for their own
mariners, others had little difficulty in putting English seamen under
the cosh.[43]

Scots soldiers in the Royal Navy and English ports

The use of Scots on land to gain more manpower for the navy was
not the only role Scottish landsmen adopted in the R.N. In the
Second Dutch War Lord George Douglas' regiment—some 1,500
men and seventy five officers in fifteen companies[44]—was stationed
in the south-east of England on return to Britain from French service, as France was allied to the Dutch at this time. This location

---

Scotland, 31 December 1702. Prince George probably meant the levy of 1692/3
as the seamen raised in 1703 were to have the usual forty-shilling bounty for volunteers (just as the levies of 1692 and 1693 had received, and as previously specified
by Charles II) as soon as they embarked at Leith. Soon after the 1703 request
Nottingham wrote that the "Queen knows that Scotland will, as formerly, *provide
considerable numbers* and that the Council there will take best and speediest methods
for raising them, if informed of her pleasure therein." See *CSPD 1702–1703*, 531.
Nottingham to Duke of Queensberry, 5 Jan 1703 [My italics]. The two R.N. frigates
detailed to cruise off the Scottish coasts were to embark the seamen at Leith at the
end of February. See *ibid.*, 586. Burchett to Richard Warre 11 February 1703.

[42] See, for example, NAS GD406/M1/19 f. 2, 'Draft of a proposed clause in
the Treaty of Union concerning the impressment of Scottish sailors into the R.N.',
c.1706–1707. It was agreed here that Scots should be legally exempt in Britain for
an initial period of seven years post-Union and that afterwards any press of Scots
should only be 'in proportion' with that of English. The draft clause also stipulated
that these terms would be unalterable by any subsequent British parliament.

[43] *The Journals of Sir Thomas Allin, 1660–1668*, 1 July 1666, I, 274.

[44] *CSPD 1667*, 506. Warrant to the Farmers of Customs, 3 October 1667.

put them in close proximity to the famous Dutch raid up the Medway in 1667. Their subsequent behaviour during the disaster elicited caustic comment from Samuel Pepys, who compared the exemplary behaviour of the Dutch troops with the rapacious Scots. The Dutch "killed none of our people nor plundered their houses", despite having ample grounds for revenge after the provocation of Sir Robert Holmes' burning and looting of unarmed civilians' (actually pacifist Mennonites') homes at Terschelling in 1666. Pepys continued: "our own soldiers [the Scots] are far more terrible to those people of the country-towns than the Dutch themselves".[45] Where they did not simply desert, Douglas' men were more concerned with rampaging through the Kent countryside and towns, slaughtering farmers' livestock and looting homes, than with opposing the enemies of their sovereign. Five companies eventually embarked from Rye for more service with Louis XIV, "to the great satisfaction of the people there, who they abused shamefully" during their couple of weeks' stay. The report primarily blamed the officers and estimated up to half the troops had deserted since their arrival.[46] The Scots had not done well in assimilating into the wider English population.

This kind of behaviour might have signalled the death knell for any goodwill towards Scots among the English maritime communities, but in fact their legacy may have been more positive. At the 1667 Medway disaster the vast majority of English seamen and dockworkers simply abandoned their posts rather than face the Dutch onslaught. The Scottish soldier Captain Archibald Douglas stood firm and was one of the very few to emerge from the debacle with a good reputation, for which he paid with his life.[47] But Douglas'

---

[45] Samuel Pepys, *Diary*, 30 June 1667.

[46] *CSPD 1667*, 489, 522, 523. Captain James Welsh to Williamson, 28 September 1667 and 12 October 1667; Richard Watts to [Williamson], 13 October 1667.

[47] Douglas was married to Frances Grey, daughter of Andrew, Lord Grey and Dame Katherine Cadell. He was sent with a few of his men aboard *Royal Oak* (76 guns) at Chatham to bolster her skeleton crew of seamen (a care and maintenance party). He stayed on her whilst his own men and the crew ran at the approach of the Dutch fleet: he refused to leave even when the Dutch fired her, and was burnt alive—*Royal Oak* was destroyed down to the waterline. See *DNB*, V, 1191; Rogers, *The Dutch in the Medway*, 105–106. Later that summer, Douglas' widow, Frances, petitioned Charles "for a gift of the prize ship *Golden Hand*, now employed in weighing the ships sunk at Chatham, where her husband lost his life in defence of the ships against the Dutch". The result is unknown, but Frances was paid £100 under

actions had far greater repercussions than bolstering his heroic memory. As Rogers pointed out, his actions were in stark contrast to the miserable cowardice prevalent all around and made an impact on the English elite.[48] Sir William Temple thought that he did this "because it should never be said, a Douglas quitted his post without order".[49] Indeed even the poet Andrew Marvell devoted a verse to Douglas in his vicious swipe at the establishment, *Last Instructions to a Painter* (1667), which juxtaposed Douglas' purity and heroism against the corruption and self-interest of virtually everyone else. The example was all the more poignant when compared by the poet to the Englishman Dolman (leading the Dutch marines) and the English pilots—'for shame'—who helped to navigate the Dutch fleet. Not content with this, Marvell dedicated a long poem purely to Douglas, *The Loyal Scott*, which repeated the view of Douglas as a heroic and erotic godlike figure, martyred defending Britannia:

> And secret joy, in his calm soul does rise,
> That Monk looks on to see how Douglas dies,
> Like a glad lover, the fierce flames he meets,
> And tries his first embraces in their sheets.
> His shape exact, which the bright flames infold,
> Like the Sun's Statue stands of burnish'd Gold . . .
> When Oeta and Alcides are forgot,
> Our English youth shall sing the valiant Scot.[50]

Marvell apologised humbly for "former satire" against the Scots and called for a pan-British union—"no more discourse of Scotch or English race"—in which Charles would husband his people and old antagonisms would be forgotten by his spreading of prosperity. After all, Marvell rather wishfully thought, there was "One king, one faith, one language, and one isle".[51] Thus within a decade of the Scots effectively fairing little better than deckhands in a very English mar-

---

the royal signet on 18 October 1667. See *CSPD 1667*, 430, August [?] 1667; *DNB*, V, 1191. *Golden Hand* was to have been used to transport the Swedish Ambassadors' horses and goods to Holland for their part in the peace negotiations.

[48] Rogers, *The Dutch in the Medway*, 105–106.

[49] *The Works of Sir William Temple* (London: 1720), II, 40; Rogers, *The Dutch in the Medway*, 106. Unfortunately the example seems to have gone unnoticed by Pepys.

[50] E. S. Donno, ed., *Andrew Marvell: The Complete English Poems* (London: 1974), 184, 185. These sections are also to be found in the verse on Douglas in *Last Instructions to a Painter*.

[51] Donno, *Andrew Marvell*, 185, 190.

itime institution, even former Cromwellians with a history of anti-Scottish rhetoric had elevated the Scots (through Douglas) to be the equal of any Englishman. Further, that long quest for the establishment of a more integrated Britain had found expression through the actions of a Scottish soldier in the Royal Navy.

Marvell wrote *The Loyal Scott* around 1669, giving it a few years to percolate through society before the outbreak of the Third Dutch War. The Scots were once more asked to contribute forces, military and naval, for the use of the R.N. For example, some 300 Scots seamen left Newcastle in mid-May 1672 for their transport south to the naval bases in two ships: 200 were crammed into one dogger (a Dutch prize) which seems to have been the only vessel suitable.[52] Another eighty four seamen were levied in Orkney in the summer of 1672, but soon found themselves in impoverished conditions.[53] We do not know whether either of these groups remained together in the same way as the crews appear to have done in the Second Dutch War. However, their desire to remain together was explicit. Robert Glasgow observed: "they grudge extreamelie to be dispersed in severall ships, wishing rather to be all together".[54] The men said nothing about resenting being in service, only that they wished not to be scattered, perhaps remembering what that had meant in terms of their reliability during the Cromwellian period. They wanted to maintain their own Scottish micro-communities within the R.N., perhaps serving together in one or two ships. As yet, it is unknown how far their wish was granted,[55] but Scots seamen served on many of the largest British warships at this time—we are afforded glimpses

---

[52] *CSPD 1671–1672*, 598. Giles Bond to Navy Commissioners, 17 May 1672. There seems to have been frequent difficulty in procuring the levies' transport from Scotland, pointing to both the relatively small size of the Scottish merchant marine overall and most of its ships individually.

[53] *RPCS 1673–1676*, 53. The men were to be clothed by the Steward of Orkney by order of the Scottish Privy Council, 15 May 1672, at a cost of £1225/9/4 Scots.

[54] PRO, SP 29/305, f. 95. Robert Glasgow to Williamson, 6 April 1672. *CSPD 1671–1672*, 288.

[55] It is almost certain that the levy was dispersed for purely coincidental reasons: the most probable is that too many ships were short manned for them to be assigned to one or two warships in large numbers—in this case they would have been placed instead in small drafts on many ships to increase the combat effectiveness of as large a part of the fleet as possible. The dispersal may also be due to the levy's arrival in England in more than one batch.

of these men from payments made to the families of some Scots seamen killed during the Third Dutch War. John Hew (Bo'ness) and
John Scott (Perth) were killed in the destruction of Sandwich's flagship
Royal James at Solebay on 28 May 1672. John Anguish of Inverkeithing
was slain the same day aboard *Monmouth*. John Richardson (Bo'ness)
was killed at the First Battle of Schoonveld on 28 May 1673 aboard
St Andrew; Robert Browne (Burntisland) later died of wounds he
received at the same battle, aboard *Henry*. Walter Jackes (Crail) was
killed aboard *Rupert*. Hugh Hamilton (Bo'ness) was killed at the Texel
on 11 August 1673, aboard *London*. All of these men were rated able
seamen—highly skilled prime hands. An Orcadian, Peter Tulloch,
was also killed at the Texel; he was of higher rank, being bosun's
mate aboard *Greenwich*.[56] Tulloch shows that Scots seamen could be
found across the R.N.'s skilled labour on the lower deck, here promoted to the 'labour elite' rank of petty officer—in this case a vital
position concerned with the handling of the ship and the maintenance of crew discipline.

A major component of the Scots in naval service was comprised
of army regiments destined for use at sea; one was stationed in East
Anglia.[57] Charles asked the Scottish Privy Council for this levy shortly
before his declaration of war, assuring the latter that the troops
would be paid at the English rates from the date of their embarka-
tion from the Forth. As conceived in the 'Zealand Design', by March
1673, the Scots would have formed 960 of the 4,660 British troops
to be landed on the Dutch coast.[58] It is likely that securing their

---

[56] PRO ADM 17/13, 'Bounty Bill Book for Men Slain'. The three Bo'ness seamen here left behind eight children between them. My grateful thanks to Dr Davies
for providing this material.

[57] This force was intended for service with the fleet, to supplement the marine
regiments intended to be landed on the Dutch coast—in the rear of their armies
facing the French—once the Dutch fleet had been quickly defeated in battle. In
the event, this never happened because of De Ruyter's genius. Marines (and soldiers used at sea under Cromwell) had already proved they could perform some
seamen's tasks: one excellent example being the Scots marine Robert Douglas, serving aboard Cornelis Tromp's flagship, *Gouden Leeuw*, in 1673. Douglas proved so
adept as a seaman that after his first two months aboard, he was paid the highest
seaman's rate for the remaining three months at sea, enjoying a very substantial
rise from eleven to seventeen guilders per month. See Nationaal Archief, Collectie
Aanwinsten van de voormalige Eerste Afdeeling van het Algemeen Rijksarchief, 438.
Pay book of *Gouden Leeuw*, 1673. My thanks to Drs Rick van Velden of the Nationaal
Archief for locating this document.

[58] *CSPD 1673*, 30. 'Zealand. The Design', note in Williamson's hand, 11 March
1673.

transport south was a factor in Charles' simultaneous assurance that no Scots seamen would be pressed.[59] The first three companies arrived at Newcastle by sea at the end of April 1672 and appeared "very handsome and able men".[60] Colonel Villiers visited the troops shortly after their arrival and commented that they were "somewhat untemperate, now that they are so very flush of money".[61] This, combined with the smouldering of nationalist tensions and local resentment at the expense of quartering the troops, could only lead to trouble. Indeed, on Villiers' departure, the Newcastle apprentices and Scottish troops rioted.[62] Nine companies were later quartered at Ipswich and "greatly oppressed" the town: "the inns and alehouses being few, 14 and 16 are quartered together in a house, and the children and servants have to be lodged out of doors". Besides the expense of maintaining them and the quantity of free beer the soldiers expected, the Scots "wear daggers with which they terrify the poor; they have stabbed several, and last Saturday evening killed a joiner".[63] Discipline broke down: the Scots soldiers drew on their own officers and attacked the local constables. Three other companies were quartered at Yarmouth and there was immediate conflict with the local people, with a particular fear of worse trouble between the Scots and English fishermen on the influx of the latter in the coming fishing season, especially when the "town is so much incensed against them [the Scots] being so abusive".[64] Apart from alienating the inhabitants of the English coastal communities they lived in, desertion was also a problem from the start and continued throughout their stay

---

[59] *CSPD 1671–1672*, 154, 174. Charles II to Privy Council of Scotland, 22 February 1672 and Robert Glasgow to Williamson, 2 March 1672. For the names of the captains and junior officers, see *ibid.*, 198, 418.

[60] *CSPD 1671–1672*, 299. Charles II to Privy Council of Scotland, 9 April 1672. Some stragglers were shipped from the Forth in May (*ibid.*, 483). *CSPD 1671–1672*, 344. Warrant to Linlithgow, 18 April 1672. *CSPD 1671–1672*, 399. William Christian to Williamson, 30 April 1672; Anthony Isaacson to Williamson, 30 April 1672. The size of the Scots ship *Holy Lamb* may be worth a remark as she seems to have transported over 300 men from the Forth.

[61] *CSPD 1671–1672*, 439. Colonel Edward Villiers to Williamson, 2 May 1672. Perhaps this was exacerbated by the regiment being on the higher English pay.

[62] *CSPD 1671–1672*, 82, 452, 461, 557. Anthony Isaacson to Williamson, 3 May 1672 and Colonel Edward Villiers to Williamson, 4, 14 and 28 May 1672.

[63] *CSPD 1672*, 509. John Wright to Sir William Dorley, 19 August 1672.

[64] *CSPD 1672*, 404, 555. J. Knight to Williamson, 26 July 1672; Richard Bower to Williamson, 2 September 1672.

in England. Two hundred of the troops deserted during their stay in England up to August, forcing Charles II to ask the Scottish Privy Council to recruit more men to replace the deserters—who were clearly thought to have returned to Scotland—and to demand severe exemplary punishment.[65] The Scots' own officers confirmed "that those left were unfit to serve the King at sea, for they are Highlanders that cannot speak a word of English".[66]

Eventually Charles decided to ship the regiment to France to get them into the fighting, but the regiment, always "unhappy", at first mutinied.[67] Once brought into line, in what Lockhart termed the "greatest persecution of ill-fortune imaginable", two companies were wrecked near Rye *en route* to France and another six were intercepted by Dutch privateers. The Dutch pillaged the Highlanders and landed most of the troops back at scattered places along the Sussex and Kent coast, with some officers and men carried as prisoners to Holland.[68] The Scottish Highland regiment had run the whole gamut of military and natural disaster. They were culturally, linguistically and actually 'foreigners'. Even had they wished to integrate into the wider naval community, they were incapable of it both by their own disposition and the reluctance of the English communities to accept them.[69] Yet while these Scots remained alienated and confrontational

---

[65] *CSPD 1673–1675*, 51, 492. Charles II to Lauderdale and Privy Council of Scotland, 15 August and 9 December 1673.

[66] *CSPD 1672*, 151. Giles Bond to Navy Commissioners, 4 June 1672. Thus the regiment was doomed to lie idle in quarters whilst command stuck to the original plan of the seaborne descent: English-speaking landlubbers could be induced to haul on the correct rope if required, but using the Gaelic-speaking Highlanders as regular members of a ship's company would surely have been an expensive mistake. Lockhart, who seems to have been appointed at a late date (initially the regiment was under no officer senior to captain) was frequently absent from the regiment— necessarily, as he was burdened with heavy diplomatic responsibilities and was soon to go to France as ambassador. This could not have helped discipline or morale.

[67] *CSPD 1673*, 545. William Bridgeman to Williamson, 15 September 1673.

[68] *CSPD 1673–1675*, 36. Sir William Lockhart to Williamson, 28 Nov 1673. In December Charles again ordered fresh recruitment in Scotland for the regiment, as well as a transfer of 200 men from Linlithgow's regiment, presumably to form a more experienced core, *ibid.*, 51–52. Thereafter the source is silent, so it seems the unit effectively ceased to exist. Some of those carried to the Republic as prisoners may have been tempted to join the Dutch.

[69] One wonders at the effect of the appearance in English maritime towns of 'uncivilised', Gaelic-speaking and very often Catholic soldiers, particularly during an increasingly unpopular war in alliance with Catholic France. Popular fear of impending Absolutism in Britain had already been awoken during the Second Dutch

with regard to English communities, the fact is that within the body of the R.N., Scots probably formed a larger proportion of the officer corps than ever before.

Scots Officers in the Royal Navy

A preliminary study of Scottish names in the published sea officers' list reveals a considerable volume of Scots commissioned during the Second Dutch War—reflecting what we might term the 'normal rehabilitation' of Scots in the wake of the Restoration—with substantial numbers continuing to enter the officer corps right up to the Union of 1707 [Figure 1]. The demands of the enormous wartime expansion of the navy and the consequent employment opportunities are made manifest. It may appear at first glance that after the early high peak, Scots were less likely to enjoy a successful naval career. Closer examination, however, reveals that a greater frequency of promotion took place at the end of our period—particularly when we view the promotion of Scots officers overall in alternate periods of peace and war [Figure 2/2a]. More Scots officers entered the R.N. in the last two decades pre-Union than in the two decades post-Restoration, the highest level being reached during William's War. Very soon after, another large group of Scots entered during Anne's War. Taking into account officers' life expectancy and career length this second influx is more significant, as many of the officers promoted in the previous war would still have been alive.[70] It also reflects the rapid contemporary expansion of the R.N. Restoration and revolution either opened opportunities for officers or closed them

---

War. In some Presbyterian quarters the numbers of the 1,500 Scots for the fleet were inflated to "several thousands" and closely associated them with the imminent military repression of the English people. *CSPD 1672–1673*, 199. Information of Thomas Cullen before the Privy Council of Ireland, 20 November 1672, enclosure in Michael Boyle, Archbishop of Dublin, to [Arlington], 23 November 1672.

[70] The reduced intake during the Third Dutch War can be explained in part by the French alliance: the French were allocated one of the three squadrons in the battle fleet, reducing normal wartime employment expectations for British officers. It is also very likely to be due to the fact that most of the Scots commissioned 1664–67 would (barring dismissal, old age or death) still be around in 1672–4. The spate of promotions in the French wars is also significant because of the long peace (early 1674–1688), during which much of the earlier generation would have disappeared from the ranks.

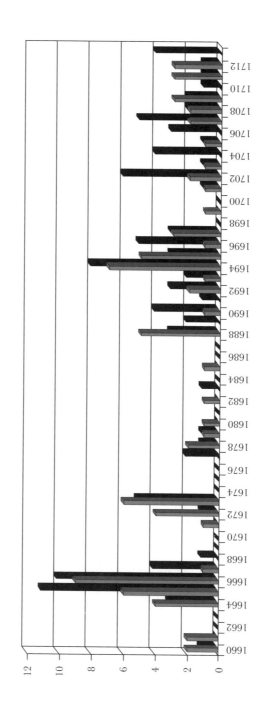

Figure 1. The Promotion of Scots RN officers, 1660–1713: commissions per year

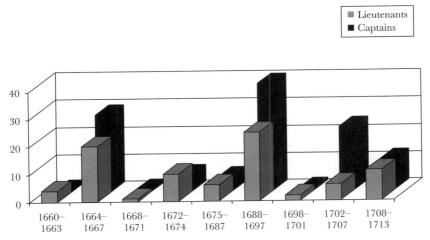

Figure 2. The Promotion of Scots RN officers, 1660–1713: total commissions in periods of peace and war (Anne's War divided pre- and post Union)

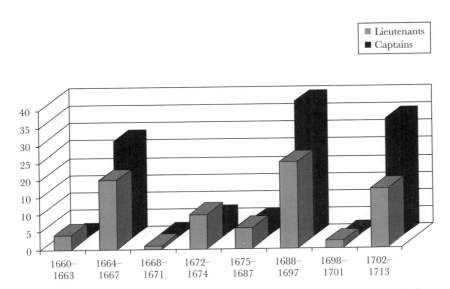

Figure 2a. The Promotion of Scots officers, 1660–1713: total commissions in periods of peace and war

according to their political reliability, so we would expect increases in promotions soon after these events.[71] Scots exploited the political turmoil whilst continually strengthening their position within (and remaining wholly incorporated into) a fully 'British' institution pre-dating the Union of 1707 by some considerable time.[72]

Pan-British absorption of the Scottish elite being already in train, there was no reason for the navy to be excluded from this process. Indeed, some Scots did particularly well from it. Throughout the Restoration period, naval administrative power devolved into the hands of a royal clique. Charles II himself exercised greater influence during the Admiralty Commission of 1673–9,[73] but the monarch and Lord High Admiral always retained the prerogative of appointing officers, exercised eagerly by Charles and James.[74] Charles had a "particular kindness" for the Scottish captain David Trotter, assign-ing him the lucrative post of convoying the Turkey fleet, "which post was given him by His Majesty to make his fortune". Unfortunately this was Trotter's last appointment, as he died of the plague whilst executing it in 1683; Lord Perth then wrote that Trotter was "a monument to our countrie".[75] Trotter's wife was Sarah Bellenden, to whom Lord Drummond had written on her intended marriage:

> For that of getting a place for your dear husband in England, I know it will be harder at this distance to procure it; but the way is to write to my Lord Bellenden whose kindnesse ought to be as great to you as any.[76]

Sarah was related to Lords Bellenden and Drummond, as well as the Duke of Lauderdale. Trotter, through his marriage, entered a

---

[71] For developments in the officers' corps see Capp, *Cromwell's Navy, passim*; Davies, *Gentlemen and Tarpaulins, passim*. We have already noted that the Restoration by its very nature increased opportunities for the Scots, but gentlemen Scots officers espe-cially, due to royal preference.

[72] It may be envisaged that the graphs would probably look very little different if the data was on English officers. However this would in itself show that the pro-motion and careers of Scots officers were 'normal' by overall R.N. standards, merely reinforcing this hypothesis.

[73] *Samuel Pepys's Naval Minutes*, 197, n4.

[74] Davies, *Gentlemen and Tarpaulins*, 60–62, 231–232.

[75] BL Add. MS 4265, ff. 186, 188. Petition of Sarah Trotter to Anne; Lord Perth to Sarah Trotter [undated]. Anne granted Sarah a pension of £20 per year. See *ibid.*, f. 186. My thanks again to Dr Davies for this material and copies of the BL references used in this chapter.

[76] BL Add. MS 4265, ff. 189–190. Lord Drummond to Mrs Sarah Bellenden.

powerful Scottish kinship network connected closely at its top with the monarch: this evidence suggests strongly that this was instrumental in advancing his naval career.

One important appointment probably had an unquantifiable impact on the promotion of Scots to the R.N. officer corps. John Maitland, 1st Duke of Lauderdale, was the Stuart Secretary for Scottish Affairs from 1660–1680. After an early inroad into the maritime sphere as Commissioner of Prize Appeals during the Second Dutch War, from 1673 he also sat as a Senior Commissioner in the English Admiralty, where he proved a useful conduit between the English and Scottish admiralties.[77] This role was made much simpler as the Lord High Admiral of Scotland, Charles Stuart, Duke of Lennox and Richmond, had also served informally in the R.N. before this time.[78] In fact, he secured the virtual detachment of R.N. units for his personal use, in conjunction with a small Scottish privateering pack which he deployed to great effect. In June 1672 the R.N. frigate *Speedwell* took six Dutch prizes bound for Copenhagen. Lennox was aboard and the prizes were taken by authority of his commission as Admiral of Scotland.[79] Under Captain Richard Borthwick, and even after Lennox's departure as British Ambassador to Denmark, *Speedwell* was contemporarily referred to as Lennox's own ship and a Scots privateer, in which capacity she brought in six prizes to Scotland whose cargoes included much-needed iron and timber.[80] Lennox also used his journey to Denmark aboard the R.N. warship *Portland* as an opportunity to dispense Scottish letters of marque, resulting in the taking of prizes that were later contested due to his ambiguous use of mixed R.N. and Scottish privateer squadrons.[81] Lauderdale and Lennox

---

[77] *CSPD 1666–1667*, 355; S. Murdoch, A. Little and A. D. M. Forte, 'Scottish Privateering, Swedish Neutrality and Prize Law in the Third Anglo-Dutch War, 1672–1674' in *Forum Navale: Skrifter utgivna av Sjöhistorika Samfundet*, nr. 59 (2003), 39.

[78] Murdoch, Little and Forte, 'Scottish Privateering, Swedish Neutrality and Prize Law', 39–40; Graham, *Maritime History of Scotland*, 21, 27; Graham, 'The Scottish Marine during the Dutch Wars', *The Scottish Historical Review*, vol. LXI, no. 171 (April 1982), 68, 72.

[79] *CSPD 1672*, 261, 272. Charles Whittington to Williamson, 24 June 1672 and Richard Bower to Williamson, 21 June 1672.

[80] *CSPD 1672*, 498. William Griffith to Williamson, 17 August 1672. See also 373, 818 and index; *CSPD 1672*, 498, 589–90; R. Dickson to Williamson, 7 September 1672. For the judgement against four of these see NAS, Register of Decreets, AC7/3 1672–1675, ff. 221–235, 4 October 1672.

[81] *CSPD 1672*, 516; *CSPD 1672*, 498. Warrant to James Hooper *et al.*, 21 August

were not contemporaries in the R.N.: Lennox died in 1672 and
Lauderdale was not appointed Admiralty Commissioner until 1673.
However, both brought their own people with them into R.N. service, and a large proportion of these were Scots such as Captain
Borthwick, as well as volunteer seamen.[82] Volunteers were, in the
main, motivated by personal loyalties to local or popular commanders, and they were highly valued as a result: being much less likely
to desert, they formed the core of a ship's company. As such, it has
been demonstrated in English cases that they could exert considerable bargaining power, for example in deciding in which ship they
were to be placed.[83] It is highly unlikely that Scottish commanders
did not attract Scots volunteer seamen around them in the same
way, particularly in the case of local magnates, as has already been
demonstrated in the Scottish context for the R.N. in the eighteenth
century.[84]

   Through the presence of Lennox and Lauderdale and their respective cliques within the R.N., extra pressure to advance Scots even
outwith their own circle can be suggested. It is unlikely that many
in the English Admiralty would have spoken out against the promotion of Scots in the presence of either Scottish nobleman.[85] A

1672. See also 373, 818 and index. *CSPD 1672*, 306. Lennox [from Copenhagen]
to Navy Commissioners, 2 July 1672.

   [82] Captain Borthwick was under the patronage of both the Lord Admiral of
Scotland and a senior English admiral, Sir Jeremy Smith, which suggests the tan-
talising prospect of close Anglo-Scottish partnership at the highest level to advance
Scots officers. Earlier in 1672 Borthwick had been recommended as master of *Success*
by both Lennox and Sir Jeremy Smith. See BL Add. MS 21,948 f. 166. His later
patron was Sir Richard Beach.

   [83] Capp, *Cromwell's Navy*, 217–219, 248, 259–262; Davies, *Gentlemen and Tarpaulins*,
69–70, 77–78, 160. Volunteers were also allowed the shore leave denied to pressed
men.

   [84] Davies, *Gentlemen and Tarpaulins*, 70, 77. Davies points out that during the Third
Dutch War, 25% to 75% of individual ships' companies were volunteers while in
1678, Sir John Kempthorne was able to man his first rate almost exclusively with
volunteers from his native Devon. For the Scottish case in the following century
see N. A. M. Rodger, *The Wooden World: An Anatomy of the Georgian Navy* (London:
1986), 156–157. Rodger notes that Scots magnates "carried their tenantry to war".
See especially the details on Douglas, M. P. for Orkney, and Maitland's crew from
the Scottish east coast, particularly Fife. On a more junior level, one of Boscawen's
lieutenants brought no less than 100 Scots into service with him.

   [85] James' penchant for Irish/Catholic officers is now known, but Davies does not
mention Scots in this respect. Scots officers are tacitly acknowledged as being present in numbers in 1688, and as showing no regional or national unity—they were
just as divided as the other regional groups on what to do or which side to join.
See Davies, *Gentlemen and Tarpaulins*, 29, 30, 113, 115, 223, 224.

review of printed and archival sources allows us a clearer picture of the Scottish presence within the officer corps and does show that there was an increase in Scottish officer numbers following the nobles' appointments, though it is impossible to definitively assess their influence until we have more evidence, particularly on the attitudes of Charles and James. Given the operational latitude Lennox exercised, the peacetime cluster of 1660–3 [Figures 1 & 2/2a] shows the immediate advancement of Scots in the wake of his appointment.[86] Similarly, the period of Lauderdale's tenure (1673–9) within the 1675–87 cluster shows a tangible increase over peacetime levels elsewhere (excepting 1660–3).[87] Unless the Scottish naval officers in the R.N. behaved differently to their colleagues in military service, or in naval service elsewhere, the likelihood is that their presence would have attracted men from their extended families into the service, adding to those Scots already serving in the navy.[88]

Andrew, Lord Rutherford, was made Earl of Teviot in 1663 for his services as Vice-Admiral and Governor of Tangiers.[89] Among the officers we also find such men as George Strachan, a R.N. captain in 1666.[90] George was also an Edinburgh merchant owner involved

---

[86] More Scots were commissioned than in the comparable peacetime interludes of 1668–71 or 1698–1701. There was of course the additional need to reward returning exiles and those deprived of employment and personal fortunes for their loyalty during the Civil Wars, though the data has not yet been systematically analysed.

[87] The demand engendered by the war scare of 1677–8 is in evidence here.

[88] See for example, Murdoch, *Britain, Denmark-Norway and the House of Stuart*, 193–210; Grosjean, *An Unofficial Alliance*, 122–135. Similarly, given the increase of Scots officers' numbers and the attainment of flag rank in the latter part of our period (see below), it is unlikely that Scots officers did not prefer fellow Scots as juniors and subordinates and have some success in advancing these under their own patronage.

[89] Letter Patent, 2 February 1663, *Register of the Great Seal of Scotland*, vol. 11, 1660–1668, 184, no. 364. Rutherford had also been Governor of Dunkirk. The source above reveals errors in David Parrott, "Rutherford, Andrew, earl of Teviot (d. 1664)", *Oxford Dictionary of National Biography* (2004) [http://www.oxforddnb.com/view/article/24360]. Pepys complained that, for the Tangier post, Rutherford, a Scot (and a Catholic), was merely preferred to Irish personnel already in situ. See *ibid.*

[90] There are two main sources for this information, Bonner Smith's printed compilation and a manuscript list of Scots in the 'English' navy dating to c.1702–1704. D. Bonner Smith, *The Commissioned Sea Officers of the Royal Navy, 1660–1815* (3 vols. Greenwich: 1950); NAS GD406/M1/19 [formerly NRAS 332, M1/19/4], f. 4. 'List of some Scotes officers belonging to the sea that are in the English Service', (no date), Cross referencing with Bonner Smith's list puts the date somewhere between January 1702 and December 1704. For George Strachan see Bonner Smith, *Commissioned Sea Officers*, III, 886; *CSPD 1666–1667*, 205, 455, 477, 554.

in supplying stores for the navy along with his relative, Captain John Strachan.[91] In 1666, John described himself as "apprenticed to his Majesty's service [for] 28 years" and previously known to Charles I as "Honest Strachan".[92] While relatives could serve and support each other in the service, so too could long-term comrades. Thomas Hamilton was made lieutenant in 1666 and soon got his 'step' to captain in 1668. His colleague, John Anderson, received his captain's commission in 1666 and served through the Revolution until 1693. His local knowledge of the west coast made him chief pilot under Thomas Hamilton, who acted as commodore for an R.N. squadron (*Kingfisher, Mermaid, Drake*) which effectively ended the 1685 Argyll Rebellion.[93] They were joined by the merchant skipper Archibald Shearer, who was persuaded by the Earl of Dumbarton to pilot *Kingfisher* in the expedition. Shearer received a commission in order to do so. A year later, Shearer was "extreamlie indigent and almost in a starveing condition having bein still out of employement since that tyme". His commander, Thomas Hamilton, certified that Shearer had been aboard *Kingfisher* and deserved his wages.[94]

These officers all appear to have come from good families, but some Scottish officers worked their way up from very lowly origins to be senior admirals. Sir David Mitchell, originally a "Scots fisherboy" and indentured apprentice to a Leith merchant master, was a master's mate in the Baltic trade when pressed into the R.N. in 1672. He became a lieutenant in January 1678 under his patron, Admiral Russell in *Defiance*, following the admiral into *Swiftsure* that same year and into *Newcastle* in 1680. He got his 'step' as captain of *Ruby* in 1683. Mitchell has been described as "the most promi-

---

[91] *CSPD 1666–1667*, 164. Strachan to Pepys, 27 September 1666. John Strachan is not in the Bonner Smith list, though he did hold a commission "of the Duke" (*i.e.* James, Duke of York, Lord High Admiral).

[92] A voluminous correspondence on Scottish maritime affairs with the Navy Commissioners survives. He was involved with procurement of naval supplies and seems to have been in partnership with Scots merchants in London. See *CSPD 1666–1667*, 258, 350, 513, 596. Samuel Pepys knew one of these men, whom Charles favoured with half the proceeds of a ship sale in 1660. See Pepys, *Diary*, 23 November 1660.

[93] *Commissioned Sea Officers*, I, 13 and II, 399; *RPCS 1686–1689*, 104. James II warrant to Anderson, 24 January 1687. Anderson received £25 reward from James for this service, and was superannuated in 1707. See also Graham, *Maritime History of Scotland*, 145–146.

[94] *RPCS 1686–1689*, 104. Petition of Shearer to Privy Council, c.1686.

nent of the lesser defectors" to the Williamites in 1688, after which his service record is quite startling.[95] Indeed, under William III, Mitchell was the commander-in-chief Russell's flag captain and captain of the fleet in *Britannia* in 1691, serving at the invasion-stopping Anglo-Dutch victory at Barfleur/La Hougue in 1692.[96] Thereafter his journey through the ranks was impressive, and he was promoted Vice-Admiral of the White in 1701.[97] Mitchell was well enough regarded to be entrusted with bringing over Tsar Peter the Great from the Dutch Republic to London in 1698.[98] More importantly from the point of view of this survey, we also find him vouching for the injured Scottish seaman, Alexander Mackduff, who had fought

---

[95] *DNB*, xiii, 513–514; Davies, *Gentlemen and Tarpaulins*, 206; Ehrman, *The Navy in the War of William III*, 136, 271, 455, 552; D. Ogg, *England in the reigns of James II and William III* (Oxford: 1955), 326. From Aberdeen, Mitchell (c.1650–1710) seems to have retired after Russell did so (on James' execution of his cousin, William Russell), and it is uncertain whether he returned to trade or acted as Russell's political agent in England and the Dutch Republic. His first command after the Revolution was *Elizabeth* (70 guns), in which he fought at the Anglo-Dutch defeat at Beachy Head/Bévéziers, 1690. See *DNB*, xiii, 513.

[96] *The Manuscripts of the House of Lords, 1692–1693* (London: 1894), 228. Although his subordinate, Mitchell was the gentleman Russell's 'tutor' in navigation and seamanship. At Barfleur, Mitchell most probably influenced Russell to make the 'general chase' order to the combined Grand Fleet, leading directly to the crushing victory. See Ehrman, *The Navy in the War of William III*, 271, 396. For his conduct at Barfleur, William made him a groom of the bedchamber, and Mitchell commanded the squadrons escorting William to and from the Dutch Republic in March and October 1693 (his flag in *Essex*). He was knighted in 1694. See *DNB*, xiii, 513.

[97] See John B. Hattendorf, 'Mitchell, Sir David (c.1650–1710)', *ODNB* [http://www.oxforddnb.com/view/article/18836]. He was made Rear Admiral of the Blue in February 1693, Rear Admiral of the Red 1693–1695, Vice Admiral of the Blue 1695, Commander-in-Chief Mediterranean 1695, Admiralty Commissioner 1699–1702. NAS, 'List of some Scotes Officers'; *CSPD 1700–1702*, 274, 283; *Commissioned Sea Officers*, II, 629–630; Ehrman, *The Navy in the War of William III*, 648. In 1693 William had wanted Mitchell advanced further: from Rear Admiral of the Blue to Vice Admiral of the Blue. A commission was accordingly issued and received by the fleet at Torbay. See *The Manuscripts of the House of Lords, 1693–1695*, 171. Admiralty Letter Book, Admirals to Admiralty, 9 July 1693. Flag appointments were temporary. The 1701 commission meant that Mitchell was the fifth most senior admiral then in the fleet (the seniority of the squadrons in descending order being Red, White, Blue). Mitchell sat on Prince George of Denmark's Council, 1702–1708. He spoke Dutch and was naval negotiator with the States General, 1702–1706, and 1709. See PRO, SP 87/2, f. 10. Duke of Marlborough to Nottingham, 15 October 1702; Hattendorf, 'Mitchell'; *DNB*, xiii, 514.

[98] A. Cross, *Peter the Great through British Eyes: Perceptions and Representations of the Tsar since 1698* (Cambridge: 2000), 15. Peter then requested that Mitchell attend him during his stay, and command the squadron escorting him back to Holland. See *DNB*, xiii, 514; Hattendorf, 'Mitchell'.

alongside him at Barfleur aboard *Britannia*.[99] Perhaps the fact that Mackduff was a Scot on his ship was merely coincidental, although it is during Mitchell's tenure at the admiralty that the 'List of Scotes officers' was drawn up, showing both an increased awareness and interest in this community within the R.N.

Mitchell was one of numerous Scots to make the transition from Stuart to Williamite service. There is little doubt that the Williamite period saw many new Scots join the service through Mitchell's close connections with devout Scottish Presbyterian refugee families, such as Sir James Wishart, whose Presbyterian father had refused to take the 'Test'. Wishart was appointed to captain in the Williamite navy on 4 July 1689, taking command of *Pearl*, and then the fourth rate *Oxford* (50 guns) at Barfleur. He eventually served as Commander-in-Chief Mediterranean 1713–1714.[100] Other prominent Scots also received their commissions after the Williamite Revolution. The Hon. Lord Archibald Hamilton, 1st lieutenant under Mitchell in *Britannia* by 1693, was ordered that September to take temporary command of *Lennox* (70 guns), despite his junior rank, on the dismissal of Captain Kerr (another Scot). Within three weeks he received his captain's commission direct from the admirals with the fleet, serving as commander of the fourth rate *Woolwich* (54 guns).[101] Mitchell probably had a hand in his countryman's advance. By April 1701 Hamilton commanded the third rate *Torbay* (80 guns), and was then short-

---

[99] *CSPD 1700–1702*, 491.

[100] He was Rear Admiral of the Blue in 1704, Admiral of the Blue 1708, Admiralty Commissioner in 1710, Admiral of the White in 1713 (*i.e.* the second most senior admiral in the fleet). See NAS, 'List of some Scotes Officers'; Bonner Smith, *The Commissioned Sea Officers*, III, 1009; *The Manuscripts of the House of Lords, 1692–1693*, 228; *DNB*, xxi, 724. He served as Captain of the Fleet (*i.e.* senior captain in the captain's list present, though seniority was subject to political favour and patronage, as with the flag ranks) to Sir George Rooke at Vigo Bay in 1702. Wishart was dismissed in 1715, after serving as Tory M.P. for Portsmouth from 1711. See *DNB*, xxi, 724. Wishart migrated to the Dutch Republic in his youth, served in the Dutch navy, reportedly as a captain, and was in the 1688 expedition. He was naval negotiator with the Dutch in 1711. See J. D. Davies, 'Wishart, Sir James (*c.*1659–1723)', *ODNB* [http://www.oxforddnb.com/view/article/29795].

[101] *The Manuscripts of the House of Lords, 1693–1695*, 169. Admiralty Letter Book, Admirals to Admiralty, 2 and 19 September 1693. Kerr seems to have been removed because of his involvement in a controversial prize dispute, but may have been reinstated later. See *ibid.*, 98–99, 102, 156, 198, 528–529. That two Scots officers were consecutively appointed to command a warship with a Scots name is probably not coincidental.

listed with twenty four other captains for the nine third rates to be
fitted out for the winter of 1701/2.[102] Having suffered some (unknown)
career setback, he was later restored to his position in the R.N. by
royal intervention, at Anne's express request in 1703.[103] He went on
to become both admiral and governor of Jamaica by 1711. During
this time numerous Hamiltons were in the R.N., and many can be
identified as related family members. Their presence resembles that
of Scottish naval dynasties in foreign service in the early seventeenth
century, such as the Clerck and Stewart families in Sweden, or the
Mowatt family in Denmark-Norway.[104] The Hamiltons did not achieve
the status within the R.N. that their countrymen did in Scandinavia,
and they have curiously been overlooked, even by Scottish maritime
historians.[105] While historians have been somehow slow to notice
their maritime importance, the presence of Mitchell and Hamilton
did not go unnoticed in some English quarters. In 1703 certain

---

[102] Bonner Smith, *The Commissioned Sea Officers*, II, 397; *CSPD 1700–1702*, 300,
468. As commander of *Lichfield* in 1696, he took *Ann* of Kirkcaldy, laden with French
wine. See Graham, *Maritime History of Scotland*, 81. *Ann* was trading illegally during
wartime with the enemies of the 'Antient Kingdome'.

[103] *CSPD 1702–1703*, 646. Sir C. Hedges to Prince's Council, 24 March 1703.
Another family member, Lieutenant Archibald Hamilton, was re-employed at sea
on the intervention of William III. See *CSPD 1700–1702*, 290. Hedges to Admiralty,
3 April 1701.

[104] Grosjean, *An Unofficial Alliance*, 133–134, but also 112–135; Murdoch, *Britain,
Denmark-Norway and the House of Stuart*, 193–210, and 98–106.

[105] Graham, *Maritime History of Scotland*, 81; T. M. Devine, *Scotland's Empire
1600–1815* (London: 2003), 41, 65. Professor Tom Devine gives the impression
that the R.N. abandoned the defence of Scotland after the Revolution of 1688.
Here are two examples that refute this position. Four R.N. frigates cruised between
Scotland and Ireland in 1689: they left Edinburgh in mid-August. Rooke was commodore of the squadron in *Dartmouth* (32 guns). Local experts were brought in especially to navigate the unfamiliar waters between Orkney and the Clyde, indicating
the extension of R.N. operations into new areas: the Privy Council ordered four
Greenock pilots from the Glasgow authorities. The 1689 case has plainly been over-
shadowed by the disaster that overtook the two hired merchantmen of the 'Scots
navy' when they operated independently of Rooke and were defeated with heavy
loss of life by a French frigate squadron. Another consideration usually overlooked
is that William III made use of the Dutch navy as Stadholder-King, and Dutch
warships escorted Forth convoys. Further, the privateer fleets Scotland sent to sea
were no small contribution to maritime defence and numbered up to twenty five
at a time. These were often deployed to defend English and Irish waters as well
as their native Scotland. See *RPCS 1689*, 83. Missive to Major General McKay,
23 August 1689; *RPCS 1689*, 38, 13 August 1689 and *passim*; Graham, *Maritime
History of Scotland*, 65–70; Grosjean and Murdoch, 'Scottish Naval Presence in the
North Sea and the Baltic'; Murdoch, Little and Forte, 'Scottish Privateering', 37–65.

sections of the English Parliament held that there were "already too
many Scotch officers among us" when the subject of foreigners was
raised whilst debating the perennial problem of manning.[106] These
isolated complaints did not stop the pre-Union penetration of the
Scots into the highest ranks of the R.N., nor the selection of those
senior Scots officers for critical diplomatic duties. Ironically, in view
of those few complaints, Mitchell was appointed Black Rod in 1698—
a full nine years before the Union. He was not only a Scot, but the
first member of the armed forces ever to hold the office. Mitchell
held it until his death in 1710.[107]

Scots in the Dutch Navy[108]

The service of Scots in the Dutch maritime sector can be traced
back to the early part of the seventeenth century. Professor Bruijn
has shown Scots forming 6% of Zeeland crews around 1600.[109] In
the Dutch East Indies, Captain James Couper commanded a small
V.O.C. fleet at Batavia in 1639–1640.[110] In Joos Banckert's Zeeland
admiralty warship supporting the W.I.C. off Brazil in 1644–48, British
seamen comprised 23.3% of the crew. The thirty Scots (including
two Shetlanders and one Orcadian) by themselves made up 14% of
the total.[111] In 1649 a 24-gun ship left Dutch service for that of

---

[106] R. D. Merriman, ed., *Queen Anne's Navy: Documents concerning the Administration of the Navy of Queen Anne, 1702–1714* (London: 1961), 187. Manly M.P. speaking in a Committee of the whole House, 4 December 1703.

[107] Hattendorf, 'Mitchell'.

[108] The Dutch navy under the Republic was characteristically decentralised in five separate admiralties by our period: Zeeland; three in Holland—Amsterdam, Rotterdam (Maze) & the North Quarter (Noorderkwartier)—and Friesland (with contributions from Groningen). In the latter four admiralties the vast bulk of the pay-muster rolls have been destroyed due to accident and circumstance. For the crews of the Zeeland admiralty see P. F. Poortvliet, *De Bemanningen der schepen van de Admiraliteit van Zeeland* (26 vols., Middelburg: 1995–98). These cover the periods 1610–1619, 1630–1633, 1643–1648 & 1680–1793.

[109] J. R. Bruijn, *The Dutch navy of the seventeenth and eighteenth centuries* (Columbia: 1993), 55; J. R. Bruijn, *Varend Verleden: De Nederlandse Oorlogsvloot in de zeventiende en achttiende eeuw* (Amsterdam: 1998), 72, citing Zeeuws Archief, Rekenkamer C 636, Payrolls of *Tonijn* and *Zeeland*.

[110] Murdoch, 'The Good, the Bad and the Anonymous', 64. This is not the same man as Admiral James Couper of the V.O.C.

[111] Poortvliet, *Bemanningen*, vol. 14b, 106–9 citing Zeeuws Archief, Rekenkamer C 6803.

Prince Rupert in Ireland; the entire crew and captain were Scots.[112] These examples give us a glimpse of small Scottish communities across the Dutch maritime sector.[113] The outbreak of the First Anglo-Dutch War presented an opportunity for these numbers to grow. The imagined Scottish presence within that navy adopted greater expression when, at the engagement with Blake off Dover in 1652, the Dutch fleet under the Orangist Maerten Tromp was observed flying "the King of Scots colours on their topsails".[114] That this represented a Scottish maritime community should not be overstated, as Charles II was called "the King of Scots" by Cromwellian propagandists as a way of distancing him from his English subjects.[115] Yet the Commonwealth thought that some 5–6,000 Britons were in the Dutch maritime sector in 1652, amongst whom many were Scots.[116] These formed the hub of a Scottish maritime community that remained in Dutch service well into the eighteenth century. Just as they did wherever they formed communities, the Scots used their networks to ensure that other members of their families or home communities could find employment long after any anti-Cromwellian motivation had died down. The religious intolerance of the Stuart regime in Scotland did, however, cause an exodus of religious refugees. While those of the political elite have been studied by Ginny Gardner among others, it will probably be impossible to establish how many of the maritime community possessed similar motivation. But given the strength of Presbyterianism in Scotland, it is unsurprising that by the conclusion of the Second Dutch War, some 3,000 English and Scots were reportedly serving in the Dutch navy.[117]

---

[112] Anderson, *The Journals of Sir Thomas Allin, 1660–1678*, II, 214, Popham to Speaker, 27 Apr 1649.

[113] J. Morrison noted how the dates of communion held in the Rotterdam Kirk were fixed to accommodate Scottish sailors engaged in the summer Greenland and the winter Levant trade, see *Scots on the Dijk* (Durham: 1981), 7. My thanks to Professor Smout for bringing this to my attention.

[114] S. C. A. Pincus, *Protestantism and Patriotism. Ideologies and the Making of English Foreign Policy, 1650–1688* (Cambridge: 1996), 71.

[115] S. Murdoch, *Britain, Denmark-Norway and the House of Stuart: A Diplomatic and Military Analysis* (East Linton: 2003), 172.

[116] *Calendar of State Papers, Venetian, 1647–1652*, 245. Lorenzo Paulucci (Venetian Secretary in England) to the Venetian Ambassador in France, 13 June 1652; Bernard Capp, *Cromwell's Navy: The Fleet and the English Revolution 1648–1660* (Oxford: 1989), 258.

[117] PRO, SP 29/206, f. 27. Colonel Titus to Arlington, 18 June 1667; C. R.

For some of the Scots we can hypothesise both the political motivation to engage in Dutch service and a desire to serve with other
Scots. The Zeeland admiralty warship *Wapen van Zeelant* was largely
manned from the Scottish staple port of Veere. Andrew Dougal of
Wemyss was one of the two pilots, and the surgeon Patrick Greeff
was almost certainly a Veere Scot of some standing. Indeed, Scots
(either from Scotland or resident at Veere) made up at least 6% of
the crew in April 1665.[118] David Reed of Wemyss, a highly literate
man, was so eager to go "to sea in thee staits servis against thee
Englishes" that he enlisted as a mere common seaman for twelve
guilders per month. Reed was careful—in case of his absence or
death—to authorise his "landladij Jannet Broun or her husband Peter
Wilson" to take what rent he owed and send the rest of his wages
to his mother in Scotland.[119] It was fortunate that he did so. *Wapen
van Zeelant* was Reed's ship from 1 August 1664 to 14 June 1665,
when he was taken prisoner on the second day of the battle of
Lowestoft. That day the Dutch lost seventeen warships and some
5,000 casualties. Reed's agents received his five and a half months'
arrears, and ten (Flemish) schellings per month (three guilders) wage
increase backdated from 20 April 1665 up to the date of his capture.[120] Andrew Skeen from Shetland was also taken prisoner; he
had enlisted on the same ship on the same day as Reed and they
were numbered consecutively in the payroll.[121]

Adrian Cunningham of Veere, another highly educated man,
started his service on 1 August 1664 aboard *Wapen van Zeelant* as a

---

Boxer, *The Anglo-Dutch Wars of the 17th Century* (London: 1974), 64; *CSPD 1667*, lx,
207. See discussion below on wages.

[118] Zeeuws Archief, Rekenkamer C 6985. Payroll of *Wapen van Zeelant*, 3 April
1665; Payroll of *Wapen van Zeelant*, 20 April 1665.

[119] Zeeuws Archief, Rekenkamer C 6985. Reed's power of attorney to Broun and
Wilson, 22 April 1665, enclosure in payment request and receipt for David Reed,
16 October 1665. Alexander Chrystie, probably Andrew Skeen's brother-in-law,
wrote the power of attorney and witnessed it. Gerrit Janssen, a Veere citizen, and
Wilson were also supposed to have witnessed but did not sign.

[120] Zeeuws Archief, Rekenkamer C 6985. Payment request and receipt for David
Reed, 16 October 1665. Reed's *slaapvrouw*, Jannet Broun, could sign her own name
reasonably well.

[121] His arrears also got the backdated increase: his sister, Margarett Christie, collected these at Middelburg. Her very elegant signature indicates that she and her
brother were of some status. See Zeeuws Archief, Rekenkamer C 6985. Payment
request and receipt for Andrew Skeen, 16 October 1665.

supernumerary (suggesting some kind of relationship with the commander, Captain de Hase), though on seaman's pay. He followed
de Hase into his new command, *Dordrecht* (also largely manned from
Veere) on 17 April 1665, receiving his arrears on 5 August.[122] The
boy James Henderson of Veere had also been aboard *Wapen van
Zeelant* and also followed de Hase into *Dordrecht*, where Scots then
made up at least 3.5% of the crew.[123] Even when they had transferred out of the first ship, Scots still comprised around 5% of *Wapen
van Zeelant*'s crew: within a few weeks Andrew Thomson of Anstruther
and John Cowey, another Veere resident, had also joined.[124]

The evidence indicates that these two ships held a small community of Scots, some of whom still maintained their links with
Scotland while fighting against their sovereign monarch. In addition
to the aforementioned two Scots prisoners taken at Lowestoft, the
battle claimed the lives of other Scots aboard *Swanenburgh*: the Dysart
seamen John and James Park and the Shetland cook Andrew Erasmus.
All had served since September 1664. The Orcadian Alexander
Williamson was particularly unfortunate; he had joined the ship only
three days before.[125]

Several explanations are possible for the behaviour of these Scots.
The first is that they were penniless exiles itching for the chance to
revenge themselves on a crypto-Catholic British monarch. The second is that they were merchant seamen deprived of their usual
employment by the seizure of British shipping in the pre-war esca-
lation periods and the wartime Dutch trade embargo, placed during the spring and early summer to facilitate recruitment for the
navy, thus making it virtually the only option.[126] In this case the
educated elite that we have seen were probably simply merchants

---

[122] Zeeuws Archief, Rekenkamer C 6985. Payment request and receipt for Cunningham, 5 August 1665.

[123] Zeeuws Archief, Rekenkamer C 6985. Payroll of *Dordrecht*, 20 April 1665. The
total will probably be higher when we are able to include Scots resident at Veere
who remain hitherto unidentified.

[124] Zeeuws Archief, Rekenkamer C 6985. Payroll of *Wapen van Zeelant*, 20 Apr
1665.

[125] Zeeuws Archief, Rekenkamer C 6984. Payroll of *Swanenburgh*, 13 June 1665.

[126] Seventy Scots who had left their ship at Delfshaven in March 1672 looking
for employment in the Greenland whale fishery found this option impossible. They
took the ship's hoy to Rotterdam and joined the navy. See PRO, SP 29/305, ff.
47, 79. Silas Taylor to Williamson, 4 and 5 Apr 1672; *CSPD 1671–1672*.

whose trade had been ruined by the embargo. Seamen and their families lived a precarious existence on a subsistence level, which brings us to a related third motivation: simple economics. Merchant pay was often uncertain,[127] and the incidence of naval pay could deteriorate severely under the strains of war, arrears running into years.[128] Furthermore, Dutch naval pay rates were market-driven and often offered 25% or even 100% increases over British basic pay to man the greatly expanded fleet in wartime.[129] This is difficult to disentangle from simple mercenary inclinations. Fourthly, it is possible that they were Scots who had more allegiance to their new country than their old one, particularly given the attitude of the British monarchy to their Presbyterian countrymen.[130] None of these can be

---

[127] See, for example, Edward Barlow, *Barlow's Journal: Of his life at sea in King's ships, East and West Indiamen & other merchantmen from 1659 to 1703*, ed. B. Lubbock (2 vols., London: 1934), *passim*.

[128] For the R.N., see especially Pepys, *Diary, passim*. Despite difficulties (especially during the First Dutch War) Dutch incidence of payment appears markedly superior in comparison, wage arrears usually running into months rather than years. In Britain the use of tickets (basically government I.O.U.s) in lieu of cash reduced the value of seamen's wages, as the seamen were forced by circumstance to sell the tickets to petty brokers for ready cash at a heavy discount. The large numbers of British seamen in the Dutch fleet in 1667, noted above, were associated with the build-up of arrears and the collapse of ticket values caused by British financial exhaustion. English seamen in the Dutch fleet at the Medway cried out to the shore "Heretofore we fought for tickets, now we fight for dollars!" See Pepys, *Diary*, 14 June 1667.

[129] Peacetime Dutch wages were in general parity with British pay. For Dutch wartime naval pay rises generally see Bruijn, *Dutch navy*, 130; Bruijn, *Varend Verleden*, 163. For general surveys of Dutch marine wages, see Johan Francke, '"Een Sware Equipage": De bemanningen van de schepen van de Admiraliteit Zeeland en de commissievaart tijdens de Negenjarige Oorlog (1688–1697)', *Tijdschrift voor Zeegeschiedenis*, Jaargang 19, nr. 2 (September 2000), 133; K. Davids, 'Maritime Labour in the Netherlands, 1570–1870', in Paul C. van Royen, J. R. Bruijn & J. Lucassen, *"Those Emblems of Hell"?*, 67. British naval seamen's basic pay rates remained static from 1652 until the great fleet mutinies of 1797. For a brief overview of Dutch/British comparative naval pay, see A. R. Little, 'British seamen in the United Provinces'.

[130] For example, Andrew Smith of Dundee, who served under Banckert, was another educated man and one who appears to have been integrated into Dutch society; he signed his name as 'Andries Smit'. See Zeeuws Archief, Rekenkamer C 6994. Payment request and receipt for Smith, 28 October 1666; Some archive 6985. Payroll of *Veere*, 23 December 1664; Payroll of *Veere*, 20 April 1665. A petty officer about whom we might theorise assimilation is the Orcadian David Grey. He served on the dispatch yacht *Souteland* through the Second Dutch war—the only Scot (or Briton, and virtually the only foreigner) in a central position as cook in a very small and therefore intimate crew. See Zeeuws Archief, Rekenkamer C 6985. Payroll of *Souteland*, 17 July 1665; Payroll of *Souteland*, 28 December 1665.

ruled out without further evidence coming to light, and combinations thereof are both possible and probable. As a corollary to the anti-Stuart motivations of some Scots, others did answer the recall home to fight the enemies of their sovereign, or at least decided to make a run for it once hostilities became official: the Bo'ness seamen Alexander Moody and Alexander Williamson, together with the Orcadian Andrew Misseth, deserted their posts aboard *Het Hoff van Zeeland* within days of the States General's declaration of war in late January 1665. They left behind at least three other Scots and a number of Englishmen.[131]

The same sets of motivations must have played a part in the service and recruitment of others, with 1,000 English and 1,500 Scots reported in the Dutch fleet in 1672.[132] These exaggerated figures reflect the impact that the smaller yet still astonishing number of British seamen in either the Dutch navy or across the Dutch maritime sector had on their countrymen at home.[133] One reason for this was that throughout 1672 Dutch recruiters specifically targeted the area in Rotterdam where Scots (and English) seamen usually lodged.[134] Douglas Catterall has conclusively demonstrated the integration of the Scots community in Rotterdam into Dutch society throughout our period, this in itself providing a conduit for Scottish entry into the navy.[135] We have already seen that this also appears to have been the case for Veere. Scots were also admitted to the English Presbyterian Church at Flushing, where the congregation

---

[131] Zeeuws Archief, Rekenkamer C 6984. Payroll of *Het Hoff van Zeeland*, 5 Jan 1666. The ship had been in commission since June 1664 and the crew do not seem to have received any pay. There were plenty of other deserters during the ship's long service so politics may not have been a feature. Conversely, war also provided new opportunities. In 1672, two Scots serving on a London merchantman stopped but released by a Flushing privateer in the Western Approaches opted to jump ship for Dutch service. See *CSPD 1672*, 21. Thomas Holden to Williamson, 20 May 1672.

[132] PRO, SP 29/305, f. 198. Silas Taylor to Williamson, 18 April 1672; Davies, *Gentlemen and Tarpaulins*, 84, citing the previous source, and PRO, SP 29/305, f. 18 and SP 29/331, f. 219; *CSPD 1671–1672*, 340.

[133] Where the British sources refer to total numbers of British either across the Dutch maritime sector as a whole or the navy in particular, they indicate that British seamen comprised roughly around 10% of the respective manpower.

[134] *CSPD 1671–1672*, 362. Richard Bower to Williamson, 22 April 1672.

[135] Catterall, *Community Without Borders: Scots migrants and the changing face of power in the Dutch Republic, c.1600–1700* (Leiden: 2002), *passim*.

intensively prayed, fasted, and sang psalms for Dutch victory (usually in company with the Dutch congregations) throughout all three of the Dutch wars.[136]

The devotion to the Dutch cause of some Scots cannot be doubted. One Scots prisoner taken at the battle of Solebay in May 1672 was more than willing to give his life spectacularly. He was taken in the magazine aboard Sir John Chicheley's flagship *Royal Katherine* (84 guns): he had tried to blow her up single-handed and was caught "match in his hand".[137] In 1672, according to two British Rotterdam merchants (a Scot and an Englishman) whose ships were embargoed at Rotterdam, 150 Scots and English were aboard one Dutch war-ship, whilst 200 Scots and English were already aboard De Ruyter's flagship, *De Zeven Provinciën*.[138] In 1673, of De Ruyter's 600 crew, some 200 were again reported to be British.[139] We can be more certain of those aboard Cornelis Tromp's flagship, *Gouden Leeuw*, the same year. British nationals comprised a very hefty 8% of the total crew; Scots made up 3%.[140] Additionally, Scots seamen (along with Englishmen) were a "significant" part of Dutch naval manpower in 1688. Davies suggests that their motivation was due to the higher Dutch wages rather than to any ideological motive, though read in combination with Ginny Gardner's chapter that argument may have to be revised.[141] We actually know very little of their service, hav-

---

[136] Gemeente Archief Vlissingen, 4469. Archief van de Engelse Kerk, Notulen van de kerkeraad [Acts of the English Presbyterian Church], *passim*, especially 12, 14, 15, 30 June 1666, 7 July 1666, 4 August 1666, 6 July 1667.

[137] *CSPD 1672*, 96, 105. Major N. Durrell (marines, Governor of Sheerness) to Williamson, 29 and 30 May 1672. In a hopeless position, *Royal Katherine* had surrendered after being cut off from the rest of the Allied fleet and surrounded by Dutch fireships. She was boarded by the Dutch and taken, her crew shut up below decks by the Dutch prize crew (of which the Scot was a member), remaining in their possession for some hours. The British prisoners later burst up through the hatches and retook her; it was soon after that the Scot was found. Unfortunately we do not yet know his name or fate.

[138] *CSPD 1671–1672*, 362. Richard Bower to Williamson, 22 April 1672.

[139] *Catalogue of the . . . Manuscripts in the Pepysian Library*, ii, 32. Pepys to Allin, 21 August 1673: Violet Barbour, 'Dutch and English Merchant Shipping in the Seventeenth Century', in P. Emmer & F. Gaastra, eds., *The Organisation of Interoceanic Trade in European Expansion, 1450–1800* (Aldershot: 1996), 126.

[140] Nationaal Archief, Collectie Aanwinsten van de voormalige Eerste Afdeeling van het Algemeen Rijksarchief, 438. Pay book of *Gouden Leeuw*, 1673.

[141] Davies, *Gentlemen and Tarpaulins*, 206, citing BL Add. MS 41816, ff. 124v, 172, 177v, 181, 189.

ing just fleeting glimpses. For instance, George Morris of Leith served throughout the Second Dutch War in the Zeeland squadron, while a few others made warrant or petty officer.[142] We already know something of Dougal and Greeff mentioned above, and foreigners achieving these ranks were already part of an established pattern. It was reported from Rotterdam in 1652 that "many of the gunners and inferior officers and several other men are English, Scots and others".[143] Matthew Stuart, a resident of Calais, was gunner's mate aboard *Vlissingen* in 1665.[144] The Scot Robert Drayby was carpenter aboard *Den Visschers Herder* during the Third Dutch War.[145] The Leith seaman John Williamson served as gunner's mate on *Zeelandia* under admirals Johan and Cornelis Evertsen.[146] During the wars against France, Scots maintained a sizeable presence in the Dutch navy. Johan Francke's comprehensive work on the Nine Years' War, 1688–1697, gives 3% Scots out of a combined British 6% total in Zeeland crews.[147] John Drummond M.P. thought that 3,000 English and 2,000 Scots had been in Dutch maritime service during "Queen Anne's time".[148] Concern over the numbers provoked the English Privy

---

[142] Zeeuws Archief, Rekenkamer C 6999.3. Payroll of *Prince te Paert*, 27 May 1666.

[143] S. R. Gardiner and C. T. Atkinson, eds., *Letters and Papers Relating to the First Dutch War, 1652–1654* (6 vols., 1898), II, 224, Letter from Rotterdam, 27 August/6 September 1652, *Mercurius Politicus*, 1848.

[144] Zeeuws Archief, Rekenkamer C 6984. Payroll of *Vlissingen*, 17 July 1665; Payroll of *Vlissingen*, September 1665.

[145] Zeeuws Archief, Rekenkamer C 8317. Payroll of *Den Visschers Herder*, 18 May 1673.

[146] Zeeuws Archief, Rekenkamer C 6984. Muster roll of *Zeelandia*, 17 July 1665 and Payroll of *Zeelandia*, (no date, but before 28 December 1665).

[147] Johan Francke, *Utititeyt voor de gemeene saake. De Zeeuwse commissievaart en haar achterban tijdens de Negenjaarige Oorlog, 1688–1697* (Middelburg: 2001), 95, citing Poortvliet, *De Bemanningen*, 10a–11b. My thanks to Drs Ivo van Loo for this reference. Minimal comparative data (two muster rolls) from the Rotterdam admiralty at this time is inconclusive. Preliminary study shows that Scots comprised at least 2.5% of the crew aboard *De Provintije van Uijtregt* in 1695; lower than the Zeeland figures, but here the Scots comprise the largest single foreign group, half the foreign contingent. See Nationaal Archief, Admiraiteitscolleges, 1104. Muster roll of *De Provintije van Uijtregt*, 1695. Another sample suggests a Scottish figure of 7%, but this is not confirmed: this analysis was on names alone, as no origins are given in the muster. See Nationaal Archief, Admiraiteitscolleges, 1108. Muster roll of *Hellevoetsluis*, 1696. With the continuing shift of Scots trade away from Veere to Rotterdam we would expect more Scots in the latter's warships: it is here that the bulk of the Rotterdam musters are particularly missed.

[148] R. Sedgewick, *The House of Commons: The History of Parliament, 1715–1754*

Council's attention, but securing the return of seamen even in an allies' fleet could be difficult.[149] Large numbers of Scots continued aboard Zeeland admiralty warships during this time: a sample of 2,463 seamen from 1700–1709 yields 201 Scots or 8.2%.[150]

Tracing the cluster of Scots aboard Commander Cornelis Evertsen the Younger's *Utrecht* in the Second Dutch War affords us a number of insights. The chief bosun, Peter Merkel of Aberdeen, enlisted in July 1664 and, judging by his wage increases, had probably risen rapidly through the junior bosun's grades (his wife was in Zeeland with him). Two of the warship's three gunners hailed from Dysart: Alexander Swaine and David Thomson. They had also received considerable wage rises in rapid succession, again marking them as key skilled crew. Also from Dysart was the seaman John Williamson, whilst gunner's mate Alan Alanson and the seaman Peter George came from Bo'ness. All joined in June/July 1664 and served aboard at least until January 1666.[151] The Scots probably exploited kinship

---

(London: 1970), 623, John Drummond M.P., speech in the House of Commons, March 1728. This may have been a guess, but it would have been a highly informed one—he had had extensive experience in Amsterdam as a merchant. My thanks to Dr Andrew MacKillop for this reference. See also Sir Edward Knatchbull, *The Parliamentary Diary of Sir Edward Knatchbull, 1722–1730*, ed., A. N. Newman, (London: 1963), 75. Date of speech given as 14 March 1728.

[149] PRO, PC 1/2/153. 'Admiralty proposal (by way of a letter from the Earl of Pembroke) for encouraging the enlistment of British seamen in Holland', 7 March 1709. In 1702, English subjects aboard *Brill* "desire to be discharged from the service of the States General. Their names are sent so that the Secretary of State may get their discharges" from the Dutch Ambassadors. See *CSPD 1702–1703*, 164, George Clarke to Nottingham, 6 July 1702 [referring to PRO, SP Naval 6, 113: names missing in MS].

[150] Poortvliet, *Bemanningen*, vol. 14c, Payrolls of *L'Aurora*, 1700–2; *Cortgeen*, 1701–2, 1704–5; *Mercurius*, 1701–5, *Orange Galleij*, 1708–9 citing Zeeuws Archief, Rekenkamer C 7293, 7314, 7324, 7333, 7344, 7353, 7354, 7373, 7383, 7384, 7423, 7502. The especially high figures for Scottish seamen here may be partly a function of Dutch warships escorting convoys to and from the Forth, but does reflect the prevalence of Scots amongst Three Kingdoms nationals (at the very least by proportion of population) that is noticeable throughout our period. See the contemporary sample from the Rotterdam admiralty given above (*Hollandt*, 1702).

[151] Zeeuws Archief, Rekenkamer C 6994. Payroll of *Utrecht*, September 1665; Payroll of C. Evertsen de Jonge's crew, 20 April 1665. Andrew Dougal's earlier service brought him to the attention of Admiral Adriaen Banckert: by 1666 Dougal had advanced to serve aboard Banckert's flagship. One of the quartermasters, Thomas Qualeth, came from Leith, as did the seaman George Morris. Other Scots seamen aboard included John Johnson, John Rams (Aberdeen), Andrew Smith (Dundee) and the Orcadian Oliver Reed. See Zeeuws Archief, Rekenkamer C 6999.3. Advance to Banckert's new crew, [?] 1666; Payment of maandgeld to Banckert's crew, 27 May 1666; Advance to Banckert's crew, 13 March 1666.

in the Dutch Republic as well as in Sweden, though in the former case it must have been based on the family connections of the host country's elite, not the Scots' own blood relations as in the spectacular Swedish examples.[152] The two Dysart gunners may have acquired a reputation within the Evertsen naval 'dynasty' during the Second Dutch War, but in the Third Dutch War Swaine and Thomson certainly secured a more advantageous and prestigious move alongside their old commander aboard his flagship; Cornelis Evertsen the Younger was now Vice-admiral. His two old loyal followers were again at the core of a cluster of Scots, this time accompanied by a number of Kirkcaldy seamen: the family members Matthew, Thomas and William Brown, plus James Bowman, Peter Bennet and Harbel Mitchelson, while Peter Adrianson hailed from Bo'ness.[153]

Conclusion

When comparing the types of Scottish communities that could form in 'foreign' maritime service, we find that the survival of evidence is uneven and hinders a complete analysis. In British archives, Scottish names and English names can be so alike that it is difficult to determine exact nationality. In the Dutch case, it was sometimes of little interest to the Dutch where a sailor came from, British names were 'Dutchified' anyway, and many archival repositories have subsequently been destroyed. For the most part we know the Scots served in the Dutch navy in their thousands, but apart from a few examples we do not yet know if they served in large concentrations or were scattered in smaller but still significant groups. The few samples cited here suggest the latter. Nonetheless, it is possible to draw conclusions about the various communities, especially when we bring in studies of Scottish maritime communities in other nations for additional comparison.

In the first half of the seventeenth century, a Scottish community

---

[152] In addition to the aforementioned Scots naval 'dynasties' in Swedish service, in 1628 64% of Swedish naval captains were Scots. See Grosjean, *An Unofficial Alliance*, 132.

[153] Zeeuws Archief, Rekenkamer C 8317. Payment of Ducatoons to Vice Admiral Cornelis Evertsen's [the Younger] crew, 23 May 1672.

of mariners could be found in the Swedish navy. It has been conclusively demonstrated that these men formed a living community
in which officers of all levels from ensign to admiral socialised together
on land and served together at sea.[154] The Swedish example belonged
to a formative period of Swedish naval development, when the Swedes
had a low level of home-grown cutting-edge naval expertise, and
thus needed to import foreign professionals. The Scots became involved
relatively early, facilitating the placement of friends and family when
opportunities arose to do so. This was not the case for either the
R.N. or the wider Dutch marine, and it was not possible to develop
the 'Swedish type' of tight, almost monopolistic 'Scottish' community
within either service. Given the sheer size of the Dutch marine, and
the additional fleets of the V.O.C. and the W.I.C., it is not surprising that the individual maritime entrepreneur could do well where
he could best serve. Hence the rise of the likes of Admiral Couper
in the V.O.C. For the same reason of scale, the existence of clusters of Scots in the Dutch navy should not surprise us. It would perhaps have been unusual in such a vast maritime environment *not* to
be able to point to such clusters, given the geographical proximity
and trade contacts between the nations. Where clusters of Scots have
been found, they compare favourably with other foreign groups, such
as Scandinavians and Germans: promoted to petty and warrant
officer, but apart from (possibly) a handful, never advancing beyond
this level. The Dutch maritime labour market was hungry for foreigners but amply supplied with commanders. The situation in the
R.N., however, was quite different.

Unlike the Dutch (or Swedish) examples, the status of Scots as
'foreigners' in the R.N. was ambiguous. This was the king's navy
and the king was the monarch of all three kingdoms. While the parliaments and organs of state adopted a national perspective, the king
wanted the best of his men running his fleet. Although Lauderdale's
appointment to the English Admiralty may be anomalous if viewed
from an exclusively English or Scottish perspective, that was not the
case when a 'British' viewpoint was taken. This was not universally

---

[154] Grosjean, *An Unofficial Alliance*, 131. Here is an account of a tempestuous night
on the town when a Scottish ensign threatened a Scottish admiral with a knife and
was killed by his own cousin (a captain) for his trouble. Interestingly, there was
only one other 'foreigner' present and no Swedes.

seen at the time, though Marvell's *The Loyal Scott* is illustrative that
the British view of the monarchs sometimes penetrated the most fer-
vently English among society. For the less educated, however, the
need to find security in an alien environment was of paramount concern. Thus, while the noble courtiers Lauderdale or Lennox could
happily adopt a British cloak in the R.N., their experience was far
from universal. Consider the Gaelic Highlander in Yarmouth, the
Bo'ness crew in Ireland, the Scottish ensign in Stockholm or the
Queensferry boys in *Hollandt*, who were always going to seek for and
stick with their own if allowed to do so.[155] Only once the 'alien'
environment became more familiar could they feel secure and dis-
perse into the wider naval community wherever they served—Admiral
Mitchell the fisher boy in the R.N., Admiral Simon Stewart the
sometime refugee in Sweden, and Admiral James Couper of the
V.O.C. in the Dutch East Indies.

---

[155] However, even volunteers who had chosen to follow a particular commander
could be dispersed—'turned over' or drafted without payment into another ship.
Scots volunteers turned over into *Norfolk* in May 1693 petitioned their admirals in
disgust at being torn from their commander. The move was especially galling as
William's earlier proclamation for seamen had stated that volunteers would not be
so used: the admirals noted the "great dissatisfaction" caused throughout the fleet,
but chose this one petition for the Admiralty's "particular observation". Perhaps the
closeness of this Scots community with their previous commander illustrated the
problem more clearly than other examples. The loss of pay due is also an issue,
but wage arrears were always a problem, with or without turnovers. Clearly, if a
seaman had to remain unpaid, it was better to be so in the loyal company of his
comrades under a loved and respected commander. See *The Manuscripts of the House
of Lords, 1693–1695* (London: 1900), 152. Admiralty Letter Book, Admirals to
Admiralty, 9 September 1693.

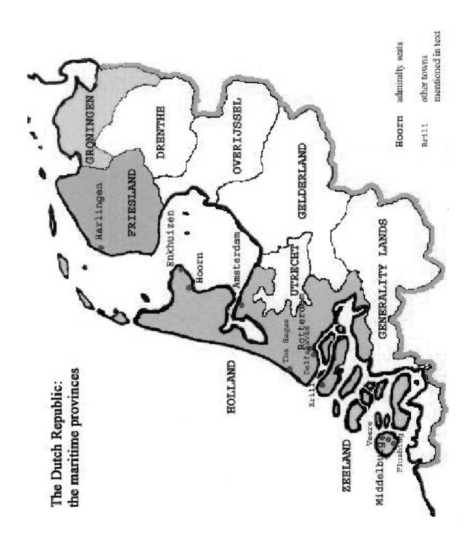

The Dutch Republic:
the maritime provinces

SCOTTISH COMMUNITIES ABROAD:
SOME CONCLUDING REMARKS

Thomas O'Connor, Sølvi Sogner and Lex Heerma van Voss

On 15 October 1917, a French firing squad executed Mata Hari. Before the war, Mata Hari had set the imagination of the European *beau monde* on fire with her striptease act, thinly veiled as oriental dances. On the suggestion of the French Secret Service she exploited her network, which included German officers, to the advantage of the Parisian government. Over time the French became convinced that Mata Hari was a double agent, and that German officers were not just paying for her company, but also for military information. Eventually, the French press suggested that she was responsible for the death of tens of thousands of French soldiers. Her conviction and execution made her name a synonym for fatal passion, predatory sexuality and high society espionage. She has subsequently been portrayed in several movies, including a memorable performance by Greta Garbo in 1931.

Mata Hari would never have died—innocently—before the firing squad had it not been for Scottish migration in previous centuries. She was born Griet Zelle in Leeuwarden on 7 August 1876. In 1895 she married Captain Rudolph MacLeod (1856–1928), a major in the KNIL (Royal Dutch Indian Army). Since the turn of the eighteenth century his ancestors had served in the Dutch and the Dutch colonial armies, as did numerous other Scots, particularly in the Scots-Dutch Brigade.[1] Rudolph's father John (1825–1868) had served as a captain in the Dutch army, his grandfather Norman (1755–1837) as a major-general, his great-grandfather John (1727–1804) as a colonel. The father of this elder John, Lieutenant Norman MacLeod (c. 1690–1729) was an ensign in Hepburn's Regiment in Holland

---

[1] J. Ferguson, ed., *Papers illustrating the history of the Scots Brigade in the service of the United Netherlands* (3 vols., Edinburgh: 1899); S. Murdoch, 'The Good, the Bad and the Anonymous: A Preliminary Survey of the Scots in the Dutch East Indies 1612–1707' in *Northern Scotland*, vol. 22, (2002), 63–76.

and later a lieutenant in the Scots-Dutch Brigade. He married Geertruid Schrassert in 1713 in Grave.[2]

Griet MacLeod-Zelle travelled with her husband to his posts in Medan (Sumatra) and Java, in the Dutch East Indies. After separating from her husband, Zelle took to dancing on the Paris stage in 1905, first as 'Lady MacLeod' and soon after as 'Mata Hari'. If the tradition of Scots in Dutch army service had not produced Rudolph MacLeod—or if Griet Zelle had not been attracted to his imposing military figure—she would not have acquired the oriental know-how which was essential for her Mata Hari performances. We will return to her in due course.

In recent years international migration studies have undergone a radical rethink.[3] In Spain, for instance, it was both French interest in French-speaking communities in the peninsula and the study of the relations between the Canaries and the Continent that kick-started the comparative study of European migrants in Iberia in the 1960s and formed a vital dimension of the Spanish historiographical renaissance during the past thirty years.[4] Migration is no longer seen as something extraordinary, released by critical circumstances. Rather migration is a normal, continuous activity, integrated into the general history of society. If it was once possible to write history without even mentioning migration this is no longer the case. In the words of one prominent migration historian, *homo migrans* has existed as long as *homo sapiens*: to migrate is as intimately a part of the human condition as birth, breeding, and death.[5] People have always been on the move, deflected, filtered but rarely bowed by borders, real or imaginary. Further, when looking for the determinants of migration, it is futile to distinguish between internal migration and migration across 'national' borders. Indeed attempts to

---

[2] http://www.macleodgenealogy.org, consulted on 18 April 2004. (The Associated Clan MacLeod Societies Genealogical Resources, The Associated Clan MacLeod Societies, Edinburgh, Scotland: 2000).

[3] Jan Lucassen and Leo Lucassen, eds., *Migration, Migration History, History: Old Paradigms and New Perspectives* (Bern: 1997), 9–37. See also N. Canny, ed., *Europeans on the Move: Studies on European Migration 1500–1800* (Oxford: 1994); T. Sowell, *Migrations and Cultures: A World View* (New York: 1996); D. Hoerder, *Cultures in Contact: World Migrations in the Second Millennium* (Durham and London: 2002).

[4] M. B. Villar García and P. Pezzi Cristóbal, eds., *Los extranjeros en la España moderna* (2 vols, Málaga: 2003), I, 15–6.

[5] Klaus J. Bade, *Europa in Bewegung: Migration vom späten 18. Jahrhundert bis zur Gegenwart* (München: 2000).

distinguish between different types of migration can be artificial and not necessarily illuminating. Migration may be a diverse human experience but all migrants choose or are obliged to undergo a similar process: the perception of possibilities elsewhere; the canny calculation of benefits; the decision to decamp and, finally, the migratory move itself. Economic as well as emotional factors come into play. The choice to migrate is usually rational but not always well-informed and constitutes only the first stage of the complex migratory experience.

In analysing migration, historians for a long time relied upon normative sources and tended to accept at face value existing restrictions on the free movement of people, goods and ideas. New research has changed our ideas completely. Legal restrictions could be modified, overlooked or dispensed with. The more we learn of our shared European past, the more the complexity of the migration experience impresses us. We now see that migration was not an exception to but rather an integral part of European social relations and that our early modern ancestors were more resourceful, ingenious and mobile than we once thought and taught. The present study is a pioneering effort to analyse the experience of one particular 'migrant producing' country, Scotland, during a particularly hectic migratory period, the seventeenth century. It looks at the Scots migrants not only as itinerants but also as settlers and community builders in the environment of 'abroad'.

The study also stresses that Scotland's migration experience was part of a great, pan-European phenomenon. During the so-called long seventeenth century crisis the overall population of Europe is believed to have stagnated, probably at some 100–120 million people.[6] However, war, disease and famine not only reduced populations but also stimulated migration in regionally varied ways. Some populations relocated within populated areas of Europe. Others colonised previously sparsely settled or virgin territories in Eastern Europe. Others again took to the high seas and headed for the New World. In few cases did they manage to shed the weight of their religious and cultural prejudices, and the new communities they founded were usually mirrors of rather than alternatives to those they left behind.[7]

---

[6] Ilja Mieck, ed., *Europäische Wirtschafts- und Sozialgeschichte von der Mitte de 17. Jahrhunderts bis zur Mitte des 19. Jahrhunderts*, Vol. 4, (Stuttgart: 1993), 45–64.

[7] Leslie Page Moch, *Moving Europeans: Migration in Western Europe since 1650* (Bloomington: 1992).

A rich range of incentives and disincentives influenced individual migration projects. Scots were certainly not the only Europeans to leave behind their paternal land and go abroad, temporarily or for good. But this should not lead us to assume that all groups within early modern European societies were equally mobile over time, even within the limits of the North Atlantic archipelago. There was, in fact, great variation over both time and space. The contrast and comparison of what until recently were regarded as the distinct and unique migration experiences of Ireland, Scotland and England have challenged accepted orthodoxies by giving local and national studies a new awareness of their inter-connectedness and also a sense of their implication in a universal phenomenon whose very essence is to breach boundaries. Parallels, symbioses and analogies now jostle for attention with inherited, hermetic certitudes, producing an exciting effervescence at conferences, in periodicals, monographs and, as here, in collections.[8] This echoes the experience in other European historiographies where comparative analysis of migration has altered not only the treatment of population movement but, more fundamentally, the way in which the history of migration itself is approached.

Set in the context of population movements in early modern Europe, migration within the British Isles and between them and both the Continent and the rest of the world emerges as a complex phenomenon that is not always reducible to the familiar topoi of victimhood, opportunism, imperialism or their avatars. For Scottish and Irish migration studies in particular, comparison has been particularly pertinent. This is not only because of geographical proximity and shared historical experience but also because the specific migration experiences of Ireland and Scotland have operated in a complex symbiosis that the emergence of religious differences and

---

[8] For an overview of the recent material on Irish migration see Patrick O'Sullivan *The Irish world wide: history, heritage, identity* (Leicester: 1992); Thomas O'Connor 'The Irish in Europe 1580–1815: some historiographical remarks' in Thomas O'Connor, ed., *The Irish in Europe 1580–1815* (Dublin: 2001), 9–26; M. Begoña Villar García 'Bibliografía sobre la emigración Irlandesa del siglo XVIII' in M. B. Villar García, ed., *La emigración irlandesa en el siglo XVIII* (Málaga: 2000), 275–89. For recent work on Scotland see D. Catterall, *Community Without Borders: Scots Migrants and the Changing Face of Power in the Dutch Republic, c.1600–1700* (Leiden: 2002); A. Grosjean, *An Unofficial Alliance: Scotland and Sweden 1569–1654* (Leiden: 2003); S. Murdoch, *Britain, Denmark-Norway and the House of Stuart, 1603–1660* (East Linton: 2003); D. Worthington, *Scots in Habsburg Service, 1618–1648* (Leiden: 2003); M. Glozier, *Scottish Soldiers in France in the Reign of the Sun King: Nursery for Men of Honour* (Leiden: 2004).

the pursuit of state building altered but did not terminate. In this context, the Ulster Plantations are the unavoidable starting point for any comparative analysis of Scotland's migration experience, not only because of their scale but also because of their impact on the subsequent relations between Ireland and Scotland as parts of the Stuart kingdoms and between Scotland and the rest of the world. Because perceptions of Hiberno-Scottish relations have traditionally been refracted through the potentially distorting Ulster lens, normalising historical analysis of Scottish migration to seventeenth-century Ireland is an essential first step in the comparative enterprise, a fact recognised by the arrangement of this book. It is important that this collection begins with an essay on 'Ulster'. Whether historians like it or not, the so-called 'Ulster' question is part of contemporary popular and political experience. While one does not want to harp on endlessly about the Good Friday Agreement or indulge in any unearned optimism, it is true that sometimes doing history is about more than history. It seems that the comparative analysis of Irish and Scottish migration experiences—which can proceed now that a head of intellectual steam has been built up via archival activity, periodical literature and monographs—possesses not only a favourable historiographical context but also a political and social aspect which could make some historians, if they desire it, appear useful. The opportunity ought to be seized, critically and sceptically, of course, but not without enthusiasm. What this means, in fact, is that 'lonely furrow' history, that hived off artificially differentiated 'national' migration experiences, can be criticised as not only distorting and partial but, more devastatingly, as unfashionable.

Nor is this just a British question. The normalisation of the study of Scots migration to Ireland is part of the maturing of European migration studies generally. The academic partners who have worked on this book hail mostly from the stable North European states whose example has traditionally been invoked, at least in Ireland, as models for emulation on the Celtic fringe. There is nothing wrong with that so long as the Irish-Scots migration case is not afforded the special status that feeds either a Celtic inferiority complex or a false sense of ideological adequacy among the Continental neighbours.[9]

---

[9] It may be the particular role of those who research Irish-Scots migration not only to normalise relations across the North Channel and within the British Isles

One aspect of this present *kairos* is the vigour of historical activity in Ireland. The past thirty years or so have been something of a historiographical rollercoaster as migration studies, along with other areas of historical research, have undergone fundamental conceptual changes, including the partial deconstruction of the traditional nationalist historiography. In this regard, it is revealing to recall the first sustained academic attempts to treat of the early modern Irish migration, in the nineteenth century.[10] They concentrated on intellectual, religious and military migrations, viewing them as consequences of Protestantism, plantation and state centralisation. This was migration as oppression and the predictably depressing monotony of the approach was only occasionally broken by a compensatory or contributory historical conceptuality that concentrated on the achievement of usually extraordinary individuals who, *contra mundum*, did their oppressed homeland proud. As a historiographical conceptuality this approach still has legs but it is accompanied nowadays by a strong tendency to treat Irish migrant studies in the field of international comparison. Comparison, of course, is cruelly exposing of inherited conceptualities and has had its fair share of shoddy practitioners. It comes as no surprise that the newer conceptuality has not gone uncontested and this is precisely as it should be, especially when well-directed criticism, often from a nationalist perspective, challenges the woolly, forced or vacuous comparisons that result from the neglect of local, regional and national studies. The latter remain as central as ever to migration studies, especially now that information technology permits the collection, manipulation and interrogation of vast bodies of first-level data. What migration studies in Ireland need most now is an integrated information technology template that permits the exploitation of the data which is already collected but still isolated in incompatible programmes.

Beyond the Atlantic archipelago too there is value in this comparative approach. Numerous countries, semi-autonomous regions and city-states around the shores of the North Sea witnessed a strong

---

but also to keep alive the awareness of the profound social, economic and ideological dysfunction that is part of any migration experience, even in jurisdictions that have traditionally enjoyed reputations for stability.

[10] See articles on the Irish intellectual, religious and military migration to the Continent reproduced in the *Irish Ecclesiastical Record*, in earlier numbers of *The Irish Sword* and in any number of local historical journals.

increase in international migration between 1550 and 1650. Migration numbers remained at a high level in the second half of the seventeenth century. In the eighteenth century they dropped off again, until by the end of the *ancien régime* they had reached the same absolute level as around 1600. Given the fact that the population figures had risen strongly in the eighteenth century as opposed to only slowly between 1550 and 1650, relative to population numbers international migration had by 1800 fallen back again to the level it had been at in 1550.[11] All countries bordering on the North Sea show this same broad movement over time, albeit with some differences, explained by the various national histories. The migration figure for the southern Netherlands rises early, as the area was plagued by social, religious, political and therefore economic troubles in the second half of the sixteenth century. Dutch out-migration, driven by the acquisition of colonies in Asia, only picked up in the first half of the seventeenth century. Overall, migration figures could be seen as an argument in favour of a European crisis in the seventeenth century.[12]

Scottish migration, then, conforms to this wider European pattern. It picks up after 1550, is high throughout the seventeenth century, and drops off, dramatically even, in the first half of the eighteenth century. What is different is that the level of out-migration is much higher than for the rest of north-west Europe. Whereas the estimates for all other countries combined climb from about half a per cent

---

[11] It is very hard to define sharply (international) migration. Do we count only those who seem to (want to) settle abroad permanently, temporary settlers, or even travellers? If we draw the line somewhere in between, where do we draw it and how do we decide on which side of it historical movers were? How do we find migrants, if some of them are only recorded by names already adapted to languages other than their original one, and others are not recorded at all? How do we handle literature based on different methodological and theoretical choices, which are not always made explicit? Given these limitations, and those of historical scholarship generally, any judgment of the kind expressed here must be tentative and somewhat impressionistic. The assessment of migrations is drawn from Jelle van Lottum, 'Migration in the North Sea region, 1550–1800' (Paper prepared for the Fifth European Social Science History Conference, March 2004, Berlin), accepted for publication to the *Northern Seas Yearbook*. Van Lottum gives an estimate for international migration figures at fifty-year intervals, based on current migration history literature. Irish out-migration is not included in Van Lottum's figures, and remains undiscussed here. The population figures are derived from Colin McEvedy and Richard Jones, *Atlas of World Population History* (Harmondsworth: 1978).

[12] Geoffrey Parker and Lesley M. Smith, eds., *The General Crisis of the Seventeenth Century* (London: 1985), 9–10; Hoerder, *Cultures in Contact*, 277–279.

of the population involved in international migration in 1550, via one per cent in 1600 to about one and a half per cent in 1650, Scottish figures are five times as high in 1550 and around ten per cent for the seventeenth century.[13] The main destinations of Scottish out-migration evolved, with what is defined in the introduction to this volume as the near-abroad dominant in the sixteenth century, the middle-abroad in the seventeenth and the far-abroad in the eighteenth. A further analysis of Scottish migration is therefore relevant for Scottish history and for migration history in general. How do we explain that the Scots were so much more prone to migrate than other nations? Perhaps it was due to the fact of Scotland being a maritime nation, where many had the know-how and the networks that enabled them to move. Situated between the Baltic, the North Sea and the Atlantic, close to the dominant economic and colonial nations of the seventeenth and of the eighteenth centuries, the Scots could profit from opportunities on offer. As opportunities within Scotland were limited, the Scots sought them elsewhere. The more developed Scottish migration networks grew to be, the easier further migration became, resulting in the formation of identifiable communities as described throughout this book.

Part of the Scottish emigrant experience resulted from the numerous military migrations which saw tens of thousands of Scots going to fight the wars which formed part of the seventeenth-century crisis.[14] Rough, mountainous areas with a relatively low level of commercialisation like Switzerland and Scotland were seen as natural suppliers of fighting men in early modern Europe. It is interesting to speculate why the Scots typically supplied fighting men to foreign princes and governments, whereas the Swedes kept down their international migration figures in a traditional sense, but were present on

---

[13] These figures alone show that the Ulster plantation did not absorb all potential for Scottish out-migration. See the introduction and the chapter by Patrick Fitzgerald in this volume.

[14] The motivations for military participation varied and ranged from political and confessional idealism to coercion and that of the simple mercenary. These motives and discussion of particular episodes are discussed in S. Murdoch, ed., *Scotland and the Thirty Years' War, 1618–1648* (Leiden: 2001); S. Murdoch and A. Mackillop, eds., *Fighting for Identity: Scottish Military Experience, c.1550–1900* (Leiden: 2002); A. Mackillop and S. Murdoch, eds., *Military Governors and Imperial Frontiers: A Study of Scotland and Empires* (Leiden: 2003); A. Grosjean, *An Unofficial Alliance: Scotland and Sweden, 1569–1654* (Leiden: 2003); D. Worthington, *Scots in Habsburg Service, 1618–1648* (Leiden: 2003).

the same battlefields as part of the Swedish national army. The traditional answer would probably be that the power of the Swedish king in Sweden's *Stormaktstiden* was more absolute than that of the Scottish kings, and that the Swedish king could therefore muster more of his national military resources.[15] Other issues like increased literacy resulting from the Calvinist nature of the Scottish Reformation should also, perhaps, be factored into the equation. Any analysis should also take into account the ease with which potential soldiers could offer their services on an international labour market, and the degree to which a capital-intensive route of state formation was available to the monarchs of Sweden and the British Isles.[16] Whatever the reasons and motivations, it is possible to compare Scottish migration and community development within the specified period with similar events in neighbouring countries, especially those which were themselves recipients of significant Scottish migration.

The Collection in a Comparative Context

If appropriate comparison is the best remedy for false particularism then migration studies stand to gain greatly from the strengthening trend towards comparative examination of population movement. Confessional issues were certainly a cause of significant migration, both pushing out and bringing in migrants from/to a variety of destinations. After the Reformation in 1536, religion was the main principle invoked when regulating access to Norway. Only the Evangelical-Lutheran religion was allowed. Jews, Jesuits, higher Catholic clergy, converts, reformists other than Evangelical-Lutheran—all had to have a special visa to be admitted. A special permit to enter was also demanded from gypsies, Romanies (*Tatere*) and vagabonds. In their case additional reasons were invoked: their way of life and their presumed criminal behavior (lying, cheating, thieving, witchcraft). In addition comedians, conjurers, illusionists and jugglers needed special permits to function in the community. The financial situation

---

[15] *Stormaktstiden* describes Sweden's 'Age of Greatness' and equates approximately to the period encompassing the reigns of Gustav II Adolf and Karl XII (1611–1718).
[16] Marjolein 't Hart, 'The Emergence and Consolidation of the "Tax State". II. The Seventeenth Century', in Richard Bonney, ed., *Economic Systems and State Finance* (Oxford: 1995), 281–293.

of the immigrant was also an important consideration. Paupers were unwanted. This consideration also applied to distinguish between Jews: Portuguese Jews were treated differently from German and Polish Jews, the latter being treated as beggars. If admitted, the person was considered as a guest, and was supposed to abide by the law of the land: *skik følge eller land fly* (follow the custom or leave the country).

The early modern Norwegian state recognized the existence of separate migrant nationalities. Norwegian law used the term 'stranger' to describe people who were not members of the state by birth.[17] This handicap could be overcome, however, and there was a definite willingness to receive the 'right kind' of immigrant. Complete outsiders, like gypsies, Romanies, beggars and vagabonds, were not allowed even a limited citizenship. But certain strangers, called temporary citizens, held limited citizenships. They might not have full commercial rights, or they might be excluded from certain privileges and benefits. But they could be regarded as being in the process of becoming full citizens. Once they had acquired full citizenship, they were no longer 'strangers'. They might still differ from the natives by birth, but they now had the same rights. They could even enjoy special privileges, if the king saw fit to bestow them—for rendered services, loans, or know-how. To show one's honest intention when applying for full citizenship, one had to settle and acquire permanent domicile in the country. If the person bought property, married or applied for permission to ply his trade, he would be considered of good intention and hence fully acceptable as a citizen. Pedersen demonstrates that many Scots, particularly in Bergen, managed to fulfill the required criteria, but Scots in Norway were only one of several immigrant nationalities in the seventeenth century, some invited, others entering on their own initiative. Elsewhere in the Scottish migrant world, they were not moving in tens or hundreds, but in thousands.

Paddy Fitzgerald's article opens this book with a deconstruction of received perceptions regarding the Scots plantation in Ulster. His concern is to normalise the event by isolating the features which per-

---

[17] This gave rise to the origin of 'stranger churches'. For a discussion of them in an English context see A. Pettegree, *Foreign Protestant Communities in Sixteenth-Century London* (Oxford: 1986).

mit a comparison between this and other migration/plantation/colonisation experiences: among the migrants the diversity of religion, social class, geographical origin and motivation; with regard to the form of the migration process, its successive wave pattern; at destination, the persistence of inherited settlement patterns, pragmatic economic motivation, creative reinterpretation of royal policy and the control of the land stock; within the global Scottish experience, high onward migration. The isolation of these common features enables this 'near-abroad' migration study to dovetail with 'middle- and far-abroad' movements examined by Kowalski and Dobson in the same section. In both these pieces, classic periodisation and simplistic causal relations break down under the weight of sheer historical evidence. They reveal the migrant Scots in colours we have come to recognise as typical of their European cousins: groups of individuals forged by family, geographical, professional, political or religious links operating opportunistically to profit from the changing strategies of the sending and the receiving jurisdictions, from evolving trade patterns and the ordinary vicissitudes of weather, food supply and disease.[18] What emerges again and again from the these pages is the picture of motivated groups doing what ideology, resources and circumstances permitted them to do and not much more. Successful migrants grab attention when they break the mould but they actually distinguish themselves by a capacity to appraise more accurately the reality of their circumstances and to develop more appropriate survival and manipulation strategies. When dealing with such individuals and communities, single-issue causality, no matter how convincingly argued, cannot do justice to either their complexity or facticity.

The issue of deliberate community-building is conceptually vital to informed comparative analysis and it is encouraging to see this issue treated in the second part of the book. While contextual description, motivational analysis and the reconstruction of lines of movement reveal much about migrant groups, the factors and circumstances

---

[18] For English, Dutch, Wallonian and German examples of the same, see H. Roseveare, ed., *Merchants and Markets of the Late Seventeenth Century: The Marscoe-David Letters, 1668–1680* (Oxford: 1987); L. Müller, *The Merchant Houses of Stockholm, 1640–1800: A Comparative Study of Early-Modern Entrepreneurial Behaviour* (Uppsala: 1998); Maj-Britt Nergård, *Mellan krona och marknad: Utländska och svenska entreprenörer inom svensk järnhantering från ca 1580 till 1700* (Uppsala: 2001); G. Haggrén, *Hammarsmeder, masugnsfolk och kolare* (Pieksamaki: 2001).

facilitating the establishment of communities are a distinct field of study. A new dynamic enters the migration phenomenon when migrants stop moving, permanently or temporarily, and begin to congregate in a particular place.[19] The interaction of push and pull factors is vitally important in this process but the historical task of unravelling them is a great challenge that obliges historians to enlist the assistance of colleagues in other disciplines. This is where the demographers come in to explain how new migrant elements of the population work within existing demographic patterns and how certain demographic configurations in the sending, itinerant and receiving populations favour or preclude migrant community formation or integration. Legal historians in particular have been instrumental in revealing what judicial means were deployed to exclude, integrate and control new migrant populations.[20] In this light it is useful to note how provocatively Ciaran O'Scea has suggested that issues of natural justice and legal obligation influenced the Spanish monarchy's acceptance of responsibility for a number of Irish noble migrant families in the early seventeenth century.[21] In eighteenth-century France, the successful integration of a number of Irish noble families was aided by the fact that the French authorities decided, after exhaustive investigation, to grant them equivalent noble status in France, thereby speeding up their integration.[22] These Irish experiences demand comparison with Scottish parallels outlined in Pedersen's look at Scots in Bergen, Murdoch and Grosjean's examination of Gothenburg, Žirgulis' analysis of Kėdainiai and Zickermann's *Überblick* of Hamburg. The deployment of inbound migrants in the political strategies of receiving jurisdictions is a subject that is likely to attract more attention in the future and the examples of the Bergen and

---

[19] See Amaia Bilbao Acedos, *The Irish Community in the Basque Country, c.1700–1800* (Dublin: 2003); M. B. Villar García, ed., *La emigración irlandesa en el siglo XVIII* (Málaga: 2000); Karin Schüller, *Die beziehungen zwischen Spanien und Irland im 16. und 17. jahrhundert* (Münster: 1999).

[20] Patrick Clarke de Dromantin, 'De l'intégration des nobles étrangers dans le second Ordre de l'ancien régime' in *Revue Historique de Droit Français et étranger* 77, 2 (April–June 1999), 223–40.

[21] Ciaran O'Scea, 'The significance of Spanish intervention in West Munster during the battle of Kinsale' in Thomas O'Connor and Mary Ann Lyons, eds., *Irish migrants in Europe after Kinsale 1602–1820* (Dublin: 2003), 32–63.

[22] Sébastien Jahan, 'An Irish family between assimilation and revolution: the Keatings of Poitiers 1777–1795' in O'Connor and Lyons, *Irish migrants in Europe after Kinsale*, 149–163.

Gothenburg Scots in particular bring several related Irish experiences to mind: the efforts of Philip II and Philip III to use the Irish seminaries as a means of keeping the Irish Gaelic nobility onside as they made peace with James I;[23] Arnošt Cardinal Harrach's efforts to use Irish Franciscans as a counterweight to imperially-supported Jesuits in 1620s and 1630s Prague;[24] the Spanish regime's special privileges for Irish merchants indirectly facilitating the English trade;[25] the de Fleury regime's efforts in 1730s Paris to use Irish clerics to replace ousted Jansenists;[26] French, Spanish, Swedish and imperial strategies to recruit Irish soldiers for military service, all involving political decisions not only with regard to England and Ireland but also concerning the abroad communities in their own jurisdictions.[27] While the circumstances are vastly different it is interesting to notice the strategic and formal similarities: contested state expansion; entrenched local privilege; available migrant community; temporary or permanent integration of migrants; development of independent abroad community concerns.

Inevitably, the comparison of different migrant communities in formation points to the definitional problems associated with the concept of 'community'. If more permanent communities of Scots were established, they could either be strong and large enough to go on as a recognizably Scottish community, or they could blend into their new receiving society. A good example of the last process is offered by the Gothenburg council, of which Murdoch and Grosjean remark that it is unclear whether certain individuals took their seats in it as occupants of a reserved seat for Scots, Dutch and Germans, or as Swedes. Moreover, the importance of such individuals to the larger communities of which they formed a part differed. Those Gothenburg Scots seem to have performed a more central role in town life than their countrymen did in Dutch towns. A Gothenburg town councillor

---

[23] Óscar Recio Morales, *El Socorro de Irlanda en 1601 y la contribución del ejército a la integración social de los Irlandeses en España* (Madrid: 2002).

[24] Jan Pařez and Hedvika Kuchařová *Hyberni v Praze: Éireannaigh i bPrág* (Prague: 2001).

[25] María del Carmen Lario de Oñate, *La colonia mercantile Británica e Irlandesa en Cádiz a finales del siglo xviii* (Cádiz: 2000).

[26] Thomas O'Connor, 'The role of Irish clerics in Paris University politics 1730–40' in *History of Universities* xv (1997–99), 193–226.

[27] See *i.a.* Óscar Recio Morales, *España y la pérdida del Ulster: Irlanda en la estrategia política de la monarquía hispánica (1602–1649)* (Madrid: 2003).

is certainly more central to town life than, say, a broker for Scots coal in Rotterdam. If this is understandable in the case of relatively large and powerful Rotterdam, it can be less easily explained for Veere, which was totally dependent on Scottish merchants.[28] Perhaps the leading Scottish merchants were relatively richer here than their fellow Scots in the Netherlands or, perhaps, a settler mentality in newly founded Gothenburg can explain this higher status. Whichever is the case it is obvious that it is vital to compare the Scots not only with the English and Irish, but also with the Germans and the Dutch in the city. This raises an interesting point regarding comparative analysis, alerting us to the benefit of the broader perspective. Scots in Sweden did not, apparently, react like their countrymen in the Netherlands, France, Spain or Portugal. They adapted to the constraints of their given location, at a particular time.

In this context it also appears pertinent to examine how Scots migrants altered or defended their inherited cultural and religious distinctiveness vis-à-vis host identities. As the various authors note, migrant Scots were themselves socially and culturally complex, holding multiple loyalties which were capable of recalibration as circumstances in the host societies demanded. Besides 'national' identities, Scots, like other Europeans, carried religious, political and cultural-ideological identities which could be adapted or tweaked as their situations altered. These, as the introduction states, could be based on "ties of blood, ethnic origin, territory, or simply lifestyle or common interest" and they were not confined by nation of birth. They could be shed or submerged and all could be "brought into play in particular situations and arenas". The Scottish students described by Esther Mijers selected their university of preference in the Dutch Republic with religious flavour and social status in mind. Scots could feel themselves to be primarily traders, students, Protestants etc., and these allegiances could become more or less pronounced depending on the circumstances. Someone like Jakob Spalding in Gothenburg can therefore easily be described as a Swedish-Scot from Mecklenburg, for instance. Indeed, students, tourists and other travellers simply

---

[28] M. P. Roosenboom, *The Scottish Staple in the Netherlands* (The Hague: 1910); V. Enthoven, 'The last straw: Trade contacts along the North Sea coast: the Scottish staple at Veere', in J. Roding and L. Heerma van Voss, eds., *The North Sea and Culture, 1550–1800* (Hilversum: 1996), 209–221; Catterall, *Community Without Borders*.

sought to balance their plural and sometimes conflicting identities. Andrew Little shows us how Scots, usually from one place, preferred to stick together on board ship, particularly as they began periods in foreign service. This was complicated by the evolution of a 'British' identity which was not confined simply to Scots. Kathrin Zickermann shows how the Englishman Joseph Averie was ousted from his position as the main representative of the British monarch in Hamburg when the Scot Robert Anstruther, the senior British diplomat to Denmark-Norway, settled there in 1630. Averie distinguished between his identity as an Englishman and Anstruther's as a Scot. Only a short while later, Averie was willing to use his Hamburg contacts on behalf of a Scottish privateer, whom he clearly considered as a fellow countryman. These national distinctions might or might not shadow political differences. During the British and Irish civil wars of the 1640s such distinctions were naturally emphasised and this almost certainly influenced migrants' identity recalibration in host jurisdictions. In more peaceful circumstances, identity was less controversial. In Middelburg in the mid-seventeenth century, for instance, a Scottish Calvinist was acceptable as a minister to a non-Calvinist English congregation. This points to identity compromises between the different British migrant groups, which was usually easier, because more beneficial, when abroad and in peacetime.

The concept of 'unbounded' communities or 'communities of the spirit' is important in this volume. It raises real definitional problems. In the final part of the present work Gardner ponders seventeenth-century Scots political exiles in the United Provinces, Little follows his itinerant Scots sailors in the 'English' and Dutch marines while Mijers traces Scottish student peregrinations between Leiden, Franeker, Groningen and Utrecht. The difficulty in defining these communities reflects their own doubts about who and what they were. All three pieces ask important questions concerning the nature of compromise within abroad communities, especially those regarding identity, integration or isolation and eventual return.[29]

---

[29] Here the distinction between bounded and unbounded communities is useful only so long as one bears in mind that all communities have both bound and unbound dimensions. In the past, Irish historians erred in confusing certain communities of the mind with bounded communities of fact but it is just as reprehensible a slip to assume, for instance, that apparently bounded trade communities were untroubled by questions of identity and meaning, or to use the old-fashioned

In this context, the comparison of student and 'ideological' migrants promises much. We learn from Mijers that the Scots university migration in the United Provinces was generally temporary, fairly well-heeled and 'fast reintegrating' into the sending society. This parallels the profile of Scandinavian students abroad in the same period.[30] The Irish equivalent in the Spanish Netherlands, Spain, Portugal, the Italian peninsula and France was somewhat different, even if the numbers involved are comparable. Irish student migration was often permanent, usually under-resourced and 'fast integrating' into the host society. Further, what historian can be insensitive to the irony that it was the Irish who replaced the medieval Scots as the quintessential British presence in the Sorbonne in the post-Reformation period?[31] Adding to the delicious complexity of this comparison is the religious inversion: the massively Protestant Scots migration to northern Europe swamping a tiny Scots Catholic current to France and Spain; the overwhelmingly Catholic Irish migration to the Latin countries obscuring the small Anglican and Presbyterian movements from Ireland to the rest of the British Isles and northern Europe. The role of art historians, philologists and cultural historians will be crucial to understanding these highly mobile migrants not only in their interaction with host societies and more permanent abroad communities but also with the sending jurisdiction to which they returned.

Conclusion

It is clear that the Scots identified themselves as different abroad only as long as it was convenient or profitable to do so. There were,

---

words, justification and destiny. The canniest Scots merchant, as long as he remained in any way identifiable as Scots, either remained attached to or was perceived as associated with something of his Scottish past, present or future. At the other end of the scale, merchants had an interest both in maintaining contacts with kin and compatriots, whom they could trust and check, and in remaining open to contacts with any other merchant who might offer lucrative trade opportunities.

[30] C. V. Jacobowsky, 'Svenska studenter i Oxford c.1620–1740' in *Personhistorisk Tidskrift*, vol. 28, (1927), 107–130; V. Helk, ed., *Danske Norske Studie Rejser: fra reformationen til enevaelden 1536–1660 Med en matrikel over studerende i utlandet* (Odense: 1987).

[31] L. W. B. Brockliss, 'Patterns of attendance at the university of Paris, 1400–1800' in *The Historical Journal* 21, 3 (1978), 503–44; L. W. B. Brockliss with Patrick Ferté 'Irish clerics in France in the seventeenth and eighteenth centuries: a statistical study' in *Proceedings of the Royal Irish Academy* section c 87, c 9 (1987).

of course, aspects of identity that they could not disown or, even more importantly, that their hosts would not allow them to discard. The contrast in deportment between older and newer members of migrant communities, the evolution in the policies of the host jurisdiction and changes in the political configuration of the sending jurisdiction are all factors affecting abroad communities, just as much as fluctuations in trade, international war, weather, and birth, death and marriage rates. In brief, if belief, sentiment and feeling have their hard-headed economic and social contexts, the inverse is also true. Is there anything particularly Scottish about this? The answer is a resounding no. Sailors and troops wanting to be paid; merchants willing to go to great lengths to make a good deal; diplomats and politicians trying to broker deals; exiles plotting revolts in the home country; students acquiring some useful knowledge and being very conscious about appearances; travellers on their individual quest along the route dictated by the travel guide, they could all be found in other north-west European nations too.

Nonetheless, while not unique (and not claiming to be), this collection offers a valuable and fresh approach to the history of migration. The formal study of the connexions between sending jurisdictions and abroad communities is bound to become more significant as research provides a more accurate picture of the sort of influence abroad communities maintained in the sending society through return travel, cultural transmission and wealth transfer. The Irish case is full of suggestive possibilities and Gardner's references to the role of returned Dutch exiles to late seventeenth-century Scotland indicate interesting Scottish parallels. In this regard, two Irish examples may turn out to be especially revealing: the clergy and the military at the end of the *ancien régime*. It is becoming apparent that the gradual eclipse of the Irish continental colleges network in the late eighteenth century was due not only to cultural, political and economic changes in Ireland, throughout the British Isles and on the Continent but, just as importantly, to the alteration in relations between the sending society and its communities abroad. The latter, which had functioned as important agents of cultural differentiation in seventeenth- and eighteenth-century Ireland, tended to lose their relevance as Ireland was sucked into the ever more powerful Atlantic system. While the Irish parliament's foundation of Maynooth in 1795 was indeed part of a complex deal involving the Irish Catholic hierarchy and the Dublin and London governments, it also expressed Irish disengagement from its near-abroad communities in the university cities of Europe, and Ireland's deepening involvement in the British Empire and America. Also suggestive is the fate of the French Irish regiments during the French Revolution. Once republican, egalitarian and fraternal ideas took hold in France, it was precisely those Irish families who had most successfully integrated into the *ancien régime* who were the most vulnerable to revolutionary zealots. The question remains: did the revolution, which had an obvious effect on Irish intellectual and military migration, signal a fundamental change in the direction of Irish migration, away from the Continent and into the New World, or did it merely accentuate trends already established? Can the Scots experience help us cope with questions like these? One thinks it might.

In this collection, finally, one notes the frequently recurring tension between the durability of the migrant community on the one hand and the inevitability of its integration into the host society on the other. An example of the complex integration processes that Scots experienced during migration can be found in the line of MacLeods that served in the Dutch army. Norman MacLeod (c.1690–1729) left the Netherlands when his regiment was disbanded in 1717. He was transferred to the British Army as lieutenant in a Company of Invalids in England, where he served in Tilbury Fort, Pendennis Castle and Plymouth. He died in London on 6 September 1729, and his widow, a Dutch woman, remarried in the Netherlands. Their son, John MacLeod (1727–1804) later became a cadet in the Dutch service in 1738. By 1779 he had risen to the rank of colonel in the Scots-Dutch Brigade. In 1782 the Scottish regiments were transferred to the Dutch Corps and Colonel MacLeod retired the following year. He had married Margaretha van Brienen in Doornspijk in 1754. Their son, Norman MacLeod, was born in Kampen in 1755 and died in Brielle in 1837, a major-general in the Dutch army. This may appear as a Dutch life, but he married Sarah Evans from St Helen (Worcester) in 1791 in England. Their son John MacLeod (1825–1868) was born in Kampen in 1825 and died in Millingen in 1868, a captain in the Dutch army. He married in 1856 at Nijmegen, Dina Louisa, Baroness Sweerts de Landas. The fact that he used his Dutch grandmother's name as part of his, John van Brienen MacLeod, might indicate that he was fully assimilated into Dutch society. Further, that his only son was not christened Norman or John, but Rudolph, may also highlight total integration with their Dutch surroundings. Rudolph married three times. The names of his other spouses, Elizabeth van der Mast and Grietje Meijer, sound every bit as Dutch as that of Griet Zelle, returning us once more to Mata Hari. As Rudolph MacLeod had no surviving sons, the family name MacLeod was only passed on for one generation after him. Because he considered himself notorious for having been married to Mata Hari, he asked to be buried in an unmarked grave. If future historians were to rely exclusively on family names to establish identities, this particular Scottish-Dutch connection would hardly emerge.[32] Elsewhere in the world, we still find communities that cling to their Scottish heritage, in Ulster, America, Canada and Australia. But it is sobering to recall that, in the long run, 'we are all dead'. Most immigrant communities integrate and are eventually assimilated. This is even more the case in our own time, when acceptance, tolerance and mutual understanding are extolled as social and political virtues and demanded of host and migrant communities alike. Migrant communities are inevitably subject to cultural and social disintegration as integration proceeds. This fact does not take from their historical significance. Rather it adds to the urgency of understanding their formation, functioning and eventual eclipse, if only to remind ourselves of the inherent vulnerability of every historical community.

---

[32] Which of course does not mean that identities and cultural links will not carry on, or cannot be re-established. In fact one of Rudolph's daughters, Non van Mourik-MacLeod, contacted MacLeods living in New Zealand after the Second World War, to inform them about the fate of Flying Officer Ian McLeod, who was shot down and killed near Arnhem in 1944. Contact between Dutch and New Zealand MacLeods was maintained until Non MacLeod died in 2000 (http://www.engelfriet.net/Alie/Gastenboek/mcleod.htm, consulted on 18 April 2004).

INDEX OF NAMES

For convenience, words beginning with or containing accented letters have been placed within the alphabetical order common to English.

INDEX OF PLACES

For convenience, words beginning with or containing accented letters have been placed within the alphabetical order common to English.

INDEX OF SUBJECTS

For convenience, words beginning with or containing accented letters have been placed within the alphabetical order common to English.